ENGLISH
DICTIONARY

ENGLISH DICTIONARY

GEDDES & GROSSET

Abbreviations used in this book

adj	adjective	*npl*	plural noun
adv	adverb	*per*	personal
cap	capital letter	*pl*	plural
def art	definite article	*poss*	possessive
comput	computing	*pp*	past participle
conj	conjunction	*prep*	preposition
demons	demonstrative	*pres p*	present participle
esp	especially	*pron*	pronoun
f	feminine	*pt*	past tense
fig	figurative	*sing*	singular
indic	indicative	*t*	tense
inf	informal	*vi*	intransitive verb
interj	interjection	*vt*	transitive verb
m	masculine	*vt, vi*	transitive and intrasitive
math	mathematics		verb
n	noun	*usu*	usually

This edition published 2002 by Geddes & Grosset,
David Dale House, New Lanark ML11 9DJ, Scotland

© 2000 Geddes & Grosset

First printed 1997
Reprinted 1997, 1998 (three times), 1999
Revised and updated 2000
Revised edition reprinted 2001 (three times), 2002 (three times), 2003

ISBN 1 85534 731 8

Printed and bound in Poland

A

a *indef art* used before a consonant (*see also* **an**); one; any; per.

aback *adv* backwards; by surprise: **taken aback** startled.

abacus *n* (*pl* **abaci** *or* **abacuses**) a square slab on the top of a column; a counting frame.

abandon *vt* to forsake entirely; to desert; to give oneself up to a desire or emotion.

abandoned *adj* deserted; depraved.

abase *vt* to bring low; to degrade; to disgrace.

abasement *n* degradation.

abash *vt* to make ashamed.

abate *vt* to lessen. * *vi* to become less.

abatement *n* reduction; decrease.

abattoir *n* a public slaughterhouse.

abbess *n* a female superior of a nunnery.

abbey *n* (*pl* **abbeys**) a monastery or convent.

abbot *n* the male superior of an abbey or monastery.

abbreviate *vt* to shorten.

abdicate *vt* to resign voluntarily; to relinquish.

abdomen *n* the lower belly.

abduct *vt* to entice; to lead away by force.

abduction *n* the unlawful carrying off of a person.

aberration *n* a wandering from the right way; derangement of the mind.

abet *vt* (*pt* **abetted**) to aid or to encourage (in evil).

abetter, abettor *n* one who abets.

abeyance *n*: **in abeyance** suspense.

abhor *vt* to shrink from with horror; to detest.

abhorrence *n* detestation.

abhorrent *adj* hateful.

abide *vb* (*pt, pp* **abode** *or* **abided**) *vi* to stay in a place; to dwell. * *vt* to wait for; to tolerate; to endure.

abiding *adj* permanent.

ability *n* the power to do a thing; skill; (*pl*) the powers of the mind.

abject *adj* mean; vile.

abjure *vt* to renounce upon oath.

ablaze *adv* on fire; in a blaze.

able *adj* capable; skilful.

ablution *n* a washing away from; cleansing.

ably *adv* with ability.

abnormal *adj* deviating from a fixed rule; irregular.

aboard *adv, prep* on board; in a ship.

abode *n* residence.

abolish *vt* to destroy; to do away with.

abominable *adj* hateful.

abominate *vt* to hate extremely; to abhor.

abomination *n* hatred; the object of hatred.

aborigine *n* the original inhabitant of a country.

abortion *n* a miscarriage, usually induced.

abortive *adj* fruitless.

abound *vi* to be, or have, in great plenty.

about *prep* around; near to; concerning. * *adv* around; nearly.

above *prep* to or in a higher place than; more than. * *adv* to or in a higher place.

aboveboard *adv* without concealment or deception.

abreast *adv* side by side.

abridge *vt* to shorten; to condense.

abridgement *n* a summary of a text without loss of meaning; a shortening.

abroad *adv* at large; in a foreign country.

abrogate *vt* to repeal; to make void.

abrupt *adj* broken off; steep; sudden; curt in manner or speech.

abruptness *n* suddenness.

abscess *n* a gathering of pus in some part of the body.

abscond *vi* to fly from justice.

absence *n* the state of being absent; inattention.

absent[1] *adj* not present; inattentive.

absent[2] *vt* to keep oneself away from.

absentee *n* one who absents himself or herself.

absolute *adj* unlimited; despotic.

absolutely *adv* unconditionally.

absolution *n* a freeing from guilt or its punishment.

absolve *vt* to free from, as from guilt or punishment; pardon.

absorb *vt* to drink in; to soak up; to engross.

absorbent *adj* imbibing; swallowing; able to soak up moisture.

absorption *n* act or process of imbibing or swallowing up; total interest in.

abstain *vi* to keep back from; to refrain.

abstemious *adj* sparing in food or drink; temperate.

abstinence *n* a refraining from anything, esp from strong drink.

abstract *vt* to draw from; to separate and consider by itself; to summarize.

abstract *adj* existing in the mind only; not concrete. * *n* a summary.

abstracted *adj* lost in thought.

absurd *adj* contrary to reason; ridiculous.

absurdity *n* the quality of being absurd; that which is absurd.

abundance *n* great plenty.

abundant *adj* abounding; plentiful.

abuse[1] *vt* to ill-use; to insult.

abuse[2] *n* misuse; insulting words.

abusive *adj* insulting.

abut *vi* to border; to meet.

abyss *n* a bottomless gulf; a chasm.

academic *adj* belonging to an academy or university; theoretical. * *n* a teacher or researcher in a university.

academy *n* a school of arts or sciences; a society of persons for the cultivation of arts and sciences.

accede *vi* to assent to; to comply with.

accelerate *vt* to hasten; to quicken the speed of.

acceleration *n* increase of velocity.

accent *n* a stress or modulation of the voice; a manner of speaking. * *vt* to express or note the accent of; to pronounce; to emphasize.

accentuate *vt* to emphasize.

accept *vt* to receive; to admit.

acceptance *n* reception; approval.

access *n* approach; admission.

accessible *adj* easy of approach; affable.

accession *n* the act of acceding; addition; succession to a throne.

accessory *adj* additional. * *n* an accomplice.

accident *n* a chance or unforeseen event; a mishap. .

accidental *adj* happening by chance.

acclaim *n* praise; enthusiastic approval. * *vt* to applaud.

acclamation *n* a shout of joy or approval.

acclimatize *vt* to accustom to a new climate; to become used to.

accolade *n* high honour; strong praise.

accommodate *vt* to make suitable; to adjust; to provide lodging for.

accommodating *adj* obliging.

accommodation *n* lodgings; loan.

accompaniment *n* the music played to accompany a singer or other performer.

accompany *vt* to go with; to perform music along with.

accomplice *n* an associate, especially in a crime.

accomplish *vt* to fulfil.

accomplished *adj* elegant; having a finished education; skilled.

accomplishment *npl* attainments.

accord *n* harmony; agreement. * *vt* to make to agree; to grant. * *vi* to agree.

accordance *n* agreement.

accordingly *adv* consequently.

accordion *n* a small keyed wind instrument.

accost *vt* to speak to first; to solicit.

account *n* a reckoning; a bill; narration. * *vt* to reckon; to value. * *vi* to give or render reasons; (*with* **for**) to explain.

accountable *adj* liable to be called to account; responsible.

accountant *n* one skilled in accounts.

accoutrements *npl* military dress and arms; special equipment.

accredit *vt* to give credit or authority to.

accredited *adj* authorized.

accretion *n* enlargement by natural growth or by external additions.

accrue *vi* to come to; to result from.

accumulate *vt* to heap up. * *vi* to increase.

accumulation *n* a heap; a collection.

accuracy *n* correctness.

accurate *adj* done with care; exact.

accursed *adj* lying under a curse; doomed.

accusation *n* a charge brought against anyone.

accusative *adj*, *n* a case in grammar.

accuse *vt* to charge with a crime; to blame.

accused *n* a person charged with a crime.

accustom *vt* to make familiar with by use.

accustomed *adj* familiar by custom; usual.

ace *n* a unit; a single point on cards or dice; an expert.

acerbity n sourness; bitterness.

acetic adj sour; like vinegar.

ache vi to be in pain. * n a gnawing pain.

achieve vt to accomplish; to win.

achievement n an accomplishment through effort.

acid adj sharp or sour to the taste. * n a sour substance; one that with certain other substances forms salts; (inf) LSD.

acidhead n (inf) name given to an individual who uses the drug LSD.

acidity n sourness.

acknowledge vt to own the knowledge of; to own or confess.

acknowledgement n recognition.

acolyte n an attendant.

acorn n the fruit of the oak.

acoustics n the science of sound; the sound properties, good or bad, of a room or hall.

acquaint vt to make to know; to inform.

acquiesce vi to rest satisfied; to comply.

acquiescence n assent.

acquiescent adj resting satisfied; submitting.

acquire vt to obtain; to gain.

acquisition n acquirement; gain.

acquisitive adj fond of getting; eager to possess things.

acquit vt to set free; to absolve.

acquittal n a setting free from a charge.

acre n a quantity of land containing 4840 square yards (4046.7 square metres).

acreage n the number of acres in a piece of land.

acrid adj sharp to the taste or smell.

acrimonious adj full of bitterness.

acrimony n sharpness or harshness of temper or tone of speech.

acrobat n a rope dancer; a gymnast.

acronym n a word made up of initial letters or parts of words.

across prep, adv from side to side; over; crosswise.

act vi to be in action; to exert power; to conduct oneself. * vt to do; to perform; to play on the stage; to pretend. * n a deed; power; a part of a play; law, as an act of parliament; pretence.

acting n performance of a part in a play. * adj taking someone's place for a time.

action n a deed; operation; a gesture; a lawsuit; a battle.

actionable adj furnishing grounds for an action at law.

active adj busy; quick; lively.

activity n nimbleness; an occupation, work or leisure a person is engaged in.

actor n one who acts; a stage player.

actress n a female stage player.

actual adj real.

actuary n a specialist in insurance statistics.

actuate vt to put into action; to incite.

acumen n sharpness of perception; sagacity.

acute adj sharp; pointed; keen; sharp in sound or of hearing; intense; of supreme importance.

adage n a proverb; a maxim.

adagio adj, adv in music, slow; with grace. * n a slow movement.

adamant n any substance of impenetrable hardness; the diamond.

adapt vt to adjust or change to suit a purpose.

adaptable adj able to be adapted.

adaptation n the result of adapting, e.g. a book for another medium.

add vt to join to; to find sum of.

addendum n (pl **addenda**) something added.

addict vt (usu passive with **to**) to be given to or dependent on. * n one addicted to something, e.g. drugs.

addition n act of adding; the thing added.

additional adj added on.

addled adj rotten; muddled.

address vt to direct; to speak to. * n verbal or written application; speech or discourse; tact; direction of a letter.

adept n, adj well skilled (person).

adequate adj sufficient; passable.

adhere vi to stick; to cling.

adherent adj sticking to. * n a follower.

adhesion n the act or state of sticking to; adherence.

adhesive adj sticking; sticky.

adieu interj farewell.

adipose adj fatty.

adjacent adj adjoining.

adjective n a word that qualifies a noun.

adjoining adj adjacent.

adjourn vt to postpone. * vi to leave off for a time.

adjournment n act of adjourning; postponement.

adjudge vt to decree.

adjudicate vt to adjudge; to determine judicially; to give a ruling on.

adjunct n something added or joined. * adj united with.

adjust vt to set right; to fit.

adjustable adj able to be adjusted.

adjustment n the act of adjusting; a settlement.

administer vt to manage; to dispense; to distribute.

administration n management; the executive part of a government.

admirable adj worthy of admiration; excellent.

admiral n the commander of a fleet or navy.

admiralty n a board for administering naval affairs.

admiration n wonder mingled with delight and respect; esteem.

admire vt to regard with delight or affection and respect.

admissible adj allowable.

admission n admittance; concession.

admit vt to allow to enter; to grant.

admittance n permission to enter; entrance; allowance; confession.

admonish vt to warn; to reprove.

admonition n gentle or solemn reproof.

adolescence n a growing up to adulthood; the age of youth.

adopt vt to take and raise as one's own (child); to embrace.

adorable adj worthy to be loved.

adoration n worship paid to God; profound reverence.

adore vt to worship; to love intensely.

adorn vt to deck with ornaments; to beautify.

adrenaline n a hormone secreted in

glands in the kidney which is released by stress and increases the heart and pulse rate.

adrift *adv* at the mercy of circumstance; floating at random.

adroit *adj* skilful; clever.

adulation *n* servile flattery.

adult *adj* full-grown. * *n* a person grown to manhood.

adulterate *vt* to debase by mixture.

adulterer *n* a person guilty of adultery.

adultery *n* unfaithfulness to marriage vows.

advance *vt* to put forward; (in commerce) to pay beforehand. * *vi* to go forward. * *n* a going forward; progress.

advanced *adj* in the van of progress.

advancement *n* improvement; promotion in station, career, etc.

advantage *n* a favourable state; gain; a term in tennis.

advantageous *adj* profitable.

advent *n* arrival; (*with cap*) the four weeks before Christmas.

adventure *n* a hazardous enterprise; an exciting experience. * *vt, vi* to risk or hazard.

adventurer *n* one who risks, hazards, or braves.

adventurous *adj* daring.

adverb *n* a word which modifies a verb, adjective or another adverb.

adversary *n* an enemy; an antagonist.

adverse *adj* hostile; contrary.

adversity *n* misfortune.

advertise *vt* to announce; to publish a notice of.

advertisement *n* information; a public notice promoting something.

advertiser *n* one who advertises.

advice *n* an opinion offered; counsel.

advisable *adj* fitting or proper to be done; expedient.

advise *vt* to counsel; to warn; to inform. * *vi* to deliberate or consider.

advised *adj* cautious; done with advice.

advisedly *adv* deliberately.

advocate *n* one who pleads for another; a barrister. * *vt* to plead in favour of; to defend, esp in a law court.

adze *n* a kind of axe, with the edge at right angles to the handle.

aegis *n* protection; sponsorship.

aerate *vt* to put air or other gas into.

aerial *adj* belonging to the air; lofty. * *n* a device, antenna to receive and transmit radio waves.

aerie, eyrie *n* the nest of a bird of prey.

aeronaut *n* one who flies, sails or floats in the air.

aeronautics *n* the science of flight.

aeroplane, airplane *n* an aircraft with wings.

aesthetics the science or philosophy of art and the beautiful.

afar *adv* at, to or from a distance.

affability *n* geniality; friendliness.

affable *adj* courteous; accessible.

affair *n* a business matter; an event; a sexual relationship, usually temporary.

affect *vt* to act upon; to move the feelings of; to pretend.

affectation *n* an assumed air put on by a person; pretence.

affection n fondness; love.

affectionate adj tender; loving.

affidavit n a written declaration upon oath.

affiliate vt to adopt; to attach to a society or other body.

affinity n relation by marriage; liking; similarity; chemical attraction.

affirm vt to assert; to declare.

affirmation n a solemn declaration (instead of an oath).

affirmative adj positive; stating a thing to be true. * n that which expresses assent; the word 'yes'.

affix vt to fasten to. * n a syllable or letter added to a word.

afflict vt to grieve; to cause pain or sorrow.

affliction n distress; grief; pain.

affluence n abundance; wealth.

affluent adj wealthy; abundant.

afford vt to yield; to supply; to be able to spend, to grant.

affray n a fight; a disturbance; a tumult.

affront vt to insult; to offend. * n an insult.

afield adv to or in the field; far away.

afloat adv, adj floating; at sea.

afoot adv on foot; in motion; happening.

aforementioned adj mentioned before.

aforenamed adj named before.

aforesaid adj said before.

afraid adj struck with fear; feeling regret.

afresh adv anew.

aft adj, adv astern.

after adj later. * prep later in time than; behind. * adv later in time.

aftermath n the result or after-effects, usu of something unpleasant; a season's second crop of grass.

afternoon n the time from noon to evening.

afterthought n reflection after an act.

afterwards adv subsequently.

again adv once more.

against prep in opposition to; in expectation of.

agate n a hard quartz-like mineral.

age n a period of time; an epoch; the length of a person's life. * vi, vt to grow or make old; to show signs of advancing age.

ageism n discrimination on grounds of age.

agency n means; a specialized or specific business; the business of an agent.

agenda npl business to be transacted at a meeting.

agent n one who acts; a deputy.

agglomeration n a heap.

aggrandize vt to magnify; to increase in power, riches, etc.

aggravate vt to intensify; to exasperate.

aggravation n the act of aggravating; provocation.

aggregate vt to collect. * adj total * n the sum of parts.

aggression n the first act of hostility; attack.

aggressive adj inclined to attacking; prone to quarrelling.

aggressor n the person who starts hostilities.

aggrieve vt to pain; to vex.

aghast adj, adv amazed; horrified.

agile adj nimble.

agility n nimbleness.

agitate vt to put in violent motion; to excite; to stir up.

agitated adj disturbed.

agitation n excitement; commotion.

agitator n one who excites discontent or revolt.

agnostic n one who disclaims any knowledge of God.

agog adv in eager excitement.

agonize vi to writhe with extreme pain.

agonizing adj giving extreme pain.

agony n extreme pain of body or mind; anguish.

agrarian adj relating to land and agriculture.

agree vi to be in concord; to suit.

agreeable adj suitable to; pleasing; grateful.

agreement n harmony; conformity; compact.

agriculture n the art or science of cultivating the ground.

aground adv stranded; on the shore.

ague n an intermittent fever with shivering.

ahead adv before; onward.

aid vt to help. * n help.

AIDS, Aids n acronym for a complex medical condition, acquired immune deficiency syndrome.

ail vt to pain. * vi to be in pain.

ailment n a pain; a disease.

aim vi to point with a weapon; to intend; to endeavour. * vt to level or direct as a firearm. * n intention; purpose.

aimless adj without aim.

air n the atmosphere; a light breeze; a tune; bearing (npl) affected manner. * vt to expose to the air; to dry.

air-conditioning n a regulating system controlling temperature, freshness and humidity of air (in a building).

aircraft n any machine that flies in the air.

airily adv in an airy manner.

airing n an exposure to the air or to a fire; an excursion in the open air.

airline n a company or organization running aeroplanes for transportation.

airplane see **aeroplane**.

airport n a place where aircraft land and take off and undergo repairs.

air pump n a machine for pumping the air out of a vessel.

air raid n an attack on ground targets by military aircraft.

airtight adj so tight or compact as not to let air pass.

airworthy adj safe to fly.

airy adj open to the air; fresh; casual; light-hearted.

aisle n a wing or side of a church; a passage in a church.

ajar adv partly open.

akin adj of the same kin; related to.

alabaster n a soft marble-like mineral.

alacrity n liveliness; eagerness.

alarm n a call to arms; sudden surprise; fright. * vt to give notice of danger.

alarming adj terrifying.

alarmist n one prone to excite alarm.

albino n a person with abnormally

white skin and hair and pink eyes.

album *n* a book for autographs, sketches, etc; a long-playing record containing several items.

albumen *n* the white of an egg.

alchemy *n* an obsolete science, aiming at changing metals into gold, etc.

alcohol *n* pure spirit of a highly intoxicating nature produced by distilling or fermenting.

alcove *n* a recess.

alderman *n* formerly a magistrate of a town.

ale *n* a fermented malt liquor; beer.

alert *adj* vigilant; quick. * *vt* to warn.

alertness *n* briskness; activity.

algebra *n* the science of computing by symbols.

alias *adv* otherwise. * *n* (*pl* **aliases**) an assumed name.

alibi *n* the plea that one was elsewhere when a crime was committed.

alien *adj* foreign. * *n* a foreigner.

alienate *vt* to transfer to another; to estrange; to cause hostility towards.

alight[1] *vi* to get down; to settle on.

alight[2] *adj*, *adv* on fire.

alike *adj* like; similar. * *adv* in the same manner.

aliment *n* nourishment; food.

alimony *n* an allowance to a woman legally separated from her husband.

alive *adj* living; lively.

alkali *n* a substance, as potash and soda, which neutralizes acids.

all *adj* every one. * *n* everything * *adv* wholly; entirely.

allay *vt* to ease; to assuage.

allegation *n* an assertion or statement made, often without having proof.

allege *vt* to assert, often without proof.

allegiance *n* loyalty.

allegorical *adj* figurative.

allegory *n* a story, etc which conveys a meaning different from the literal one.

allegro a word denoting a sprightly movement in music.

alleviate *vt* to make light; to assuage; to relieve pain.

alley *n* a narrow walk or passage.

alliance *n* state of being allied; league; the countries forming this.

allied *adj* united by treaty or marriage.

alliteration *n* the repetition of a letter at the beginning of two or more words in close succession.

allocate *vt* to distribute.

allot *vt* to give by lot; to apportion.

allow *vt* to let; to admit the truth or the possibility of; to grant.

allowance *n* a sum allotted; permission.

alloy *vt* to mix with baser metals. * *n* a mixture of metals.

allude *vi* to refer to.

allure *vt* to entice; to decoy.

allurement *n* temptation; enticement.

alluring *adj* attractive.

allusion *n* a hint; a reference.

alluvial *adj* deposited by water.

ally *vt* to unite by friendship, marriage, or treaty. * *n* an associate.

almanac *n* a calendar of days, weeks, and months, etc.

almighty *adj* omnipotent. * *n* God.

almond *n* the nut of the almond tree.

almoner *n* formerly a hospital social worker.

almost *adv* nearly.

aloft *adv* in the sky; on high.

alone *adj* solitary. * *adv* separately.

along *adv* lengthways. * *prep* by the side of.

aloof *adv* apart.

aloud *adv* loudly.

alpaca *n* a llama with long hair; cloth made from this hair.

alphabet *n* the letters of a language.

alpine *adj* pertaining to high mountains. * *n* a small plant growing on mountainsides.

already *adv* even now.

also *adv* likewise; too.

altar *n* an elevated stone on which sacrifices were offered; the communion table.

alter *vt* to change. * *vi* to vary.

alteration *n* partial change or variation.

altercation *n* a wrangle; an angry dispute.

alternate *adj* by turns. * *vt* to follow by turns.

alternative *n* a choice of two things.

although *conj* though.

altitude *n* height.

alto *adj* high. * *n* (*mus*) contralto.

altogether *adv* wholly.

altruism *n* devotion to others; unselfishness.

aluminium *n* a soft white light metal.

always *adv* at all times.

amalgam *n* a mixture of mercury with another metal, usually silver.

amalgamate *vt* to unite in an amalgam; to combine.

amass *vt* to form into a mass; to heap up.

amateur *n* a lover of any art or science or a participant in any sport or activity, but not a professional.

amaze *vt* to astonish.

amazement *n* wonder.

ambassador *n* a diplomatic representative of a country abroad.

amber *n* a mineralized yellow or yellow-brown fossil resin used for jewellery.

ambidextrous *adj* using both hands alike.

ambiguity *n* doubtfulness of meaning or interpretation.

ambiguous *adj* doubtful; obscure.

ambit *n* compass; scope.

ambition *n* desire for preferment or power.

ambitious *adj* aspiring.

amble *vi* to walk at a slow easy pace. * *n* an easy pace.

ambrosia *n* the imaginary food of the gods.

ambulance *n* a vehicle for transporting the sick or wounded.

ambulatory *adj* movable; walking.

ambush *n* the place or act of lying in wait in order to surprise.

ameliorate *vt* to make better.

amen *adv* so be it.

amenable *adj* easily led; cooperative; accountable.

amend *vt* to correct; to improve. * *vi* to grow better.

amendment *n* a change for the better; correction; reformation.

amends *npl* compensation; satisfaction; recompense.

amenity *n* pleasantness; agreeableness of situation.

amethyst *n* a precious stone of a bluish violet or purple colour.

amiability *n* sweetness of temper.

amiable *adj* loveable; pleasant; friendly.

amicable *adj* friendly; kind.

amid, amidst *prep* in the midst of.

amidships *adv* in or towards the middle of a ship.

amiss *adj* in error; improper. * *adv* improperly.

amity *n* friendship.

ammonia *n* volatile alkali.

ammonite *n* an extinct marine animal; its coiled shell found as a fossil.

ammunition *n* war stores and projectiles, e.g. bullets, rockets, fired from weapons; any helpful facts, etc, to be used in winning an argument.

amnesty *n* a general pardon.

amoeba *n* (*pl* **amoebae, amoebas**) a minute organism that constantly changes shape, found in fresh water.

among, amongst *prep* amidst.

amorous *adj* inclined to or showing love.

amorphous *adj* shapeless.

amount *vi* to mount up to; to result in. * *n* the sum total.

ampere *n* the unit of current in electricity.

amphibian *n* an animal able to live either on land or in water.

amphibious *adj* able to live in water or on land; (of a vehicle) built to operate on land and water.

amphitheatre *n* a building of an oval form, with rows of seats all round, rising one above the other.

ample *adj* spacious; abundant; sufficient.

amplification *n* enlargement.

amplifier *n* a device that amplifies or enlarges or makes the sound louder.

amplify *vt, vi* to enlarge; to make louder; to fill out.

amplitude *n* ampleness; extent; abundance.

amply *adv* fully; copiously.

amputate *vt* to cut off, as a limb.

amuck, amok *n, adv*: **to run ~** to attack all and sundry.

amulet *n* a charm against evils.

amuse *vt* to entertain; to beguile; to cause laughter.

amusement *n* diversion; entertainment.

amusing *adj* droll; diverting.

an *adj* the indefinite article, used before words beginning with a vowel sound.

anachronism *n* the error of assigning an event or circumstance out of its time.

anaemia *n* bloodlessness.

anaesthetic *adj* producing unconsciousness. * *n* a substance (drug or gas) that produces unconsciousness.

anagram *n* a word formed from the letters of another, e.g. rood from door.

analogous *adj* corresponding.

analogy *n* similarity.

analyse *vt* to resolve into its elements.

analysis *n* (*pl* **analyses**) a breaking up of a thing into its elements.

analyst *n* one who analyses.

anarchic *adj* without rule or government.

anarchist *n* one who opposes all forms of government.

anathema *n* an object of detestation.

anatomical *adj* relating to anatomy.

anatomy *n* the science dealing with physical structure of animals and plants; the art of dissection.

ancestor *n* a forefather.

ancestral *adj* relating or belonging to ancestors.

ancestry *n* lineage; descent.

anchor *n* an iron instrument that grips the sea or river bed and holds a ship at rest in water. * *vt* to hold fast by an anchor.

anchorage *n* a place where a ship can anchor.

ancient *adj* old; antique.

ancillary *adj* subservient or subordinate.

and *conj* a word joining words or phrases; also; in addition, consequently.

andante *adj* in music, with slow, graceful movement.

anecdote *n* a short often amusing story.

anemometer *n* an instrument for measuring the force of the wind.

aneroid *adj* a kind of barometer.

aneurysm *adj* dilatation of an artery.

anew *adv* once more.

anger *n* wrath. * *vt* to enrage.

angle *n* the inclination of two lines that meet in a point; a corner; a viewpoint.

angler *n* one who fishes with hook and line.

Anglican *adj* pertaining to the Church of England. * *n* a member of the Church of England.

Anglicize *vt* to make English.

angling *n* fishing with hook and line.

Anglophobia *n* an excessive hatred of English people, customs, etc.

angry *adj* full of anger; wrathful.

anguish *n* extreme pain, body or mind.

angular *adj* sharp-cornered; (of a person) thin and bony.

animal *n* a living being having sensation and voluntary motion.

animate *vt* to give life to; to enliven; to produce moving objects and figures by animation.

animated *adj* lively; living; (film, etc) made by animation.

animation *n* life; vigour; vivacity; the art of drawing objects and filming them to create moving images on film or tape.

animosity *n* violent hatred; active enmity.

ankle *n* the joint which connects the foot with the leg.

annals *npl* a yearly record of events.

annex *vt* to unite at the end; to subjoin; to take possession of.

annexation *n* the act of annexing.

annexe *n* an extension to a building, built on to it or erected nearby.

annihilate *vt* to reduce to nothing.

annihilation *n* the act of annihilating; nonexistence.

anniversary *n* a day on which some event is annually celebrated.

annotate *vt* to write notes upon.

announce *vt* to make known.

announcement *n* declaration.

annoy *vt* to hurt; to vex.

annoyance *n* act of annoying; state of being annoyed.

annual *adj* yearly; lasting a year. * *n* a book published yearly.

annuitant *n* one who receives an annuity.

annuity *n* a sum of money payable yearly.

annul *vt* to make of no effect; to repeal.

anoint *vt* to consecrate with oil; to rub with or apply oil to.

anomalous *adj* irregular; exceptional.

anomaly *n* irregularity.

anonymous *adj* nameless; unsigned.

another *adj* not the same.

answer *vt* to reply to; to suit. * *n* a reply; a solution.

answerable *adj* accountable.

antagonism *n* opposition; hostility.

antagonist *n* an opponent.

antagonistic *adj* hostile.

Antarctic *adj* of or near the South Pole.

antecedent *adj* going before. * *n* that which goes before; (*pl*) ancestors; a person's history.

antechamber *n* anteroom.

antedate *vt* to date before the true time.

antediluvian *adj* before the flood.

antelope *n* a kind of deer.

antemeridian *adj* before midday; a.m.

antenna *n* (*pl* **antennae**) one of the feelers of an insect; an aerial.

anterior *adj* prior.

anteroom *n* a room leading to another.

anthem *n* a piece of Scripture set to music.

anthology *n* a collection of poems or prose.

anthracite *n* a kind of coal which burns almost without flame.

antics *npl* buffoonery and posturing.

anticipate *vt* to forestall.

anticipation *n* act of anticipating; expectation.

anticlimax *n* a tame ending to a striking beginning.

anticyclone *n* an opposite state of atmospheric conditions to what exists in a cyclone, presaging good weather.

antidote *n* a remedy for poison or any evil.

antipathy *n* aversion; dislike.

antipodes *npl* the opposite side of the globe.

antiquarian *adj* pertaining to antiquaries.

antiquated *adj* old-fashioned; out of date.

antique *adj* old. * *n* an ancient relic, object of value or work of art.

antiquity *n* ancient times; great age; (*pl* **antiquities**) remains of ancient times.

antiseptic *adj* counteracting contamination.

antithesis *n* (*pl* **antitheses**) contrast.

antler *n* a branch of a stag's horn.

anus *n* the excretory opening of the alimentary canal.

anvil *n* an iron block used by smiths.

anxiety *n* concern; worry.

anxious *adj* troubled; worried; eager.

any *adj* one indefinitely.

aorta *n* the artery leading from the heart.

apace *adv* fast.

apart *adj*, *adv* separate; aside; in pieces.

apartment *n* a room; a flat.

apathetic *adj* indifferent.

apathy *n* want of feeling; indifference.

ape *n* a monkey. * *vt* to mimic.

aperture *n* an opening.

apex *n* (*pl* **apexes, apices**) the summit.

apiary *n* a place where bees are kept.

apiece *adv* in a separate share.

aplomb *n* self-possession.

apocalypse *n* a disastrous happening.

apocryphal *adj* fictitious.

apologetic *adj* excusing.

apologize *vi* to make an excuse.

apology *n* that which is said in defence or as an expression of regret.

apoplexy *n* a shock involving paralysis.

apostasy *n* departure from one's faith or party.

apostate *n* one who renounces his religion or his party.

apostrophe *n* a mark (') indicating contraction of a word, or the possessive case.

apotheosis *n* a deification.

appal *vt* to dismay.

appalling *adj* causing dread or terror.

apparatus *n* (*pl* **apparatus**) tools or equipment for doing work or for a special purpose.

apparel *n* clothing. * *vt* to dress.

apparent *adv* evident; seeming.

apparition *n* a ghost or phantom.

appeal *vi*, *vt* to entreat; to carry to a higher court. * *n* entreaty.

appear *vi* to become visible; to seem.

appearance *n* act of coming into sight; semblance.

appease *vt* to pacify; to calm.

appellant *n* one who appeals.

appellation *n* a name; a title.

append *vt* to add; to attach.

appendage *n* something added; an external organ, e.g. a tail.

appendicitis *n* inflammation of the vermiform appendix of the bowels.

appendix *n* (*pl* **appendices**) an adjunct; a supplement; a prolongation; (*pl* **appendixes**) a small tube of tissue that forms an outgrowth of the intestine (vermiform appendix).

appertain *vi* to belong.

appetite *n* a desire or relish for food.

appetize *vt* to whet the appetite.

applaud *vt* to praise by clapping the hands.

applause *n* praise loudly expressed.

apple *n* a fruit.

appliance *n* the act of applying; the thing applied; a device or machine usually for domestic use.

applicability *n* relevance.

applicable *adj* suitable.

applicant *n* one who applies, e.g. for work.

application *n* the act of applying; perseverance; (*comput*) a program.

apply *vt* to fasten or attach. * *vi* to suit; to make application.

appoint *vt* to fix; to nominate.

appointment *n* office; engagement.

apposite *adj* suitable.

appraise *vt* to fix or set a price or value on.

appreciable *adj* that may be appreciated.

appreciate *vt* to value; to be grateful to or thankful for. * *vi* to rise in value.

appreciation *n* the act of appreciating; a just valuation; approval; gratitude; a rise in value.

apprehend *vt* to take hold of; to arrest; to fear; to understand.

apprehension *n* seizure; dread.

apprehensive *adj* fearful.

apprentice *n* one who is learning a trade or occupation. * *vt* to bind as an apprentice.

apprise *vt* to inform.

approach *vt*, *vi* to come near. * *n* the act of drawing near; an avenue.

approbation *n* approval.

appropriate *vt* to take to oneself as one's own. * *adj* suitable.

appropriateness *n* peculiar fitness.

approval *n* praise; a favourable opinion.

approve *vt* to consider good; to sanction. * *vi* (with **of**) to express approbation.

approximate *adj* near; almost right or good. * *vt* to bring near. * *vi* to come near.

approximately *adv* nearly.

apricot *n* a stone fruit, allied to the plum.

April *n* the fourth month of the year.

apron *n* a garment worn in front to protect the clothes.

apt *adj* suitable; liable.

aptitude *n* natural facility.

aquarium *n* (*pl* **aquariums, aquaria**) a vessel or tank or building for aquatic plants and animals.

Aquarius *n* the water bearer, a sign in the zodiac.

aquatic *adj* living or growing in water; (*pl*) water sports.

aqueduct *n* a conduit made for conveying water.

aqueous *adj* watery.

aquiline *adj* hooked like the beak of an eagle.

Arab *n* a native of Arabia; an Arabian horse.

arabesque *n* a species of ornamentation consisting of fanciful figures in dance and music, and floral forms in art.

arable *adj* fit for ploughing and growing.

arbiter *n* an umpire.

arbitrarily *adv* by will or caprice only; despotically.

arbitrary *adj* despotic; capricious.

arbitrate *vi* to act as an arbiter; to decide.

arbitrator *n* a person chosen to decide a dispute; referee.

arboriculture *n* the art of cultivating trees and shrubs.

arc *n* a part of a circle or curve.

arcade *n* a covered passage with shops.

arcane *adj* understood only with inside knowledge; secret; mysterious.

arch¹ *adj* chief; expert; roguish; sly.

arch² *n* a curved structure supporting a bridge or roof.

archaeology *n* the science of antiquities; knowledge of ancient art.

archaic *adj* antiquated; obsolete.

archbishop *n* a chief bishop.

archdeacon *n* a church dignitary, next in rank to a bishop.

archer *n* a person who shoots with a bow and arrow.

archery *n* the art of the archer.

archipelago *n* a sea abounding in islands.

architect *n* one who plans buildings.

architecture *n* the art or science of building.

archive *n* a record; (generally *pl*) public records.

archness *n* roguishness; slyness.

archway *n* a passage under an arch.

Arctic *adj* pertaining to the regions about the North Pole; frigid; cold.

ardent *adj* fervent; eager.

ardour *n* warmth; eagerness; passion.

arduous *adj* difficult.

arduously *adv* with effort.

area *n* any open surface; surface measurement; any enclosed or sunken space.

arena *n* an open space of ground for contests or games.

argue *vt*, *vi* to discuss; to dispute.

argument *n* a reason offered; a plea; a controversy.

argumentative *adj* prone to argument.

arid *adj* dry; parched.

Aries *n* the ram, the first of the twelve signs in the zodiac.

arise *vi* (*pp* **arisen**, *pt* **arose**) to rise up; to come about.

aristocracy *n* government by the nobility; the nobility.

aristocrat *n* a noble.

arithmetic *n* the science of numbers; computation.

ark *n* a large floating vessel; a place of refuge.

arm *n* the limb from the shoulder to the hand; a weapon; (*pl*) war; armour; armorial bearings. * *vt* to furnish with arms. * *vi* to take up arms.

armada *n* a fleet of armed ships.

armament *n* a force armed for war; war equipment of an army, ship or vehicle.

armistice *n* a truce.

armorial *adj* relating to arms in heraldry.

armour *n* defensive arms.

armoury *n* a place for keeping arms.

armpit *n* the hollow place under the shoulder.

army *n* a body of men armed for war.

aroma *n* perfume.

aromatic *adj* fragrant.

around *prep* about; encircling. * *adv* on every side.

arouse *vt* to stir up.

arraign *vt* to indict; to censure.

arrange *vt* to put in order; to prepare for; to plan; to adjust a musical work for different instruments.

arrangement *n* orderly disposition; classification; agreement.

arrant *adj* downright; thorough.

array *n* order; apparel. * *vt* to draw up in order; to adorn.

arrear n (generally pl) that which remains unpaid.

arrest vt to stop; to apprehend. * n a seizure by warrant.

arrival n the act of coming to a place.

arrive vi to come; to reach; to succeed.

arrogance n haughtiness; insolent bearing.

arrogant adj haughty; overbearing; self-important.

arrow n a barbed shaft shot from a bow.

arsenal n a public establishment for making or storing weapons of war.

arsenic n a virulent mineral poison.

arson n the malicious setting on fire of a house, etc.

art n practical skill; cunning; profession of a painter, etc.

arterial adj pertaining to arteries; pertaining to a main road, railway, etc.

artery n a tube which conveys blood from the heart; a main road, etc, or means of communication.

artesian adj applied to wells made by boring.

artful adj skilful; crafty.

arthritis n painful inflammation of a joint.

article n a separate item; composition (in newspaper); a part of speech, as the. * vt to bind by articles. * vi to stipulate.

articulate adj distinct; clear and intelligible. * vi to utter distinct sounds.

artifice n an artful device or deception.

artificial adj made by art; not natural.

artillery n cannon and heavy guns in general; the troops who manage them.

artist n one skilled in some art, esp the fine arts.

artistic adj characteristic of art; aesthetic.

artless adj unaffected.

as adv, conj, prep like; for example; because; in the same way; playing the part of.

asbestos n a mineral fibrous incombustible substance.

ascend vi to rise. * vt to climb.

ascendancy, ascendency n controlling power; sway.

ascendant adj superior. * n superiority.

ascension n act of ascending.

ascent n rise; upward slope.

ascertain vt to make certain; to find out.

ascetic adj unduly rigid in self-denial and self-discipline.

ascribe vt to attribute.

aseptic adj not liable to putrefy; rendered free of germs.

ashamed adj affected by shame or guilt.

ashen adj made of ash; pale.

ashes npl the remains of anything burned; (fig) a dead body.

ashore adv, adj on or to the shore.

aside adv on one side; apart. * n words spoken by an actor to an audience only.

asinine adj belonging to or resembling the ass; stupid.

ask vt to request. * vi to make inquiry.

askance adv awry; obliquely.

askew adv, adj awry.

asleep adj, adv sleeping.

aspect n appearance; outlook.

asperity n roughness; harshness.

aspersion n calumny, lie; (esp pl) slander; defamation.

asphalt n a kind of pitch used for paving.

aspirant n a candidate.

aspirate vt to pronounce with an audible breath; to add an h sound to.

aspiration n ardent desire; ambition.

aspire vi to aim at high things.

ass n a long-eared animal akin to the horse.

assagai, assegai n a light African throwing spear.

assail vt to attack.

assailant n one who assails; an attacker.

assassin n one who kills by surprise or secretly.

assassinate vt to murder by surprise or treacherously.

assault n an attack. * vt to assail.

assay n proof; analysis of ores. * vt to try.

assemblage n a collection of persons or things.

assemble vt to bring together. * vi to come together.

assembly n a gathering of people to consult together; a putting together of many parts to make a whole.

assent n consent. * vi to agree.

assert vt to affirm.

assertive adj affirming confidently.

assess vt to rate; to value or estimate amount, worth, etc.

assessable adj that may be assessed.

assessment n the act of assessing; the sum levied.

asset n a useful or valuable thing.

assiduity n close application; diligence.

assiduous adj constantly diligent.

assign vt to designate; to allot; to make over to another.

assignable adj that may be assigned.

assignation n an appointment to meet; a making over by transfer of title.

assignee n one to whom an assignment is made.

assignment n an allotment or legal transfer; a task assigned to someone.

assimilate vt to make like to; to digest.

assist vt to help. * vi to lend help.

assistance n help; aid.

assistant n one who assists.

assize n an assessment court; (pl) periodical courts for administering justice.

associate vt to join in company with. * vi to keep company with. * n a companion; a business colleague or partner.

association n act of associating; union.

assort vt to arrange. * vi to suit.

assortment n a varied collection.

assuage vt to allay; to calm.

assume vt to take for granted; to usurp. * vi to claim more than is due.

assumption n act of assuming; the thing assumed.

assurance n secure confidence; impudence; insurance.

assure vt to confirm; to insure.

assuredly adv certainly.

asterisk n a star-shaped mark used in printing (*) to indicate an omission, cross-reference, footnote, etc.

astern adv in or at the hinder part of a ship.

asteroid n a small planet.

asthma n a disease marked by shortness of breath.

astigmatism n a defect in the eyes preventing proper focusing.

astir adv awake or stirring; active.

astonish vt to amaze.

astonishment n amazement.

astound vt to astonish; to stun.

astrakhan n a rough cloth with a curled pile made from lambs bred in Astrakhan.

astral adj belonging to the stars.

astray adv straying.

astride adv with the legs apart or on either side of something.

astringent n a medicine that contracts the tissues. * adj binding; constricting; harsh; sharp; bracing.

astrologer n one versed in astrology.

astrology n the art of foretelling future events from the stars.

astronomer n one versed in astronomy.

astronomical adj pertaining to astronomy; very large.

astronomy n the science of the heavenly bodies.

astute adj shrewd; crafty.

astuteness n shrewdness.

asunder adv apart; into parts.

asylum n a place of refuge; an institution for the care of the insane.

at prep denoting nearness, presence or location.

atheism n the disbelief in the existence of God.

atheist n one who disbelieves the existence of God.

athenaeum n a literary or scientific club.

athlete n one skilled in exercises of agility or strength.

athletic adj pertaining to an athlete; strong; active.

athletics npl sporting events of track and field; physical exercises.

atlas n a collection of maps.

atmosphere n the air surrounding the earth; pervading influence.

atmospheric adj pertaining to the atmosphere.

atoll n a ring-shaped coral reef or islands.

atom n a minute particle, esp of a chemical element; anything extremely small.

atomic adj pertaining to or consisting of atoms; extremely minute.

atone vi to make up for; to expiate.

atrocious adj abominable; very wicked.

atrocity n horrible wickedness.

atrophy n a wasting away.

attach vt to join; to affix. * vi to adhere.

attaché n one attached to the suite of an ambassador or a diplomatic mission.

attachment *n* fidelity; tender regard.

attack *vt* to assault. * *n* an assault; seizure by a disease.

attain *vi* to arrive at. * *vt* to reach; to gain.

attainable *adj* that may be attained.

attainment *n* accomplishment.

attempt *vt* to try to do. * *n* an essay; effort.

attend *vt* to wait on; to be present at. * *vi* to pay regard.

attendance *n* the act of attending; the persons attending.

attendant *adj* accompanying * *n* one who waits on or accompanies.

attention *n* heed; courtesy.

attentive *adj* heedful; courteous; diligent.

attenuate *vt* to make slender; to weaken.

attest *vt* to bear witness to.

attestation *n* testimony.

attic *n* a garret; a room or storing space under the roof of a house.

attire *vt* to dress. * *n* dress.

attitude *n* posture; a position or viewpoint taken on some matter.

attorney *n* (*pl* **attorneys**) a lawyer.

attract *vt* to draw to; to entice.

attraction *n* allurement; charm.

attractive *adj* having the power of attracting; enticing; pretty.

attributable *adj* that may be attributed.

attribute *vt* to ascribe, to impute. * *n* a quality; an adjectival word or clause.

attributive *adj* that attributes.

attrition *n* the act of wearing down by rubbing.

attune *vt* to put in tune; to adjust to or acclimatize.

auburn *adj* reddish brown.

auction *n* a public sale.

auctioneer *n* the person who sells at auction.

audacious *adj* daring; impudent.

audacity *n* daring; impudence.

audible *adj* that may be heard.

audience *n* an assembly of hearers; reception.

audit *n* an examination of accounts.

auditor *n* one who examines accounts.

auditory *adj* pertaining to the sense of hearing. * *n* an audience.

auger *n* a tool for boring holes.

aught *n* anything.

augment *vt* to make larger; to increase; * *n* increase; a prefix to a word.

augmentation *n* increase.

augur *n* one who foretold the future; a soothsayer. * *vt* to foretell.

august *adj* regal; imposing.

August *n* the eighth month of the year.

aunt *n* the sister of one's father or mother.

aura *n* a quality or atmosphere surrounding a person or thing.

aureole *n* in art, a golden disk or halo round the head of saints.

auricle *n* the external ear; one of the two ear-like cavities of the heart.

aurora borealis *n* the northern lights.

auscultation *n* detecting heart conditions by listening to beats.

auspices *npl* omens; patronage.

auspicious *adj* fortunate; favourable.

austere *adj* stern; severe.

austerity *n* sternness; severity; living without luxuries.

authentic *adj* genuine.

authenticate *vt* to attest; to confirm.

authenticity *n* genuineness.

author *n* the writer of a book, etc.

authoress *n* a female author.

authoritative *adj* official; decisive.

authority *n* legal power or right; person exercising this power.

authorize *vt* to sanction.

autobiography *n* memoirs of a person written by himself or herself.

autocracy *n* absolute government by one person.

autocrat *n* an absolute ruler.

autograph *n* a signature.

automatic *adj* self-acting; carried out without conscious thought.

automaton *n* (*pl* **automata**) a self-moving machine, or a person acting like one.

autonomy *n* self-government.

autopsy *n* an examination of a dead body to discover the cause of death.

autumn *n* the third season of the year.

auxiliary *adj* helping. * *n* a person or thing that helps.

avail *vt*, *vi* to profit; to be of use. * *n* advantage; use.

available *adj* attainable.

avalanche *n* a vast snow slide.

avarice *n* greed of gain.

avaricious *adj* covetous; greedy.

avenge *vt* to take satisfaction for; to harm in retaliation.

avenue *n* an approach to; a broad street.

aver *vt* to assert.

average *n* medium. * *adj* medial; moderate; not outstanding in ability. * *vi* to form a mean.

averse *adj* disinclined.

aversion *n* dislike.

avert *vt* to turn aside or away from.

aviary *n* a place for keeping birds.

aviation *n* the art of flying.

aviator *n* one who flies aeroplanes.

avocation *n* a person's regular business or occupation.

avoid *vt* to shun.

avoirdupois *n*, *adj* a system of weight, in which a pound contains sixteen ounces.

avow *vt* to declare with confidence; to confess frankly.

avowal *n* an admission.

avowedly *adv* openly.

await *vt* to wait for; to expect.

awake *vt* (*pp* **awaked** *or* **awoken**, *pt* **awoke**) to rouse from sleep. * *vi* to cease from sleep. * *adj* not sleeping.

awaken *vt*, *vi* to awake.

award *vt* to adjudge. * *vi* to make an award. * *n* a judgment; a reward or prize.

aware *adj* informed; cognizant.

away *adv* absent; at a distance.

awe *n* fear; fear mingled with reverence. * *vt* to strike with fear.

awful *adj* very bad; terrible.

awhile *adv* for some time.

awkward *adj* inexpert; inelegant; deliberately unhelpful; difficult.

awl *n* a tool for piercing small holes in leather.

awning *n* a canvas covering.

awry *adj*, *adv* twisted; distorted; gone wrong.

axe *n* an instrument for hewing and chopping.

axiom *n* a self-evident truth.

axiomatic *adj* self-evident.

axis *n* (*pl* **axes**) the line on which a body revolves; a partnership.

axle *n* the pole on which a wheel turns.

azure *adj* sky-blue.

B

babble *vi* to talk idly; to prate. * *n* idle talk; murmur, as of a stream.

babel *n* confusion.

baboon *n* a large kind of monkey.

baby *n* a child just born; a young animal.

baby-sit *vt*, *vi* to look after a child during the parents' absence.

bachelor *n* an unmarried man; a graduate of a university or college.

bacillus *n* (*pl* **bacilli**) a microscopic organism; a microbe.

back *n* the hind or (in beasts) the upper part of the body. * *vt* to support; to cause to recede. * *adv* to the rear.

backbite *vt* to speak evil of secretly.

backbone *n* the spine; strength.

background *n* the ground behind; the setting of a picture, etc; what has taken place beforehand; social status.

backslide *vi* to degenerate; to relapse.

backward *adj* looking backwards; lagging behind in progress or ability; shy, reserved.

backwards *adv* towards the back; with the back foremost; in a way opposite the usual; into a less good state or condition; into the past.

backwoods *npl* outlying forest districts; an isolated thinly populated area.

bacon *n* pig's flesh cured and dried.

bacteriology *n* the study of bacteria.

bacteria *npl* microbes; germs.

bad *adj* wicked; immoral.

badge *n* a distinguishing mark or emblem.

badger *n* a burrowing quadruped. * *vt* to worry; to pester.

badminton *n* a game like lawn tennis played with shuttlecocks as balls.

baffle *vt* to frustrate; to defeat.

bag *n* a sack; a pouch; a purse.

bagatelle *n* a trifle.

baggage *n* luggage.

bagpipe *n* a musical wind instrument.

bail *vt* to liberate from custody on security for reappearance; to free (a boat) from water, to bale. * *n* security given for release; the small bar placed on the stumps in cricket.

bailiff *n* a subordinate civil officer; a landowner's or landlord's steward or agent.

bait *n* food to trap or lure animals or fish; an enticement. * *vt* to furnish with a lure; to harass, esp by verbal teasing.

bake vt to dry and harden by fire; to cook in an oven.

balance n a pair of scales; equilibrium; difference of two sums; the sum due on an account. * vt to bring to an equilibrium; to settle. * vi to hesitate.

balance sheet n a statement of assets and liabilities.

balcony n a railed or walled platform projecting from a window; an upper tier of seats in a theatre or cinema.

bald adj wanting hair; bare; paltry.

baldly adv nakedly; meanly.

baldness n state of being bald; meagreness.

bale n a bundle or package of goods. * vt to free a boat from water; (with out) to escape from aircraft by parachute; to bail.

baleful adj deadly.

balk, baulk n a ridge; a great beam; part of a billiard table. * vt to baffle.

ball n a round body; a bullet; a dance.

ballad n a narrative poem; a popular sentimental song.

ballast n heavy matter carried in the bottom of a ship to keep it steady.

ballet n a theatrical dance.

balloon n a large bag filled with a gas which makes it float in the air.

ballot n a system of voting. * vi to vote by ballot.

balmy adj (of weather) pleasantly mild and calm.

balsam n soothing ointment.

baluster n a small column or pillar supporting a rail.

balustrade n a row of pillars joined by a rail.

bamboo n a tropical plant of the reed kind.

bamboozle vt to hoax; to confuse.

ban n a prohibition; an edict. * vt to curse; to forbid.

banal adj commonplace; vulgar.

banana n an edible plant with yellow fruit growing in hanging bunches.

band n that which binds; a company of people acting together, e.g. a group of musicians. * vt to unite in a troop.

bandage n a band; a cloth for a wound, etc. * vt to bind with a bandage.

bandit n a robber.

bandoleer n a shoulder strap for carrying cartridges.

bandy vt to exchange, esp words in anger; to pass to and fro.

bandy-legged adj having crooked legs.

baneful adj pernicious; poisonous.

bang vt to thump. * n a heavy blow.

bangle n a bracelet or anklet.

banish vt to drive away; to exile.

banishment n act of banishing; exile.

banjo n a six-stringed musical instrument.

bank n ground rising from the side of a river, lake, etc; place where money is deposited. * vt to deposit in a bank.

banking n the business of a banker.

bankrupt n one who cannot pay his or her debts. * adj unable to pay debts; insolvent.

banner n a flag; a cloth with a slogan.

bannister n a form of baluster that supports the uprights of a staircase.

banns npl the proclamation of marriage.

banquet n a feast.

banter vt to chaff; to rally. * n raillery.

baptise vt to administer baptism to; to christen.

baptism n an immersing in or sprinkling with water as a religious ceremony.

baptismal adj pertaining to baptism.

bar n a bolt; obstacle; a long piece of wood or metal; a tribunal; a body of barristers; anything that prohibits or obstructs; a counter where liquors are served. * vt to prohibit.

barb n the notched tip of a fishing hook or arrow.

barbarian adj savage; uncivilized. * n a savage

barbarism n extreme cruelty, coarseness or ignorance; an impropriety of speech.

barbarity n the state or qualities of a barbarian; ferociousness.

barbarous adj cruel; inhuman.

barbed adj jagged with hooks or points.

barber n a hairdresser.

bare adj uncovered; empty; worn. * vt to make naked; to reveal.

barebacked adj unsaddled.

barefaced adj shameless.

barefoot adj, adv with the feet bare.

bargain n something sold at a price favourable to the buyer, a gainful transaction.

barge n a flat-bottomed boat for freight used on canals and rivers; a canal pleasure boat. * vi to push in bodily.

bark n the outer rind of a tree; a barque; the noise made by a dog. * vt to strip bark off; to treat with bark; to make the cry of dogs.

barley n a species of grain used for making malt, beer, whisky, puddings, etc.

barmaid, barman n a woman, man who tends a bar.

barn n a building for storing grain, etc.

barometer n an instrument for measuring the weight of the atmosphere.

baron n a peer of the lowest rank.

baroness n a baron's wife.

baronet n the lowest order of hereditary titles.

barrack n (usu pl) buildings for housing soldiers. * vt to jeer loudly at.

barrage n a bar or dam constructed across a river; the firing of heavy artillery; a continuous onslaught as of words or blows.

barrel n a round wooden cask; the tube of a gun.

barren adj unfruitful; sterile.

barrenness n the state or quality of being barren.

barricade n a temporary fortification; a barrier. * vt to bar.

barrier n a fence; a bar.

barrister n a lawyer qualified to plead at the bar.

barrow n a small handcart; a burial mound.

barter vi to traffic by exchange. * vt

to exchange in commerce. * *n* traffic by exchange.

baritone *n* a male voice between tenor and bass.

basalt *n* a dark volcanic rock, often found in columnar form.

base *adj* low; worthless. * *n* foundation; support; chief ingredient of a compound. * *vt* to place on a basis; to found.

baseball *n* an American game with four bases set in diamond shape, played with bat and ball.

baseless *adj* groundless.

basement *n* the ground floor.

baseness *n* meanness; vileness.

bashful *adj* modest; shy.

basic *adj* relating to a base; fundamental.

basil *n* an aromatic herb.

basilica *n* a hall or church with double colonnades.

basin *n* a broad shallow container for liquid; its contents; a reservoir; a dock; land drained by a river.

basis *n* (*pl* **bases**) a base; groundwork.

bask *vi* to lie in the sun.

basket *n* a wicker container.

bass *n* the lowest part in musical harmony; the lowest male voice.

bassoon *n* a musical wind instrument.

bastard *adj* illegitimate; not genuine. * *n* a person whose parents are unmarried.

baste *vt* to beat with a stick; to drip fat on meat while roasting; to sew with temporary stitches.

bastion *n* a fortification standing out from a rampart.

bat *n* a flying mammal like a mouse; a club used to strike the ball in cricket, etc. * *vi* (*pt* **batted**) to play with a bat.

batch *n* the quantity of bread baked at one time; a quantity.

bath *n* a place to bathe in; immersion in water.

bathe *vt* to immerse in water. * *vi* to take a bath.

baton *n* a staff; a truncheon; a thin stick used by a conductor of music.

battalion *n* a military body three or more companies strong.

batten *n* a board for flooring; strip of wood to fasten down the hatches; a plank. * *vt* to fasten with battens.

batter *vt* to beat with violence. * *n* a cooking mixture of flour, eggs and milk.

battery *n* a fully equipped artillery unit; an apparatus for originating an electric current; a violent assault.

battle *n* encounter of two armies; a combat.

battlement *n* a parapet with openings to discharge missiles through.

battleship *n* a large warship furnished with heavy artillery.

bauble *n* a trifle.

bawl *vi* to shout; to weep loudly.

bay *adj* reddish-brown. * *n* an inlet on the shore of the sea or a lake; the laurel tree; the bark of a dog. * *vt* to bark at; (*with* **at**) with back to the wall.

bayonet *n* a dagger-like weapon fixed to a rifle.

bay window *n* a projecting window which forms a recess or bay within.

bazaar n a place of sale; a sale of articles for a charitable purpose.

be vi (pres t I **am**, you/we/they **are**, he/she/it **is**, pres p **being**, pt I/he/she/it **was**, you/we **were**, pp **been**) to exist; to remain.

beach n the shore of the sea. * vt to run (a vessel) on a beach.

beached adj stranded.

beacon n a flare; a signal of danger. * vt to light up.

bead n a little ball strung on a thread; a small drop of liquid; a small projection for sighting a gun.

beadle n a minor officer of a parish, church, or college.

beak n the bill of a bird.

beaker n a large drinking cup; a glass vessel.

beam n a main timber in a building; part of a balance which sustains the scales; a ray of light. * vi to shine; to smile broadly.

beaming adj emitting beams or rays; radiant.

bean n a name of several kinds of pulse or peas.

bear[1] vb (pt **bore**, pp **borne**) vt to carry; to suffer; to bring forth; to permit. * vi to suffer; to produce.

bear[2] n a large shaggy quadruped.

beard n the hair on the chin etc.

bearer n a carrier of anything.

bearing n manner, appearance and general behaviour.

beast n an animal; a brutal man.

beat vb (pt **beat**, pp **beaten**) vt to strike; to overcome. * vi to throb; to sail against the wind. * n a stroke; a rhythmic stroke of the heart; musical rhythm; the area patrolled by a police officer.

beatify vt to make happy; to pronounce a person worthy of canonization.

beating n act of striking; defeat.

beauteous adj beautiful.

beautiful adj full of beauty.

beautify vt to make beautiful; to adorn.

beauty n loveliness; elegance; a beautiful thing or person.

becalm vt to make calm.

because conj by cause of; on this account that; since.

beckon, beck vi to make a sign to approach by nodding, etc.

become vb (pt **became**, pp **become**) vi to come to be. * vt to suit.

becoming adj fitting; graceful.

bed n something to sleep or rest on; the channel of a river; a layer; a stratum. * vt to lay in a bed; to sow. * vi to go to bed.

bedding n the materials of a bed.

bedeck vt to adorn.

bedraggle vt to soil by drawing through the mud.

bedroom n a sleeping room.

bedsit n one room with cooking and sleeping facilities.

bedstead n a frame for supporting a bed.

beef n the flesh of an ox or cow.

beefeater n a yeoman of the royal guard.

beeline n a direct line or way.

beer n a fermented liquor made from barley and hops.

beeswax n the wax secreted by bees for their combs.

beet *n* a vegetable with fleshy roots, yielding sugar.

beetle *n* a common insect; a wooden mallet. * *vi* to jut; to hang over.

beetle-browed *adj* having prominent brows.

befall *vt* to happen to.

befit *vt* to suit.

before *prep, adv* in front of; earlier than; rather than; onward.

beforehand *adv* in advance.

befriend *vt* to act as a friend to.

beg *vt* to ask in charity; to ask earnestly; to avoid answering a question; to take for granted.

beget *vt* (*pt* **begot** *or* **begat**, *pp* **begotten**) to procreate; to produce.

beggar *n* one who begs. * *vt* to reduce to poverty; to be beyond, esp description.

begin *vb* (*pt* **began**, *pp* **begun**) *vi* to commence. * *vt* to enter on.

beginner *n* one who begins; a novice.

beginning *n* the first stage; commencement.

begrudge *vt* to envy the possession of.

beguile *vt* to dupe; to while away; to charm.

behalf *n* interest; support.

behave *vt* to conduct (oneself). * *vi* to act.

behaviour *n* conduct.

behead *vt* to cut off the head.

behest *n* a command.

behind *prep* in the rear of. * *adv* backwards.

behold *vt* (*pt, pp* **beheld**) to look upon; to regard with attention.

beholden *adj* obliged.

being *n* existence; a creature.

belabour *vt* to beat soundly.

belated *adj* arriving or made late.

belay *vt* (*naut*) to fasten a rope by winding round something.

belch *vt* to cast forth violently; to expel wind through the mouth.

beleaguer *vt* to besiege.

belfry *n* a bell tower.

belie *vt* to represent falsely; to fail to be equal to.

belief *n* faith; trust; opinion.

believe *vt* to accept as true; think.

belittle *vt* to make smaller; to disparage.

bell *n* a metallic vessel for making ringing sounds when struck; anything in the form of a bell. * *vt* to put a bell on.

bellicose *adj* pugnacious.

belligerent *adj* waging war; quarrelsome. * *n* a nation waging war.

bellow *vi* to roar like a bull. * *n* a roar.

bellows *npl* an instrument for blowing fires, supplying wind to organ pipes, etc.

belly *n* that part of the body which contains the bowels; the abdomen. * *vt, vi* to swell; to bulge.

belong *vi* to be the property of; to appertain to; to be a member.

belongings *npl* personal possessions.

beloved *adj* greatly loved.

below *prep* under; beneath. * *adv* in a lower place.

belt *n* a girdle; a band; a stripe; area, e.g. of trees.

bemoan *vt* to lament.

bemused *adj* muddled.

bench *n* a long seat; a long work table; seat of justice; body of judges.

bend *vt* (*pt, pp* **bent**) to curve; to direct to a certain point; to adjust for one's own purpose. * *n* a curve.

beneath *prep, adv* below; under.

benediction *n* a solemn blessing.

benefactor *n* a person who confers a benefit.

benefice *n* an ecclesiastical living.

beneficent *adj* kind; bountiful.

beneficial *adj* helpful; bringing about improvement.

beneficiary *n* a person who is benefited or assisted or gains.

benefit *n* an act of kindness; a favour; something that brings improvement; an allowance from government, an employer, etc. * *vt* (*pt* **benefited**) to do a service to.

benevolence *n* kindness; active love of mankind.

benevolent *adj* kind; charitable.

benign *adj* gracious; kind.

bent *n* bias of mind; aptitude; a wiry grass.

benumb *vt* to deprive of sensation.

benzene *n* a liquid used to remove grease and as an insecticide.

bequeath *vt* to leave by will.

bequest *n* a legacy.

bereave *vt* to deprive of someone dear by death.

bereavement *n* loss by death.

berry *n* a pulpy fruit containing seeds.

berserk *adj* frenzied.

berth *n* a place in which a moored ship lies; a place for sleeping in a train, ship, etc. * *vt* to moor.

beseech *vt* (*pt, pp* **besought** *or* **beseeched**) to entreat.

beseechingly *adv* imploringly.

beset *vt* (*pt, pp* **beset**) to surround; to attack from every direction.

besetting *adj* habitual.

beside, besides *prep* by the side of; near. * *adv* moreover.

besiege *vt* to lay siege to.

besotted *adj* infatuated.

bespatter *vt* to spatter over.

bespeak *vt* to speak for beforehand.

best *adj* the superlative degree of 'good'. * *adv* the superlative of 'well'. * *vt* to defeat; to beat.

bestial *adj* brutish.

bestiality *n* brutish conduct.

bestir *vt* to rouse oneself to action.

bestow *vt* to gift; to present with.

bestraddle *vt* to bestride.

bestride *vt* to stride over or across; to span.

bet *n* a wager. * *vt* (*pt, pp* **bet** *or* **betted**) to wager.

betide *vi* to befall; to happen.

betoken *vt* to imply; to foreshadow.

betray *vt* to prove false to; to entrap.

betrayal *n* act of betraying.

betroth *vt* to pledge in marriage.

betrothal *n* mutual promise to marry.

better *adj* comparative of 'good'. * *adv* comparative of 'well'. * *vt* to advance; to outdo.

between *prep* in the middle.

bevel *n* an instrument for setting angles.

beverage *n* a drink.

bevy *n* a flock of birds.

bewail *vt* to lament.

beware *vi* to take care.

bewilder *vt* to perplex.

bewilderment *n* perplexity.

bewitch *vt* to enchant.

bewitching *adj* fascinating.

bewitchment *n* fascination.

beyond *prep* on the farther side of; post; not within reach. * *adv* at a distance; further on.

bias *n* weight on one side; a bent; a prejudice. * *vt* to incline to one side.

biased, biassed *adj* prejudiced.

bib *n* a cloth or plastic cover tied round the neck (of a child) to protect clothing from food spillage.

Bible *n* the Holy Scriptures of the Christian faith.

biblical *adj* pertaining to the Bible.

bibliographical *adj* pertaining to bibliography.

bibliography *n* an account, description or reference list of books on a subject.

bibliomania *n* a passion for possessing books.

bibliophile *n* a lover of books.

bibulous *adj* given to tippling.

bicentenary *n* two hundred years.

biceps *npl* muscles of the forearm.

bicker *vi* to quarrel.

bicycle *n* a two-wheeled vehicle propelled by pedals.

bicyclist *n* one who rides a bicycle.

bid *vt* (*pt* **bade**, *pp* **bidden**) to ask; to order; (*pt*, *pp* **bid**) to offer. * *n* an offer, as at an auction.

biddable *adj* obedient.

bidding *n* an invitation; a command.

biennial *adj* lasting for two years; taking place once in two years.

biennially *adv* once in two years.

bier *n* the frame on which a corpse rests or is carried.

bifurcate, bifurcated *adj* forked or divided into two.

big *adj* great; large.

bigamist *n* one who commits bigamy.

bigamy *n* the crime of having two wives or husbands at once.

bigot *n* a person obstinately wedded to particular ideas.

bigoted *adj* prejudiced.

bigotry *n* intolerance.

bilateral *adj* two-sided.

bile *n* the bitter secretion of the liver; ill-nature.

bilge *n* the bulging part of a cask; the breadth of a ship's bottom.

bilge water *n* water in the bilge of a ship.

bilingual *adj* in two languages.

bilious *adj* affected by bile.

bill *n* the beak of a bird; an instrument for pruning; an account of money due; draft of a new law; a poster or leaflet.

billet *n* a small note in writing; lodgings; a situation. * *vt* to quarter, as soldiers.

billet-doux *n* (*pl* **billets-doux**) a love letter.

billiards *npl* a game played on a table with balls and cues.

billion *n* a million of millions.

billow *n* a great wave of the sea.

bimonthly *adj* every two months.

bin *n* a receptacle.

binary *adj* twofold.

bind *vb* (*pt*, *pp* **bound**) *vt* to tie; to

oblige; to cover (a book); to make firm; to bandage. * *vi* to grow hard, tight or stiff; to be obligatory.

binding *n* the cover and sewing of a book. * *adj* obligatory.

bingo *n* a gambling game with numbered cards for several people in which numbers called are covered by players until a card is full.

binocular *adj* adapted for both eyes. * *npl* field or opera glasses.

binomial *adj, n* (of) an algebraic expression with two terms.

biochemistry *n* the study of the chemistry of living organisms.

biogenesis *n* the doctrine that living matter springs only from living matter.

biographer *n* a writer of biography.

biography *n* written life of a person.

biologist *n* one skilled in biology.

biology *n* the study of the science of living organisms.

bipartite *adj* having two parts.

biped *n* an animal with two feet.

bird *n* a feathered, egg-laying vertebrate with wings.

birth *n* the act of bearing or coming into life.

birthright *n* any right to which a person is entitled by birth.

biscuit *n* a hard, flat, sweet or plain cake.

bisect *vt* to half.

bishop *n* the head of a diocese.

bishopric *n* the office of a bishop; a diocese.

bit *n* a morsel; the metal part of a bridle; a boring tool used with a brace.

bitch *n* a female dog or wolf.

bite *vt* (*pt* **bit**, *pp* **bitten**) to crush or sever with the teeth; to cause to smart; to wound by reproach, etc; to corrode. * *n* a wound made by biting; a mouthful.

biting *adj* sharp; piercingly cold; sarcastic.

bitter *adj* sharp to the taste; severe; painful.

bitterness *n* the quality of being bitter.

bitumen *n* a pitch-like substance.

bivalve *n* a two-valved animal.

bivouac *n* an encampment of soldiers for the night in the open air.

biweekly *adj* occurring every two weeks.

bizarre *adj* fantastic; odd; strange

black *adj* having no light; dark; gloomy; sullen; atrocious; wicked. * *n* the darkest colour. * *vt* to make black.

blackboard *n* a board for writing on with chalk.

blacken *vt* to make black. * *vi* to grow black or dark; to speak ill of.

blackguard *n* a scoundrel. * *vt* to revile.

blackleg *n* one who works during a strike.

blackmail *n* money extorted by threats. * *vt* to commit the crime of blackmail.

black market *n* illegal buying and selling when restrictions are in force.

blackout *n* total darkness when lighting has failed or been switched off; a loss of consciousness temporarily.

blacksmith *n* a smith who works in iron.

bladder *n* a membrane in animals containing the urine; a blister.

blade *n* a leaf; the cutting part of a sword, knife; the flat part of an oar.

blame *vt* to censure. * *n* censure; fault.

blameless *adj* free from blame.

blanch *vt* to make white. * *vi* to grow white.

blancmange *n* a white jelly.

bland *adj* mild; gentle.

blandish *vt* to soothe; to flatter.

blandishment *n* flattery.

blank *adj* white; empty. * *n* a void space.

blanket *n* a woollen covering.

blank verse *n* verse without rhyme.

blare *vi* to give forth a loud, harsh sound.

blarney *n* flattery; insincere talk.

blasé *adj* satiated; used up; bored.

blaspheme *vt* to speak irreverently of something held sacred.

blasphemous *adj* impious; irreverent.

blast *n* a gust of wind; the sound of a wind instrument; a violent explosion; harsh criticism. * *vt* to blight.

blatant *adj* noisy and loud; glaringly obvious.

blaze *n* a flame; a fire; brilliance. * *vi* to flame. * *vt* to noise abroad.

bleach *vt* to make white. * *vi* to grow white.

bleak *adj* dreary; dark and gloomy.

blear *adj* sore; dimmed.

blear-eyed, bleary-eyed *adj* sore or watery-eyed.

bleat *vi* to cry as a sheep. * *n* the cry of a sheep.

bleed *vb* (*pt, pp* **bled**) *vi* to emit or lose blood, etc; to ooze sap, dye, etc. * *vt* to take blood, sap, etc, from; (*inf*) to extort money from.

bleeding *n* a flow of blood; the operation of letting blood; the drawing of sap from a tree.

blemish *vt* to mar; to tarnish. * *n* a stain; dishonour.

blend *vt* to mix together. * *n* a mixture.

bless *vt* (*pp* **blessed** *or* **blest**) to make happy; to invoke a blessing.

blessed *adj* happy; holy.

blessing *n* a benediction; a prayer of thanks; good wishes.

blight *n* that which withers up or destroys wholesale; mildew. * *vt* to wither up; to blast; to cause failure.

blind *adj* destitute of sight; having no outlet. * *n* a screen; a pretext. * *vt* to make blind.

blindfold *adj* having the eyes covered.

blindly *adv* heedlessly.

blindness *n* lack of sight; ignorance.

blink *vi* to wink; to twinkle. * *vt* to shut the eyes upon.

blinker *n* a flap to prevent a horse from seeing sideways.

bliss *n* perfect happiness.

blissful *adj* full of bliss.

blister *n* a watery bubble on the skin; a swelling as on paint. * *vt* to raise a blister; to castigate vigorously.

blithe *adj* joyful.

blizzard *n* a violent snowstorm.

bloated *adj* inflated.

blob *n* a small globe of liquid.

block *n* a heavy piece of wood; a

lump of solid matter; a piece of wood in which a pulley is placed; buildings in a group; an obstacle. * vt to shut up; to obstruct.

blockade n a close siege by troops or ships. * vt to besiege closely.

blockhead n a stupid fellow.

blockhouse n a building used for defence.

blond, blonde adj having fair hair; of a fair complexion.

blood n the red fluid which circulates in animals; kindred. * adj pertaining to blood.

bloodless adj without blood; lifeless.

bloodshot adj inflamed.

bloodthirsty adj eager to shed blood.

blood vessel n an artery or a vein.

bloody adj stained with blood; cruel.

bloom n a blossom; a flower; state of healthy youthfulness. * vi to blossom.

blossom n the flower of a plant. * vi to bloom.

blot vt to spot; to stain; to dry. * n a spot or stain; a disgrace.

blotch n a spot or discoloured patch.

blouse n a loose upper garment.

blow vb (pt **blew**, pp **blown**) vi to make a current of air; to pant; to bloom. * vt to impel by wind; to inflate. * n a blast; a blossoming; a heavy punch; a stroke; a misfortune.

blowpipe n a tube for heating flame by blowing air into it; a tube for blowing poison darts.

blubber n the fat of whales. * vi to weep noisily.

bludgeon n a short club.

blue n the colour of the sky; one of the seven primary colours; a university athletic distinction. * adj of a blue colour; sky-coloured; depressed. * vt to dye a blue colour.

blueprint n a print of plans, etc, photographed on a blue background; a plan used as a basis of future work.

bluestocking n a learned woman.

bluff adj hearty; blunt. * n a steep projecting bank. * vt, vi to persuade or deceive by a show of boldness or strength.

bluish adj slightly blue.

blunder vi to err stupidly. * n a mistake; an error.

blunt adj not sharp; unceremonious; rude; straightforward. * vt to make blunt or dull.

blur n a stain; a blot; a hazy impression. * vt to stain; to obscure.

blurt vt to utter suddenly or unadvisedly.

blush vi to redden in the face. * n a red colour in the face caused by shame, embarrassment, etc.

bluster vi to roar like wind; to swagger; to boast and bully. * n swaggering.

blustering adj noisy; windy.

boa n a large snake without fangs; a feathery or fur scarf.

boar n the male of the pig or hog.

board n a strip of timber broad and thin; a table; food; persons seated round a table; a council; a group of people in charge of a company; the deck of a ship. * vt to cover with boards; to supply with food; to enter a train, bus, ship, etc.

boarder n one who receives food and lodging at a stated charge.

boarding house n a house where board and lodging are provided for payment.

boarding school n a school where the pupils are boarders.

boast vi to brag. * vt to magnify. * n a bragging utterance.

boastful adj given to boasting.

boat n a small open vessel, usually impelled by oars; a small ship.

boatswain n a petty officer or warrant officer on board ship.

bob n something that hangs or plays loosely; a short jerking motion; a woman's short haircut. * vt to move with a short jerking motion. * vi to play to and fro or up and down; to curtsey.

bobbin n a winding pin; a reel.

bode vt to portend.

bodice n the upper part of a dress; an inner vest; a corset.

bodily adv wholly; entirely.

body n the trunk or main part of an animal or human being; matter; a person; a dead person; a group of people; any solid figure.

bodyguard n one appointed to guard the safety of another.

bog n a marsh.

bogus adj sham.

boil vi to bubble from the action of heat; to seethe. * vt to heat to a boiling state. * n a sore swelling or tumour.

boisterous adj stormy; noisy; loud and high-spirited.

bold adj daring.

boldness n courage.

bole n the body or stem of a tree.

bolster n a long pillow. * vt to hold up; to give support to a person.

bolt n an arrow; a thunderbolt; a bar of a door. * vi to leave suddenly. * vt to fasten; to swallow hastily.

bomb n an explosive shell.

bombard vt to attack with continual fire and bombs; to attack with words and questions.

bombast n high-sounding words.

bombastic adj inflated; turgid; pompous.

bona fide adv, adj in good faith; genuine.

bond n that which binds; obligation; a legal deed; (pl) chains; a place where dutiable goods are stored. * vt to grant a bond in security for money; to store till duty is paid.

bondage n slavery.

bonded adj liable to pay duty.

bone n the hard part of the skeleton. * vt to take out bones from.

bonfire n an open-air fire.

bon mot n (pl **bons mots**) a witticism.

bonnet n a headdress.

bonny adj beautiful.

bonus n a premium; extra gift to shareholders; an addition to a salary.

book n a collection of printed sheets bound together. * vt to enter in a book; to reserve beforehand; to note a person's particulars for a minor offence.

booking office n an office where people buy tickets in advance.

bookish *adj* fond of study.

book-keeper *n* one who keeps accounts.

booklet *n* a little book.

bookmaker *n* a person who takes bets on events and pays out winnings.

bookseller *n* one who sells books.

bookworm *n* one who pores over books.

boom *n* a long pole to extend the bottom of a sail; a chain barrier across a river or harbour; a hollow roar; prosperity in commerce; in film studies, a long pole with a microphone at the end. * *vi* to roar; to make a loud, deep noise; to boost; to prosper.

boomerang *n* an Australian missile that when thrown returns to the thrower.

boon *n* a favour; something helpful; a blessing.

boor *n* a rustic; a rude, unhelpful person.

boorish *adj* clownish; rude.

boot *n* a covering for the foot.

booth *n* a temporary shed; a stall; a cubicle for voting or for a telephone.

bootless *adj* useless, unavailing.

booty *n* spoil; plunder.

border *n* the outer edge of anything; the boundary line between two countries. * *vi* to approach near. * *vt* to surround with a border.

bore *vt* to make a hole in; to pester; to weary by being dull, uninteresting or repetitious. * *n* the hole made by boring; the diameter of a tube; a

tiresome person; a great tidal wave.

boreal *adj* northern.

born *pp of* **bear** to bring forth.

borne *pp of* **bear** to carry.

borrow *vt* to ask or receive as a loan.

bosom *n* the breast; the seat of the affections. * *adj* beloved.

boss *n* a knob; a master; a manager. * *vt* to be domineering; to be or act as a boss.

botanic, botanical *adj* pertaining to botany.

botanist *n* one skilled in botany.

botany *n* the science which treats of plants.

botch *vt* to perform clumsily.

both *adj, pron* the two. * *conj* as well.

bother *vt* to annoy. * *vi* to trouble oneself. * *n* a trouble.

bothersome *adj* causing trouble.

bottle *n* a narrow-mouthed vessel of glass or plastic; the contents of a bottle.

bottom *n* the lowest part; the ground under water; foundation. * *vt* to found or build upon.

boudoir *n* a woman's private room.

bough *n* a branch of a tree.

boulder *n* a large roundish stone or rock.

boulevard *n* a wide street planted with trees.

bounce *vi* to spring or rush out suddenly; to rebound; to boast. * *n* springiness; a boast.

bouncing *adj* big; strong; boastful.

bound *n* a boundary; a leap. * *vt* to limit. * *vi* to leap. * *adj* obliged; sure; ready; destined.

boundary n a bounding line; a border.

bounden adj obligatory.

boundless adj unlimited.

bounteous adj liberal.

bountiful adj generous.

bounty n liberality; a premium to encourage trade; a reward.

bouquet n a bunch of flowers; a perfume from wine.

bourgeois n a middle-class citizen.

bout n a contest; a spell.

bovine adj dull, stupid.

bow[1] vt to bend. * vi to make a reverence. * n a bending of the head or body; the curved forepart of a ship.

bow[2] n a weapon to shoot arrows; the rainbow; a stick for playing on violin strings; a slipknot.

bowdlerize vt to expurgate.

bowed adj bent like a bow.

bowels npl the lower intestines.

bower n an arbour.

bowl[1] n a ball of wood; (pl) the game played with such bowls. * vi to play with bowls; to deliver a ball at cricket.

bowl[2] n a large roundish dish.

bow-legged adj bandy-legged.

bowler[1] n one who plays bowls; to deliver a ball at cricket.

bowler[2] n a stiff felt hat.

bowling green n a smooth lawn for the game of bowls.

bowman n an archer.

bowsprit n a spar projecting over the bow of a ship.

bow window n a bay window.

box n a case of wood, metal, etc; a seat in a theatre; a blow; a tree or shrub. * vt to put in a box; to strike. * vi to fight with the fists.

boxer n a pugilist.

boy n a male child.

boycott vt to refuse dealings with.

boyhood n the state of being a boy.

brace n a support; a bandage; a couple; a boring tool; (pl) suspenders. * vt to tighten; to straighten up; to strengthen.

bracelet n an ornament for the wrist.

bracing adj invigorating.

bracken n a species of fern.

bracket n a support for something fixed to a wall; a mark—() or []—in writing or printing to enclose words. * vt to place within or connect by brackets; to group.

bracketing n grouping together.

brackish adj salt; saltish.

brag vi to talk big. * n a boast.

braggart adj boastful. * n a boaster.

braid vt to weave together strands of hair, thread, etc. * n a plaited band.

braided adj edged with braid.

brain n the centre of thought and sensation; the soft matter within the skull.

braise vt to cook in a covered pan.

brake n a device on a wheel to reduce speed or to stop motion; a type of wagon.

bran n the husks of ground corn.

branch n the offshoot of a tree; the offshoot of anything, as of a river, family. * vi to spread in branches; (with **out**) to broaden or increase one's activities.

brand n a burning piece of wood; a mark made with a hot iron; a trade-

mark; a particular make (of goods).
* *vt* to mark with a hot iron; to denounce.

brandish *vt* to shake; wave.

brandy *n* a spirit distilled from wine or fruit such as apricot, plum, etc.

brass *n* a yellow alloy of copper and zinc; brass section of an orchestra or band; impudence.

brassiere *n* a woman's undergarment protecting and supporting the breasts; a bra.

brat *n* an ill-behaved child.

bravado *n* bluster.

brave *adj* daring; valiant. * *vt* to defy.

bravery *n* courage.

brawl *vi* to quarrel noisily. * *n* uproar.

brawn *n* the flesh of a boar; muscle; strength.

brawny *adj* muscular.

bray *vi* to make a loud harsh sound, as an ass. * *n* the cry of an ass.

brazen *adj* made of brass; impudent.

brazier *n* a worker in brass; a portable fire.

breach *n* the act of breaking; quarrel. * *vt* to make a gap in.

bread *n* food made of flour or meal baked.

breadth *n* width.

break *vb* (*pt* **broke**, *pp* **broken**) *vt* to sever by fracture; to rend; to tame; to interrupt; to dissolve any union; to tell with discretion. * *vi* to come to pieces; to burst forth. * *n* an opening; a breach; a pause; the dawn.

breakage *n* a breaking.

breakdown *n* a failure or stoppage due to mechanical malfunction; a nervous or mental collapse; an analysing and classifying of a project, etc, into its separate parts.

breaker *n* a large, crested wave.

breakfast *n* the first meal in the day.

breakneck *adj* dangerously fast.

breakwater *n* a mole or bar to break the force of the waves.

breast *n* the front part of a body; a mammary gland in the female. *vt* to face.

breastbone *n* the bone of the breast.

breath *n* the air drawn into and expelled from the lungs; life; pause; a gentle breeze.

breathe *vt, vi* to take breath; to live; to utter.

breathing *n* respiration.

breathless *adj* out of breath.

bred *pp* of **breed**.

breech *n* the hinder part (of a gun, etc); (*pl* **breeches**) garment for men.

breed *vt, vi* (*pt, pp* **bred**) to bring forth; to educate; to rear. * *n* offspring; kind.

breeding *n* the raising of a breed; good manners.

breeze *n* a light wind.

brethren *npl* of **brother**.

breve *n* a note in music.

brevity *n* shortness.

brew *vt* to prepare from malt; to concoct; to scheme. * *vi* to make beer; to infuse tea. * *n* the mixture formed by brewing.

brewery *n* the place where beer brewing is carried on.

bribe n a gift to corrupt the conduct or judgment. * vt to gain over by bribes.

bribery n the giving or taking of bribes.

bric-a-brac n ornamental or rare odds and ends.

brick n a rectangular block of baked clay or other material used in building.

bricklayer n one who builds with bricks.

bridal n a wedding. * adj belonging to a bride or a wedding.

bride n a woman about to be or newly married.

bridegroom n a man about to be or newly married.

bridesmaid n a woman who attends on a bride during a wedding.

bridge n a roadway across a river; a structure to carry people, vehicles, railways across; something that serves to fill a gap or helps communication; a platform on a ship from which the captain issues commands; a card game like whist. * vt to build a bridge over.

bridle n the headgear of a horse; a curb; a check. * vt to put a bridle on; to restrain.

brief adj short. * n a summary of a client's case; (pl) underpants without legs.

brigade n a group of two or more regiments.

brigadier n the officer who commands a brigade.

bright adj clear; shining; lively; clever.

brighten vt, vi to make bright.

brilliance n the state of being brilliant; splendour.

brilliant adj sparkling. * n a diamond.

brim n the rim of anything.

brimful adj full to the brim.

brindled adj marked with brown streaks.

brine n salt water.

bring vt (pt, pp **brought**) to lead; to fetch; to produce; to cause to happen.

brink n the edge; the margin; the moment before a happening, often a disaster.

brisk adj lively.

brisket n the breast of an animal.

briskly adv actively.

bristle n a stiff hair. * vt, vi to stand on end; to show anger.

brittle adj apt to break.

broach n a roasting spit. * vt to pierce, as with a spit; to tap; to open up.

broad adj wide.

broaden vi to grow broad. * vt to make broad.

broadside n a discharge of all the guns on one side of a ship.

brocade n a silk stuff with raised pattern.

brochure n a pamphlet.

brogue n a strong shoe formerly of raw hide; the Irish accent.

broil n a brawl. * vt to cook over a fire.

broken adj crushed; ruined.

broker n an agent who buys and sells for others.

brokerage n the business of a broker.

bromide n a drug; a platitude.

bronchi npl the tubes branching from the windpipe to the lungs.

bronchial adj belonging to the air tubes.

bronchitis n inflammation of the bronchial tubes.

bronze n an alloy of copper and tin; a colour.

brooch n an ornament to pin on a dress.

brood vi to sit on eggs; to ponder anxiously. * n offspring.

brook n a small stream. * vt to bear.

broom n a shrub with yellow flowers; a brush.

broth n a meat soup with vegetables.

brother n a son of the same parents; an associate; a fellow creature; a working or lay member of a male religious order.

brotherhood n the relationship of a brother; an association.

brow n the ridge over the eye; the forehead; the edge of a cliff.

browbeat vt to bully.

brown adj dusky; tanned. * n a colour resulting from the mixture of red, black, and yellow.

brownie n a junior Guide; a small nutty, chocolate cake.

browse vt to feed upon; to read through casually.

browser n someone that browses; a computer software package which allows the user to locate and read hypertext files.

bruise vt to crush; to injure and cause discoloration of the skin without drawing blood. * n a skin discoloration from a blow.

brunette n a woman with a dark complexion and dark hair.

brunt n the main area to bear the shock of an attack, etc.

brush n an implement with bristles for cleaning by rubbing or sweeping or for painting; a skirmish; a thicket; the tail of a fox. * vt, vi to sweep; to touch lightly.

brushwood n small trees and shrubs growing together.

brusque adj abrupt; rude.

brutal adj cruel.

brutality n savageness; cruelty.

brute adj purely physical; sheer, as in brute force. * n a beast; a brutal person.

brutish adj brutal; sensual.

bubble n a fluid film enclosing air; a swindle. * vi to rise in bubbles.

buccaneer n a pirate.

buck n the male of deer, goats; a lively, stylish young fellow. * vi to jump violently.

bucket n a pail.

buckle n a strap or belt fastener. * vt to fasten; to bend.

buckshot n lead shot for hunting big game.

bucolic adj pastoral; rustic.

bud n a young shoot or flower. * vi to put forth buds.

budding n a method of grafting buds. * adj promising.

budge vt to move; to stir.

budget n a financial statement; an estimate for expenditure. * vt, vi to put on a budget; to plan; to make a budget.

buff n a yellow colour; the bare skin. * adj light yellow. * vt to clean or shine by rubbing.

buffer n anything for deadening the shock of collision, etc.

buffet[1] n a sideboard; a refreshment bar; a meal where people serve themselves.

buffet[2] n a blow; a slap. * vt to box; to contend against.

buffoon n a clown; one who plays the fool to amuse; a fool.

buffoonery n the antics of a buffoon.

bugle n a hunting horn; a kind of trumpet.

bugler n one who plays the bugle.

build vb (pt, pp **built**) vt to construct; to establish. * vi to form a structure. * n make; form.

building n an edifice; the art or trade of building.

building society n a financial company where deposits of money are paid interest and loans are made, esp for house buying.

bulb n a round root.

bulbous adj swelling out.

bulge n a swelling; a rounded projection. * vt to swell out.

bulk n size; the main mass; cargo.

bulky adj large and awkwardly shaped.

bull n the male of cattle, elephant and whale; an edict of the pope.

bulldog n a species of dog; a never-say-die person.

bullet n a metal missile shot from a firearm.

bulletin n an official report.

bullion n uncoined gold or silver.

bull's-eye n the centre of a target; a shot hitting this; any aim that is achieved.

bully n an overbearing quarrelsome fellow. * vt to insult and threaten.

bulwark n a rampart; a person or thing acting as a strong buffer.

bump[1] n a heavy blow, or the noise of it; a lump produced by a blow. * vt to crash or knock against.

bump[2] vt to decline a pre-booked passenger their seat on a flight, due to overbooking.

bumper n a full glass; a protective metal bar fixed at the front and rear of a vehicle to absorb shock.

bumptious adj self-assertive.

bun n a small cake; a round coil of hair worn at the nape of the neck.

bunch n a cluster.

bundle n a package. * vt, vi to tie in a bundle; to hurry off.

bungalow n a one-storeyed house.

bungee jumping n a sport which involves jumping from a great height (a bridge) with only a rubber wire secured to the ankles.

bungle vi to botch. * n a clumsy performance.

bunion n a lump on the ball of the big toe.

bunk n a sleeping berth; a narrow bed.

bunker n a large bin; a sandpit hazard on a golf course; an underground shelter.

bunting n stuff of which flags are made; flags.

buoy n a floating navigation mark. * vt to keep afloat; (with **up**) to give support or encouragement to.

buoyancy n capacity for floating; cheerfulness; resilience.

buoyant adj floating; light; cheerful.

burden n a load; something hard or wearisome to bear; a chorus. * vt to load; to oppress.

bureau n (pl **bureaux**) a writing table;

a chest of drawers; a government office.

bureaucracy n government through state departments; unnecessary officialdom.

burgeon vt, vi to flourish; to grow rapidly and profusely.

burglar n a housebreaker.

burglary n the act of housebreaking.

burgundy n a red or white wine produced in Burgundy.

burial n the act of burying; interment.

burlesque adj comic. * n a caricature; a satirical play caricaturing some subject. * vt to turn into ridicule.

burly adj stout; portly; of a strong build.

burn vt, vi (pt, pp **burnt** or **burned**) to consume with fire; to be on fire; to rage fiercely. * n a hurt caused by fire; a rivulet.

burning adj fiery; vehement.

burnish vt to polish. * n polish.

burr n a prickly fruit, seed case or flower head; a gruff pronunciation of the letter r.

burrito n a tortilla baked with a savoury filling.

burrow n a hole in the earth made by rabbits, etc. * vi to excavate.

bursar n a treasurer; a student who holds a scholarship.

bursary n a scholarship.

burst vb (pt, pp **burst**) vi to fly or break open; to rush forth. * vt to break by force.

bury vt to put into a grave; to cover; to conceal.

bus n (pl **buses**) a large vehicle designed to carry passengers along a route; an omnibus.

bush n a shrub; a thicket.

business n occupation; concern.

busk vi to entertain for money.

bust n a woman's bosom; a sculpture of a person's head, shoulders and chest.

bustle vi to hustle. * n hurry.

busy adj occupied. * vt to employ.

busybody n a meddler.

but conj, prep, adv yet, except, only.

butcher n one who kills or sells animals for food. * vt to slaughter.

butler n a male servant in charge of a wine cellar.

butt n the end of a thing; a mark to be shot at; an object of ridicule; a cask of wine. * vt to strike with the head.

butter n the substance obtained from cream by churning. * vt to spread with butter; to flatter grossly.

buttercup n a wild yellow cup-shaped flower.

butterfly n a winged insect often brightly coloured; a showy person; a swimming stroke.

buttermilk n the milk that remains after the butter is separated.

button n a knob or disc for fastening; a badge. * vt to fasten with buttons.

buttress n a construction to support and strengthen a wall; a prop. * vt to support by a prop.

buxom adj jolly; large.

buy vt (pt, pp **bought**) to purchase.

buzz vi to hum. * n a humming noise.

by prep, adv used to denote the instrument, agent, or manner; at the rate of; not later than.

bye n in certain games, reaching the second round without playing an opponent in the first; a ball scoring a run in cricket without being hit by a batsman.

bygone *adj* past.

bylaw *n* a local law.

bypass *n* a road that skirts a town; a re-channelling, esp of blood flow into the heart. * *vt* to go round so as to avoid.

byre *n* a cow house.

bystander *n* a spectator.

byway *n* a side way.

byword *n* a common saying; a proverb.

C

cabal *n* an intrigue; a party clique. * *vi* to combine in plotting.

cabbage *n* a vegetable.

cabin *n* a hut; a room in a ship. * *vt* to confine.

cabinet *n* a closet; a showcase; the ministers of state.

cabinet-maker *n* a maker of furniture.

cable *n* anchor rope; a submarine telegraph wire. * *vt* to send by cable.

cackle *vi* to utter a cry (as of a hen); to chatter. * *n* clucking; idle talk or laughter.

cadaverous *adj* ghastly, deathlike.

cadence *n* a fall of the voice at the end of a sentence.

cadet *n* a younger brother; a military pupil.

cadge *vt vi* to go about begging.

cadmium *n* a whitish metal.

Caesarean section *n* the removal by surgery of a baby from the womb.

café *n* a small informal restaurant; a coffee bar.

cage *n* a wire frame to confine birds or beasts.

cairn *n* a heap of stones as landmark or memorial.

cairngorm *n* a yellow-brown rock crystal used as a gem.

caisson *n* a structure used to raise sunken vessels or to lay foundations in deep water.

cajole *vt* to wheedle; to persuade by smooth words.

cake *n* baked dough in various forms; fancy bread; a flat compact mass.

calamitous *adj* disastrous.

calamity *n* misfortune; disaster.

calcareous *adj* containing lime.

calculate *vt* to count; to think out; to estimate.

calculating *adj* scheming.

calculus *n* (*math*) a method of calculation.

calendar *n* a means of calculating years, months, days; an almanac; a list of coming events.

calf *n* (*pl* **calves**) the young of the cow; the fleshy lower part of the leg.

calibre *n* the diameter of the bore of a gun; quality.

calico *n* a cotton cloth, usu not bleached.

call *vt* to name; to summon. * *vi* to utter a loud sound; to make a short visit. * *n* a summons; a short visit; a bird's note; a need; a demand.

calligraphy *n* the art of writing.

calling *n* a vocation.

callipers *n, npl* compasses for measuring calibre; a metal support strapped to the leg for support.

callisthenics *n* exercises for strength or grace of movement.

callous *adj* hardened; unfeeling.

callow *adj* young and immature.

calm *adj* still; quiet; windless. * *n* tranquillity. * *vt* to soothe; to pacify.

calmness *n* composure, stillness.

calorie *n* a unit of heat; a unit measuring the energy of food.

calorific *adj* causing heat.

calumnious *adj* slanderous.

calumny *n* slander; defamation.

calve *vi* to give birth to a calf.

calypso *n* a West Indian story in song to a syncopated rhythm.

camber *n* the slight curve upward towards the centre of a road surface.

cambered *adj* curved.

cambric *n* a fine white linen.

cameo *n* a precious stone carved in relief.

camera *n* an apparatus for taking photographs or cinema and television pictures; a judge's private chamber.

camisole *n* an under bodice.

camp[1] *n* the ground on which tents are pitched; the collection of tents; those who support a cause or party.

camp[2] *adj* (*inf*) theatrical, exaggerated; effeminate; homosexual.

campaign *n* the operations of an army in war.

campaigner *n* an old soldier.

campus *n* the grounds (and buildings) of a university.

can[1] *n* a metal vessel; a tin.

can[2] *vi* (*pt* **could**) to be able.

canal *n* an artificial watercourse for boats; a duct or channel in the body.

canard *n* a false rumour.

canary *n* a light wine; a song bird.

cancel *vt* to strike out; to delete; to annul; to undo or call off.

cancer *n* one of the signs of the zodiac; a malignant growth.

candelabrum *n* (*pl* **candelabra**) a branched ornamental candlestick.

candid *adj* frank; outspoken; fair and unprejudiced.

candidate *n* an applicant for a post or office; someone worthy to be chosen; someone taking an examination.

candidly *adv* sincerely.

candle *n* a stick of wax with a wick for lighting.

candlestick *n* a candle-holder.

candour *n* frankness.

candy *vt* to conserve with sugar. * *n* a sweetmeat.

cane *n* a walking stick; the stem of some plants as bamboo; a thin stick for supporting plants. * *vt* to beat with a cane.

canine *adj* pertaining to dogs.

canister *n* a small box; an explosive shell.

canker *n* an ulcer; a blight.

cannabis *n* a drug from the hemp plant.

cannibal *n* a person who eats human flesh. * *adj* relating to cannibalism.

cannon *n* a large gun mounted on a

carriage; a shot in billiards when the cue ball strikes two other balls; an impact and rebound. * *vt* to collide with.

cannonade *n* a bombardment.

cannot the negative of **can**.

canny *adj* cautious; wary.

canoe *n* a skiff driven by paddles.

canon *n* a decree; a law; a rule or criterion; a list of an author's works accepted as genuine; a cathedral cleric.

cañon *n* a canyon.

canonize *vt* to declare a person to be a saint.

canopy *n* a covering over a throne, bed, etc.

cant *n* insincere talk; jargon.

cantankerous *adj* cross.

cantata *n* a short oratorio.

canteen *n* a restaurant within or attached to a place of work, school etc; (the box holding) a full set of cutlery; a place in camp or barracks for the sale of food and drink; a flask for water.

canter *n* a moderate gallop. * *vi* to move at a moderate gallop.

cantilever *n* a large supporting bracket; a principle applied in bridge making.

canto *n* a division of a poem.

canvas *n* a coarse cloth; sails of ships; a painting.

canvass *vt* to solicit the votes of.

canyon *n* a long, narrow mountain gorge.

cap *n* a covering for the head; a top piece. * *vt* to put a cap on; to excel; to outdo.

capability *n* capacity; competence.

capable *adj* efficient; able.

capacious *adj* wide; roomy.

capacity *n* volume; ability.

cape *n* a headland; a sleeveless coat.

caper *vi* to skip. * *n* a leap; a prank.

capillary *adj* minute; hair-like. * *n* a small blood vessel.

capital *adj* chief; punishable with death. * *n* the top of a column; the chief city; wealth.

capitalist *n* a man of wealth.

capitalize *vt* to convert into capital.

capitation *adj, n* per head, esp of a tax.

Capitol *n* the US senate house.

capitulate *vi* to surrender on conditions.

caprice *n* a whim.

capricious *adj* fickle; unreliable.

Capricorn *n* the goat, one of the signs of the zodiac.

capsize *vt, vi* to upset or overturn.

capstan *n* an apparatus for winding in anchors, etc.

capsule *n* a gelatin case containing a drug to be swallowed; a covering; the part of a spacecraft, often manned, that gathers information and is recovered later.

captain *n* a commander, a leader.

caption *n* a headline of a newspaper or book; the explanatory text under an illustration; a subtitle.

captivate *vt* to fascinate.

captive *n* a prisoner.

captivity *n* the state or condition of being a captive.

capture *n* arrest. * *vt* to seize.

car *n* a motor vehicle; the compartment for passengers on a train, aircraft, cable railway etc.

carafe n a glass water bottle.

caramel n burnt sugar as colouring matter; a caramel flavoured sweet.

carat n unit of purity for gold.

caravan n a company travelling together; a house on wheels.

carbide n a compound of carbon with a metal.

carbine n a cavalry rifle.

carbohydrate n a compound of carbon, hydrogen and oxygen found in sugar, starch etc.

carbolic adj an antiseptic acid obtained from coal tar.

carbon n pure charcoal.

carbonaceous adj containing carbon.

carboniferous adj carbon-bearing.

carbonize vt to convert into carbon.

carbuncle n a large boil.

carburettor n the device in an internal combustion engine making and controlling the mixture of air and fuel.

carcass adj the body of a dead animal.

card n a piece of pasteboard for various purposes. * vt to comb wool, etc.

cardboard n a thick card.

cardiac adj pertaining to the heart.

cardigan n a knitted garment with front fastenings.

cardinal adj chief. * n a Roman Catholic dignitary.

care n solicitude; attention. * vi to be anxious; to have regard; to look after; to provide for.

career n a race; a profession. * vi to

proceed rapidly and without control.

careful adj anxious; cautious.

careless adj heedless; thoughtless; carefree.

caress vt to fondle. * n an embrace.

caret n an omission mark, thus (^).

cargo n freight.

caricature n a ludicrous portrait. * vt to burlesque; to parody.

caries n bone decay; tooth decay.

carmine n a bright crimson colour.

carnage n slaughter.

carnal adj sensual; sexual; worldly.

carnally adv lustfully.

carnation n flesh-colour; a rose-pink flower.

carnival n a gala day; public merry-making; a travelling funfair.

carnivorous adj feeding on flesh.

carol n a song of joy, esp one sung at Christmas.

carotid (artery) n one of two great arteries in the neck.

carousal n a noisy revel.

carouse vi to drink freely.

carp vi to find fault. * n a voracious fish.

carpenter n a worker in timber.

carpentry n the trade of a carpenter.

carpet n a woven cover for floors.

carpeting n cloth for carpets.

carriage n a vehicle; the price of carrying; behaviour; bearing.

carrion n putrid flesh.

carrot n a reddish vegetable of a tapering shape; something offered as a reward.

carry vt to bear; to convey; to gain; to behave.

cart *n* a vehicle with two wheels for carrying goods.

carte blanche *n* (*pl* **cartes blanches**) a blank paper; unconditional terms.

cartel *n* a challenge; a written agreement for the exchange of prisoners; a union formed to promote and achieve common aims.

cartilage *n* gristle.

cartography *n* science of making maps.

carton *n* a cardboard box.

cartoon *n* a humorous or satirical topical sketch; a comic strip often animated.

cartridge *n* a case containing the charge for a gun.

carve *vt* to cut; to engrave.

carver *n* one who carves; a large knife for carving.

cascade *n* a waterfall.

case *n* a box; a covering; an event; a suit in court; an ailment or disease being medically treated; the patient undergoing treatment; a form in the inflection of nouns. * *vt* to put in a case.

case-hardened *adj* callous.

casement *n* a hinged window.

cash *n* money. * *vt* to turn into money.

cashier *n* one who has charge of money. * *vt* to dismiss.

cashmere *n* a soft wool or woollen fabric woven from the hair of Kashmir goats.

casino *n* a gaming hall.

cask *n* a barrel.

casket *n* a jewel case.

casque *n* a helmet.

casserole *n* a covered dish for cooking; the food stewed in a casserole.

cassock *n* a garment worn by clerics and choristers.

cast *vt* (*pt, pp* **cast**) to throw; to throw off; to let fall; to condemn; to model. * *n* a throw; a squint; a mould; a company of actors.

castaway *n* a shipwrecked person.

caste *n* social class and distinctions.

castigate *vt* to reprimand severely; to chastise.

casting *n* that which is cast in a mould; the allotting of actors to their roles.

cast iron *n* iron formed in moulds.

castle *n* a fortress; an imposing mansion.

castor *n* a small cruet; a small wheel.

castor oil *n* a medicinal oil used as a purgative.

castrate *vt* to neuter.

casual *adj* accidental; occasional; informal; careless.

casually *adv* by chance.

casualty *n* an accident; the person injured or killed in an accident or a war.

cat *n* a domestic feline animal; a related animal such as a lion or tiger.

cataclysm *n* a deluge; an upheaval.

catacomb *n* an underground vault.

catalogue *n* a list; a register.

catapult *n* a sling.

cataract *n* a waterfall; a disease of the eye.

catarrh *n* a cold in the head, due to inflammation of a mucus membrane in the nose.

catastrophe *n* disaster; finale.

catch vt (pt, pp **caught**) to lay hold on; to grasp; to entangle; to receive by contagion; to get. * n a grasping; a song; play on words; a type of fastening; a hidden obstacle.

catching adj infectious.

catechise vt to instruct by question and answer; to question.

catechism n a manual of instruction by questions and answers, esp of religious tenets.

categorical adj positive.

categorically adv absolutely.

category n a class or order or division.

cater vi to provide provisions, etc.

catgut n a cord made from intestines of animals and used as strings for violins, harps, guitars, etc.

cathedral n the main church in a diocese.

cathode n the negative pole of an electric current.

catholic adj universal; general.

Catholic n a member of the Roman Catholic church. * adj relating to the Roman Catholic church.

Catholicism n adherence to the Roman Catholic church.

cattle npl oxen; livestock.

caucus n a party organization or clique.

caulk vt to stop up seams of a ship.

causal adj implying cause.

causation n the relation of cause and effect.

cause n that which produces an effect; reason; origin; suit; an enterprise. * vt to bring about.

causeway n a paved way.

caustic adj burning; biting; sarcastic.

caustically adv scathingly.

cauterize vt to sear or burn, esp in treating a wound.

caution n care; pledge. * vt to warn.

cautious adj wary; careful.

cavalcade n a procession of persons on horseback or in cars; a dramatic sequence.

cavalier adj careless; offhand; haughty. * n a horseman; a lady's escort; (with cap) a royalist in the English Civil War.

cavalry n mounted troops.

cave n an underground hollow. * vt, vi (with **in**) to collapse; to give in or yield.

caveat n a warning.

cavern n a large cave.

cavernous adj hollow.

cavity n a hollow place, esp a hole in a tooth.

CD abbr compact disc; corps diplomatique.

CD-ROM abbr compact disc read only memory: a CD used for distributing text and images in electronic publishing, for computer software, and for permanent storage of computer data.

CDV abbr CD-video; compact video disc.

cease vi to leave off; to stop. * vt to put a stop to.

ceaseless adj incessant.

cede vt to give up.

cedilla n the mark (ç) of the soft c.

ceiling n the upper inside surface of a room.

celebrant n the officiating priest; one

taking part in a religious ceremony.

celebrate vt to commemorate; to accord high praise to.

celebrated adj famous.

celebrity n fame; a famous person.

celerity n speed; quickness.

celestial adj heavenly.

celibacy n the unmarried state.

celibate n one vowed to celibacy. * adj unmarried.

cell n a small room; a cave; a unit mass in living matter.

cellar n an apartment underground.

cellophane n a thin transparent paper used as protective wrapping.

cellular adj consisting of cells.

Celsius adj pertaining to a thermometer scale with a freezing point of 0 degrees and a boiling point of 100 degrees.

cement n mortar; a bond of union. * vt to unite closely.

cemetery n a burial place.

cenotaph n a monument to one who is buried elsewhere.

censor n a critic; a supervisor (of books, films, etc) who advocates removal of anything obscene, treasonable, etc.

censorious adj fault-finding.

censure n blame; reproof. * vt to judge; to blame.

census n an official count of people.

cent n a coin worth a hundredth of a dollar.

centaur n a mythical being, half man and half horse.

centenarian n one a hundred years old.

centenary n a hundredth anniversary or its commemoration.

centigrade adj Celsius.

centimetre n the hundredth part of a metre.

central adj at the centre; most important; principal.

centralize vt to move to the centre; to cause to be under a central jurisdiction, authority, government.

centre n the middle point; a nucleus. * vt to collect to a point. * vi to have as a centre.

centreboard n a movable keel.

centrifugal adj tending to fly from a centre.

century n a hundred years.

ceramic adj pertaining to pottery. * npl the art of pottery.

cereal adj pertaining to corn. * n a grain plant; a breakfast food from the grains of such a plant.

cerebral adj of the brain; requiring use of the brain.

ceremonial adj pertaining to ceremony. * n rites and their observance; form of duty.

ceremonious adj formal.

ceremony n pomp; observance.

certain adj sure; particular.

certainly adv without doubt.

certainty n truth; fact.

certificate n a written testimony.

certify vt to declare; to attest.

cervix n the neck of the womb.

cessation n stoppage.

cesspool n a receptacle for sewage.

chafe vt to warm by rubbing; to irritate (skin) by rubbing; to enrage. * vi to fret.

chaff n the husk of corn; banter. * vt to banter; to make fun of laughingly.

chagrin n vexation.

chain n a series of links; a measure of length; pl bondage. * vt to confine with chains.

chair n a movable seat; an official seat; professorship.

chalet n a Swiss cottage; a ski lodge or holiday house modelled on this.

chalice n a cup; a communion cup.

chalk n a soft limestone. * vt to mark with chalk.

challenge n a defiance; a calling in question; a demand esp to fight; a task or request requiring special effort. * vt to defy; to call in question.

challenger n one who challenges.

chamber n an apartment; a public body.

chamberlain n an officer of state; a city treasurer.

chamois n a species of antelope; a soft leather.

champ vt to chew; to bite.

champagne n a brisk sparkling wine.

champion n a defender of a cause; a vindicator. * vt to uphold.

championship n state of being a champion; a contest held to find a champion.

chance n accident; opportunity; luck. * vi to happen. * adj casual.

chancel n the altar end of a church.

chancellor n a high government official; the head of a university court.

chandelier n a branching lamp with many lights that hangs from a ceiling.

change vt, vi to alter; to exchange; to put on fresh clothes; to continue one's journey in a different vehicle. * n alteration; variety; a fresh set, esp of clothes; small coins; balance of money returned after payment.

changeable adj variable; capricious.

channel n a watercourse; a narrow sea; a band of radio frequencies allotted for a purpose, such as broadcasting. * vt to groove; to convey; to guide.

chant vt, vi to sing; to intone. * n a song.

chaos n disorder; total confusion.

chapel n a place of worship.

chaperon n a female guardian or escort.

chaplain n an army or navy clergyman.

chapter n a division of a book.

char vt to burn. * n a fish.

character n a letter or figure; the distinguishing attributes of a person or thing; nature; quality; a part in a play.

characteristic adj distinctive.

characterize vt to describe; to mark or be characteristic of.

charade n a word puzzle acted out in syllables followed by all of the word; a travesty.

charcoal n charred wood.

char vt to blacken by fire.

charge vt to load; to fill; to price; to entrust; to accuse; to command; to attack. * n care; cost; attack; order; accusation.

chargeable adj imputable.

chargé d'affaires n an ambassador's deputy.

charger n a large dish; a warhorse.

chariot n a state carriage.

charioteer n a chariot driver.

charitable adj benevolent; generous in giving; lenient.

charity n love; benevolence; generosity to the needy; a money-raising fund or institution.

charlatan n a quack.

charm n a spell. * vt to delight.

charming adj enchanting.

charnel house n a burial vault.

chart n a map; a table of information.

charter n a warrant; a hire. * vt to hire.

chary adj careful; cautious.

chase vt to pursue; to emboss. * n pursuit; hunt; a printer's frame.

chasm n a deep cleft.

chassis n the frame of a motor vehicle.

chaste adj pure.

chasten vt to discipline by punishment; to tame; to make repentant.

chastise vt to punish.

chastity n purity; virginity.

chat vi to gossip. * n talk.

château n a castle.

chattel n (usu in pl) belongings.

chatter vi to talk idly; to jabber. * n talk.

chauffeur n one employed to drive a car.

chauvinism n jingoism.

cheap adj of a low price; common; inferior.

cheapen vt reduce in price; to belittle.

cheat vt to deceive; to swindle. * n a trick; a swindler.

check vt, vi to stop; to curb; to chide; to control. * n position in chess; a control.

checkmate n the winning move in chess. * vt to frustrate.

cheddar n a type of cheese.

cheek n the side of the face; impudence.

cheer n gaiety; happiness; good spirits; a shout of joy. * vt to brighten; to gladden; to applaud.

cheerful adj happy, blithe.

cheering adj encouraging.

cheerless adj gloomy; dejected.

cheese n the curd of milk dried and pressed.

cheeseparing adj mean.

chef n a head cook.

chemical n any substance obtained by a chemical process.

chemise n an undergarment worn by females.

chemist n one skilled in chemistry; a pharmacy.

chemistry n the science of the properties and nature of substances.

cheque n an order for money.

chequer n a square pattern; (pl) draughts.

chequered adj varied; fluctuating.

cherish vt to treasure.

cheroot n a kind of cigar.

cherry n a tree and its small red fruit; a bright red colour.

chess n a game played on a squared board.

chessman n a piece used in chess.

chest n a large box; the breast.

chestnut n a tree; its edible nut; its wood; a stale joke. * adj reddish-brown.

chew vt to masticate.

chic n style. * adj stylish.

chicane, chicanery n trickery.

chick, chicken n the young of birds.

chicken-hearted adj timid.

chickenpox n an eruptive fever.

chicory n a plant with a root that when ground is used for or with coffee.

chide vt, vi to reprove; to scold.

chief adj first; leading. * n a leader.

chieftain n the head of a clan.

chilblain n a painful swelling on the hands or toes produced by cold.

child n an infant; offspring.

childhood n the stage between birth and adolescence.

childish adj like a child; trifling.

childlike adj innocent.

chill n a cold fit. * adj cold. * vt to discourage.

chime n a harmony of bells; (pl) a set of bells. * vi to accord.

chimerical adj fanciful.

chimney n a smoke escape.

chimpanzee n a large ape.

chin n the lower part of the face.

china n porcelain.

chink n an opening; a crack. * vt, vi to jingle as of coins.

chintz n calico, patterned and coloured.

chip n a fragment. * vt to cut into chips.

chiropody n the treatment of the feet.

chirp vi to cheep.

chisel n a cutting tool. * vt to cut or engrave.

chiselled adj clear-cut.

chivalrous adj gallant; knightly.

chivalry n knighthood; gallantry.

chloride n a chlorine compound.

chlorine n a gaseous element used in bleaching and disinfectants.

chloroform n a volatile liquid anaesthetic.

chlorophyll n the green colouring matter of plants.

chocolate n a beverage and sweet from cacao; its colour.

choice n option; selection; preference. * adj select; precious.

choir n a band of singers; the place where they sit, esp in church.

choke vt to suffocate. * vi to be blocked up.

cholera n a highly infectious and deadly disease.

choleric adj bad-tempered; peevish.

choose vt (pt **chose**, pp **chosen**) to prefer; to select.

chop vt to cut to pieces. * vi to turn suddenly. * n a piece of meat.

chopsticks n two wooden sticks used to eat, esp by the Chinese.

choral adj belonging to, sung by or written for a choir.

chord n three or more musical notes played together.

chorister n a singer in a choir.

chorus n a company of singers; musical refrain.

chosen adj select.

Christ n Jesus of Nazareth, the Christian Messiah.

christen vt to baptize; to name.

Christendom n the whole body of Christians.

Christian n a professed follower of Christ.

Christianity n the religion of Christians.

Christmas n the festival of Christ's nativity, 25 December.

chrome, chromium n a hard metal used in steel alloys and electroplating.

chronic adj permanent.

chronicle n a diary of events; history. * vt to record.

chronological *adj* arranged in order of happening.

chronology *n* the science of time; the sequence of events and their arrangement.

chronometer *n* a timepiece.

chrysalis *n* the grub stage of certain insects.

chubby *adj* plump.

chuck *vt* to tap under the chin; to toss; to pitch; to give up; to throw away.

chuckle *vi* to laugh in the throat; to exult. * *n* a half-suppressed laugh.

chum *n* a close friend.

chunk *n* a short thick piece.

church *n* a building consecrated to the worship of God; the body of clergy.

churchyard *n* a cemetery.

churlish *adj* surly; sullen.

churn *n* a vessel that is vigorously turned and shaken to make butter; a milk container.

chute *n* a sloping channel or slide for water, rubbish, logs etc.

cicatrix, cicatrice *n* a scar.

cider *n* fermented apple juice.

cigar *n* a roll of tobacco leaf for smoking.

cigarette *n* a paper cylinder of shredded tobacco.

cinchona *n* a tree whose bark yields quinine.

cinder *n* a burned coal.

cinema *n* a building where films are shown; the art or industry of film-making.

cinnamon *n* a tree and the aromatic spice from it; a yellow-brown colour.

cipher, cypher *n* the figure 0; any numeral; a person or thing of no importance; a secret writing.

circle *n* a round figure; a group; its bounding line; a ring; a class. * *vt, vi* to move round; to enclose.

circuit *n* area; extent; journey of judges to hold courts; a detour; the path of an electric current.

circuitous *adj* roundabout.

circular *adj* round. * *n* a notice.

circulate *vi* to move in a circle; to pass from person to person or place to place. * *vt* to spread.

circulation *n* circulating; the area centred and the number sold, of a newspaper etc; the flow of blood through the arteries and the veins; currency.

circulatory *adj* circulating.

circumcise *vt* to cut off the foreskin.

circumference *n* the bounding line of a circle.

circumflex *n* an accent (^) on vowels marking contraction, etc.

circumlocution *n* a roundabout mode of speaking.

circumlocutory *adj* diffuse.

circumnavigate *vt* to sail round.

circumscribe *vt* to enclose; to limit.

circumspect *adj* wary.

circumspection *n* caution.

circumstance *n* an event; (*pl*) state of affairs; condition.

circumstantial *adj* indirect; incidental.

circumvent *vt* to avoid by going round; to evade; to outwit.

circus *n* (*pl* **circuses**) an enclosed area or place for games etc; a travelling show of entertainers and animals.

cirrus n (pl **cirri**) a thin, trailing cloud.

cistern n a water tank.

citation n quotation; summons.

cite vt to summon; to quote.

citizen n an inhabitant of a city.

citizenship n the rights of a citizen.

citrus n a type of tree including the orange and lemon; the fruit.

city n a large town.

civet n an African and Asian catlike animal; the perfume obtained from it.

civic adj pertaining to a city or citizen.

civil adj municipal; non-military; of the state; polite; internal.

civilian n one engaged in civil, not military pursuits.

civility n courtesy.

civilization n culture; social development; the modern world.

civilize vt to convert from a savage or wild state; to refine.

clad pp of clothe.

claim vt to demand as due; to assert outright to; to state one's ownership of. * n a formal demand; the thing claimed.

claimant n one who claims.

clairvoyance n the supposed power of seeing things not present to the senses.

clamber vi to scramble over.

clammy adj sticky; damp; moist.

clamorous adj noisy.

clamour n shouting; uproar. * vi to demand with shouts.

clamp n a gripping appliance. * vi to fasten or grip.

clan n a family; a tribe.

clandestine adj secret; underhand.

clang n a ringing noise.

clank n a dull metallic ring as of chains.

clannish adj united; belonging to a group and excluding others.

clap vt to strike together noisily, esp the hands; to pat. * n explosive sound as of thunder.

clapper n the tongue of a bell.

claret n a red wine. * adj claret-coloured.

clarify vt, vi to make clear; to purify by heating.

clarinet n a reed musical instrument.

clarion n a shrill trumpet. * adj rousing.

clash vi to make a noise by collision; to be antagonistic to or incompatible. * n noisy collision; jarring.

clasp n an embrace; a hook. * vt to fasten; to embrace.

clasp-knife n a knife with blades that fold into the handle.

class n a rank; a group; a body of students learning together, a standard or grade of worth. * vt to arrange in classes.

classic adj of the first rank. * n a work of the first rank in any of the arts.

classical adj refined; standard; pertaining to or in keeping with the great masterpieces of Greece and Rome; traditional.

classification n organization into classes or categories.

classify vt to arrange; to categorize; to restrict, esp information, to an inner group for security reasons.

clatter vi to make rattling noises; to talk noisily. * n a rattling noise.

clause n a part of a sentence; a single item of a treaty, contract, bill, etc.

claustrophobia n a morbid fear of confined spaces or being shut in.

clavicle n the collarbone.

claw n a hooked nail; a crab's pincer. * vt to scratch or dig with claws or nails.

clay n heavy soil.

claymore n a large two-edged sword; a basket-hilted sword.

clean adj free from dirt; pure. * vt to purify; to cleanse.

cleanliness n state of being clean.

cleanse vt to make clean or pure.

clear adj bright; shining; limpid; fair; plain; shrill. * adv manifestly. * vt to make clear; to free from suspicion.

clearance n a setting free; an emptying; a discharge.

clearing n the act of making clear; a settling up; land cleared of trees.

cleavage n a splitting or tendency to split; the hollow between the breasts.

cleave[1] vi vb (pt **clove** or **cleft**, pp **cloven** or **cleft**) to stick; to adhere.

cleave[2] vt (pt, pp **cleaved**) to split; to sever.

cleaver n a butcher's axe or knife.

clef n a mark to show the key in music.

cleft n a crevice; a fissure.

clemency n mercy.

clench vt to hold tight; to close (teeth) tightly.

clergy npl the ministers of the Christian religion.

cleric n a clergyman.

clerical n pertaining to the clergy, or to a clerk.

clerk n an office employee; an official who looks after records.

clever adj adroit; talented.

cleverness n ability.

click vi to clink; to make a faint sharp sound.

client n a customer.

clientele n clients collectively.

cliff n a steep rock face.

climacteric n a critical period in life; the menopause.

climate n weather characteristics or conditions; a prevailing atmosphere, mood or feeling.

climax n the highest point; an ascending scale.

climb vi, vt to ascend; to mount.

clinch vt to settle finally (a deal, an argument); to fasten; to grasp. * n a grip hindering the use of the arms; a tight embrace.

cling vi (pt, pp **clung**) to adhere; to cleave.

clinic n a place for the care of outpatients; a private hospital; doctors practising in a group.

clinical adj of or pertaining to the treatment, progress and medical observation of patients; objective; detached.

clink vt to jingle.

clinker n burnt brick or hard cinders.

clip vt (pt **clipped**) to shear; to trim with scissors; to shorten or cut off words when speaking; to grip or fasten with a clip or clasp. * n a clasp to hold, fasten or hook together; an extract from a film.

clique n a party; a set; an exclusive group.

clitoris n a small sensitive erectile organ of the vulva.

cloak n a loose outer garment; a pretext. * vt to hide; to veil.

clock n a timepiece.

clockwork n the machinery of a clock; unfailing regularity.

clod n a lump of earth; a stupid fellow.

clog n a shoe with a wooden sole.

cloister n a monastery or convent; a covered walk there or in a college.

close[1] vt to shut; to finish. * vi to end. * n the end.

close[2] adj shut fast; tight; dense; near; stingy; secretive. * n an enclosed place; a courtyard or its entrance; the precincts of a cathedral.

closet n a small room or recess. * vt (pl **closeted**) to shut up.

closure n a stoppage; a closing.

clot n a curdled or coagulated mass (of blood). * vi (pt **clotted**) to become thick.

cloth n a woven fabric.

clothe vt to attire.

clothes n dress; coverings.

cloud n a mass of visible water vapour high in the air; a crowd; gloom. * vt to darken; to obscure; to hide.

cloudless adj clear.

cloudy adj overcast; indistinct; muddy.

clove n a spice; one segment of a bulb of garlic.

clover n a three-leaved plant used as fodder.

clown n a lout; a jester; a circus entertainer.

clownish adj boorish.

cloy vt to glut; to surfeit with sweetness.

club n a cudgel; a golf stick; a society of people; their meeting place; a suit at cards; an association for some common object. * vt to beat with a club. * vi to join together.

clue n a guide or help to solve a puzzle.

clump n a thick cluster; the sound made by heavy or clumsy footsteps.

clumsy adj awkward; graceless; tactless; a collection of eggs hatched at the one time; a brood of chickens.

cluster n a bunch. * vi to keep close together.

clutch vt to seize; to grasp. * n the lever that puts an engine in or out of action.

coach n a four-wheeled closed vehicle; a long-distance bus; a sports trainer.

coagulate vt, vi to curdle; to clot; (liquid) to thicken to a semisolid state.

coal n a black mineral used as fuel.

coalesce vi to unite; to fuse; to merge.

coalition n a party union; an alliance.

coal mine n a mine containing coal.

coal tar n a black liquid from distilled coal.

coarse adj rude; gross; crude.

coast n the seashore. * vi to sail along a shore; to travel without mechanical power, esp downhill.

coaster n a vessel that trades along the coast; a protective mat placed under a glass or bottle.

coastguard n a coast police force.

coasting adj a brakeless downhill ride.

coat n an outer garment; a covering; a layer. * vt to cover.

coax vt to wheedle; to persuade by gentleness or flattery.

cobble vt to mend coarsely. * npl a road surfaced with rounded stones.

cobbler n a mender of shoes.

cobweb n a spider's web.

cocaine n a drug injected to deaden pain.

cochineal n an insect; the scarlet dye got from it.

cock n a male bird; a tap; the hammer of a gun. * vt to set erect.

cockney n, adj (of) a native of London.

cockpit n a pit where game cocks fight; a pilot's compartment in an aeroplane.

cocktail n an alcoholic drink composed of a mixture of spirits and other ingredients.

cocoa n cacao seeds; the beverage made from them.

coconut n the fruit of the coco palm.

cocoon n the case spun by the silkworm.

coddle vt to be overprotective; to cook in water below boiling point.

code n a collection of laws, rules, or signals; letters, numbers, symbols arranged to transmit secret messages.

codicil n a supplement to a will.

codification n the collection (of laws, etc) into a system.

codify vt to collect or arrange (laws, rules, etc) into a system.

coefficient adj cooperating. * n (math) a numerical or constant factor in an algebraic term.

coerce vt to force; to compel.

coercion n the act of compulsion; government by force.

coexecutor n a joint executor.

coexist vi to live together, esp peacefully; at the same time.

coffee n a drink made from the seeds of the coffee tree.

coffer n a chest, esp one for holding valuables.

coffin n the coffer or chest for holding a corpse.

cog n the tooth of a wheel.

cogency n force.

cogent adj convincing.

cogitate vi to ponder.

cognac n French brandy.

cognition n perception.

cognizable adj capable of being known or perceived.

cognizance n knowledge; judicial notice.

cognizant adj having knowledge of.

cohabit vi to dwell together.

cohere vi to stick together.

coherent adj connected; intelligible, of speech; logical and consistent.

cohesion n the force keeping the particles of bodies together.

cohort n a company of soldiers.

coiffure n a hairstyle.

coil vt to wind into a ring. * n a ring or rings into which a rope, etc, is wound, or a spiral of a thing wound, esp a wire for electric current.

coin n a piece of money. * vt to mint; to invent a new word or phrase.

coinage n coined money.

coincide vi to correspond in space or time; to agree exactly.

coincidence n concurrence; the occurrence by chance of two events at the same time.

coincident adj corresponding.

colander n a strainer for food.

cold adj not hot; chill; indifferent. * n absence of heat; an illness due to cold.

coleslaw n raw cabbage shredded and mixed in a dressing as a salad.

colic n an acute pain in the abdomen.

collaborator n an associate in literary or scientific labour; one who works against one's country in wartime.

collage n a picture or piece of artwork composed of random scraps of paper, material etc pasted on a surface.

collapse n a breakdown; a fall; a failure. * vi to fall; to break down.

collar n a band worn round the neck; the neckband of a garment.

collarbone n one of the two bones that connect the shoulder blades with the neck.

collate vt to examine and compare, as books, etc.

collateral adj side by side; indirect.

collation n the collating of texts etc.

colleague n an associate in office, a fellow worker.

collect[1] vt, vi to bring together; to infer; to arrange; to accumulate things as a hobby.

collect[2] n a short prayer.

collected adj self-possessed.

collection n act of collecting; that which is collected; an accumulation of things of value or interest; money gathered for a purpose.

collective adj taken as a whole.

collectivism n the doctrine of the state ownership of land and all means of production.

college n an institution of scholars; a centre of higher learning.

collide vi to strike against each other.

collier n a coal miner; a coal ship.

colliery n a coal mine.

collision n act of striking together; conflict.

colloquial adj conversational; informal and non-literary of talk.

collude vi to connive.

collusion n fraud by agreement; conspiracy.

collusive adj fraudulently concerted.

colon n a mark of punctuation, thus (:); the large intestine.

colonel n the commander of a regiment.

colonial adj pertaining to a colony. * n a person belonging to a colony.

colonist n an inhabitant of a colony.

colonization n act of colonizing.

colonize vt to found a colony.

colonnade n a range of columns.

colony n a settlement in a new country.

colophon n the device or emblem of a publisher on a book.

colossal adj huge.

colour n the hue or appearance of a body to the eye; a pigment; complexion; pretence; pl a flag. * vt to tinge; to varnish; to embellish. * vi to blush.

colouring n act of giving a colour; colour applied; a false appearance.

colourist n a painter who excels in use of colour.

colt n a young horse.

column n a pillar; a body of troops; a section of a page; a line of figures; an article or feature appearing regularly in a newspaper etc.

coma n a stupor; a lengthy period of unconsciousness.

comatose adj torpid; deathlike.

comb n a toothed appliance for dressing hair, wool, etc. * vt to arrange hair with a comb; to search for thoroughly.

combat vi to fight * vt to oppose. * n a fight; a contest.

combatant adj contending. * n a fighter.

combative adj disposed to fight.

combination n a union; an alliance of persons; numbers arranged to open the combination lock of a safe.

combine vt to join. * vi to league together. * n a machine that cuts and threshes crops.

combustible adj inflammable.

combustion n a burning.

come vi (pt **came**, pp **come**) to move forward; to draw near; to arrive; to happen.

comedian n an actor of comic roles; one who entertains by telling jokes.

comedy n drama written to amuse.

comely adj good-looking; becoming.

comestible n an eatable.

comet n a heavenly body having a luminous tail.

comfort vt to console; to gladden. * n consolation.

comfortable adj contented; at ease; having adequate money to live well.

comic adj relating to comedy; amusing.

comical adj funny.

comma n a mark of punctuation, thus (,).

command vt to order; to govern; to have at one's disposal. * vi to have chief power. * n order; authority.

commandant n the military officer in charge of men or an establishment.

commandeer vt to appropriate.

commander n one who commands.

commanding adj dominating; authoritative.

commandment n a precept of moral law.

commando n a soldier belonging to a special attacking force.

commemorate vt to celebrate the memory of someone or something.

commemoration n a solemn celebration as a memorial to.

commence vi, vt to take the first step; to begin.

commend vt to praise; to recommend.

commendable adj worthy of praise.

commendation n praise.

commensurate adj proportional.

comment *vi* to make remarks or criticisms. * *vt* to annotate. * *n* an explanatory note.

commentary *n* a book of comments or notes; a spoken explanation of events as they take place.

commentator *n* one who reports and explains events, as on television.

commerce *n* exchange of goods, trade.

commercial *adj* trading; pertaining to commerce; intended to be profit-making. * *n* a broadcast advertisement on television, etc.

commingle *vt* to blend.

commiserate *vt* to pity, condole with.

commiseration *n* pity; sympathy.

commissariat *n* the stores department of an army; the supplies themselves.

commission *n* trust; warrant; a percentage; a body of commissioners; the appointment of a soldier to officer's rank; a business or task given or entrusted to someone. * *vt* to require the services of.

commissionaire *n* a porter or messenger.

commissioner *n* one appointed to perform some office.

commit *vt* to entrust; to consign, esp to custody; to perpetrate.

commitment *n* a pledge; imprisonment.

committal *n* the act of committing.

committee *n* a body appointed to manage any matter on behalf of a larger body.

commodious *adj* spacious and suitable.

commodity *n* any article of commerce.

commodore *n* the commander of a squadron.

common *adj* general; usual; of no rank; of little value. * *n* an open public ground.

commonly *adv* usually.

commonplace *adj* ordinary; trite.

common sense *n* sound judgment.

commonwealth *n* the public good; the state; a republic; a federation of states.

commotion *n* tumult; disorder.

communal *adj* belonging to a community or commune; shared; common to.

commune[1] *vi* to confer with privately or spiritually.

commune[2] *n* a group of people living together and sharing everything.

communicable *adj* capable of being imparted to another.

communicant *n* a partaker of the Lord's supper.

communicate *vt, vi* to impart.

communication *n* news; a message; (*pl*) the passing and exchange of information, ideas etc by means of speech, telecommunications, the media etc.

communicative *adj* candid; talkative.

communion *n* intercourse; celebration of the Lord's Supper.

communism *n* the doctrine of a community of property.

communist *n* an advocate of communism.

community *n* the body of the people;

a body of people living in the same locality.

commutable *adj* exchangeable.

commutation *n* exchange; change; lessening.

commute *vt, vi* to travel a distance daily between home and work; to exchange; to lessen; to reduce the length of a prison sentence.

compact *adj* solid; dense. * *vt* to consolidate. * *n* an agreement.

compact disc *n* a mirrored disc containing recordings that are read by a laser beam.

companion *n* a comrade; a friend.

companionable *adj* sociable.

company *n* a body of guests, of traders, or of soldiers; a business; a ship's crew.

comparable *adj* similar.

comparative *adj* relative.

compare *vt* to examine side by side; to liken; to form degrees of comparison.

comparison *n* relation; simile; illustration; inflection in an adjective.

compartment *n* spaces divided off (in drawers etc); a division of a railway carriage; something separate; a category.

compass *n* a circuit; limit; range; an instrument with a magnetic needle pointing to the north; (*often pl*) an instrument for drawing circles.

compassion *n* sympathy.

compatible *adj* consistent; in keeping; able to live with agreeably; of like mind.

compatriot *n* one of the same country.

compel *vt* (*pt* **compelled**) to drive; to urge; to force.

compendium *n* a summary.

compensate *vt* to make amends for; to requite. * *vi* to atone.

compensation *n* recompense.

compete *vi* to strive (as rival); to contend.

competence *n* sufficiency, ability.

competent *adj* well qualified; fit.

competently *adv* adequately.

competition *n* rivalry; a contest; a, match.

competitor *n* a rival.

compilation *n* the act of compiling; the thing compiled.

compile *vt* to collect (facts, figures, etc).

complacence, complacency *n* satisfaction; self-satisfaction.

complacent *adj* pleased, with oneself.

complain *vi* to grumble at; to be dissatisfied with; to lament; to make a charge; to feel unwell.

complainant *n* a plaintiff.

complaint *n* a grumble; an accusation; an ailment.

complement *n* the full quota, allowance or number.

complementary *adj* completing.

complete *adj* finished. * *vt* to finish; to fulfil.

completion *n* the fulfilment; the finishing.

complex *adj* involved; difficult. * *n* a whole composed of many parts e.g. buildings or units.

complexion *n* the colour of the face; aspect.

complexity n intricacy.

compliance n concurrence; acquiescence.

compliant adj yielding; docile.

complicate vt to make complex or difficult.

complication n a complex situation; something that worsens or adds to a difficulty; a medical condition following on and arising from the original malady.

complicity n state of being an accomplice.

compliment n an expression of praise or admiration. * vt to praise; to congratulate.

comply vi to acquiesce.

component adj constituent. * n a constituent part.

compose vt to write, esp music; to calm.

composed adj calm; serene.

composer n a writer of music.

composite adj compound.

composition n a putting together; the thing composed, as a piece of music or literature; the make-up of something.

compositor n one who sets types.

composure n calmness.

compound vt, vi to put together; to mix; to adjust. * adj composed of two or more parts. * n a mass composed of two or more elements; an enclosure.

comprehend vt to understand.

comprehensible adj intelligible.

comprehension n understanding.

comprehensive adj inclusive; of wide scope. * n a secondary school accepting pupils of all abilities.

compress vt to press together. * n a soft pad to apply to a wound.

compressed adj flattened; condensed.

compression n a condensing; the increasing of pressure in an engine to compress the gases so that they explode.

comprise vt to contain; to consist of.

compromise n a settlement by agreement. * vt to settle by mutual concessions; to endanger.

comptroller n a controller.

compulsion n force; an overpowering urge.

compulsive adj compelling; acting as if forced.

compulsory adj obligatory.

compunction n remorse.

computation n reckoning.

compute vt to count; estimate.

computer n an electronic device that processes data according to instructions fed into it.

comrade n a mate; companion.

concave adj curving inwards.

conceal vt to hide.

concealment n a hiding place.

concede vt to yield; to grant.

conceit n vanity; an exaggerated opinion of oneself.

conceited adj vain.

conceivable adj thinkable; imaginable.

conceive vt, vi to comprehend; to think; to become pregnant.

concentrate vt to collect to one point; to direct the mind solely to one aim or object; to condense in order to increase the strength of something.

concentric *adj* having a common centre.

concept *n* a general idea; an abstract idea.

conception *n* act of conceiving; an idea.

concern *vt* to interest oneself in; to apply to; to cause anxiety to. * *n* anxiety.

concert *n* agreement; harmony; a musical performance.

concerted *adj* planned; combined.

concertina *n* a musical instrument.

concerto *n* a musical composition for solo instrument and orchestra.

concession *n* a grant; the act of yielding.

conch *n* a marine shell.

conciliate *vt* to reconcile; to propitiate.

conciliatory *adj* persuasive.

concise *adj* brief; pointed.

conclave *n* the assembly of cardinals for the election of a pope; a close assembly.

conclude *vt, vi* to end; to deduce.

conclusion *n* inference; the end; a final judgment or opinion.

concoct *vt* to devise; to plot; to produce from a mixture of ingredients; to fabricate.

concoction *n* a mixture; an invention.

concomitant *adj* accompanying. * *n* a connected circumstance.

concord *n* union; harmony.

concordance *n* agreement; a complete index.

concourse *n* a gathering; a crowd; a large area where crowds can gather.

concrete *adj* solid; real, not abstract. * *n* a mass of stones and mortar.

concretion *n* a compacted mass.

concur *vi* to unite; to agree.

concurrence *n* agreement; association; joint action.

concurrent *adj* happening at the same time; agreeing; attendant.

concussion *n* a violent shock, esp caused by an explosion or heavy blow; unconsciousness because of a heavy blow to the head.

condemn *vt* to censure; to sentence.

condemnatory *adj* condemning.

condensation *n* act of condensing; state of being condensed; an abridgement.

condense *vt* to compress; to liquefy; to reduce by cutting esp of text or speech.

condenser *n* a chamber in which steam is condensed; a vessel for condensing or accumulating electricity.

condescend *vi* to stoop; to deign; to be patronizing.

condescension *n* graciousness; patronizing behaviour.

condiment *n* a seasoning or spice.

condition *n* physical state of health; case; stipulation; illness; *pl* circumstances. * *vt* to stipulate; to make fit; to make accustomed (to).

conditional *adj* depending on conditions; not absolute; (*gram*) expressing condition. * *n* a conditional clause or conjunction.

conditioner *n* a substance for bringing the hair into a glossy condition.

condole *vi* to sympathize.

condolence *n* expression of sympathy.

condom *n* a sheath for the penis, used to prevent conception and infection.

condone *vt* to overlook; to pardon an offence.

conducive *adj* leading to; contributing to.

conduct *n* behaviour; management; escort. * *vt* to lead; to manage; to behave; to direct an orchestra; to transmit, e.g. heat or electricity.

conduction *n* property by which bodies transmit heat or electricity.

conductor *n* a leader; a director of an orchestra; one who is in charge of a train.

conduit *n* a channel; a subway for pipes.

cone *n* a pointed figure with a circular base; the fruit of firs, etc.

confection *n* a mixture; a sweet.

confectioner *n* a maker of sweets.

confederacy *n* a league.

confederate *adj* allied. * *n* an ally; a fellow conspirator. * *vt, vi* to unite.

confederation *n* an alliance.

confer *vb* (*pt* **conferred**) *vi* to consult together. * *vt* to give or bestow.

conference *n* a meeting for consultation.

confess *vt* to own; to admit. * *vi* to make a confession.

confessedly *adv* avowedly.

confession *n* admission of a fault or sin, esp to a confessor; a creed.

confessional *n* the place where a priest hears confessions.

confessor *n* a priest who hears confession.

confidant *m*, **confidante** *f* a trusted friend.

confide *vi, vt* to trust wholly; to entrust.

confidence *n* trust; assurance.

confidential *adj* private; privy to secrets.

confidently *adv* with assurance.

confiding *adj* trusting.

configuration *n* shape brought about by arranging of parts.

confine *n* a boundary. * *vt* to restrain; to shut up.

confinement *n* imprisonment; childbirth.

confirm *vt* to ratify; to corroborate; to admit to communion in church.

confirmation *n* proof; the receiving into full communion.

confirmatory *adj* corroborative.

confirmed *adj* fixed; settled.

confiscable *adj* liable to forfeiture.

confiscate *vt* to seize as forfeit.

conflagration *n* a great fire.

conflict *n* a struggle; a fight; strife; an upset. * *vi* to be at variance.

conflicting *adj* contradictory.

confluence *n* a flowing together; the meeting of streams.

confluent *adj* mingling.

conform *vt, vi* to adapt; to comply.

conformation *n* structure.

conformity *n* agreement; likeness; keeping to established rules.

confound *vt* to confuse; to astound; to overthrow.

confront *vt* to face; to oppose; to challenge face to face.

confuse *vt* to mix together; to derange; to perplex; to embarrass.

confusion n disorder.

confute vt to disprove.

congeal vt to coagulate; to thicken.

congenial adj kindred; having like natures or tastes; compatible.

congenital adj hereditary.

congested adj overcrowded; clogged with blood etc; blocked.

congestion n undue fullness (esp of blood); overcrowding; a blockage of traffic.

conglomerate adj stuck together in a mass.

conglomeration n a mixed mass.

congratulate vt to compliment; to felicitate.

congratulatory adj complimentary.

congregate vt, vi to meet together.

congregation n an assembly.

Congregationalism n church government in which each church manages its affairs.

congress n an assembly; (with cap) the legislature of the USA.

congressional adj pertaining to a congress.

congruence, congruency n agreement; suitability.

congruent adj suitable; agreeing; corresponding.

congruous adj accordant; corresponding; appropriate.

conic, conical adj cone-like; cone-shaped.

coniferous adj bearing cones.

conjectural adj reaching an opinion by guesswork.

conjecture n supposition. * vt to surmise.

conjoin vt to unite.

conjoint adj united.

conjugal adj pertaining to marriage.

conjugate vt to inflect (a verb). * adj joined in pairs.

conjugation n the inflection of verbs.

conjunction n connection; a connecting word.

conjunctive adj uniting

conjuncture n a crisis.

conjure vt to summon up by magic. * vi to juggle.

conjurer, conjuror n one who entertains with magic tricks and juggling.

connect vt to join; to associate; to link by telephone; to transfer from one vehicle to another to continue journey.

connective adj binding together. * n a conjunction.

connection n a relation by blood or marriage; relationship; the vehicle timed to connect with another.

connive vi to concur in a wrong.

connoisseur n an expert; a judge of fine arts.

connotation n the implied meaning; the resultant meaning.

conquer vt to gain by force; to vanquish. * vi to overcome.

conqueror n a victor.

conquest n subjugation; that which is conquered.

conscience n the sense of right and wrong.

conscientious adj high principled; regulated by conscience; thorough; diligent.

conscious adj aware; sensible of.

consciousness n awareness.

conscript n one compulsorily enrolled to serve in the army or navy.

conscription n a compulsory enrolment for military or naval service.

consecrate vt to set apart for sacred use; to dedicate.

consecutive adj following in order.

consent n concurrence; agreement; permission. * vi to assent; to acquiesce; to permit.

consequence n result; inference; importance.

consequent adj following; resulting.

consequential adj pompous.

conservancy n a board controlling a port, fishery, countryside, etc.

conservation n preservation, esp of the environment and natural resources.

conservative adj averse to change. * n one opposed to political change.

conservatory n a greenhouse.

conserve vt to keep in a sound state; to keep safe; to preserve or pickle food.

consider vt, vi to think on; to ponder; to weigh up; to examine.

considerable adj worth considering; fairly large.

considerate adj thoughtful of others.

consideration n serious deliberation.

considering prep in view of; allowing for; seeing that.

consign vt to hand over to another.

consignee n the person to whom goods are consigned.

consigner n one who consigns.

consignment n goods consigned.

consist vi to be composed of.

consistency n a degree of density or firmness; harmony; being true to one's previous ideas, behaviour etc.

consistent adj fixed; compatible; reliably unchanging in deed or thought.

consolation n solace; a comfort.

consolatory adj giving consolation.

console vt to comfort.

consolidate vt to make solid; to strengthen.

consonance n concord; agreement.

consonant adj accordant; consistent. * n a letter or sound that is not a vowel.

consort n a partner; a wife or husband; a companion. * vi to associate with unsuitable people; to agree; to accord.

consortium n a combining for a special purpose.

conspicuous adj outstanding; noticeable.

conspiracy n a plot.

conspire vi to plot together.

constable n a policeman or woman of the lowest rank.

constabulary n the body of constables.

constancy n steadfastness.

constant adj steadfast; faithful. * n a fixed quantity.

constellation n a group of stars.

consternation n dismay.

constipation n difficulty in moving the bowels.

constituency n the body of voters; the voters of an area.

constituent adj component; being a part of a whole. * n an elector; one essential part of a whole.

constitute *vt* to set up; to compose; to appoint.

constitution *n* the condition of the body; a system of government.

constitutional *adj* of, pertaining to a constitution; legal. * *n* a walk taken for one's health.

constrain *vt* to force; to necessitate; to restrain; to imprison.

constrained *adj* forced; embarrassed.

constraint *n* necessity; embarrassment; inhibition; confinement.

constrict *vt* to contract; to compress; to limit free movement.

constriction *n* contraction; a feeling of tightness; compression.

construct *vt* to build; to devise.

construction *n* a structure; meaning; interpretation.

constructive *adj* having ability to construct; develop; improve.

construe *vt* to arrange words so as to discover the sense of a sentence; to interpret.

consul *n* a state agent in foreign towns.

consulate *n* the office or residence of a consul.

consult *vi, vt* to take counsel; to consider; to seek advice.

consultant *n* a consulting physician.

consultation *n* a seeking of advice from a doctor or lawyer.

consume *vt, vi* to eat or drink; to destroy; to use up; to squander.

consumer *n* one who buys goods and uses services.

consummate[1] *vt* to finish, to perfect.

consummate[2] *adj* complete; perfect.

consummation *n* end; perfection.

consumption *n* expenditure.

contact *n* a touching together; close union; a business acquaintance; one who has been close to a person with a contagious disease. * *vt* to get in touch with.

contagious *adj* infectious, spread by touch.

contain *vt* to hold; to restrain.

contaminate *vt* to corrupt; to pollute.

contamination *n* pollution.

contemplate *vt* to meditate on; to intend.

contemplation *n* meditation.

contemplative *adj* thoughtful.

contemporaneous *adj* concurrent.

contemporary *adj* belonging to the same time. * *n* one who lives at the same time; a person of the same age.

contempt *n* scorn; disregard.

contemptible *adj* mean; worthy of contempt.

contemptuous *adj* scornful.

contend *vi* to strive; to vie; to dispute.

content *adj* satisfied. * *vt* to please; to satisfy. * *n* satisfaction; capacity; *pl* things held by a container.

contented *adj* satisfied.

contention *n* a struggle; a quarrel.

contentious *adj* quarrelsome.

contest *vt, vi* to call in question; to strive; to contend; to emulate. * *n* a competition.

context *n* the setting (of a passage of text).

contiguity *n* nearness.

contiguous *adj* touching; adjacent.

continent¹ adj chaste; moderate; able to control urination and defecation.

continent² n a large mass of land; (*with cap*) the mainland of Europe.

contingency n a possible event; accident.

contingent adj incidental; conditional; that may happen. * n a quota; a detachment of troops; a possible happening.

continual adj incessant.

continuance n duration.

continue vi to remain; to persevere. * vt to prolong; to extend.

continuity n unbroken sequence; the whole script and scenario of a film.

continuous adj uninterrupted.

contort vt to twist, pull out of shape.

contortion n a twisting out of shape.

contortionist n an entertainer who twists his body into unnatural positions.

contour n outline; form; a line on a map joining all points at the same height above sea level.

contraband n smuggled goods.

contract vt to reduce; to incur; to shorten (a word); to be affected by a disease. * vi to shrink; to make a mutual agreement. * n an agreement; a bond.

contraction n shrinking; a shortening; tensing of a muscle.

contractor n a firm that arranges sale of materials or goods or manpower.

contradict vt to deny; to say the contrary.

contradictory adj inconsistent.

contralto n the lowest voice of a woman.

contraption n a devise; a gadget; an improvised or complicated contrivance.

contrary adj opposite; adverse; opposed; perverse. * n the opposite.

contrast vt to set in opposition; to show up the differences in. * vi to stand in contrast to * n opposition; difference.

contravene vt to oppose; to transgress.

contravention n violation.

contribute vt to give; to write magazine articles; to make suggestions.

contribution n something given; a gift.

contributor n one who contributes; a writer to a periodical.

contributory adj aiding; partly responsible for.

contrite adj penitent.

contrition n sorrow for sin; repentance.

contrivance n a scheme; a plan; an invention, often mechanical.

contrive vt to invent; to devise; to achieve, often by unusual means.

control n restraint; authority; a standard to compare with and check against. * vt to regulate; to be in command.

controller n a supervisor of public accounts.

controversial adj disputable.

controversy n a dispute.

contusion n a severe bruise.

conundrum n a riddle.

convalesce vi to recover health.

convalescence n gradual recovery after illness.

convalescent n one recovering from sickness.

convene vi to assemble; to call a meeting. * vt to convoke.

convenience n ease; comfort; something useful and labour saving; a public lavatory.

convenient adj suitable.

convent n a monastery; a nunnery.

convention n an assembly; an agreement; a recognized social custom.

conventional adj customary; unoriginal; following accepted rules.

converge vi to tend to the same point.

convergent adj approaching; meeting; arriving at the same point or result.

conversant adj familiar with; versed in.

conversation n easy talk.

conversationalist n a good talker.

conversazione n a social meeting.

converse vi to talk familiarly. * n conversation; the very opposite.

conversion n a change of religion, party, etc.; an alteration to a building.

convert vt, vi to transform; to change. * n one who has changed his opinion, practice, or religion.

convertible adj transformable * n a car with a folding or detachable roof.

convex adj curved outwards.

convey vt to transport; to carry; to transfer, esp the title of a property; to make known.

conveyance n any means of transport; a transference of property by deed.

convict vt to prove to be guilty. * n a criminal undergoing sentence.

conviction n a proving guilty; a strong belief.

convince vt to persuade; to satisfy.

convincing adj conclusive; believable beyond doubt.

convivial adj festive; jovial; sociable.

convolute, convoluted adj rolled, coiled on itself; involved; difficult to follow.

convolution n a winding; a spiral.

convoy vt to escort. * n a protecting force of ships or vehicles.

convulse vt to agitate violently * vi to cause spasms of helpless laughter.

convulsion n a shaking fit; a disturbance.

convulsive adj spasmodic.

cook vt to prepare food; to concoct. * n one who prepares food.

cookery n the art of preparing food.

cool adj moderately cold; self-possessed. * vt to make cool.

coolly adv with assurance.

coolness n calm assurance.

coop n a cage or pen for poultry.

cooper n one who makes barrels.

cooperage n the work or workshop of a cooper.

cooperate vi to act, work together with another.

cooperation n copartnership.

cooperative adj operating jointly; helpful.

co-opt vt to elect into a body, committee etc by vote of its members.

coordinate adj equal in rank. * vt to arrange in the same order; to integrate.

coordination n act of coordinating; harmonious movement of parts of the body.

cope vt to cover; to grapple (with); to manage something successfully.

copestone n the topmost stone.

copier n a transcriber; a machine that makes copies; an imitator.

copilot n a second pilot in an aircraft.

coping n the topmost course of a wall, etc.

copious adj abundant.

copper n a reddish metal.

copperplate n an engraver's plate; the print from it; perfect handwriting.

coppersmith n one who works in copper.

coppice, copse n a thicket.

copulate vi to have sexual intercourse.

copulative adj that unites. * n a conjunction.

copy n an imitation; matter to be set up in type. * vt to imitate; to transcribe.

copyright n the sole right to publish (a book, etc).

coquetry n flirtation.

coracle n a boat made of skin-covered wickerwork.

coral n a sea rock built up from the skeletons of minute organisms.

cord n a thin rope; a band.

cordial adj hearty. * n a refreshing drink.

cordiality n heartiness.

cordon n a line or chain of police or soldiers barring entry to an area; a knight's ribbon.

corduroy n a thick cotton stuff corded or ribbed.

core n the heart; the essence; the seed-bearing centre of fruit; the centre of the earth below the mantle.

co-respondent n a joint respondent in divorce proceedings.

cork n a tree or its bark; a stopper. * vt to stop with a cork.

corm n a bulb-shaped root.

corn n grain (as wheat, oats, etc); a horny growth on the foot.

cornea n the transparent membrane over the eye.

corned adj salted.

corner n an angle; the place where two lines, sides, streets etc meet; a difficult or dangerous position; a free kick from the corner of the pitch in football, hockey; a nook.

cornerstone n the indispensable stone, part, or basis.

cornet n a brass instrument of the trumpet family; a cone-shaped wafer for ice cream.

cornice n the upper moulding of a column, a room, a wall, etc.

cornucopia n the horn plenty full of fruit and vegetables.

corolla n the inner envelope; the petals of a flower.

corollary n an additional inference from a proved proposition.

corona n the halo round the sun in total eclipse; a circle of florets.

coronation n the ceremony of crowning.

coroner n an officer who holds an inquest in a case of sudden death.

corporal n the second lowest non-commissioned officer. * adj pertaining to the body; physical; material.

corporate adj formed into a legal body; united; joint.

corporately adv in a corporate capacity.

corporation n a body corporate, empowered to act as an individual.

corporeal adj material, not spiritual.

corps n a body of troops.

corpse n the dead body of a human being.

corpulence n excessive fatness.

corpulent adj portly; fat.

corpuscle n a red or white blood cell in the body.

corpuscular adj pertaining to corpuscles.

corral n a pen for cattle; an enclosure or stockade.

correct adj right. * vt to make right; to chastise.

corrective adj intended to correct * n that which corrects; restriction.

correlate vi to be reciprocally related. * vt to determine the relations between.

correlation n reciprocal relation.

correlative adj having a mutual relation, as father and son. * n a word that relates to another word, as: either and or.

correspond vi to be like or similar; to agree; to write to.

correspondence n agreement; exchange or writing of (letters, etc).

corridor n a passage in a building or train linking rooms, compartments, etc.

corroborate vt to strengthen; to confirm.

corroboration n confirmation.

corrode vt to eat or wear away by degrees; to rust.

corrosion n wearing away through chemical action.

corrosive adj gnawing; blighting. * n a corroding agent.

corrugate vt to wrinkle; to fold into parallel ridges.

corrugated adj wrinkled; ridged.

corrupt vt to taint morally; to infect; to bribe. * vi to become debased or vitiated. * adj tainted; depraved.

corruptible adj subject to decay, destruction, debasement.

corruption n act or process of corrupting; depravity; bribery.

corset n a close-fitting undergarment supporting the lower body.

cortege n a train of attendants; a funeral procession.

cortex n the bark of a tree; a membrane.

coruscate vi to flash; to glitter.

corvette n a escort ship of war.

cosy adj snug. * n a teapot cover.

cosmetic n a skin beautifier. * adj beautifying; correcting; improving.

cosmic adj relating to the universe.

cosmography n a description of the world.

cosmology n the science of the world or the universe.

cosmonaut n a Russian astronaut.

cosmopolitan n a citizen of the world; a much travelled person; someone without national prejudices. * adj unprejudiced.

cosmopolite n a cosmopolitan person.

cosmos n the universe and its system.

cost vt (pt, pp **cost**) to be bought for; to cause; (pt, pp **costed**) to set a price on. * n charge; price; trouble.

costal adj pertaining to the ribs.

costive adj constipated.

costume n an established mode of dress; garb; attire; clothing worn by actors.

costumier n a dealer in costumes.

cot n a small house; a small bed.

coterie n a small social group of people with like interests; a clique.

cottage n a small house.

cotton n a soft substance in the pods of several plants; cloth made of cotton.

cotton wool n cotton in the raw state bleached and sterilized.

couch vt to express in specific language or mode of speech. * n a bed; a sofa.

couchant adj lying down.

cough n a noisy explosion of air from the lungs. * vt, vi to make a violent effort to expel the air from the lungs.

could pt of **can**.

council n an assembly; a governing or advisory body elected or appointed.

councillor n a member of a council.

counsel n deliberation; advice; design; a barrister. * vt to advise; to recommend.

counsellor n an adviser; a barrister.

count vt to number; to judge. * vi to reckon; to rely on; to matter or be of importance; to mark time. * n reckoning.

countenance n the face; air; aspect; favour. * vt to favour.

counter n a shop table; (pl) tokens for card games. * vt to parry. * adj rival; opposite.

counteract vt to act in opposition to; to hinder; to check; to neutralize.

counterbalance vt to weigh against with an equal weight or power.

counterfeit vt, vi to forge; to copy; to feign. * adj fraudulent. * n a forgery.

counterfoil n a part of a cheque, etc, kept for reference.

countermand vt to annul a former command. * n a contrary order.

counterpane n a cover for a bed.

counterpart n a corresponding part or person; a duplicate.

counterpoint n the art of musical composition; the sounding or playing of two or several melodies or parts at the same time.

countersign vt to sign with an additional signature. * n a password.

countess n the wife of an earl or count.

countless adj innumerable.

country n a large tract of land; a region; a kingdom or state; the public; rural parts. * adj rural.

country dance n a folk dance usually with partners facing each other in line.

county n a shire or division of a country.

coup n a stroke or blow; a masterstroke.

coupé *n* a four seater closed car with two doors and a sloped back.

couple *n* a pair; a brace; a man and his wife. * *vt, vi* to unite; to copulate.

couplet *n* two lines that rhyme.

coupling *n* the links connecting railway carriages or machine parts.

coupon *n* a ticket entitling holder to some money, service, or privilege.

courage *n* bravery.

courageous *adj* bold; fearless.

courier *n* an express messenger.

course *n* a running; a passage; a route; career; ground run over; line of conduct; a track; a series of lectures, etc; range of subjects taught; a layer of stones in masonry; part of a meal served at one time.

court *n* an enclosed area; the retinue of a sovereign; judges in session; flattery. * *vt* to woo; to flatter; to seek.

courteous *adj* polite.

courtesy *n* politeness.

courtier *n* an attendant at a royal court.

courtliness *n* dignity mingled with graciousness.

courtly *adj* dignified.

court martial *n* (*pl* **courts martial**) a court to try military or naval offences.

courtship *n* wooing.

cousin *n* the child of an uncle or aunt.

cove *n* a small inlet.

covenant *n* a contract; a compact. * *vi, vt* to enter into a formal agreement.

cover *vt* to overspread; to cloak; to shelter; to defend; to wrap up; to brood on; to include; to understudy; to write a newspaper report. * *n* a cloak; disguise; shelter; insurance against loss etc.

coverlet *n* the cover of a bed.

covert *adj* secret; private. * *n* a shelter.

covet *vt* to desire eagerly; to envy.

covetous *adj* grasping; greedy.

cow *n* a female of domestic cattle, whale, elephant etc. * *vt* to terrorise; to dishearten; to intimidate.

coward *n* one who is not brave.

cowardice *n* timidity.

cower *vi* to crouch; to waver or tremble through fear.

cowl *n* a monk's hood; a covering over a chimney to aid ventilation.

cowpox *n* an eruption on the teats of cows from which the smallpox vaccine is obtained.

coxcomb *n* a fop; a vain fellow.

coxswain *n* the person who steers a boat or has charge of a ship's boat.

coy *adj* shy; reserved.

crab *n* a crustacean; a sign of the zodiac.

crabbed *adj* perverse.

crack *n* a chink; a sudden sharp sound; a sounding blow; a chat. * *vt, vi* to split; to break; to open a safe forcibly; to open a bottle; to make a joke; to decipher a code; to chat; to give in under pressure.

cracker *n* a small firework; a hard biscuit.

crackle *vi* to make small sharp noises.

cradle *n* an infant's bed on rockers; a

framework under a ship for launching or supporting it; a frame for a broken limb. * *vt* to lay or rock in a cradle.

craft *n* ability; guile; manual art; trade; a ship or aircraft.

craftily *adv* artfully; cunningly.

craftsman *n* an skilled worker.

crafty *adj* cunning.

crag *n* a steep rugged rock.

cram *vt, vi* to stuff; to coach for an examination.

cramp *n* a spasmodic contraction of a muscle; a clamp. * *vt* to affect with spasms; to restrain; to hamper.

cramped *adj* restrained; restricted; of handwriting, small and hard to read.

crane *n* a long-legged, long-necked bird; a machine for raising heavy weights. * *vi* to stretch out one's neck.

cranial *adj* relating to the skull.

cranium *n* the skull.

crank *n* a contrivance for producing a horizontal or perpendicular motion by means of a rotary motion, or the contrary; a bend or turn; an eccentric person. * *adj* liable to be overset; loose. * *vt* to wind.

cranny *n* a chink.

crash *vi* to fall with a clatter; to collide with or fall violently; to gate-crash. * *n* a noise of breakage; a collapse esp financial; a failure; a violent impact or descent.

crass *adj* gross; dense; stupid.

crate *n* a wooden packing case.

crater *n* the bowl-shaped mouth of a volcano; a hole or depression caused by a bomb or meteor explosion.

cravat *n* a neckcloth.

crave *vt* to ask earnestly; to have an intensely strong desire for.

craven *n* a coward. * *adj* cowardly.

craving *n* a morbid desire.

craw *n* the crop of fowls.

crawl *vi* to creep on hands and knees; to be servile towards. * *n* a crawling motion; slow motion; a swimming stroke.

crayon *n* a pencil of coloured chalk; a coloured drawing.

craze *vt* to shatter; to derange. * *vi* to become crazy. * *n* an inordinate desire or enthusiasm; a passing fashion.

crazy *adj* deranged.

creak *vi* to make a grating sound. * *n* a sharp, grating sound.

cream *n* the oily part of milk from which butter is made; the best of anything. * *vt* to take off cream from.

creamery *n* a place where milk is made into butter and cheese.

crease *n* a mark made by folding; the lines marking the batman's stance (in cricket). * *vt* to make creases in.

create *vt* to make out of nothing; to cause to be; to shape; to invent; to appoint.

creation *n* the universe; an original work of any kind.

creative *adj* original; imaginative.

creator *n* the Supreme Being; a producer.

creature *n* a human being; a mere tool.

creche *n* a public nursery for children.

credence *n* credit; trust.

credential *n* warrant; voucher (*pl*) testimonials.

credibility *n* reliability.

credible *adj* worthy of belief.

credit *n* belief; reputed integrity; transfer of goods on trust; side of an account in which payment is entered; money possessed or at one's disposal; distinction given to an examinee for good marks. * *vt* to trust; to believe; to sell or lend in trust.

creditable *adj* estimable; praiseworthy.

creditor *n* one to whom a debt is due.

credulity *n* simplicity; overtrustfulness.

credulous *adj* easily imposed on.

creed *n* belief.

creek *n* a small bay.

creel *n* a fisherman's basket.

creep *vi* (*pt*, *pp* **crept**) to crawl; to move stealthily; to be servile; to shiver.

creeper *n* a creeping plant.

cremate *vt* to consume by burning.

creosote *n* an oily liquid, antiseptic and wood preservative.

crepuscular *adj* pertaining to twilight.

crescent *n* a figure shaped like the new moon. * *adj* increasing.

crest *n* a tuft on the head of certain birds; the plume of feathers on a helmet; a device or symbol of a family or office; the top of a hill.

crestfallen *adj* dejected.

cretaceous *adj* chalky.

cretin *n* one afflicted with deficiency of thyroid hormone resulting in mental retardation.

crevice *n* a cleft; a fissure.

crew *n* a company; a gang; the personnel of a ship or aircraft.

crib *n* a child's bed; a small habitation; a rack; a stall for cattle; a literal translation or list of answers often used illicitly by students in examinations. * *vt* to confine; to pilfer; to copy illicitly.

crick *n* a cramp in the neck.

cricket *n* a chirping insect; a game played with bat and ball at a wicket.

crime *n* a breach of law.

criminal *adj* guilty; wicked. * *n* a malefactor; one who has broken the law.

crimp *vt* to curl; to seize; to pinch or fold together.

crimson *n* a deep red colour. * *adj* of a deep red. * *vt* to dye a deep red colour. * *vi* to blush.

cringe *vi* to fawn; to crouch.

crinkle *vi* to wrinkle. * *vt* to be corrugated or crimped. * *n* a wrinkle.

cripple *n* a lame person. * *vt* to lame; to disable.

crisis *n* (*pl* **crises**) a turning point; a critical moment; an emergency.

crisp *adj* brittle; friable; fresh and bracing. * *n* a thin potato chip.

criterion *n* (*pl* **criteria**) a standard; a rule regarded as a measure of judgment.

critic *n* a judge; a reviewer; a censor.

critical *adj* skilled in judging; crucial; exacting.

criticism n the art or act of judging or the exposition of it.

criticize vi, vt to judge critically; to censure.

critique n a review.

croak vi to make a low hoarse noise in the throat. * n the cry of raven or frog.

crochet n a type of knitting, some with a hooked needle.

crock n an earthen vessel; a pot.

crockery n china dishes; earthenware pots.

croft n a small plot of land with a farmhouse.

crone n an old woman.

crony n a familiar friend.

crook n a bend; a hooked staff; a shepherd's staff; a pastoral staff; a dishonest person; a swindler.

crooked adj bent; deceitful.

crop n the stomach or craw of birds; grain while growing; a riding whip. * vt to clip or cut short; to browse; to cultivate; (with up) to appear unexpectedly.

crop-eared adj having the ears cut short.

croquet n an open-air game played with mallets, balls and hoops.

croquette n a ball of mashed potato, meat or fish fried until brown.

cross n two straight lines crossing each other; a monument in the form of a cross; the symbol of the Christian religion; the meeting place of roads, the town centre; adversity. * vt to mark with a cross; to pass over; to intersect; to cancel; to vex or thwart. * adj peevish.

crossbow n a bow fixed crosswise on a stock.

crossbreed n a mixed breed.

cross-examination n the examination of a witness by the opposing lawyer.

cross-purpose n a contrary purpose or aim; a misunderstanding.

cross-question vt to cross-examine.

crossroad n a road that crosses another; (pl) the point where two roads cross.

cross section n a surface exposed after cutting a solid at right angles to its length; a representative group (of people) chosen at random.

crosswise adv transversely.

crossword n a word puzzle on a grid with clues in which words reading down must fir in with those reading across.

crotch n the part of the body where the legs fork; the area of the genitals.

crotchet n a note in music; a half a minim.

crotchety adj perverse; bad-tempered.

crouch vi to bend low; to squat.

croupier n the dealer at a gaming table.

crow n a large black bird with croaking voice; the cock's cry. * vi to make the cry of a cock; to exult.

crowbar n a bar of iron used as a lever.

crowd n a throng. * vt to press together. * vi to throng.

crown n royal headgear; a king's power and symbol of office; the completion; the top of the head; a wreath or garland; a reward; the centre of a road; the upper part of a tooth. * vt to invest with a crown; to adorn; to perfect.

crowning adj highest; final.

crow's-feet npl the wrinkles about the eyes.

crucial adj decisive; critical.

crucible n a vessel or pot for heating substances to high temperatures.

crucifix n a figure of Christ upon the cross.

Crucifixion n the death of Christ.

cruciform adj cross-shaped.

crucify vt to put to death by nailing to a cross.

crude adj raw; unripe; rough; vulgar.

cruel adj unmerciful; harsh; fierce.

cruelty n severity; barbarity.

cruet n a small bottle for holding oil, vinegar etc.

cruise vi to sail hither and thither; to travel at a moderate speed. * n a sailing to and fro; a pleasure voyage.

cruiser n a swift armed warship.

crumb n a fragment; a small piece.

crumble vt, vi to break into small fragments; to pulverize; to decay.

crumple vt, vi to press into wrinkles; to crease; to collapse.

crunch vt to crush between the teeth.

crusade n an enterprise or serious activity to further a cause.

crush vt to squeeze; to bruise; to overpower; to stamp out. * vi to press forward. * n a crowding; an infatuation.

crushing adj overwhelming.

crust n the hard outer coating of anything. * vt, vi to cover with a crust.

crustacean n any aquatic animal with a hard shell, including crabs, lobsters, etc.

crusty adj covered with a crust; surly.

crutch n a stick with arm rests to support the body and allow mobility to a lame person; the crotch.

crux n the crucial or deciding point.

cry vi to utter the loud shrill sounds of weeping, joy, etc; to weep. * vt to proclaim. * n a shriek or scream; weeping; an appeal for help; a catchword.

crypt n an underground vault used as chapel or burial place.

cryptic adj hidden; secret; mysterious.

cryptogram n secret characters or cipher.

crystal n pure transparent quartz; articles made of this; the geometrical form assumed by certain bodies in solidifying.

crystallize vt, vi to form into crystals.

cub n the young of the bear, fox, etc; a junior boy scout.

cube n a regular solid body, with six equal square sides; the third power of a number. * vt to raise to the third power.

cubic, cubical adj cube-shaped.

cubicle n a compartment with a bed partitioned off in a dormitory.

cubism n a style of painting representing subjects from different viewpoints at the same time using geometrical shapes, cubes etc.

cud *n* the food which ruminants bring up to chew again.

cuddle *vt* to hug closely; to curl up comfortably.

cudgel *n* a short thick stick.

cue *n* the last words of an actor's speech as a sign to a following actor; catchword; hint; the straight rod used in billiards.

cuff *n* a blow; a slap; part of a sleeve near the hand. * *vt* to beat with the fist or open hand.

cuisine *n* style of cooking.

cul-de-sac *n* a blind alley.

culinary *adj* relating to cookery.

cull *vt* to gather; to reduce numbers of certain animals by killing.

culminate *vi* to reach the highest point.

culmination *n* the highest point; acme.

culpability *n* blame; guilt.

culpable *adj* blameworthy.

culprit *n* an accused person; a criminal.

cult *n* a system of worship often with special or secret rites.

cultivate *vt* to till; to refine; to civilize.

culture *n* refinement; appreciation of the arts; the whole range of skills of a people at a certain period; artificial rearing of bees, bacteria, etc.

cultured *adj* educated; refined.

culvert *n* an arched waterway or drain.

cumbersome *adj* burdensome; awkward; heavy.

cumin, cummin *n* an aromatic plant.

cummerbund *n* a girdle or waistband.

cumulate *vt* to heap together.

cumulative *adj* growing by additions.

cumulus *n* (*pl* **cumuli**) a cloud formation resembling snowy mountains.

cuneiform *adj* wedge-shaped. * *n* the wedge-shaped characters of ancient Assyrian and Persian writing.

cunning *adj* astute; crafty. * *n* craftiness.

cup *n* a small drinking vessel with a handle; its contents; a cup-shaped trophy, often silver or ornamental.

cupboard *n* a shelved cabinet for crockery, food, etc.

cupidity *n* a longing to possess; avarice.

cur *n* a mongrel dog; a low fellow.

curate *n* an assistant clergyman.

curative *adj* tending to cure.

curator *n* a superintendent; a custodian.

curb *vt* to control; to check. * *n* a check; part of a bridle; the edge of the pavement.

curd *n* coagulated milk. * *vt, vi* to curdle; to congeal.

curdle *vt, vi* to change into curds; to thicken.

cure *n* healing; a remedy. * *vt* to heal; to preserve food by salting, pickling etc.

curfew *n* an evening bell rung as a signal to put out lights.

curio *n* a rare or unusual object.

curious *adj* inquisitive; strange; singular.

curl *vt* to form into ringlets. * *vi* to go into coils; to play at the game of curling. * *n* a ringlet of hair; a twist.

curling n a game played on ice with large, heavy, smooth stones.

currency n circulation; circulating medium; the time when a thing is current or prevalent; the money used in a particular country.

current adj running; circulating. * n a running; a stream; progressive motion of water, electricity, etc.

curriculum n a course of study (at school, university, etc).

curriculum vitae n a (written) statement or summary of a person's career.

curry n a highly spiced sauce; a dish spiced with this. * vt to flavour with curry; to comb a horse; to seek (favour).

curse vt to call down evil on; to blight; to torment. * vi to swear. * n an oath.

cursed adj execrable; detestable.

cursive adj running; flowing. * n running script.

cursory adj hasty; careless; superficial.

curt adj short; rude; abrupt.

curtail vt to cut short; to cut down, e.g. privileges.

curtain n a screen for a window, etc; the moving screen of a theatre stage; (pl) the end; death. * vt to enclose with curtains.

curtsy, curtsey n an obeisance or bow.

curvature n a curving.

curve n a bent line; an arch. * vt, vi to bend.

cushion n a pillow for a seat; the padded rim of a snooker table; any buffer against shock. * vt to furnish with cushions; to protect against; to lessen shock or impact.

cusp n a point or sharp horn, as of moon.

custard n a mixture of milk, eggs, and sugar prepared as a pudding or sauce.

custodian n a guardian; a keeper.

custody n care; security; imprisonment.

custom n habit; fashion; business patronage; (pl) duties on merchandise imported or exported.

customary adj habitual; usual.

customer n a regular purchaser at a shop or from a business.

cut vb (pt, pp **cut**) vt to divide into pieces; to mow; to clip; to reduce prices etc. * vi to make an incision; to stop filming. * adj gashed. * n a wound; act of dividing a pack of cards; form; fashion or shape of a garment; a reduction in price; a share of gains, etc.

cutaneous adj pertaining to the skin.

cuticle n the skin at the base of fingernails and toenails; epidermis.

cutlass n a broad, curving sword.

cutlery n instruments used for eating; forks, knives and spoons.

cutlet n a piece of meat cut off the ribs, leg or neck; a chop.

cutter n a light sailing vessel; a ship's boat; one who cuts cloth.

cutting n a piece cut off; an incision; a passage; a piece cut off a plant for propagating; an excerpt cut from a newspaper; film editing.

cyanide n a highly toxic poison.

cyberspace n all of the data stored on a large computer or network through which a virtual reality user can move.

cycle *n* a period of time; a series; a bicycle. * *vi* to ride a bicycle.

cyclic, cyclical *adj* recurring in series.

cyclist *n* one who rides a bicycle.

cyclone *n* a storm moving in a circle; a hurricane.

cylinder *n* a solid or hollow roller-shaped body.

cymbal *n* a musical instrument of two brass plates that are clashed together.

cynic *n* a sneering, censorious person.

cynic, cynical *adj* sceptical; surly; sneering; captious.

cynicism *n* surliness; heartlessness.

cypher *see* **cipher**.

cyst *n* a sac in animal bodies containing morbid matter.

czar, tsar *n* the former emperor of Russia.

Czech *n* a native of the Czech Republic; its language.

D

dab *vt* (*pt* **dabbed**) to hit lightly with something soft or moist. * *n* a gentle blow; a small mass of anything soft or moist; an adept.

dabble *vt* to wet; to sprinkle; to move hands or feet in water. * *vi* to trifle.

dado *n* the decorative border round the lower part of the walls of a room.

dagger *n* a short sharp-pointed sword.

daily *adj* happening every day. * *adv* day by day. * *n* a newspaper published every weekday.

dainty *adj* nice; delicate; elegant. * *n* a delicacy.

dairy *n* a place where milk is sold, or converted into butter or cheese.

dais *n* the high table where principal guests or speakers are seated; a raised platform.

dale *n* a valley.

dalliance *n* lovemaking; trifling.

dally *vi* to trifle; to delay; to lose time by idleness.

dam *n* a mother (of a four-footed animal); a barrier to confine water. * *vt* (*pt* **dammed**) to confine by a dam.

damage *n* hurt; injury; money; compensation. * *vt* to injure; to harm.

damask *n* a figured cloth, usually of silk or linen. * *adj* of a pink or rosy colour.

dame *n* a lady.

damn *vt* to condemn; to curse; to consign to eternal punishment.

damnation *n* condemnation.

damned *adj* hateful; detestable; consigned to hell.

damp *adj* moist; humid. * *n* moist air. * *vt* to moisten; to dispirit; to stifle.

dampness *n* moisture.

damsel *n* a girl.

dance *vi* to move in time to music; to skip or leap lightly. * *n* a party for dancing; a dance performance of an artistic nature; music for dancing.

dandruff *n* scurf on the head under the hair.

dandy *n* a fop; a coxcomb.

danger *n* risk; hazard; peril.

dangle *vi* to hang loose. * *vt* to swing.

dank *adj* damp; moist.

dapper *adj* small and neat.

dappled *adj* spotted.

dare *vt, vi* to be bold; to defy; to venture on; to challenge. * *n* a challenge.

daredevil *n* a reckless fellow. * *adj* daring; bold.

daring *adj* bold; fearless. * *n* courage.

dark *adj* without light; gloomy; secret; ignorant; having brown or black skin or hair. * *n* darkness; ignorance.

darkness *n* absence of light; gloom.

darling *adj* dearly beloved. * *n* one much beloved.

darn *vt* to mend holes in clothes.

dart *n* a pointed missile thrown by the hand; a sudden bound. * *vt* to shoot. * *vi* to move rapidly; (*pl*) an indoor game in which darts are thrown at a target.

dash *vt, vi* to shatter; to rush; to frustrate. * *n* a violent striking; a rushing or onset; a mark in writing (—); a small quantity of something added to food; a tinge.

dashboard *n* an instrument panel in a car.

dashing *adj* spirited; showy; stylish.

data *see* **datum**.

data processing *n* the analysis of information stored in a computer for various uses.

date *n* the time when any event happened; an appointment, esp with one of the opposite sex; era; age. * *vt, vi* to note the time of; to have origin to affix a date to.

dative *adj, n* (of) a grammatical case.

datum *n* (*pl* **data**) a fact granted as basis for further inference.

daub *vt* to smear; to paint without skill. * *n* poor painting; a smear.

daughter *n* a female child.

daughter-in-law *n* a son's wife.

daunt *vt* to intimidate; to scare; to cow.

dauntless *adj* fearless.

dawdle *vi* to waste time; to saunter.

dawn *vi* to grow light. * *n* the break of day; first appearance.

day *n* the time between the rising and setting of the sun; light; time; a particular period of success or influence.

daybreak *n* the dawn.

daydream *n* a reverie.

daylight *n* the light of the sun; dawn; a visible gap; a sudden realization or understanding.

daytime *n* the time of daylight.

daze *vt* to stupefy; to stun; to perplex. * *n* confusion; bewilderment esp produced by a blow or a shock.

dazzle *vt* to overpower with light or splendour. * *vi* to be intensely bright.

deacon *n* a church official.

dead *adj* without life; perfectly still; cold; unerring; exact. * *n* stillness; gloom.

deadbeat *adj* quite exhausted.

deaden *vt* to make numb; to muffle.

dead-end *n* a cul-de-sac; a hopeless situation; a job without prospects.

dead heat *n* a race in which the competitors finish at the same time.

deadline *n* the time or date by which a thing must be done.

deadlock *n* a complete standstill; a clash of interests making progress impossible.

deadly *adj* mortal; implacable.

deadpan *adj* deliberately expressionless.

dead weight *n* a heavy or oppressive burden; weight of a body without its load.

deaf *adj* unable to hear; inattentive.

deafen *vt* to stun with noise.

deaf-mute *n* a deaf and dumb person.

deal *n* an indefinite quantity; a business transaction; the distribution of playing cards. * *vt* (*pt, pp* **dealt**) to distribute; to behave; to do business with; to solve.

dealer *n* a trader; one who deals cards; a seller of illegal drugs.

dealing *n* conduct; behaviour; business.

dean *n* the head of the chapter of a cathedral; an officer in a university.

deanery *n* the office or residence of a dean.

dear *adj* costly; valuable; beloved.

dearth *n* scarcity; want.

death *n* extinction of life; decease; the destruction of something.

deathless *adj* immortal.

death rate *n* the proportion of deaths in a town, country, etc.

debacle *n* a sudden break-up; a crash; a rout.

debar *vt* to shut out from something.

debase *vt* to lower; to degrade.

debatable *adj* open to question.

debate *n* a discussion; a formal argument; controversy. * *vt, vi* to dispute; to deliberate.

debauch *vt* to corrupt. * *vi* to revel. * *n* excess in eating or drinking.

debauched *adj* profligate.

debauchery *n* intemperance; depraved overindulgence; corruption; lewdness.

debenture *n* interest-bearing bonds in return for a loan.

debilitate *vt* to enfeeble.

debility *n* weakness.

debit *n* a recorded item of debt; the left-hand page or debtor side of a ledger.

debonair *adj* suave; carefree; sprightly.

debris *n* (*sing or pl*) fragments; rubbish; wreckage.

debt *n* what is owing; an obligation.

debtor *n* one who owes.

debut *n* a first appearance in public.

decade *n* a period of ten years.

decadence *n* a falling off; decay; deterioration esp of morality.

decamp *vi* to leave without notice.

decant *vt* to pour from one vessel into another.

decanter *n* a stoppered bottle in which wine is brought to table.

decapitate *vt* to behead.

decay vi to fall away; to waste; to wither; to fail. * n decline; putrefaction.

decease n death. * vi to die.

deceased adj dead.

deceit n fraud; guile; treachery.

deceive vt to mislead; to cheat.

December n the twelfth and last month of the year.

decency n propriety.

decent adj quite good; kind; generous.

decentralize vt to transfer power from central to local authority.

deception n the act or state of being deceived; fraud.

deceptive adj misleading; ambiguous.

decide vt, vi to determine; to settle; to resolve; to give a judgment on.

deciduous adj (of trees) shedding all leaves annually.

decimal adj by tens; having 10 as the basis of numeration.

decimate vt to destroy a large number.

decipher vt to decode; to solve.

decision n determination of a judgment; verdict; firmness of character.

decisive adj conclusive; absolute.

deck vt to clothe; to adorn. * n the floor of a ship, aircraft, bus or bridge; a pack of playing cards; the turntable of a record-player; the ground.

declaim vi to make a formal speech; to harangue.

declamatory adj grandiloquent.

declaration n assertion; affirmation.

declare vt, vi to make known; to assert; to admit possession of (dutiable goods).

declared adj avowed.

declension n a falling off; (gram) the variation in form that nouns etc undergo.

decline vi to bend downwards; to swerve; to fail. * vt to refuse; to inflect a noun, etc.; to diminish; to draw to an end; to deviate. * n a falling off; decay; consumption.

declivity n a downward slope.

decode vt to decipher.

decompose vt to resolve into original elements. * vi to decay.

decomposition n analysis; decay.

decor n a general decorative effect or appearance, esp of a room.

decorate vt to adorn; to deck.

decoration n ornamentation; a mark or badge of honour.

decorative adj ornamental.

decorator n one who paints houses.

decorous adj seemly; becoming.

decorum n propriety; seemliness.

decoy n an animal or bird trained to lure others into a snare; one who lures others into a trap. * vt to lure into a snare.

decrease vi, vt to become or make less. * n a diminution; a reduction.

decree n an edict; an order or law. * vt to enact; to award.

decrepit adj broken down with age.

decry vt to cry down; to disparage.

dedicate vt to consecrate; to devote (often refl); to inscribe to a friend.

dedication n consecration; inscription or address.

deduce *vt* to infer; to arrive at by reasoning.

deduct *vt* to subtract from.

deduction *n* inference; discount.

deductive *adj* that is or may be deduced from premises.

deed *n* an act; feat; a written agreement.

deem *vt* to judge. * *vi* to be of opinion.

deep *adj* being far below the surface; involved; engrossed; profound; intense; secret; artful. * *n* the sea.

deepfreeze *n* a refrigerator in which food is frozen and stored.

deeply *adv* at a great depth; profoundly.

deer *n* (*pl* **deer**) a quadruped with antlers on the males.

deerstalking *n* the hunting of deer.

deface *vt* to disfigure; to erase.

defalcation *n* misappropriation of funds.

defamation *n* slander.

defame *vt* to slander.

default *n* an omission; neglect; absence; lapse. * *vi* to fail to meet payment or keep contract.

defaulter *n* one who fails to answer a summons or to make payment due.

defeat *n* overthrow; loss of battle; frustration of one's plans; loss of a game, race etc. * *vt* to frustrate; to conquer.

defect *n* a want; a blemish.

defection *n* abandonment of a person or cause.

defective *adj* faulty; incomplete.

defence *n* a protection; fortification; vindication; apology; plea; defending the goal etc against attacks from the opposing side; the defending players in a team.

defenceless *adj* unprotected.

defend *vt* to guard; to support; to act as defendant.

defendant *n* one sued at law.

defensible *adj* justifiable.

defer *vb* (*pt* **deferred**) *vt* to postpone. * *vi* to yield to another's opinion, wishes, judgment.

deference *n* regard; respect.

deferential *adj* respectful.

defiance *n* wilful disobedience; a challenge to fight; contempt of danger.

defiant *adj* bold; insolent; challenging.

deficiency *n* want; defect; deficit.

deficient *adj* defective; lacking.

deficit *n* shortage; the amount by which a sum falls short of what is needed; an excess of expenditure over income.

defile *vt* to pollute. * *n* a narrow pass.

define *vt* to limit; to explain exactly.

definite *adj* precise; exact.

definition *n* an explanation or description.

definitive *adj* limiting; positive; final.

deflate *vt* to release gas or air from; to reduce in size or importance; to reduce inflation in the economy.

deflect *vi* to deviate. * *vt* to turn aside.

deflection *n* deviation.

deflower *vt* to strip of flowers; to ravish.

defoliation *n* the shedding of leaves.

deform *vt* to disfigure.

deformed *adj* misshapen.

defraud *vt* to cheat.

defray *vt* to bear the charges of.

deft *adj* apt; clever; nimble.

defunct *adj* deceased; no longer functioning. * *n* a dead person.

defuse *vt* to disarm an explosive by removing its fuse; to decrease tension in a crisis or other situation

defy *vt* (*pt* **defied**) to dare; to challenge; to set at nought; to resist attempts at; to elude.

degeneracy *n* decline in good qualities.

degenerate *vi* to decline in good qualities. * *adj* depraved; base. * *n* a degenerate or immoral person.

degradation *n* a depriving of rank; disgrace; humiliation.

degrade *vt* to depose; to dishonour.

degraded *adj* debased; dishonoured.

degree *n* a step; rank; grade; measure; the 360th part of the circumference of a circle; a university distinction.

dehydrate *vt* to remove water from. * *vi* to lose water esp from body tissue.

deify *vt* (*pt, pp* **deified**) to make a god of; to idolize.

deign *vi* to condescend to give or do something.

deity *n* a god.

deject *vt* to dispirit; to depress.

dejected *adj* cast down; discouraged.

dejection *n* lowness of spirits.

delay *vt, vi* to defer; to retard; to stop; to linger. * *n* a stay; a hindrance.

delectable *adj* delightful.

delegate *vt* to send as a representative; to depute. * *n* a representative; an agent.

delegation *n* a body of delegates.

delete *vt* to erase; to efface.

deleterious *adj* hurtful.

deletion *n* the act of deleting; a word, phrase, etc, deleted from a text.

deliberate *vi, vt* to weigh well; to consider; to debate. * *adj* cautious; well advised; intentional.

deliberation *n* careful consideration; thorough discussion; caution.

delicacy *n* refinement of taste; tenderness; a luxurious food.

delicate *adj* pleasing; fine; minute; tender; not robust.

delicious *adj* highly delightful esp to the taste.

delight *n* great joy or pleasure. * *vt, vi* to charm; to take great pleasure.

delightful *adj* charming; giving pleasure.

delineate *vt* to draw in outline; to sketch.

delinquency *n* a fault; wrongdoing; a crime.

delinquent *adj* neglecting duty. * *n* culprit; an offender, esp a young law breaker.

delirious *adj* raving; frenzied.

delirium *n* temporary disorder of the mind.

deliver *vt* to set free; to rescue; to hand over; to carry and distribute regularly; to give birth; to launch or throw.

deliverance *n* release; rescue; a legal judgment.

delivery *n* childbirth; rescue; distribution (of letters); manner of speaking; the act of giving birth; the bowling of a ball in cricket.

dell n a small valley.

delta n the space between diverging mouths of a river; the fourth letter of the Greek alphabet.

delude vt to deceive; to trick.

deluge n a flood; the flood; heavy rain. * vt to inundate; to drown.

delusion n a mistaken idea; a fallacy.

delusive adj deceptive.

delve vt, vi to dig.

demagogue n a voluble political orator deriving power from appealing to popular prejudices.

demand vt to claim by right; to question. * n a claim, often urgent; a challenging; the desire shown by consumers for particular goods or services.

demarcate vt to define the bounds of.

demarcation n a boundary; a fixed limit.

demean vt to lower in dignity; to debase.

demeanour n behaviour.

demented adj insane; infatuated.

demise n death; termination.

demit vt to resign (an office).

demobilize vt to discharge from the armed forces; to disband.

democracy n government by the people through elected representatives; political, social or legal equality.

democrat n a friend to popular government.

demolish vt to pull down; to defeat.

demon n an evil spirit.

demonstrable adj that may be demonstrated or proved.

demonstrate vt to prove beyond doubt; to exhibit * vi to show support for a cause by public protest and parades.

demonstration n proof; show of feeling; a display of feeling by public protest, mass meetings etc.

demonstrative adj open; unreserved.

demoralization n corruption; loss of morale.

demoralize vt to corrupt; to dispirit.

demur vi to hesitate; to object. * n pause; objection.

demure adj affectedly modest.

demy n a size of paper for printing or writing.

den n a cave; a dell; a lair of a wild beast.

denial n contradiction; refusal of a request; reluctance to admit the truth of something.

denim n a hard-wearing cloth esp for jeans; pl trousers of this.

denomination n class; religious sect.

denominator n the divisor in a vulgar fraction.

denote vt to indicate; to imply; to mean.

denouement n the unfolding, the final outcome of the plot in a play; the issue.

denounce vt to threaten; to condemn; to accuse publicly.

dense adj thick; close.

density n compactness; stupidity; the ratio of mass to volume.

dent n a mark made by a blow or pressure. * vt to mark.

dental *adj* pertaining to the teeth.

dentist *n* one qualified to treat disorders of the teeth.

denude *vt* to make bare; to strip.

denunciation *n* the utterance of a threat, censure or menace.

deny *vt* to contradict; to disavow.

deodorant *n* a preparation that masks unpleasant smells.

deodorize *vt* to rid of smell.

deoxidize *vt* to deprive of oxygen.

depart *vi* to go away; to deviate; to die.

department *n* a separate part; a division; a branch; a place of activity.

department store *n* a large shop with many departments each selling different types of goods.

departure *n* act of going away; withdrawal, death.

depend *vi* to hang from; to be reliant on; to trust.

dependant *n* one who depends on another; a retainer.

dependence *n* reliance; trust; subordination.

dependency *n* a subject territory.

dependent *adj* relying on; contingent.

depict *vt* to portray; to describe.

depilate *vt* to strip of hair.

deplete *vt* to empty; to exhaust.

deplorable *adj* shocking; pitiable.

deplore *vt* to regret deeply; to deprecate.

deploy *vt* to open out; to distribute and position strategically (soldiers etc).

depopulate *vt* to reduce the population of.

deport *vt* to expel (an undesirable person) from a country; to conduct (oneself).

deportation *n* banishment from a country.

deportment *n* carriage; behaviour.

depose *vt* to dethrone; to divest of office.

deposit *vt* to lay down; to lodge in a place. * *n* something deposited; money left in a bank; money left in security.

deposition *n* affidavit; testimony; displacement.

depot *n* a storehouse; a warehouse; a place for storing military supplies; a military training centre; a railway or bus station.

deprave *vt* to corrupt.

depraved *adj* profligate; perverted.

deprecate *vt* to disapprove of.

deprecation *n* disapproval.

depreciate *vt* to lower the value of; to undervalue. * *vi* to fall in value.

depreciation *n* a fall in value, esp of an asset through wear and tear.

depress *vt* to press down; to deject.

depression *n* dejection; an economic phase characterized by stagnation, unemployment, etc; a lowering of atmospheric pressure; a hollow.

deprivation *n* want; bereavement.

deprive *vt* to take from; to dispossess.

deprived *adj* lacking the essentials of life, e.g. food, housing, etc.

depth *n* deepness; a deep place; intensity; profoundness.

deputation *n* persons sent to act for others.

depute vt to appoint as a substitute.

deputy n a substitute; a representative.

derange vt to displace; to disorder; to unbalance; to make insane.

deranged adj distracted.

derelict adj abandoned. * n the thing or person abandoned.

dereliction n failure; wilful neglect.

deride vt to ridicule; to jeer.

derision n mockery.

derisive adj mocking.

derivation adj source or origin.

derivative adj derived. * n a derivative word; an offshoot.

derive vt, vi to obtain; to draw; to trace to its origin; to come from.

dermatology n the study of skin and its diseases.

derogatory adj disparaging.

descant n a discourse; a melody. * vi to sing; to discourse.

descend vi, vt to climb down; to invade; to be derived; to sink morally.

descendant n an heir; offspring.

descent n act of descending; declivity; invasion; lineage.

describe vt to portray; to relate.

description n a verbal account; relation; kind; sort.

descriptive adj graphic.

desecrate vt to violate a sacred place.

desecration n profanation.

desert[1] adj waste. * n a sandy barren region.

desert[2] vi to leave; to quit. * vi to run away, esp from the armed forces. * n (usu pl) a deserved reward or punishment.

deserter n a runaway.

deserve vt, vi to merit.

deservedly adv justly.

desiccate vt to dry.

design vt to plan; to propose; to make working drawings for. * vi to intend. * n a drawing or sketch; purpose; aim.

designate vt to point out; to name; to mark; to appoint or nominate for a position.

designation n name; title; nomination.

designedly adv purposely.

designer n one who designs; a creator of high-class fashion clothes. * adj of the latest fashion or trend.

designing adj artful; scheming.

desirable adj longed for; advisable.

desire n longing; craving; love. * vt to wish for; to covet.

desist vi to stop; to leave off.

desk n a (sloping) table designed for writer's or reader's use; the section of a newspaper responsible for a particular topic.

desktop publishing n the use of a microcomputer with sophisticated page-layout programs and a laser printer to produce professional-looking printed matter.

desolate adj forlorn; forsaken; waste. * vt to lay waste.

desolation n ruin; gloom; loneliness.

despair n hopelessness. * vi to give up all hope.

despatch, dispatch vt to send away in haste; to kill; to perform quickly. * n an official message; speed.

desperate adj reckless; hopeless; urgently needing money; extreme; dangerous.

despicable *adj* contemptible.

despise *vt* to scorn; to disdain.

despite *prep* not withstanding; in spite of.

despoil *vt* to rob; to rifle; to plunder.

despondent *adj* dejected; hopeless.

despondency *n* dejection.

despot *n* a tyrant.

despotic *adj* autocratic.

dessert *n* the fruit or sweet course at the end of a meal.

destination *n* a goal; the place to which one is going.

destiny *n* fate; a predetermined course of events.

destitute *adj* in want; forlorn.

destitution *n* want.

destroy *vt* to pull down; to overthrow; to kill.

destroyer *n* a small swift warship to destroy submarines.

destruction *n* ruin; death; slaughter.

destructive *adj* ruinous causing destruction; negative or adverse (of criticism).

desultory *adj* casual; rambling.

detach *vt* to separate; to release.

detached *adj* separate; (of a house) not joined to another; aloof; unbiassed.

detachment *n* separation; a body of troops away from the main army.

detail *vt* to recount; to particularize; to set apart. * *n* an individual fact; an item; a small part of a picture, statue etc.; a small detachment for special duties.

detailed *adj* minute; thorough.

detain *vt* to keep back; to arrest; to place in confinement.

detect *vt* to discover; to notice.

detective *n* a police officer whose duty is to detect criminals.

detention *n* act of detaining; confinement; being kept in (school) after hours.

deter *vt* (*pt* **deterred**) to hinder; to discourage.

detergent *adj* cleansing; purging. * *n* a cleaning agent.

deteriorate *vi* to grow worse. * *vt* to depreciate.

determination *n* firm resolution; conclusion.

determine *vt* to bound; to fix permanently; to resolve; to bring to an end.

deterrent *n* a warning; a curb; a nuclear weapon to deter attack through fear of retaliation. * *adj* deterring.

detest *vt* to abhor; to loathe.

detestable *adj* odious.

dethrone *vt* to depose.

detonate *vt, vi* to explode.

detonation *n* an explosion.

detour *n* a roundabout way.

detract *vt, vi* to disparage; to defame.

detractor *n* a slanderer; a muscle which detracts.

detriment *n* loss; damage.

devastate *vt* to lay waste; to overwhelm.

develop *vt* to unfold; to make visible; to make to grow; to treat a photographic film or plate to reveal an image. * *vi* to grow or expand.

development *n* growth; land or property that has been improved.

deviate *vi* to stray; to wander; to diverge.

device *n* a contrivance; an emblem.

devil *n* an evil spirit; Satan; a wicked

person; a difficulty. * vb (pt **dev-
illed**) vt to pepper and broil. * vi to
drudge for another, esp a barrister.

devilment n mischief.

devilry n extreme wickedness.

devious adj circuitous; deceitful; underhand.

devise vt to plan; to contrive; to invent.

devoid adj destitute; free from.

devolution n a transfer of business,
duties or authority, esp from a central government to regional govern-
ments.

devolve vt to transfer; to depute.

devote vt to dedicate; to give or use
for a particular activity or purpose.

devoted adj zealous; attached; loyal.

devotion n consecration; attachment;
strong affection; piety.

devour vt to eat ravenously; to swallow up; to absorb eagerly.

devout adj pious; sincere.

dew n atmospheric vapour deposited
on cool surfaces at night.

dexterity n adroitness; skill.

dexterous adj skilful; expert.

dhow n an Arab trading vessel.

diabolic, diabolical adj fiendish.

diagnose vt to identify a disease from
symptoms.

diagnosis n the identification of an
illness from symptoms.

diagonal adj applied to a line drawn
from corner to corner.

diagram n an illustrative figure in
outline.

dial n a time recorder; the face of a
clock; the numbered disc on some
telephones for connecting some
calls.

dialect n the form of a language peculiar to a province.

dialectic, dialectical adj relating to
dialectics; pertaining to a dialect.

dialectics npl the art of reasoning;
logical skill.

dialogue n a conversation between
two or more.

diameter n the line passing through
or across the centre (esp of a circle).

diamond n the most valuable of
gems; a suit of playing cards; the
playing field in baseball.

diaphragm n the midriff, a muscle
separating thorax and abdomen; a
disc or plate closing partly or
wholly a tube; a contraceptive cap.

diarrhoea n looseness of the bowels.

diary n a daily record of events.

diastole n dilation of the heart in
beating.

diatribe n a tirade.

dice see **die**[2].

dictaphone n an instrument for recording and reproducing speech.

dictate vt to read for reproduction by
another person or by a recording
machine; to prescribe; to order.

dictation n act, art, or practice of dic-
tating; command.

dictator n one invested with absolute
authority.

diction n a way of speaking or enun-
ciating; a choice of words.

dictionary n a book with the words
of a language arranged alphabeti-
cally with their meanings, pronun-
ciations, etc.

didactic adj instructive.

diddle vt (inf) to trick.

die¹ *vi* (*pres p* **dying**) to cease to live; to expire.

die² *n* (*pl* **dice**) a cube with sides marked 1, 2, 3, 4, 5, 6, used in games of chance.

die³ *n* (*pl* **dies**) an engraved stamp for pressing coins, etc.

diesel *n* a vehicle driven by a diesel engine.

diesel engine *n* an internal combustion engine where ignition is produced by the heat of highly compressed air alone.

diet *n* food; a course of feeding. * *vt, vi* to eat or cause to eat according to special guidelines.

differ *vi* to be unlike; to disagree.

difference *n* dissimilarity; a dispute; a disagreement; remainder (in subtraction).

different *adj* distinct; dissimilar.

differential *adj* discriminating; variable; relating to increments in given functions. * *n* an infinitesimal difference between two states of a variable quantity; the difference in wage rates for different types of labour esp within an industry.

differentiate *vt* to mark or distinguish by a difference.

difficult *adj* arduous; perplexing; hard to please; hard to understand.

diffidence *n* want of confidence; reserve.

diffident *adj* wanting confidence; bashful.

diffuse *vt* to pour out and spread; to proclaim. * *adj* widely spread; not concise.

diffusion *n* dispersion; circulation.

dig *vb* (*pt, pp* **dug**) *vt* to turn up with a spade. * *vi* to work with a spade; to excavate; to investigate; to nudge; to understand; to approve.

digest *vt* to assimilate; to think out; to dissolve in the stomach. * *n* a summary.

digestible *adj* capable of being digested.

digestion *n* process of making food assimilable.

digit *n* a finger; any of the figures 0 to 9.

digital *adj* of or using digits, e.g. a clock.

dignified *adj* stately; grave.

dignify *vt* to ennoble; to grace; to exalt.

dignitary *n* one holding high rank.

dignity *n* honour; rank; formality in manner and appearance.

digress *vi* to depart from main subject; to deviate.

dike, dyke *n* a ditch; an embankment.

dilapidated *adj* in a ruinous condition.

dilapidation *n* decay; ruin.

dilation *n* expansion; enlargement.

dilate *vt, vi* to expand; to distend.

dilatory *adj* tardy; putting off.

dilemma *n* a fix; a quandary.

diligence *n* application.

diligent *adj* industrious; persevering.

dilute *vt* to reduce in strength by adding water or some qualifying matter. * *adj* weak; diluted.

dilution *n* reduction in strength.

dim *adj* obscure; faint. * *vt* (*pt* **dimmed**) to dull; to make dark.

dimension n the measure of a thing, size, extent, capacity.

diminish vt, vi to lessen; to decrease.

diminutive adj small. * n a word denoting smallness.

dimple n a small hollow on the cheek or chin.

din n a loud sound long continued. * vt to stun with noise; to teach with constant repetition.

dine vi to eat dinner.

dinghy n a small ship's boat.

dingy adj dull; faded.

dinner n the principal meal of the day.

diocese n the see of a bishop.

dip vb (pt **dipped**) vt to plunge quickly in and out of a liquid; to immerse. * vi to incline. * n a bathe; downward slope; a mixture in which to dip something.

diphtheria n an infectious throat disease.

diphthong n the blending of two vowel sounds.

diploma n a document conferring a degree of honour.

diplomacy n the art of negotiating esp between nations; tact.

diplomat n a diplomatist.

diplomatic adj prudent, tactful.

dire adj dreadful; urgent.

direct adj straight; express; sincere. * vt to point or aim at; to show; to conduct; to order; to instruct; to address a letter.

direction n course; guidance; command; management; address on a letter; the way in which one is pointing.

directly adv without delay; expressly.

director n a superintendent; a counsellor; one who directs the production of a stage or screen show.

directory n a book that lists names, addresses, telephone numbers etc.

dirge n a lament.

dirt n any filthy substance; scandal.

dirty adj soiled with dirt; mean; dishonest; obscene. * vt to soil; to sully.

disable vt to deprive of power; to injure.

disabled adj handicapped physically.

disabuse vt to free from a mistaken impression.

disadvantage n inconvenience; loss.

disaffect vt to estrange; to make discontented.

disaffection n disloyalty.

disagree vi to differ; to fall out; to dissent.

disagreeable adj offensive; displeasing.

disagreement n difference; discord.

disappear vi to vanish from sight.

disappearance n removal from sight.

disappoint vt to fail to fulfil the hopes of a person; to frustrate; to foil.

disapprobation n disapproval; censure.

disapproval n dislike; blame.

disapprove vt to censure as wrong; to blame.

disarm vt, vi to deprive of arms; to disband.

disarmament n the laying down of arms.

disarrange *vt* to derange; to upset.

disarray *vt* to throw into disorder. * *n* disorder.

disaster *n* a calamity; a failure.

disavowal *n* denial.

disband *vt* to disperse. * *vi* to break up.

disbelief *n* want of belief; distrust.

disbelieve *vt* to refuse to credit.

disburse *vt* to pay out.

disc *n* the flat face of a thin, round body (e.g. coin, sun, counter, etc).

discard *vt* to throw away.

discern *vt, vi* to perceive; to judge.

discerning *adj* sharp-sighted; acute.

discharge *vt* to unload; to fire; to dismiss; to perform; to acquit. * *n* a dismissal; release; matter coming from a sore or wound.

disciple *n* a learner; a follower.

disciplinarian *n* one who enforces discipline; a martinet.

disciplinary *adj* intended for discipline.

discipline *n* training; order; subjection to laws; punishment; correction. * *vt* to train; to punish to enforce discipline; to bring under control.

disclaim *vt* to disown, reject.

disclaimer *n* disavowal; denial.

disclose *vt* to open; to uncover; to reveal.

disco *n* a discotheque.

discoloration *n* stain.

discolour *vt* to change the colour; to stain.

discomfiture *n* rout; disappointment.

discomfort *n* uneasiness; its cause; lack of comfort.

disconcert *vt* to embarrass.

disconnect *vt* to disunite; to separate.

disconsolate *adj* comfortless.

discontentment *n* dissatisfaction.

discontinue *vt, vi* to leave off; to cease.

discord *n* want of harmony; strife.

discordant *adj* harsh sounding.

discotheque *n* a gathering for dancing to recorded music; a club or party for this.

discount *n* a sum deducted from the cost. * *vt* to cash a bill at present worth; to take away from.

discourage *vt* to dishearten; to dissuade.

discourse *n* a speech; a treatise; a sermon. * *vi* to talk.

discourteous *adj* rude.

discover *vt* to lay open to view; to detect; to find or learn about for the first time.

discredit *n* want of credit; distrust. * *vt* to damage the reputation of.

discreditable *adj* dishonourable.

discreet *adj* prudent.

discrepancy *n* variance; a disagreement as between figures in a total.

discretion *n* prudence; judgment.

discretionary *adj* left to one's discretion.

discriminate *vt* to distinguish; to select.

discrimination *n* discernment.

discursive *adj* rambling.

discus *n* a quoit; a disc.

discuss *vt* to debate; to examine by argument.

discussion *n* a debate.

disdain *vt* to scorn. * *n* contempt.

disdainful *adj* contemptuous.

disease *n* an ailment.

disembark *vt, vi* to put or go ashore.

disembody *vt* to divest of the body.

disenchant *vt* to disillusion.

disengage *vt* to detach; to release; to extricate.

disentangle *vt* to extricate.

disfavour *n* want of favour.

disfiguration *n* defacement.

disfigure *vt* to mar the appearance of.

disfigurement *n* a blemish.

disgorge *vt* to vomit; to empty; to surrender.

disgrace *n* shame; dishonour.

disgraceful *adj* shameful.

disguise *vt* to conceal; to dissemble; to change the appearance of. * *n* pretence; false appearance.

disgust *n* loathing; repugnance. * *vt* to offend; to sicken.

disgusting *adj* repulsive; sickening.

dish *n* an open vessel for serving food; the meat served. * *vt* to put in a dish.

dishearten *vt* to discourage.

dishevelled *adj* disarranged; untidy.

dishonest *adj* fraudulent; untrustworthy.

dishonesty *n* fraudulence.

dishonour *n* disgrace. * *vt* to bring shame on; to refuse payment of.

dishonourable *adj* base; vile.

disinclined *adj* unwilling.

disinfect *vt* to cleanse from infection.

disinfectant *n* a substance that destroys infectious germs.

disingenuous *adj* crafty; cunning.

disinherit *vt* to cut off from inheriting.

disintegrate *vt* to break up into parts.

disinter *vt* to take out of a grave.

disinterested *adj* impartial.

disjointed *adj* unconnected; incoherent.

disk *n* a storage device in a computer, either floppy or hard.

dislike *n* aversion; distaste. * *vt* to feel aversion to.

dislocate *vt* to displace a joint; to upset the working of.

dislodge *vt* to remove; to oust.

disloyal *adj* faithless; untrustworthy.

dismal *adj* dark; gloomy.

dismantle *vt* to strip; to take apart.

dismay *vt* to terrify; to appal. * *n* terror; consternation.

dismember *vt* to sever limb from limb.

dismiss *vt* to send away.

dismissal *n* discharge.

dismount *vi* to descend from a horse.

disobedience *n* neglect or refusal to obey.

disobedient *adj* failing, refusing to obey; unruly.

disobey *vt* to neglect or refuse to obey.

disobliging *adj* unaccommodating.

disorder *n* confusion; disease. * *vt* to disarrange.

disorganize *vt* to throw into confusion.

disown *vt* to repudiate; to refuse to acknowledge as one's own.

disparage *vt* to depreciate; to belittle.

disparate *adj* unlike.

disparity *n* inequality.

dispatch *see* **despatch**.

dispassionate *adj* cool; impartial.

dispel *vt* to scatter; to banish.

dispensary *n* a place where medicines are made up and dispensed.

dispensation *n* distribution; exemption.

dispense *vt* to deal out; to administer; to exempt.

disperse *vt, vi* to scatter; to diffuse; to vanish.

dispirited *adj* dejected.

displace *vt* to derange; to supersede.

displacement *n* quantity of water displaced by a floating body.

display *vt* to unfold; to show; to parade. * *vi* to make a show. * *n* exhibition; parade; a computer monitor.

displease *vt* to offend; to disgust.

displeased *adj* annoyed.

displeasing *adj* unpleasant.

displeasure *n* annoyance.

disport *n* pastime. * *vi* to sport; to gambol.

disposable *adj* designed to be discarded after use; available.

disposal *n* control; arrangement.

dispose *vt, vi* to arrange; to incline; to regulate; to give, sell or transfer to another; to throw away.

disposed *adj* inclined.

disposition *n* order; character; inclination; arrangement.

dispossess *vt* to deprive of possession.

disproportion *n* inequality.

disproval *n* disproof.

disprove *vt* to prove to be wrong; to confute.

dispute *vi* to argue; to debate. * *vt* to impugn. * *n* controversy; strife.

disqualify *vt* to make ineligible through violation of rules; to incapacitate.

disquiet *n* unrest; anxiety.

disregard *n* neglect. * *vt* to slight; to ignore.

disrepair *n* neglect.

disreputable *adj* of bad character.

disrepute *n* disgrace.

disrespect *n* discourtesy.

disrobe *vt* to undress; to uncover.

disruption *n* disorder; confusion.

dissatisfaction *n* discontent.

dissatisfied *adj* discontented.

dissect *vt* to cut up; to examine minutely.

dissemble *vt, vi* to hide; to disguise.

disseminate *vt* to spread abroad esp ideas, information etc.

dissemination *n* propagation.

dissension *n* discord.

dissent *vi* to disagree; to separate from an established church. * *n* disagreement.

dissenting *adj* disagreeing.

dissertation *n* a formal discourse or treatise.

disservice *n* an ill-service.

dissident *adj* dissenting. * *n* one who disagrees with government policies so strongly as to suffer imprisonment.

dissimilar *adj* unlike.

dissimulate *vt, vi* to dissemble.

dissipate *vt, vi* to scatter; to squander.

dissipated *adj* dissolute.

dissociate *vt* to disunite; to repudiate a connection with.

dissolute *adj* profligate.

dissolution n melting; break up (of a parliament); death.

dissolve vt, vi to liquefy; to break up legally; to annul; to be overcome with emotion.

dissuade vt to exhort against; to deter by argument.

distance n remoteness in place or time; space between two points or places; reserve. * vt to outstrip.

distant adj far off; cold; shy.

distaste n dislike.

distemper n a disordered state of mind or body; a dog disease; a method of painting on plaster without oil.

distend vt, vi to stretch; to swell.

distention n inflation.

distil vi, vt to extract the essence of; to fall in drops; to rectify or purify.

distiller n a maker of alcoholic spirit.

distillery n a distilling factory.

distinct adj separate; clear; definite.

distinction n difference; eminence; honour.

distinctive adj distinguishing.

distinctness n clearness; precision.

distinguish vt, vi to mark a difference; to perceive; to differentiate; to honour.

distinguished adj eminent; of elegant appearance.

distort vt to twist; to misrepresent.

distract vt to draw the attention aside; to bewilder; to confuse.

distracted adj frantic; maddened.

distraction n derangement; diversion; an amusement; extreme agitation.

distrain vt to seize (goods) for debt.

distraught adj distracted; agitated.

distress n anguish; destitution. * vt to afflict with pain.

distressed adj afflicted; extremely agitated, pained or poor.

distressing adj grievous.

distribute vt to deal out; to apportion; to classify.

distribution n division; sharing.

district n a region marked off for some special purpose.

distrust vt to doubt; to suspect. * n doubt; suspicion.

distrustful adj suspicious.

disturb vt to throw into disorder; to agitate.

disuse n neglect. * vt to cease to use.

ditch n a long narrow trench.

dither vi to hesitate, vacillate. * n a state of confusion; uncertainty.

divan n a sofa or bed without back or sides.

dive vi to plunge into water head foremost; to descend steeply (of aircraft); to submerge; to dash headlong.

diverge vi to deviate; to digress.

divergent adj diverging; dissimilar.

diverse adj different; unlike.

diversified adj varied.

diversify vt to vary; to invest in a broad range of securities or a variety of commercial operations to reduce risk of loss.

diversion n amusement; a feigned attack.

diversity n variety.

divert vt to turn aside; to amuse.

diverting adj amusing.

divest vt to strip; to unclothe.

divide vt to separate into parts; to share; to sever; to estrange * vi to part; to vote.

dividend n a number to be divided; share of profit.

divider n a distributor; (pl) compasses.

divination n prediction.

divine adj of or belonging to God. * n a member of the clergy. * vt, vi to foretell; to guess; to dowse.

divining rod n a wand used by dowsers to locate underground water.

divinity n any god; theology; the quality of being God or a god.

divisible adj capable of division.

division n act of dividing; separation; a separation into two opposing sides to vote; disunion; portion; a process in arithmetic.

divisive adj creating division or discord.

divisor n the number by which a dividend is divided.

divorce n a dissolution of marriage; a separation. * vt to dissolve a marriage.

divulge vt to disclose.

dizzy adj giddy.

do v aux (pres t he/she/it **does**, pt **did**, pp **done**) to perform; to bring about; to prepare. * vi to act or behave; to fare in health; to cheat; to rob. * n a party.

docile adj easily taught; tractable.

dock n an enclosed basin for ships; an enclosure in court for prisoners. * vt to cut off; to put a ship in dock.

docket n a summary; a bill tied to goods. * vt to make or attach an abstract of.

dockyard n an area with docks and facilities for repairing and refitting ships.

doctor n a learned person; a physician.

doctorate n the degree of a doctor.

doctrine n a principle or belief; the teaching of a person, school, or church.

document n written evidence or proof.

dodge vt, vi to move nimbly aside; to evade a duty; to quibble. * n a trick.

dog n a domestic quadruped. * vt to follow closely.

dogged adj obstinate; relentless.

doggerel n worthless verse.

dogma n a body of opinion; authoritative belief.

dogmatic, dogmatical adj positive; overbearing.

dogmatism n assertion without proof.

doldrums npl the dumps; equatorial region of calms.

dole n money received from the state while unemployed; what is dealt out. * vt to deal out in small quantities.

doleful adj woeful; gloomy; sad.

doll n a child's toy in human form.

dollar n an American unit of money.

dolman n a table-shaped ancient stone structure.

dolorous adj mournful.

dolt n a blockhead.

domain n an estate; a province; a sphere of activity etc.

dome n an arched roof; a large cupola.

domestic *adj* belonging to the home; tame. * *n* a household servant.

domesticate *vt* to make domestic or tame.

domicile *n* a habitation.

dominant *adj* ruling; prevailing over others; overlooking from a superior height.

dominate *vt* to rule.

domineer *vi* to lord over others.

domineering *adj* overbearing.

dominion *n* territory with one ruler or government; authority.

domino *n* (*pl* **dominoes**) a masquerade dress; a half-mask; (*pl*), a game played with dotted ivory or bone rectangles.

don *n* a fellow of a college. * *vt* to put on.

donate *vt* to bestow.

donation *n* a gift.

donor *n* one who gives something; one who donates blood, organs etc for medical purposes.

doom *n* fate; ruin. * *vt* to condemn to failure or ruin.

door *n* the entrance of a house, room, carriage, etc; the frame closing it.

Doric *adj, n* (of) an order of architecture; (of) a rustic dialect.

dormant *adj* sleeping; inactive.

dormitory *n* a sleeping room with many beds.

dorsal *adj* pertaining to the back.

dose *n* the quantity of medicine given at one time.

dot *n* a small point, as made with a pen, etc. * *vt* to mark with a dot.

dotage *n* the feeble-mindedness of old age.

dote *vi* to be excessively fond of.

double *adj* twice as large, as strong etc.; designed or intended for two; made of two similar parts; having two meanings, characters, etc. * *adv* twice; in twos. * *n* a number or amount that is twice as much; a person or thing identical to another. * *vt, vi* to make or become twice as much or as many; to fold, to bend; to bend sharply backwards; to have an additional purpose.

double bass *n* the lowest-toned instrument of violin class.

double-dealing *n* duplicity.

double-cross *vt* to betray an associate; to cheat.

doubt *vi* to waver; to question; to suspect. * *vt* to believe to be uncertain. * *n* uncertainty; suspicion.

doubtful *adj* feeling doubt; uncertain; suspicious.

doubtless *adv* unquestionably.

douche *n* a jet of water applied to the body.

dough *n* flour moistened with water or milk and kneaded to make bread.

douse *vt, vi* to plunge into water.

dovetail *n* a wedge-shaped joint resembling a dove's tail used in woodwork. * *vt, vi* to join as above; to fit exactly.

dowager *n* a title given to the widow of a nobleman.

dowdy *adj* ill-dressed; not stylish.

down *n* the fine soft feathers of birds; a hill. * *adv* toward or in a lower physical position; toward or to the ground, floor, or bottom; or in a lower status or in a worse condition; in cash; to or in a state of less activity. * adj occupying a low position, esp lying on the ground; depressed, dejected. * n a low period (as in activity, emotional life, or fortunes); (inf) prejudice. * vt, vi to defeat; to swallow.

downcast adj dejected.

downfall n ruin.

downpour n a heavy fall of rain.

downright adj plain; blunt; utter.

downtrodden adj oppressed.

downward, downwards adv in a descending course. * adj descending.

dowry n a wife's marriage portion.

dowse vt, vi to search for water, treasure, etc, with a divining rod.

doze vi to be half asleep. * n a light sleep.

dozen n twelve.

drab adj of a dull brown colour; dull; uninteresting.

draconian adj very severe.

draft n a detachment of men or things; an order for money; the first sketch or outline of a speech or other writing; conscription in USA. * vt to sketch; to select.

drag vb (pt **dragged**) vt to draw along slowly and with force; to search with a dragnet or a hook. * vi to protract. * n a brake; a check.

dragnet n a net to be drawn along the bottom.

dragon n a fabulous winged monster.

dragoon n a cavalry man. * vt to harass; to persecute.

drain vt, vi to draw off; to filter; to flow off; to drink the entire contents

of. * n a sewer; a channel for liquids.

drainage n a system of drains.

dram n a unit of weight; a small draught of spirits.

drama n a stage, radio or television play.

dramatic adj pertaining to the drama; theatrical.

dramatize vt to turn into a drama.

drape vt to cover or hang with cloth.

drastic adj acting with strength or violence.

draught n the quantity drunk at once; a sketch; the depth a ship sinks in water; a current of air; (pl) a game on a squared board using 24 round pieces.

draughtsman n one who makes detailed drawings or plans.

draw vt, vi (pt **drew**, pp **drawn**) to pull along or towards; to cause to come; to attract; to sketch; to infer; to end a game with equal scores; to shrink. * n the act of drawing; a drawn game.

drawback n a defect; a hindrance, handicap.

drawbridge n a movable (up and down or sideways) bridge.

drawer n one who draws a cheque; a sliding box in a table, chest or desk; pl an undergarment.

drawing n a pencil sketch.

drawing room n a reception or living room.

drawl vi, vt to speak slowly with drawn-out vowel sounds. * n affected slowness of speech.

dread n fear; terror. * adj exciting

great fear; terrible. * *vt* to fear greatly.

dreadful *adj* terrible.

dream *n* a vision in sleep; an idle fancy; an ambition. * *vt, vi* (*pt, pp* **dreamed** *or* **dreamt**) to have dreams; to fancy.

dreary *adj* cheerless.

dredge *n* a dragnet. * *vt* to scoop up, esp from the bottom of a river etc.

dredger *n* a floating vessel for dredging and deepening.

dregs *npl* lees; grounds.

drench *vt* to soak.

dress *vt* to clothe; to set in order; to decorate; to wash and bandage; to prepare food. * *n* clothes; a woman's one-piece garment; style or manner of clothing.

dresser *n* a kitchen sideboard; a surgeon's assistant.

dressing *n* a bandage, ointment, etc, applied to a wound; a sauce.

dribble *vi* to trickle. * *vt* (in games) to move the ball little by little with the foot, hand, stick, etc.

drift *n* a heap of snow, sand, etc, deposited by the wind; natural course, tendency; the general meaning or intention (of what is said); an aimless course. * *vt* to cause to drift. * *vi* to be driven or carried along by water or air currents.

drill[1] *vt, vi* to pierce a hole with a drill; to train (soldiers); to furrow; to sow in rows. * *n* a hole borer; a furrow; exercise; procedure; routine.

drill[2] *n* a cotton cloth.

drink *vt, vi* (*pt* **drank**, *pp* **drunk**) to swallow liquid. * *n* a beverage; alcoholic liquor.

drip *vi* (*pt* **dripped**) to fall in drops. * *n* a liquid that falls in drops; its sound; a device for injecting a fluid slowly and continuously into a vein.

dripping *n* the fat from roasting meat.

drive *vb* (*pt* **drove**, *pp* **driven**) *vt* to urge, push or force onward; to convey in a vehicle; to carry through strongly; to propel (a ball) with hard blow. * *vi* to be forced along; to be conveyed in a vehicle. * *n* a trip in a vehicle; a stroke to drive a ball (in golf, etc.); a driveway; an intensive campaign; the transmission of power to machinery.

driver *n* one who drives; a golf club.

drizzle *vi* to rain in small fine drops. * *n* a fine rain.

droll *adj* comic; amusing; whimsical.

drone *n* the male or non-working bee; a humming sound; monotonous speech. * *vi* to hum; to speak in a monotonous tone.

droop *vi* to hang down; to languish.

drop *n* a globule of any liquid; a distance to fall. * *vt, vi* (*pt* **dropped**) to pour or let fall in drops; to fall; to let fall; to sink; to set down from a vehicle; to mention in passing; to give up (an idea etc).

dropsy *n* an unnatural collection of water in the body.

dross *n* the scum of metals; refuse; rubbish.

drought *n* a period of very dry weather.

drove *n* a herd or flock in motion.

drown *vt, vi* to suffocate or be suffocated in water.

drowse *vi* to doze.

drowsy *adj* sleepy, heavy.

drudge *vi* to toil; to slave. * *n* a menial servant.

drudgery *n* distasteful toil.

drug *n* any substance used in medicine. * *vt* (*pt* **drugged**) to dose with drugs.

drum *n* a sound percussion instrument; a stretched membrane in the ear. * *vi, vt* (*pt* **drummed**) to beat a drum; to teach or instruct by constant repetition.

drunk *adj* intoxicated.

drunkard *n* one given to drink.

drunkenness *n* intoxication.

dry *adj* free from moisture; thirsty. * *vt, vi* (*pt* **dried**) to free from moisture; thirsty; marked by a matter-of-fact, ironic or terse manner of speech; uninteresting.

dry rot *n* a timber disease.

dual *adj* consisting of two; twofold.

dub *vt* to confer a knighthood on by touching with a sword.

dubiety *n* doubtfulness.

dubious *adj* wavering; uncertain; untrustworthy.

duchess *n* a duke's wife.

duchy *n* a country ruled by a duke.

duck *vt, vi* to plunge in water; to bow. * *n* a waterfowl; a kind of canvas.

duct *n* a narrow tube in the body; a channel or pipe for fluids, electric cables etc.

due *adj* owed; owing; proper. * *adv* directly. * *n* a fee; a right; a just title.

duel *n* a set fight between two persons; any conflict between two people, sides, etc. * *vi* (*pt* **duelled**) to fight in a duel.

duet *n* a piece of music for two performers.

duke *n* one of the highest order of nobility.

dukedom *n* the lands or title of a duke.

dulcet *adj* sweet; melodious.

dull *adj* stupid; drowsy; cheerless. * *vt* to make dull; to stupefy; to blunt; to sully.

dulse *n* an edible seaweed.

duly *adv* properly; suitably.

dumb *adj* mute; silent.

dumbbells *n* weights used for developing the muscles of the arm.

dumbfound, dumfound *vt* to astonish; to confuse.

dummy *n* a stupid person; a figure used to display clothes; the exposed hand in a game of bridge; a sham.

dump *n* a place for refuse; a temporary store; a thud; a dirty, dilapidated place; *pl* (*inf*) low spirits. * *vt* to get rid off; to drop.

dunce *n* a stupid person.

dune *n* a sand hill on the sea coast.

dung *n* the excrement of animals. * *vt* to manure.

dungeon *n* an underground prison.

duodenum *n* the first portion of the small intestines.

dupe *n* one easily cheated. * *vt* to impose on; to deceive; to trick.

duplex *adj* double; twofold.

duplicate *adj* double. * *n* a copy. * *vt* to double; to make an exact copy.

duplicity *n* guile; trickery.

durable *adj* lasting; permanent.

duration *n* continuance; the period in which an event continues.

duress *n* constraint; imprisonment.

during *prep* for the time of; throughout.

dusk *n* twilight.

dusky *adj* darkish.

dust *n* fine dry particles of earth, etc; earth as symbolic of mortality. * *vt* to free from dust; to sprinkle.

duster *n* a cloth, etc, for removing dust.

duty *n* what one is bound to do; service; a tax on goods.

dux *n* the head of a class in a school.

DVD *abbr* *d*igital *v*ideo *d*isc.

dwarf *n* one noticeably undersized. * *vt* to make (or make seem) small.

dwell *vi* (*pt, pp* **dwelt** *or* **dwelled**) to live in a place; to continue; to focus the attention on; to think, talk, write at length about.

dwelling *n* habitation; abode.

dwindle *vi* to diminish gradually.

dye *vt* to stain; to give a new colour to. * *n* a colouring matter; tinge; hue.

dynamic *adj* relating to force that produces motion; forceful; energetic

dynamics *n* the science of force or power.

dynamite *n* a powerful explosive.

dynamo *n* a machine for producing an electric current.

dynasty *n* a line of rulers of the same powerful family.

dysentery *n* a disorder of the intestines.

dyspepsia *n* indigestion.

E

each *adj, pron* everyone separately.

eager *adj* keen; ardent earnest.

ear *n* the organ of hearing; the power of appreciating musical sounds; heed; a spike of corn.

earache *n* a pain in the ear.

earl *n* a member of the British nobility.

early *adv, adj* before the expected time; of or occurring in the first part of a period or series; timely, soon.

earn *vt* to gain by labour; to deserve.

earnest *adj* ardent; eager; serious.

earnings *npl* wages.

earring *n* an ornament worn in the ear.

earth *n* the globe we inhabit; dry land; the ground; the burrow of a badger, fox etc. * *vt* to cover with earth.

earthenware *n* ware made of clay; pottery.

earthquake *n* a shaking or trembling of the earth.

earthwork *n* a rampart of earth.

earthy *adj* consisting of or resembling earth; crude.

earwig n an insect with a pincer-like appendage at the end of the body.

ease n freedom from toil, pain, etc; rest; comfort. * vt to calm; to alleviate; to shift a little.

easel n a stand to support pictures while they are being painted.

east n that part of the sky where the sun rises; the countries east of Europe. * adj in or towards the east.

Easter n the festival commemorating Christ's Resurrection.

easterly adj coming from the east, as winds; moving towards the east.

eastern adj belonging to the east; oriental.

easy adj free from pain or anxiety; simple; relaxed in manner; lenient; compliant; unhurried.

eat vt (pt **ate**, pp **eaten**) to chew and swallow, as food; to wear away; to corrode.

eaves npl that part of the roof overhanging the walls.

eavesdrop vi to try to hear or to listen in to a private conversation.

ebb n the flowing back of the tide; decline. * vi to flow back; to decline.

ebony n a hard, heavy, dark wood.

ebullient adj enthusiastic; exuberant; boiling.

eccentric adj not conforming to the usual pattern; unconventional; odd; whimsical.

eccentricity n oddity of conduct, dress, etc.

ecclesiastic, ecclesiastical adj belonging to the church or clergy. * n a clergyman.

echo n the repetition of sound by reflection of sound waves; imitation. * vt, vi to repeat; to resound; to imitate.

eclectic adj selecting the best of everything (esp in philosophy and the arts).

eclipse n an obscuring of the light of the sun, moon etc, by some other body; an overshadowing. * vt to darken; to surpass.

economic, economical adj pertaining to economics or the economy; showing a profit; frugal; careful.

economics n the science of the application of wealth and concerned with the production, and consumption and distribution of goods and services.

economize vt, vi to manage money with prudence to save.

economy n thrift; prudent management; the management of finances and resources of a business, industry, etc; the economic system of a country.

ecstacy n rapture; enthusiasm; the synthetic amphetamine-based drug MDMA, which reduces social and sexual inhibitions.

ecstatic adj entrancing; transporting.

ecumenic, ecumenical adj of the whole Christian church; seeking Christian unity worldwide

eczema n a skin disease.

eddy n a whirling current of water or air. * vi to move round and round.

edge n the sharp side; an abrupt border or margin; keenness; force; effectiveness. * vt to put an edge or fringe on; to move gradually.

edged adj sharp; keen.

edgeways adv sideways.

edible *adj* eatable.

edict *n* a decree; a manifesto.

edifice *n* a large building.

edify *vt* to improve morally or mentally.

edit *vt* to prepare a text for publication; to prepare a final version of a film by selecting, cutting and arranging sequences.

edition *n* the number of copies of a book printed at one time.

editor *n* one who is responsible for the issue of a book or newspaper.

editorial *n* a leading article in a newspaper expressing the opinions of its editor or owner.

educate *vt* to train and instruct; to provide schooling.

education *n* instruction and training, as imparted in schools, colleges and universities; the theory and practice of teaching.

eerie *adj* awesome; weird.

efface *vt* to blot out; to erase; to make oneself inconspicuous through shyness, humility or false modesty.

effect *n* a result; an impression; (*pl*) belongings. * *vt* to bring about; to accomplish.

effective *adj* efficient; making a striking impression; forceful; fruitful.

effectual *adj* producing the desired result.

effeminacy *n* a display or impression of feminine qualities in a man; weakness; timidity.

effeminate *adj* womanish; unmanly.

effervesce *vi* to bubble or sparkle.

effervescent *adj* bubbling; sparkling.

effete *adj* worn out; feeble; decadent.

efficacious *adj* achieving the desired result.

efficiency *n* competence.

efficient *adj* capable; competent.

effigy *n* a portrait; a sculpture or figure of a person, esp one crudely executed to ridicule or show contempt.

effluent *adj* flowing out. * *n* a stream from a river or lake; liquid waste discharged from a sewer, an industrial plant, a nuclear station etc.

effluvium *n* (*pl* **effluvia**) noisome vapour.

effort *n* exertion; strenuous endeavour.

effrontery *n* brazen impudence.

effusion *n* a pouring out; copious utterance.

effusive *adj* profuse; gushing.

egg *n* the shell-covered embryo laid by birds, snakes, insects, etc. * *vt* to urge on.

ego *n* the 'I'; the self, self-image; conceit.

egoist *n* a self-centred person.

egotism *n* self-importance; self-centredness.

egotist *n* one always talking of him or herself.

egregious *adj* conspicuously bad or flagrant.

egress *n* exit.

egret *n* a species of heron.

eiderdown *n* the down or soft feathers of the eider duck used for stuffing quilts etc.

eight *adj n* a cardinal number and its symbol (8); the crew of an eight-oared rowing boat.

eighteen *adj, n* eight and ten (18).

eighteenth *adj, n* the ordinal number of 18.

eighth *adj, n* the ordinal number of 8.

eightieth *adj, n* the ordinal number of 80.

eighty *adj* eight times ten (80).

either *adj, pron* one or the other; one of two. * *conj* used as correlative to or.

ejaculate *vt, vi* to emit a fluid (as semen); to exclaim.

eject *vt* to throw out; to expel. * *vi* to escape from an aircraft or spacecraft using an ejection seat.

ejection seat *n* an escape seat in an aircraft, that can be ejected with its occupant in an emergency by means of explosive bolts.

eke *vt* (with **out**) to supplement; to use frugally; to make a living with difficulty.

elaborate *vt* to work out; to explain in detail. * *adj* highly detailed.

elapse *vi* to by, of time.

elastic *adj* springy; rebounding; flexible.

elated *adj* exultant.

elation *n* joy; exultation.

elbow *n* the joint between the forearm and upper arm; a sharp turn or bend. * *vt* to push away with the elbow.

elder *adj* older. * *n* an older person; an office bearer in the Presbyterian Church.

elderly *adj* quite old.

eldest *adj* oldest.

elect *vt* to choose by voting; to make a selection (of); to make a decision on. * *adj* chosen for an office.

election *n* the public choice of a person for office, esp a politician.

electioneering *n* the arts used to secure the election of a candidate.

elector *n* one who has a vote in an election.

electoral *adj* of elections or electors.

electorate *n* the body of electors.

electric, electrical *adj* containing, conveying, worked or produced by electricity.

electricity *n* the force that is developed by friction, and by chemical, thermal or magnetic action.

electrify *vt* to charge with electricity; to thrill; to astonish.

electrocute *vt* to kill by electricity.

electrode *n* a conductor through which an electric current enters or leaves a gas discharge tube etc.

electrodynamics *n* the science that treats of electric currents.

electrolysis *n* chemical decomposition by electricity.

electromagnetic *adj* having electric and magnetic properties.

electron *n* a negatively charged elementary particle that forms the part of the atom outside the nucleus.

electronic *adj* of or worked by streams of electrons flowing through semiconductor devices, vacuum or gas.

electronic mail *n* messages, etc, sent and received via computer terminals.

electronics *n* the study, development and application of electronic devices.

elegance n beauty; refinement; grace.

elegant adj graceful; refined; dignified.

elegy n a lament.

element n a constituent part; a favourable environment for a plant or animal; a wire that produces heat in a electric cooker, kettle, etc; pl atmospheric conditions (wind, rain, etc); pl basic principles, rudiments.

elementary adj basic, simple.

elevate vt to lift up; to raise in rank; to improve in intellectual or moral stature.

elevation n a raised place; the height above the earth's surface or above sea level; the angle to which a gun is raised above the horizon; a drawing that shows the front, the rear, the front view of something.

elevator n a cage or platform for moving something from one level to another; a moveable surface on the tailplane of an aircraft to produce motion up or down; a lift; a building for storing grain.

eleven adj one more than ten (11).

eleventh adj, n the ordinal number of 11.

elicit vt to draw out by inquiry.

elide vt to omit a letter or syllable at the beginning or end of a word.

eligible adj qualified; suitable.

eliminate vt to get rid of; to eradicate; to exclude a competitor from a competition by defeat.

elite n the pick; the best.

elixir n the specific sought after by alchemists to prolong life or transmute metals.

ellipse n an oval figure; a closed plane figure formed by the plane section of a right-angled cone.

elocution n the art of effective speaking.

elongate vt to lengthen.

elope vi to run away secretly, esp of lovers to be married.

eloquence n skill in speaking and the use of words; persuasive speech.

else adj, adv other; besides.

elsewhere adv in some other place.

elucidate vt to make clear.

elude vt to avoid by artifice; to baffle.

elusive adj evasive; deceptive; difficult to contact.

emaciate vi, vt to become or make lean.

email, e-mail n electronic mail.

emanate vi to flow out; to issue.

emanation n outflowing; effluvium.

emancipate vt to free from restraint; to liberate, esp from slavery.

emasculate vt to castrate; to enfeeble.

embalm vt to preserve (corpse) with drugs, chemicals, etc.

embankment n a protecting mound to hold back water or to carry a roadway.

embargo n a prohibition on ships from sailing; restraint; a restriction of commerce by law; a prohibition

embark vt, vi to go or put on board; to begin an activity or enterprise.

embarrass vt to confuse; to harass; to burden; to make a person uncomfortable.

embarrassment n confusion; entanglement; trouble; abashment.

embassy *n* the office or residence of an ambassador.

embellish *vt* to adorn.

embellishment *n* decoration; ornament.

embers *n* live remains of a fire.

embezzle *vt* to misapply funds.

embezzlement *n* fraudulent use of funds.

embitter *vt* to make bitter.

emblem *n* a symbol; a heraldic device.

emblematic, emblematical *adj* symbolic.

embody *vt* to give concrete form to; to incorporate in a single book, law, system, etc.

emboss *vt* to mould or adorn in relief.

embrace *vt* to clasp in the arms; to accept an idea etc eagerly.

embroider *vt* to adorn with patterned needlework.

embroidery *n* decorative needlework.

embroil *vt* to involve a person in trouble.

embryo *n* unborn or unhatched offspring.

embryonic *adj* rudimentary; imperfect.

emendation *n* correction (in texts, etc).

emerald *n* a bright green precious stone, its colour. * *adj* bright green.

emerge *vi* to come forth; to issue; to be revealed as the result of investigation.

emergency *n* a crisis requiring immediate attention.

emetic *n* a medicine that induces vomiting.

emigrant *n* one who leaves one's country to settle in another.

emigrate *vi* to go to reside in another country.

eminence *n* a height; fame; a title for a cardinal.

eminent *adj* exalted; prominent.

emissary *n* an agent sent on a mission; a messenger.

emit *vt* to send or throw out; to utter.

emollient *adj* soothing; softening.

emolument *n* salary; remuneration.

emotion *n* a strong feeling of joy, sadness, anger, fear etc.

emperor *n* the sovereign of an empire.

emphasis *n* a particular stress placed on anything; force, vigour.

emphasize *vt* to lay stress on.

emphatic *adj* impressive; decisive.

empire *n* dominion; sway; states ruled by an emperor.

empirical *adj* based on observation, experiment or experience only, not theoretical.

employ *vt* to give work to; to keep at work

employee *n* one who works for an employer.

employer *n* a person, business, etc, that employs people.

employment *n* occupation or profession.

emporium *n* (*pl* **emporia, emporiums**) a commercial centre; a large shop selling goods of all types.

empower *vt* to authorize.

empress *n* the consort of an emperor; a female ruler of an empire.

empty *adj* void; vacant; lacking in

substance, value or reality; hungry. * vt to take everything out of.

emulate vt to strive to equal; to vie with.

emulsion n a mixture of mutually insoluble liquids in which one is dispersed in droplets throughout the other; a light-sensitive substance on photographic paper or film.

enable vt to empower; to authorize.

enact vt to establish by law; to decree; to act.

enactment n a decree; an act.

enamel n an ornamental or preservative glasslike coating on metals, etc.; the hard outer layer of a tooth. * vt to cover with enamel.

enamour vt to inspire with love.

encampment n a camp.

enchant vt to charm; to fascinate.

enchanter n a sorcerer; a bewitching person.

enchanting adj charming.

enchantment n magic; fascination.

encircle vt to encompass; to embrace.

enclose vt to shut up or in; to put in a wrapper or parcel, usu with a letter.

enclosure n a space fenced in; a thing enclosed with a letter in a parcel or envelope.

encompass vt to encircle; to sail round.

encore adv again; once more. * n a call for a performance to be repeated.

encounter n an unexpected meeting; a conflict. * vt, vi to confront; to fight against.

encourage vt to inspire with hope; to urge on; to promote the development of.

encroach vi to trespass on rights, lands, etc, of others.

encroachment n trespass; intrusion.

encrust vt to cover with a crust.

encumber vt to burden; to hamper.

encumbrance n a burden; a mortgage.

encyclopaedia, encyclopedia n a book or books of general knowledge.

end n the extreme point; the close; the stopping place; death; result; aim. * vt to bring to an end. * vi to come to an end; to result in. * adj final, ultimate.

endanger vt to put in danger.

endear vt to make dear or more loved.

endeavour n effort; attempt. * vi to try; to strive; to aim.

endemic adj peculiar to a people or region.

endless adj not ending; very numerous.

endorse vt to write one's name on the back of (cheques, etc); to ratify; to support; to record an offence on a driving licence.

endorsement n a docket; signature; approval.

endow vt to settle money or property on; to enrich; to provide with special power.

endurance n fortitude; patience.

endure vi, vt to bear patiently; to tolerate; to last; to continue in existence.

enemy n one who is unfriendly; an

antagonist; a hostile army; something harmful.

energetic *adj* forceful; vigorous; lively.

energy *n* power; force; vigour; capacity to do work.

enervate *vt* to enfeeble.

enforce *vt* to urge with energy; to impose; to compel compliance with threats.

enfranchise *vt* to give the right of voting to.

engage *vt* to bind by pledge; to attach; to promise to marry; to attract; to enter into; to attack. * *vi* to bind one's self.

engagement *n* a contract; a betrothal; an appointment arranged with someone; a fight.

engaging *adj* winning; attractive.

engender *vt* to breed; to occasion.

engine *n* a power machine; a locomotive; a contrivance.

engineer *n* a maker or designer or operator of machinery. * *vt* to plan or construct; to contrive; to plan.

engineering *n* the art or business of an engineer.

engrave *vt* to cut or carve on metal; to imprint.

engraving *n* a print from an engraved plate.

engross *vt* to absorb.

engulf *vt* to swallow up.

enhance *vt* to increase in value, importance, attractiveness.

enigma *n* a puzzle; a mystery.

enigmatic, enigmatical *adj* puzzling; obscure; mysterious.

enjoin *vt* to command; prescribe.

enjoy *vi* to take delight in; to experience.

enjoyment *n* pleasure; satisfaction.

enlarge *vt, vi* to make large; to grow large; to speak or write.

enlighten *vt* to make clear; to instruct.

enlightened *adj* instructed; cultured.

enlist *vi* to enter on a list; to enrol (in army). * *vt* to ensure support of.

enliven *vt* to brighten; to gladden.

enmity *n* hostility; ill-will.

ennoble *vt* to exalt; to dignify.

enormity *n* great wickedness, a serious crime.

enormous *adj* huge.

enough *adj* adequate, sufficient. * *n* a sufficiency. * *adv* tolerably.

enrage *vt* to make very angry.

enrapture *vt* to fill with delight.

enrich *vt* to make rich; to fertilize.

enrol *vt* to write in a roll; to record; to admit as a member of a society.

enrolment *n* act of enrolling; a register; a record.

enshrine *vt* to enclose; to cherish.

ensign *n* a badge; an emblem; a flag.

enslave *vt* to make a slave of; to subjugate.

ensnare *vt* to entrap.

ensue *vi* to result from.

entail *vt* to involve as a result; to settle land on individuals in succession so that all are life-renters. * *n* this mode of settlement.

entanglement *n* disorder; a relationship between a man and a woman considered to be unsuitable.

enter *vi* to go or come in or into; to come on stage; to begin, start; (*with* for) to register as an entrant. * vt to come or go into; to pierce, penetrate; (*organization*) to join; to insert; (*proposal etc*) to submit; to record (*an item*) in a diary etc.

enteric adj belonging to the intestines.

enterprise n a venture; boldness.

entertain vt, vi to receive as a guest; to please; to amuse; to consider; to have in mind.

entertaining adj pleasing; amusing.

entertainment n entertaining; amusement; an act or show intended to amuse and interest.

enthral vt to enslave; to charm; to captivate.

enthusiasm n ardent feeling; fervent zeal; keen interest.

enthusiast n a person full of enthusiasm for something.

entice vt to tempt; to allure; to lure away by promise of reward.

enticing adj attractive; tempting; fascinating.

entire adj whole; complete.

entitle vt to give a title to; to empower.

entity n being; existence.

entomology n the science of insect life.

entrails npl the intestines.

entrance n coming or going in; the place of entry; the power or authority to enter; an admission fee.

entrance vt to enrapture; to fill with delight.

entreat vt to beg earnestly; to implore.

entreaty n urgent prayers or plea.

entrench vt to dig in; to establish oneself in a strong defensive position.

entry n act of entering; entrance; an item recorded in a diary, account or dictionary.

enumerate vt to count one by one; to list.

enunciate vt to utter; to pronounce (clearly).

enunciation n clear utterance; statement; expression; declaration; public attestation.

envelop vt to wrap up.

envelope n a cover (of letter, etc).

enviable adj exciting envy.

environment n conditions and surroundings that influence our development and that of plants and animals.

environs npl neighbourhood.

envisage vt to picture to oneself.

envoy n one sent on a mission.

envy n jealousy; discontent caused by another's possessions, achievements, etc. * vt to begrudge.

enzyme n a complex protein produced by living cells that induces or speeds chemical reactions in plants and animals.

ephemeral adj short-lived.

epic adj heroic; in the grand style. * n a heroic poem.

epidemic adj a disease affecting a whole community. * n a disease which attacks many people at the same period.

epidermis n the outer skin.

epiglottis n the valve covering the larynx.

epigram n a pointed, witty, or sarcastic saying.

epilepsy n a disorder of the nervous system marked by convulsions and loss of consciousness.

epilogue n a speech addressed to audience at the close of a play; the concluding section of a book.

episcopacy n church government by bishops; bishops collectively.

episcopal adj relating to bishops.

episode n an incident in a sequence of events; a piece of action in a book or drama.

epistle n a letter.

epitaph n an inscription on a tomb.

epithet n a descriptive adjective.

epitome n a typical example; personification; a brief summary.

epoch n a period of time.

equable adj uniform; even; hot extreme; even tempered.

equal adj the same in all respects. * n one not inferior or superior to another. * vt to make or be equal to ; to do something equal to.

equality n sameness; evenness.

equalize vt to make equal.

equanimity n evenness of temper.

equate vt to make equal; to make, treat or regard as compatible

equation n an act of equalling; the state of being equal; (chem) an expression representing a reaction in symbols.

equator n an imaginary circle passing round the globe, equidistant from the poles.

equestrian adj on horseback. * n a horseman.

equidistant adj equally distant.

equilateral adj equal sided.

equilibrium n a state of balance, weight, power, force etc.

equine adj pertaining to a horse.

equinox n the two times at which the sun crosses the equator and day and night are equal.

equip vt to furnish; to provide with all necessary tools, supplies etc.

equipment n everything needed for a particular task, expedition etc.

equitable adj fair; just.

equity n fairness; just dealing; (pl) ordinary shares in a company.

equivalent adj, n equal in value amount, force, meaning etc; virtually identical, esp in function as effect. * n an equivalent thing.

equivocal adj ambiguous; questionable.

equivocate vi to quibble.

era n a fixed reckoning date; a period of time.

eradicate vt to root out; to obliterate.

erase vt to rub out; to remove a recording from magnetic tape; to remove data from a computer memory or storage medium.

erect adj upright; (of the sex organs) rigid from sexual stimulation. * vt to build.

erection n act of erecting; formation; anything erected; structure; a swelling and rigidity of the penis due to sexual excitement.

erode vt to eat or wear away gradually.

erosion n a wearing away (as of sea cliffs).

erotic adj of sexual love; amatory.

err vi to wander; to stray.

errand n a message; a short journey to carry out a task.

errant adj roving; wandering.

erratic adj irregular; eccentric; unreliable.

erratum n (pl **errata**) an error in printing, etc.

erroneous adj wrong; mistaken.

error n a mistake; a fault.

erudite adj deeply read; learned.

erupt vi to burst out; to break out into a rash; to explode ejecting ash and lava from a volcano.

eruption n a bursting forth; a breaking out.

escapade n a mad prank.

escape vt, vi to get out of the way of; to avoid; to be free. * n a getting away by flight; a leakage e.g. of gas etc.; a temporary respite.

escarpment n the steep side of a hill, rock, or rampart.

eschew vt to shun; to avoid.

escort n a guard; an attendant. * vt to attend and guard.

esoteric adj private; select; understood only by elite minority.

especial adj distinct; chief.

espionage n spying.

esplanade n a seaside terrace or promenade.

espouse vt to marry; to adopt a cause etc.

espy vt to catch sight of.

essay vt to try. * n an endeavour or experiment; a short literary composition.

essence n the nature or being of any-thing; a substance extracted from another without the loss of the qualities of the original; perfume.

essential adj vital; indispensable; volatile (oil).

establish vt to fix firmly; to institute; to set up (a business etc) permanently; to settle a person in a position; to have generally accepted; to place beyond doubt.

established adj legally confirmed (church); assured.

establishment n household staff; a place of business; (with cap) those in power whose aim is to preserve the status quo.

estate n landed property; a large area of residential or industrial development; a person's total possessions, esp at their death; a social or political class.

estate agent n a person whose business is selling and leasing property.

esteem vt to value on; to regard highly; to prize. * n judgment; estimation; regard.

estimable adj worthy; respected.

estimate vt to calculate; to appraise. * n valuation; an approximate calculation; a judgment or opinion.

estrangement n withdrawal of friendship.

estuary n the mouth of a river; a firth.

etch vt to portray on metal plates by use of acids.

etching n the impression taken from an etched plate.

eternal adj everlasting.

eternity n infinite time; future life.

ether n a volatile liquid used as an anaesthetic or solvent; the invisible elastic substance formerly believed to be distributed through space.

ethereal adj airy; heavenly; aerial; intangible.

ethic, ethical adj moral.

ethics n the science of morals; principles.

ethnic adj of races or large groups of people classed accordingly to common traits and customs.

etiquette n code of manners; decorum.

etymology n the study of the history and development of words.

Eucharist n the Christian sacrament of communion; the consecrated elements in this.

eugenics n the science of the improvement of the human race.

eulogize vt to praise; to extol.

eulogy n praise; panegyric.

euphemism n the use of a mild for a harsh term ('fairy tale' for 'lie'.)

euphonic adj pleasing to the ear.

euro n the monetary unit of the European Union.

euthanasia n painless killing, esp to relieve incurable suffering.

evacuate vt to make empty; to quit; to move people from a danger to a safe area; to discharge wastes from the body.

evade vt to avoid; to escape from.

evaluate vt to assess; to determine the value carefully.

evangelist n a preacher of the gospel.

evaporate vi to change into vapour; to remove water from; to disappear.

evasion n avoidance; an equivocal reply or excuse.

evasive adj shuffling; equivocating.

eve, even n evening; the evening before as (Christmas Eve).

even adj level; smooth; equal; divisible by two. * vt to equalize; to make even; to balance (debts etc). * adv just; exactly; fully; quite; at the very time.

evening n the close of the day.

event n an incident; a happening; contingency; an item or contest; an item or contest in a sports programme.

eventful adj memorable.

eventuality n a possible result.

ever adv always; at any time; in any case.

evergreen n a tree or plant always in leaf. * adj always green.

everlasting adj eternal; never ending.

every adj each of all.

everybody n every person.

everyday adj happening daily; commonplace; worn or used every day.

everything pron all things; all; something of the greatest importance.

everywhere adv in every place.

evict vt to dispossess by law; to expel.

eviction n expulsion (of tenant).

evidence n testimony; proof.

evident adj clear; plain; understandable.

evil adj wicked; bad. * n sin; harm.

evince vt to show; to prove.

eviscerate vt to disembowel.

evoke vt to call forth.

evolution n a process of change in a particular direction; the process by which something attains its distinctive characteristics; a theory that existing types of plants and animals have developed from earlier forms.

evolve *vt, vi* to unfold; to open out; to develop.

exacerbate *vt* to aggravate; to make something worse.

exact *adj* accurate; precise. * *vt* to compel payment; to demand and obtain.

exacting *adj* severe; greatly demanding; requiring close attention and precision.

exactly *adv* in an exact manner; precisely. * *interj* quite so! indeed!

exaggerate *vt* to overstate.

exalt *vt* to raise in power, rank, etc; to extol.

examination *n* an interrogation; a testing by set questions.

examine *vt* to scrutinize; to inquire into; to question (witness); to test.

example *n* a sample; pattern; model; a warning to others.

exasperate *vt* to enrage; to annoy intensely.

excavate *vt* to hollow out by digging; to unearth; to expose to view (remains, etc) by digging.

exceed *vt* to surpass; to overstep (the limit).

excel *vb* (*pt* **excelled**) *vt* to surpass. * *vi* to be preeminent.

excellent *adj* of high quality; choice.

except *vt* to omit; to exclude. * *vi* to object. * *prep* without.

excepting *prep* excluding; except.

exceptional *adj* unusual; rare; superior.

excerpt *n* an extract. * *vt* to extract from a book, etc.

excess *n* surplus; intemperance.

excessive *adj* undue; extreme.

exchange *vt* to give and take (one thing in return for another). * *n* the conversion of money from one currency to another; a place where things and services are exchanged, esp a marketplace for securities; a centre or device in which telephone lines are interconnected.

excision *n* a cutting out.

excitable *adj* easily agitated.

excite *vt* to arouse the feelings of, esp to generate feelings of pleasurable anticipation; to cause to experience strong emotion; to rouse to activity; to stimulate a response, e.g. in a bodily organ.

excitement *n* strong pleasurable emotion; agitation; commotion.

exclaim *vi, vt* to call out; to declare loudly, suddenly and with emotion.

exclamation *n* a loud outcry; an emotional utterance; an interjection.

exclude *vt* to shut out.

exclusion *n* a shutting out; a ban; omission.

exclusive *adj* excluding all else; reserved for particular persons; snobbishly aloof; fashionable; high-class, expensive; unobtainable or unpublished elsewhere; sole, undivided.

excommunicate *vt* to bar from church privileges and rites.

excrement *n* waste matter discharged from the body.

excretion *n* ejection of waste matter.

excruciating *adj* intensely painful or distressful.

excursion *n* a pleasure trip.

excuse *vt* to let off; to forgive; to overlook. * *n* an apology; that which excuses; a reason or explanation of.

execrable *adj* hateful; detestable.

execute *vt* to perform; to carry out; to put to death; to make valid.

execution *n* the act or manner of performing; skill in music; capital punishment.

executive *n* a person or group concerned with administration or management of a business or organization. * *adj* having the power to execute decisions, laws, decrees etc.

executor *n* one who carries out provisions of will.

exemplary *adj* model; worthy of imitation.

exemplify *vt* to show by example.

exempt *vt* to free from; excuse. * *adj* free; immune.

exemption *n* release; immunity.

exercise *n* the use or application of a power or right; regular physical or mental exertion; something performed to develop or test a specific ability or skill. * *vt* to use, exert, employ; to engage in regular physical activity; to engage the attention of; to perplex.

exert *vt* to put forth strength etc; to strive.

exertion *n* effort.

exhale *vt, vi* to breathe out.

exhaust *vt* to use up; to make empty; to use up; tire out; (subject) to deal with or develop completely. * the escape of waste gas or steam from an engine.

exhaustion *n* extreme weariness.

exhaustive *adj* full; thorough.

exhibit *vt* to display, esp in public; to present to a court in legal form. * *n* an act or instance of exhibiting, something exhibited; something produced and identified in court for use as evidence.

exhibition *n* display; any public show.

exhilarate *vt* to elate; to enliven.

exhort *vt* to encourage; to warn.

exhume *vt* to disinter.

exigence *n* pressing necessity; urgency.

exile *n* banishment; the person banished. * *vt* to banish from one's country.

exist *vi* to be; to live; to manage one's life with difficulty.

existent *adj* being; existing.

exit *n* a going out; a way out.

exonerate *vt* to free from blame.

exorbitant *adj* excessive esp of prices.

exorcise *vi* to drive out evil spirits.

exotic *adj* foreign; excitingly different or unusual.

expand *vt, vi* to spread out; to swell; to describe in fuller detail; to become more friendly and genial.

expanse *n* a wide area.

expansion *n* enlargement; increase.

expansive *adj* wide; genial.

expatiate *vi* to speak or write about at length.

expatriate vt to exile oneself or banish another. * adj, n (a person) living in another country, or self-exiled or banished.

expect vt to anticipate, to regard as likely to arrive or happen; to consider necessary, reasonable or due; to suppose.

expectancy n hope; expectation.

expectant adj awaiting; anxious; hopeful.

expectation n something that is expected to happen; pl prospects for the future, esp of inheritance.

expectorate vt to spit or cough out.

expediency n fitness; suitability under the circumstances.

expedient adj suitable for the present time or circumstances. * n a means to an end; a means used for want of a better.

expedite vt to accelerate.

expedition n promptness; an enterprise or those who undertake it.

expeditious adj speedy; prompt.

expel vt to drive out; to banish.

expend vt to spend; to use up; to consume.

expenditure n outlay; cost.

expense n cost; charge; price.

expensive adj costly; lavish.

experience n personal trial; knowledge gained from contact with life or work; an effecting event. * vt to try; to meet with.

experiment n a trial; a practical test; a controlled procedure carried out to discover, test or demonstrate something.* vi to carry out experiments.

experimental adj of, derived from or proceeding by experiment; provisional.

expert adj skilful; knowledgeable through training and experience. * n a specialist.

expertise n expert knowledge or skill.

expiate vt to atone for.

expire vt to breathe out; to exhale. * vi to die; to end.

explain vt to make clear; to expound. * vi to account for.

explanation n interpretation; reason.

explanatory adj serving to explain.

expletive n an oath.

explicable adj explainable.

explicit adj definite; expressly or frankly stated or shown.

explode vt, vi to burst with a loud noise; to expose; discredit.

exploit n a brilliant deed; a bold achievement. * vt to make use of; to take unfair advantage of.

exploitation n successful application of industry to any object, as land, mines, etc.

explore vt to search; to examine closely; to travel through to discover.

explorer n a traveller in unknown regions.

explosion n a violent detonation; an outburst (of feeling).

explosive adj liable to explode. * n material that explodes.

exponent n a person who explains or interprets something.

export vt to send goods abroad for sale. * n the commodity exported.

expose vt to deprive of protection or shelter; to uncover; to display; to endanger.

exposed adj unmasked; not sheltered.

exposition n explanation; exhibition.

exposure n a laying open to view or weather or danger; the time during which light reaches and acts on a photographic film, paper or plate; publicity.

expound vt to explain.

express vt to declare; to utter; to make known; to squeeze out. * adj swift, special; explicit; plain. * n a swift messenger, service or conveyance; an express train. * adv with haste; at high speed; by express service.

expression n a phrase or mode of speech; facial look; taste and feeling (in music); (math) a collection of symbols serving to express something.

expressive adj striking; full of expression.

expressly adv of set purpose; explicitly.

expulsion n ejection; discharge.

expunge vt to blot out; to erase.

expurgate vt to purify (from sin, etc); cut out offensive passages from (books, etc).

exquisite adj beautiful; incomparable; acutely felt, as pain or pleasure.

extend vt, vi to stretch out; to prolong in time; to spread; to accord; to reach; to hold out, e.g. the hand.

extension n extent, scope; an added part, e.g. to a building; an extra period; a programme of extramural teaching provided by a college, etc; an additional telephone connected to the principal line.

extensive adj far-reaching; large.

extent n compass; size; range; scope.

extenuate vt to make excuses for.

extenuation n mitigation.

exterior adj external; outside.

exterminate vt to destroy utterly.

external adj on the outside; visible.

extinct adj dead; extinguished; no longer existing or active.

extinction n destruction.

extinguish vt to put out; quench.

extinguisher n a device for putting out a fire.

extol vt (pt **extolled**) to praise highly; to glorify.

extort vt to exact by force, e.g. money, promises.

extortionate adj exorbitant; harsh.

extra adj, adv additional. * n something additional; a special edition of a newspaper; a person who plays a non-speaking part in a film.

extract vt to take or pull out by force; to withdraw by chemical or physical means; to abstract. * n the essence of a substance obtained by extraction; a passage taken from a book, play, film, etc.

extraction n lineage; a drawing out.

extradite vt to give up foreign criminals to police of their own country.

extramural adj connected with a university but not as regular students.

extraneous adj foreign; irrelevant; inessential.

extraordinary *adj* unusual; remarkable.

extravagance *n* excess; overspending; flamboyance; wastefulness.

extravagant *adj* lavish in spending; excessively, high of prices; unrestrained; wasteful; profuse.

extravaganza *n* a fantastic literary or musical composition.

extreme *adj* of the highest degree or intensity; excessive, immoderate, unwarranted; very severe, stringent; outermost. * *n* the highest or furthest limit or degree.

extremely *adv* in the utmost degree.

extremist *n* a supporter of extreme measures.

extremity *n* the farthest point; the utmost need; (*pl*) the hands or feet.

extricate *vt* to set free; to disentangle.

exuberance *n* high spirits.

exuberant *adj* high-spirited; lively.

exude *vt, vi* to ooze out.

exult *vi* to rejoice exceedingly; to triumph.

exultant *adj* jubilant.

eye *n* the organ of vision; mind; perception; a small hole; a catch; a shoot. * *vt* to regard closely.

eyebrow *n* the hairy arch above the eye.

eyelash *n* the hair that edges the eyelid.

eyelid *n* the cover of the eye.

eyesight *n* power of sight.

eyesore *n* something offensive to the sight.

eye-witness *n* a person who sees an event.

eyrie *n* an eagle's nest.

F

fable *n* a short story with a moral; a falsehood.

fabled *adj* legendary.

fabric *n* frame of anything; a building; texture; cloth.

fabricate *vt* to fashion; to invent.

fabrication *n* construction; forgery.

fabulous *adj* told in fables, mythical; incredible; (*inf*) very good.

façade *n* front view of an edifice.

face *n* the front part of the head; the countenance; aspect; assurance; dial of a watch. * *vt* to front; to oppose.

facet *n* one of many sides (of gems); an aspect.

facetious *adj* humorous.

facilitate *vt* to make easy.

facility *n* ease; dexterity.

facsimile *n* an exact copy.

fact *n* a deed; event; truth.

faction *n* an unscrupulous and self-interested party; discord.

factor *n* an agent; a land steward; an essential element; a measure of a number.

factory *n* a building or buildings where goods are manufactured.

factual adj based on or containing facts; actual.

faculty n capacity; power; special aptitude; a department of a university.

fad n personal habit on idiosyncrasy.

fade vt, vi to (cause to) lose vigour or brightness or intensity gradually; to vanish gradually.

fail vi to weaken; to fade away; to stop operating; to become bankrupt; not to succeed; to miss; vt to disappoint the expectations on hope.

failure n failing, non-performance, lack of success; an unsuccessful person or thing.

faint vi to become feeble; to swoon. * adj dim, indistinct; weak; feeble. * n the act of fainting.

fair adj pleasing to the eye; light in colour; just; favourable (weather); moderately good or large; average * adv justly. * n a regular market or gathering for the sale of goods

fairly adv honestly, justly; moderately.

fairy n an elf; a sprite.

faith n belief; trust; religious conviction; system of beliefs; fidelity to one's promises.

faithful adj loyal; trusty; accurate.

faithless adj false; unfaithful.

fake vt to disguise and so cheat; to pretend; to simulate.* n a faked article; a forgery; an impostor.

fall vi (pt **fell**, pp **fallen**) to drop down; to descend; to collapse; to sin; to lose power, status, office; to be injured or die in battle; to happen. * n a drop; a decrease; a decline in status or position; overthrow.

fallacious adj deceitful; misleading.

fallacy n a false argument or idea.

fallible adj liable to err; make mistakes.

fallout n a deposit of radioactive dust from a nuclear explosion; a byproduct.

fallow adj left uncultivated for one or more seasons; yellowish-brown.

false adj not true; forged; treacherous; deceitful; artificial.

falsehood n untruth; a lie.

falsetto n an unnaturally high-pitched voice.

falsification n wilful misrepresentation.

falsify vt to make false by altering in order to deceive.

falter vi to hesitate; to waver; to move unsteadily.

fame n reputation; renown.

familiar adj well-acquainted; friendly; common; well-known; presumptuous. * n an intimate; a spirit said to assist a witch.

familiarity n intimacy; presumptuous.

family n parents and their children; a set of relatives; the descendants of a common ancestor; a group of related plants or animals.

famine n extreme scarcity of food.

famish vt, vi to starve; to suffer extreme hunger.

famous adj renowned.

fan[1] n an instrument or device for creating a current of air. * vt (pt fanned) to cool by moving; to ventilate; to stir up or excite; to spread out like a fan.

fan² n an enthusiastic follower of a person, a sport or a hobby.

fanatic adj frenzied, bigoted. * n a zealot; an over-enthusiastic person.

fancy n imagination; caprice; whim; delusion. * vt, vi to imagine; to like. * adj elegant; unreal.

fancy dress n a costume representing an animal, historical character, etc.

fanfare n a flourish of trumpets.

fang n a long, sharp, pointed tooth.

fanlight n a window over a door.

fantastic adj unrealistic; fanciful; unbelievable; imaginative.

fantasy n imagination; a product of this; an imaginative poem, play or novel.

far adj remote; extreme in political views. * adv very distant in space, time or degree; very much.

farce n a ludicrous situation.

farcical adj droll; ludicrous.

fare vi to be in a specified condition. * n food; the cost of a journey.

farewell interj, n goodbye.

farinaceous adj starchy; mealy.

farm n land (with buildings) on which crops and animals are raised. * vt, vi to cultivate; to lease out; to subcontract.

farmer n one who manages and operates a farm.

farther adj comp more remote. * adv to a greater degree.

farthest adj super most distant. * adv at the greatest distance.

fascia n the instrument panel of a motor vehicle, the dashboard; the flat surface above a shop front with the name etc.

fascinate vt to charm; to captivate.

fascination n charm; spell.

fashion n a current style of dress, conduct, speech etc; the manner of form of appearance or action. * vt to make in a particular form; to suit or adapt.

fashionable adj stylish; in keeping with the prevailing fashion.

fast adj firm; fixed; steadfast; swift; lasting. * vt to abstain from food. * n a period of doing without food.

fasten vt, vi to fix firmly; to become fixed.

fast food n food, such as hamburgers, kebabs and pizzas, prepared and served quickly.

fastidious adj hard to please; overrefined.

fat adj plump; oily; rich; fertile. * n oily substance in animal bodies; the richest or best point of anything.

fatal adj deadly; disastrous.

fatalist n one who holds all things are predetermined.

fatality n a fatal occurrence; a death caused by disaster or accident; a person so killed.

fate n destiny; necessity; death; doom; lot.

fateful adj having important, often unpleasant, consequences.

father n a male parent; an ancestor; name given to Roman Catholic priests. * vt to adopt; to found; to originate.

fatherhood n state of being a father.

father-in-law n the father of one's husband or wife.

fatherland n one's native country.

fathom n a nautical measure of length (6 feet/1.83 metres). * vt to try the depth of; to sound; to comprehend.

fatigue n tiredness from physical or mental effort; the tendency of a material to break under repeated stress. * vt, vi to make or become tired.

fatten vt to make fat.

fatuous adj foolish; idiotic.

fault n a slight offence; a flaw; a break of strata; an incorrect stroke in tennis.

faulty adj defective; imperfect.

fauna n a collective term for the animals of a region or specific environment.

favour n goodwill; kindness; leave; a token of goodwill; a gift presented at a party. * vt to befriend; to show support for; to oblige with; to facilitate.

favourable adj kindly disposed; propitious; conductive to.

favoured adj regarded with favour.

favourite n a person habitually preferred; a darling; a competitor expected to win; a minion. * adj preferred; beloved.

favouritism n showing undue partiality.

fawn n a young deer. * vi to cringe or flatter to gain favour. * adj light brown.

fax n a facsimile; a method of sending printed matter through the telephone system; a document sent in this way. * vt to send a fax.

fear n dread; terror; awe; anxiety. * vt, vi to dread; to hesitate; to reverence.

feasibility n practicability.

feasible adj practicable; possible.

feast n a sumptuous meal; a periodic religious celebration. * vi, vt to have or take part in a feast; to entertain with a feast.

feat n an exploit; a notable act.

feather n any of the light outgrowths forming the covering of a bird, a hollow central shaft with a vane of fine barbs on each side. * vt to ornament with feathers.

feature n any of the parts of the face; a trait of something; a special attraction or distinctive quality of something; a prominent newspaper article etc. * vt, vi to make or be a feature of (something).

February n the second month in the year.

fecund adj fruitful; prolific.

federal adj united in a league for national purposes but each partner having independent powers in local affairs.

federation n a union of independent bodies or states to take common action on certain matters.

fee n a reward for services; a payment; charge. * vt to pay a fee to.

feeble adj weak; infirm.

feed vb (pt, pp fed) vt to give food to; to fatten. * vi to take food; to eat; to graze. * n food for animals; material fed into a machine.

feedback n a return to the input of part of the output of a system; information about a product, service, etc, returned to the supplier for evaluation.

feel n the sense of touch; feeling; a quality as revealed by touch. * vt, vi (pt, pp **felt**) to perceive or explore by the touch; to find one's way by cautious trail; to be conscious of, experience; to be affected by; to convey a certain sensation when touched.

feeler n an organ of touch in insects etc; a remark etc made to probe a situation.

feeling adj sensitive; sympathetic. * n the sense of touch; emotion; sympathy; a belief; an opinion arising from emotion; pl emotions; sensibilities.

feign vt, vi to pretend; to invent.

feint n a pretence (of doing); a sham blow.

felicitate vt to congratulate.

felicitous adj happy; apt.

felicity n happiness; aptness.

feline adj catlike.

fell adj cruel; savage. * n a skin; a stony hill. * vt to strike down.

fellow n a partner; one of a pair; a man; a member of the governing body of a college etc; a member of a learned society.

fellowship n companionship; an association; the status of a college fellow.

felon n a criminal.

felony n a serious crime.

felt n a fabric made of wool.

female n a girl or woman. * adj of the sex that produces young.

feminine adj womanly; womanish.

feminism n the movement to win political, economic and social equality for women.

femoral adj belonging to the thigh.

femur n the thigh bone.

fen n a marsh; a bog.

fence n a barrier put round land to mark a boundary, or prevent animals, etc from escaping; a receiver of stolen goods. * vt, vi to surround a fence; to keep (out) as by a fence; to make evasive answers; to act as a fence for stolen goods.

fencing n the practice of sword play; material for fences.

fend vt to keep or ward off; (with **for**) to provide a livelihood for.

fender n a hearth guard; a buffer along a ship's side; the part of a car body over the wheel.

ferment n that which causes fermentation, as yeast; tumult; agitation. * vt, vi to cause or subject to fermentation; to cause agitation or excitement.

fermentation n the breakdown of complex molecules in organic components caused by the influence of yeast or other substances.

ferocious adj fierce; savage.

ferocity n savagery; fury.

ferret n a species of weasel. * vt to drive out (rabbits); to search out (secrets).

ferry n a boat used for ferrying; a ferrying service; the location of a ferry. * vt to convey (passengers etc) over a stretch of water; to transport from one place to another, esp along a regular route.

fertile *adj* fruitful; inventive.

fertilize *vt* to enrich (soil) by adding nutrients; to impregnate.

fertilizer *n* natural organic or artificial substances used to enrich the soil.

fervent *adj* burning; ardent; passionate.

fervid *adj* zealous; eager.

fervour *n* zeal; earnestness.

fester *vi* to suppurate; to rankle.

festival *n* a feast; a gala day; performances of music, plays etc given periodically.

festive *adj* joyous; merry.

festivity *n* festive gaiety.

fetch *vt* to go and bring back; to heave.

fête *n* a festival. * *vt* to honour; to make much of.

fetid *adj* stinking; offensive.

fetish *n* anything excessively reverenced.

fetter *n* a shackle for feet; restraint. * *vt* to hobble; to restrict.

feu *n* land held in fee.

feud *n* a quarrel esp between individuals, families, clans.

feudalism *n* the holding of land in return for military service.

fever *n* a disease marked by high temperature; restless excitement.

few *adj* not many; a small number.

fiancé *m*, **fiancée** *f n* a person engaged to be married.

fiasco *n* an ignominious failure.

fibre *n* a natural or synthetic thread, e.g. from cotton, nylon, which is spun into yarn; a material composed of such yarn; texture; strength or character; roughage.

fibreglass *n* a glass composed of fibres often bonded with plastic used in making various products.

fickle *adj* vacillating; inconstant.

fickleness *n* inconstancy.

fiction *n* a made-up story; novels; plays collectively.

fictitious *adj* imaginary; false.

fiddle *n* a violin. * *vt* to play the violin; to swindle.

fidelity *n* faithfulness; loyalty.

fidget *vi* to be restless. * *n* a restless person.

field *n* land suitable for tillage or pasture; range; sports ground; an area affected by electrical, magnetic or gravitational influence etc; the area visible through an optical lens; all competitors in a contest; in a computer; a section of a record in a database. * *vt, vi* to catch and return the ball in cricket etc; to handle (e.g. questions) successfully.

field marshal *n* an army officer of the highest rank.

fiend *n* a demon; a cruel person; an avid fan.

fiendish *adj* like a fiend.

fierce *adj* wild; savage; violent; intense.

fiery *adj* burning; passionate; irascible.

fight *vi, vt* (*pt, pp* **fought**) to contend; to strive for victory. * *n* a struggle; a battle.

fighter *n* a person who fights; a person who does not yield easily; an aircraft designed to destroy enemy aircraft.

figment n a fiction; a falsehood.

figuration n shape; form.

figurative adj using figures of speech; metaphorical.

figure n form; outline; diagram; pattern; person; statue; symbol; price; digit; a set of steps on movements (pl) arithmetic. * vt, vi to represent in a diagram or outline to imagine; to estimate; to appear.

figurehead n the carved figure on the bow of ships; a nominal head or leader.

filament n a slender thread; the fine wire in a light bulb.

filch vt to pilfer; to steal.

file n a container for holding papers; an orderly arrangement of papers; a line of persons or things; in computer, a collection of related data under a specific name; a smoothing or polishing or grinding tool. * vt, vi to put on public records, to march in file; to wear down.

filial adj of or relating to a son or daughter.

filigree n delicate tracery in gold or silver.

filings npl particles rubbed off by a file.

fill vt, vi to make or become full; to pervade; to hold; to satisfy.

fillet n a thin boneless strip of fish or meat. * vt to bone meat, etc.

filling n a substance used to fill a tooth cavity; the contents of a sandwich, pie etc. * adj substantial (of a meal).

filly n a female colt.

film n a fine, thin skin, coating etc; a flexible cellulose material covered with a light-sensitive substance used in photography; a haze or blur; a motion picture.

filter n a device or substance straining out solid particles, impurities etc; a traffic signal that allows cars to turn left or right while the main lights are red. * vt, vi to pass through or as through a filter, to remove with a filter.

filth n dirt; pollution; obscenity.

filthy adj dirty; foul; obscene.

filtrate vt to filter.

fin n an organ by which a fish etc steers itself and swims; any fin-shaped object used as a stabilizer, as on an aircraft.

final adj last; conclusive. * n (often pl) the last of a series of contests; a final examination.

finale n the last piece; the end, esp of any public performance; the last section in a musical composition.

finance n the management of money. * vt to supply or raise money for.

financier n one skilled in finance.

find vt (pt, pp **found**) to come upon; to discover; to have; to supply; to declare. * n a discovery.

finding n a verdict; a discovery.

fine adj slender; minute; keen; delicate. * n a money penalty. * vt to punish by a fine.

finery n showy apparel or jewellery.

finesse n delicacy or subtlety of performance; skilfulness, diplomacy in handling a situation. * vt to achieve by finesse.

finger n one of the five digits of the

hand usually excluding the thumb; anything finger-shaped. * *vt* to touch.

fingerprint *n* the impression of the ridges on a fingertip, esp as used for purposes of identification.

finish *n* the last part, the end; anything used to finish a surface; the finished effect; means or manner of completion or perfecting; polished manners, speech etc. **vt, vi* to bring to an end, to come to the end of; to consume entirely; to perfect; to give a desired surface effect to.

finite *adj* limited; bounded.

fiord, fjord *n* an inlet of the sea.

fire *n* the flame, heat and light of combustion.

fire alarm *n* a device that uses a bell, hooter etc, to warn of a fire.

firearm *n* a gun or rifle.

firebrand *n* a flaming piece of wood; one who causes mischief or disturbance.

fire brigade *n* an organisation of men and women trained to extinguish fires.

fire escape *n* a means of exit from a building, esp a stairway, for use in case of fire.

fireplace *n* a place for a fire, esp a recess in a wall; the surrounding area.

fireproof *adj* incombustible.

fireside *n* the hearth; home.

firework *n* a device packed with explosive and combustible material used to produce noisy and colourful displays.

firing squad *n* a detachment with the task of firing a salute at a military funeral or carrying out an execution.

firm *adj* steady; strong; hard; resolute. * *n* a business partnership.

firmament *n* the sky or heavens.

first *n* a person or thing that is first; the beginning; the winning place, as in a race; the highest award in a university degree. * *adj* before all others in a series; foremost, as in rank, equality etc. * *adv* before anyone or anything else.

first aid *n* emergency treatment for an injury etc, before regular medical aid is available.

first-class *adj, n* of the highest quality, as in accommodation, travel.

first-hand *adj* obtained directly.

first-rate *adj, adv* of the best quality; (*inf*) excellent.

firth *n* a wide river mouth.

fiscal *adj* relating to public finance. * *n* a public prosecutor.

fish *n* a cold-blooded animal living in water, having backbones, gills and fins. * *vi* to catch or try to catch fish.

fisherman *n* one who fishes for a living or for sport.

fishery *n* the business of fishing; fishing ground.

fishing *n* the art of catching fish.

fishmonger *n* a dealer in fish; his shop.

fishy *adj* like a fish in odour, taste etc; creating doubt or suspicion.

fission *n* a split or cleavage; the splitting of the atomic nucleus resulting in the release of energy, nuclear fission.

fissure *n* a cleft; a chasm.

fist *n* the hand clenched.

fit *n* a spasm; convulsion; right size; caprice. * *adj* suitable; proper; healthy. * *vt, vi* (*pt* **fitted**) to make fit; to suit; to adapt; to equip.

fitful *adj* spasmodic; uncertain.

fitment *n* a piece of equipment, esp fixed furniture.

fitter *n* one who fits; one who puts the parts of machinery together.

fitting *adj* becoming; appropriate. * *npl* fixtures.

five *adj, n* one more than four; the symbol for this, 5.

fix *vt, vi* to make fast or firm; to settle; to appoint; to direct one's eyes steadily at something; to repair; to arrange or influence a result. * *n* a dilemma.

fixed *adj* firm; fast.

fixture *n* what is fixed to anything, as to land or to a house; a fixed article of furniture; a firmly established person or thing; a fixed or appointed time or event.

fizz *vi* to make a hissing sound.

flabby *adj* soft; limp.

flaccid *adj* flabby.

flag[1] *n* a square or oblong piece of material with a pattern on it representing a country, party, etc; a coloured cloth or paper used as a sign or signal. * *vt* (*pt* **flagged**) to decorate with flags; to signal to (as if) with a flag; (*usu with* **down**) to signal to stop.

flag[2] *n* a flat paving stone.

flag[3] *vi* (*pt* **flagged**) to droop; to languish.

flag[4] *n* a plant with a sword-shaped leaf, the iris; a long thin plant blade.

flagellate *vt* to whip.

flagellation *n* a scourging.

flagon *n* a jug-shaped metal or pottery vessel.

flagrant *adj* glaring; shameful; notorious.

flail *n* a hand-threshing implement.

flair *n* natural ability; aptitude; discernment; stylishness.

flake *n* a scale; a fleecy particle (snow). * *vi* to peel off. * *vt* to form into flakes.

flamboyant *adj* florid; flaming; strikingly elaborate; dashing; exuberant.

flame *n* a sheet of fire; a blaze; passion. * *vi* to blaze; to become red in the face with emotion.

flan *n* an open case of pastry or sponge cake with a sweet or savoury filling.

flange *n* a raised edge on wheel.

flank *n* the fleshy part of the side; from the ribs to the hip; the side of (army, mountain, etc). * *vt* to be at the side of; to menace on the side.

flannel *n* a soft woollen cloth, a small cloth for washing the face; nonsense; equivocation; (*pl*) trousers made of flannel.

flap *n* the beat of wings or a similar sound; anything hanging loose (esp part of a garment); agitation; panic. * *vi, vt* (*pt* **flapped**) to move like wings; to flutter; to panic.

flare *n* a sudden flash; a bright light used as a signal or illumination; a widened part or shape. * *vi* to burn with a sudden, bright, unsteady flame; to widen our gradually.

flash n a sudden gleam; a brief moment, display, news item. * vi, vt to shine out suddenly; to signal.

flashback n an interruption in the continuity of a story etc, by telling or showing an earlier episode.

flashbulb n a small bulb giving an intense light used in photography.

flashlight n a torch.

flash point n the ignition point.

flashy adj gaudy; showy.

flask n a kind of bottle; a vacuum flask.

flat adj level; prostrate; tasteless; below pitch; deflated; dull; tedious; (of battery) drained of electric current. * n a storey or set of rooms in a house.

flatten vt to make flat.

flatter vt to praise unduly or insincerely.

flattery n undeserved praise.

flatulence n wind in the stomach.

flaunt vi, vt to show off.

flautist n a flute player.

flavour n distinctive taste. * vt to season; to give flavour to.

flaw n a crack; a defect.

flax n a plant cultivated for its fibres.

flaxen adj of or like flax; fair; pale yellow.

flay vt to strip off (skin).

flea n a jumping, blood-sucking insect.

fleck n a spot; a streak. * vt to streak.

fledgling n a young bird; a trainee.

flee vi (pt, pp **fled**) to run away from danger, etc; to disappear.

fleece n a sheep's coat. * vt to shear the wool from; to rob; to defraud.

fleet n a squadron of ships; navy; a group of cars, ships, buses under one management. * adj swift; nimble.

fleeting adj transient; passing.

flesh n the soft part of the body; the pulpy part of fruits and vegetables; meat; the body and its appetites.

fleshy adj plump; fat.

flex vt to bend.

flexible adj pliable; supple; adaptable.

flick n a touch with a whip; a flip. * vt to flip; to strike with a flick.

flicker vi to burn unsteadily. * n an unsteady light; a flickering movement.

flight[1] n the act, manner, or power of flying; distance flown; an aircraft scheduled to fly a certain trip; a set of stairs, as between landings.

flight[2] n an act or instance of fleeing.

flighty adj fickle; giddy.

flimsy adj thin; slight; weak; light and thin; unconvincing * n copying paper.

flinch vi to shrink; to quail; to drawback.

fling vb (pt, pp **flung**) vt to hurl; to scatter. * vi to kick out violently; to move quickly or impetuously. * n a throw; a Highland dance.

flint n a hard stone; a pebble.

flinty adj hard; cruel.

flip n a flick. * vt to flick; to flick with the thumb.

flippancy n undue levity; frivolity.

flippant adj saucy; heedless; frivolous.

flirt *vt, vi* to throw or jerk; to make insincere amorous approaches; to trifle or toy e.g. with an idea. * *n* one who toys amorously with the opposite sex.

flit *vi* (*pt* **flitted**) to fly or dart; to vacate premises.

float *n* a cork or other device used on a fishing line to signal that the bait has been taken; a low flat vehicle decorated for exhibit in a parade; a small sum of money available for cash expenditures. * *vt, vi* to rest on the surface of or be suspended in liquid; to put into circulation.

floe *n* floating ice.

flog *vt* (*pt* **flogged**) to whip; to thrash.

flood *n* a deluge; a river; abundance. * *vt* to overflow; to deluge.

floodgate *n* a gate or lock in a waterway.

floodlight *n* a strong beam of light used to illuminate a stage, stadium, etc. * *vt* to illuminate with floodlights.

floodmark *n* high-water mark.

flood tide *n* the rising tide.

floor *n* the inside bottom surface of a room; the bottom surface of anything; as the ocean; a storey in a building; the lower limit, the base. * *vt* to provide with a floor; (*inf*) defeat; (*inf*) to shock, to confuse.

flop *vi* (*pt* **flopped**) to sway or bounce loosely; to move in a heavy, clumsy or relaxed manner; (*inf*) to fail. * *n* a flopping movement; a collapse; (*inf*) a complete failure.

floppy *adj* limp; hanging loosely.

floppy disk *n* a disk of flexible material for storing data in a computer.

flora *n* the plant life of a region or district.

floral *adj* pertaining to flowers.

florid *adj* flowery; ruddy of complexion.

florist *n* a cultivator or seller of flowers.

flotation *n* the act or process of floating; a launching of a business venture.

flotilla *n* a small fleet.

flotsam *n* floating wreckage.

flounce[1] *vi,* to move in an emphatic or impatient manner.

flounce[2] *n* a frill of material sewn to the skirt of a dress. * *vt* to add flounces to.

flounder *n* a flat fish. * *vi* to move awkwardly and with difficulty; to be clumsy in thinking in speaking.

flour *n* the meal of grain.

flourish *vi* to grow luxuriantly; to thrive; to live and work at a specified period. * *vt* to brandish. * *n* showy expression; fanciful stroke of the pen; brandishing.

flout *vt* to disobey openly; to treat with contempt.

flow *vi* to move, as water; to issue; to glide smoothly; to hang loose; to circulate; to be plentiful. * *n* a stream; current.

flow chart *n* a diagram representing the sequence of and relationships between different steps or procedures in a complex process, e.g. manufacturing.

flower *n* the blossom of plants; youth; the prime. * *vi* to blossom; to bloom.

flowery *adj* full of or decorated with flowers; figurative; elaborate of language.

fluctuate *vi* (of prices) to be continually varying in an irregular way; to waver; to be unstable.

fluctuating *adj* varying.

flu *n* influenza.

flue *n* a smoke vent.

fluent *adj* flowing; voluble; able to speak and write a foreign language with ease; articulate; graceful.

fluff *n* light down or nap; a mistake.

fluid *adj* capable of flowing. * *n* that which flows, as water or air.

fluke *n* the barb of an anchor; a lucky stroke; a flat fish; a flattened parasitic worm.

fluoride *n* any of various compounds of fluoride.

flurry *n* a sudden gust of wind, rain or snow; bustle; hurry. * *vt, vi* to (cause to) become flustered.

flush[1] *n* a rapid flow, as of water; sudden, vigorous growth; a sudden excitement; a blush. * *vt, vi* to cause to blush; to excite; to flow rapidly.

flush[2] *vt* to make game birds fly away suddenly.

flush[3] *n* (in poker etc) a hand of cards all of the same suit.

fluster *vt* to agitate; to confuse.

flute *n* an orchestral woodwind instrument with finger holes and keys held horizontally and played through a hole located near one end; a decorative groove. * *vi* to play or make sounds like a flute.

flutter *vi* to flap; to quiver; to beat irregularly or spasmodically (of the heart) * *n* a tremor; stir; nervous excitement; commotion, confusion; (*inf*) a small bet.

fly[1] *n* a two-winged insect; a natural or imitation fly attached to a fishhook as bait.

fly[2] *vi, vt vb* (*pt* **flew**, *pp* **flown**) to move through the air, esp on wings; to travel in an aircraft; to control an aircraft; to take flight, as a kite; to escape, flee from; to pass quickly; (*inf*) to depart quickly. * *n* a flap that hides buttons; a zip, etc, on trousers; material forming the outer roof of a tent.

fly[3] *adj* (*inf*) sly, astute.

flying *adj* capable of flight; fleeing; fast-moving. * *n* the act of flying an aircraft.

flying start *n* a start in a race when the competitor is already moving at the starting line; a promising start.

flyleaf *n* (*pl* **flyleaves**) a blank leaf at the beginning or end of a book.

flyover *n* a bridge that carries a road or railway over another; a fly-past.

fly-past *n* a processional flight of aircraft.

foal *n* young of horse, ass.

foam *n* froth or fine bubbles on the surface of liquid. * *vi* to cause or emit foam.

fob *n* a watch pocket in a trouser waistband. * *vt* (with **off**) to cheat; to put off; to palm off.

focal *adj* belonging to a focus.

focus *n* (*pl* **foci** *or* **focuses**) the point in which reflected rays converge; correct adjustment of the eye or lens to form a clear image; a centre of activity or interest. * vt (pt **focused**) to bring into focus, to concentrate; to adjust the focus of.

fodder n food for cattle.

foe n an enemy.

foetus n the unborn young of an animal, esp in later stages; in humans, the offspring in the womb from the fourth month until birth.

fog n a thick mist; cloudiness on a developed photograph.

foible n a weakness or failing; an idiosyncrasy.

foil vt to frustrate; to baffle. * n defeat; a sword used in fencing; a leaf of metal; a background to set things off.

foist vt to palm off.

fold¹ vt, vi to cover by bending or doubling over so that one part covers another; to interlace (one's arms); to incorporate (an ingredient) into a food mixture by gentle overturning. * n something folded, as a piece of cloth; a crease or hollow made by folding.

fold² n a pen for sheep.

foliage n leaves.

folio n a sheet once folded; a leaf in a ledger; a book of largest size.

folk n people in general; relatives.

folklore n popular tales, songs, etc, of a people.

follow vt, vi to go or come after; to pursue; to accompany; to succeed; to result from; to understand; to practise; to be occupied with.

follower n a disciple or adherent; a person who imitates another.

following n a body of followers, adherents or believers. * adj succeeding; next after; now to be stated.

folly n foolishness; madness; an extravagant or fanciful building serving no practical purpose.

foment vt to stir up strife or agitation.

fond adj tender; loving; doting.

fondle vt to caress.

font n the receptacle for baptismal on holy water; set of type.

food n nourishment; provisions.

fool n a simpleton; a jester; a cold pudding of whipped cream and fruit purée. * vi to trifle. * vt to deceive.

foolhardy adj rash; venturesome.

foolproof adj proof against failure; easy to understand; easy to use.

foolscap n a size of paper.

foot n (pl **feet**) that upon which anything stands; the lower end of the leg; the lower part or edge of something; the bottom; a measure of 12 inches; a group of syllables serving as a unit of metre in verse. * vt to pay; to walk; to dance.

football n a large ball; game played with it by two teams.

foothold n a ledge etc, for placing the foot when climbing etc; a place from which further progress may be made.

footing n foothold; basis; status.

footlights n a row of lights in front of the stage floor.

footpath n a narrow path for pedestrians.

footprint n impression of the foot.

footsore adj having painful feet from excessive walking.

footstep n a track; a footprint.

for prep, because of, as a result of; as the price of, or recompense of; in order to be, to serve as; to quest of; in the direction of; on behalf of; in place of; in favour of; with respect to; in spite of; to the extent of; throughout the space of; during. * conj because.

forage n fodder. * vt to collect or go in search of provisions.

foray vt to pillage. * n a sudden raid.

forbear vi to endure; to avoid. * vt to hold oneself back from.

forbearance n patience; restraint.

forbid vt (pt **forbad** or **forbade**, pp **forbidden**) to prohibit; to oppose.

forbidding adj unfriendly; solemn; strict; repulsive.

force n strength, power, effort; (physics) (the intensity of) an influence that causes movement of a body or other effects; a body of soldiers, police etc prepared for action; effectiveness; violence, compulsion. * vt to compel by physical effort, superior strength etc; to achieve by force; to press or drive against resistance; to produce with effort; to break open; to impose, inflict.

forced adj affected; overstrained.

forceful adj powerful, effective.

forceps n an instrument for grasping and holding firmly, or exerting traction upon objects, esp by jewellers and surgeons.

ford n a crossing place in a river. * vt to wade across.

fore adj in front of; prior. * adv before.

forearm[1] n the arm from elbow to wrist.

forearm[2] vt to arm beforehand.

forebode vt to foretell; to portend.

forecast vt to foresee; to predict events, weather etc through national analysis. * n a prediction.

foreclose vt to preclude; to stop.

forecourt n an enclosed space in front of a building, as in a filling station.

forefathers pl n ancestors.

forefront n the foremost part.

foregoing adj preceding.

foregone adj past; inevitable; preceding.

foreground n the front part of a picture.

forehead n the brow.

foreign adj alien; native belonging to another country; introduces from outside.

foreman n an overseer; the spokesman in a jury.

foremost adj first; chief; most advanced.

forensic adj belonging to or used in courts of law.

forensic medicine n the application of medical expertise to legal and criminal investigations.

forerunner n a herald; precursor.

foresee vt to be aware of beforehand.

foreshadow vt to prophesy; to augur.

foreshore n the shore between high- and low-water marks.

foresight n forethought; provision for the future.

forest n an extensive wood; something resembling this.

forestall vt to prevent by taking action beforehand.

forestry n the science of planting and cultivating forests.

foretaste n a taste beforehand.

forever adv always; eternally.

foreword n a preface to a book.

forfeit vt to lose by fault; to be penalized by forfeit. * n a penalty.

forge¹ n a furnace; a smithy. * vt, vi to shape by heating and hammering; to falsify; to counterfeit a signature, etc.

forge² vt to move steadily forward with effort.

forgery n the fraudulent copying of something; a forged copy.

forget vt (pt **forgot**, pp **forgotten**) to cease to remember.

forgetful adj apt to forget; inattentive.

forget-me-not n a small blue flower.

forgive vt to pardon; to stop feeling resentment. * vi to be merciful or forgiving.

forgiving adj compassionate.

forgo vt to go without; to abstain from.

fork n a small, usu metal, instrument with two or more thin prongs set in a handle, used in eating and cooking; anything that divides into prongs or branches; the point of separation. * vt, vi to divide into branches; to follow a branch of a fork in the road etc.

forklift truck n a vehicle with power-operated prongs for raising and lowering loads.

forlorn adj deserted; hopeless.

form n general structure; the figure of a person or animal; arrangement; a printed document with blanks to be filled in; a class in school; condition of mind or body; changed appearance of a word to show inflection. * vt, vi to shape; to train; to develop (habits); to constitute; to be formed.

formal adj in conformity with established rules or habits; regular; relating to outward appearance only; ceremonial; punctilious; stiff.

formality n accordance with custom.

format n the size, form, shape in which books, etc are issued; the general style or presentation of something; (comput) the arrangement of data on magnetic disk etc of access and storage. * vt to arrange in a particular form, esp for a computer.

formative adj pertaining to formation and development; shaping.

former adj comp past; preceding.

formidable adj terrifying; difficult.

formula n (pl **formulas, formulae**) a set of symbols expressing the composition of a substance; a general expression in algebraic form for solving a problem; a prescribed form; a fixed method according to which something is to be done.

formulate vt to express clearly or in a formula.

forsake vt (pt **forsook**, pp **forsaken**) to abandon; to renounce.

fort n a fortress.

forte adv (mus) loudly. * n a person's strong point.

forth adv forward; abroad.

forthcoming adj about to appear.

forthright adv frank; straightforward; outspoken.

forthwith adv without delay.

fortification n the act of fortifying; defensive works.

fortify vt to strengthen; to erect defences; to add alcohol to.

fortitude n endurance; courage; patience.

fortnight n two weeks.

fortress n a stronghold; a castle.

fortuitous adj chance; accidental.

fortunate adj lucky; prosperous.

fortune n chance; luck; fate; vast wealth; prosperity.

fortune-teller n a person who claims to foretell a person's future.

forum n an assembly or meeting to discuss topics of public concern; a medium for public debate, as a magazine.

forward adv towards the front. * adj in advance, ready; bold; pert. * n a first-line player. * vt to hasten; to advance; to send on.

fossil adj petrified and preserved in rocks. * n petrified remains of plants and animals; an out-of-date person or thing.

foster vt to nourish; to promote; to bring up a child not one's own.

foul adj dirty; filthy; stormy; impure; obscene; contrary to rules. * vt, vi to defile; to dirty; to strike against. * n unfair play.

found vt to lay the base of; to establish; to institute; to cast (in a mould). * vi to rest on.

foundation n an endowment for an institution; such an institution; the base of a house, wall, etc; an underlying principle etc; a supporting undergarment.

founder n an originator; an endower; a moulder of metals. * vi, vt to fill with water and sink; to fall; to collapse.

foundry n a workshop for casting metal.

fount n a set of printing type on characters of one style and size; a source.

fountain n a spring; an artificial jet; source.

fowl n a bird; poultry.

fox n a doglike animal, red-furred and bushy-tailed; a sly person. * vt to deceive by cunning.

fracas n an uproar.

fraction n a small part, amount etc; (math) a quantity less than a whole, expressed as a decimal or with a numerator and denominator.

fractious adj snappish; peevish.

fracture n a break; breaking of a bone. * vt to break.

fragile adj easily broken; frail; delicate.

fragment n a part broken off. * vt, vi to break or cause to break into fragments.

fragmentary adj consisting of fragments; incomplete.

fragrance, fragrancy n a perfume.

fragrant adj sweet-smelling.

frail adj easily broken; weak; fragile.

frame vt to form according to a pattern; to construct; to put into words;

to enclose (a picture) in a border; (*sl*) to falsify evidence against (an innocent person). * *n* something composed of parts fitted together and united; the physical make-up of an animal esp a human body; the case enclosing a window, door etc; an ornamental border, as round a picture; (*snooker*) a single game.

franc *n* the former unit of French currency.

franchise *n* the right to vote in public elections; authorization to sell the goods of a manufacturer in a particular area. * *vt* to grant a franchise.

frank *adj* free and direct in expressing oneself; honest, open. * *vt* to mark letters etc with a mark denoting free postage. * *n* a mark indicating free postage.

frankincense *n* incense; perfume.

frantic *adj* mad; distracted; furious; wild.

fraternal *adj* of or belong to a brother or a fraternity; brotherly; friendly.

fraternity *n* brotherly feeling; a society of people with common interests.

fraternize *vi* to associate as brothers.

fratricide *n* murder of a brother.

fraud *n* criminal deception; a deceitful person; an impostor.

fraudulent *adj* dishonest.

fraught *adj* full of; loaded with.

fray *n* an affray; a fight. * *vt, vi* to wear away or become worn.

freak *n* an unusual happening; (*inf*) a person who dresses or acts in a notably unconventional manner.

freakish *adj* grotesque.

freckle *n* a brownish spot on the skin.

free *adj* not under the control or power of another; having social and political liberty; independent; able to move in any direction; not exact; generous; frank; with no cost or charge; clear of obstruction. * *adj* without cost; in a free manner. * *vt* (*pt* **freed**) to set free.

freedom *n* liberty; privilege; frankness; undue familiarity.

freehand *adj* drawn by hand.

free-handed *adj* generous.

freehold *n* land with no burdens except taxes.

freelance, freelancer *n* a person who pursues a profession without longterm commitment to any employer * *vt* to work as a freelance.

Freemason *n* a member of the secretive fraternity dedicated to mutual aid.

free trade *n* trade based on the unrestricted international exchange of goods with tariffs used only as a source of revenue.

freeway *n* in North America, a fast road, a motorway.

freewheel *vi* to ride a bicycle with the gear disconnected; to drive a car with the gear in neutral.

free will *n* freedom of human beings to make choices that are not determined by prior causes or by divine intervention.

freeze *vi, vt* (*pt* **froze**, *pp* **frozen**) to be formed into, or become covered by ice; to become motionless; to be made speechless by strong emotion; to become formal and unfriendly; to convert from a liquid to a solid with cold.

freezer *n* a container that freezes and preserves food for long periods.

freezing point *n* the temperature at which a liquid solidifies.

freight *n* cargo (ship); load (train); the cost of transport.

freighter *n* a ship or aircraft carrying freight.

French fries, french fries *npl* thin strips of potato fried in oil etc, chips.

French windows, French doors *npl* a pair of floor-length casement windows in an outside wall, opening on to a patio, garden etc.

frenzied *adj* distracted; maddened.

frenzy *n* madness; passion; wild excitement.

frequent *adj* coming, happening often; numerous; common. * *vt* to visit often.

frequency *n* repeated occurrence; the number of occurrences, cycles etc, in a given period.

fresco *n* a painting on plaster while wet or fresh.

fresh *adj* new; brisk; unfaded; not salt; not stale; pure; cool.

freshen *vt* to make fresh. * *vi* to grow fresh.

freshman *n* a novice; newcomer; a student in the first year at a university etc.

fret *vt* to eat into; to vex. * *vi* to be vexed. * *n* irritation; peevishness; one of a series of ridges along the fingerboard of a guitar, banjo etc

used as a guide for depressing the strings.

fretful *adj* peevish; petulant.

fretwork *n* ornamental and perforated woodwork.

friable *adj* easily crumbled.

friar *n* a member of certain RC religious orders.

fricassé *n* a dish of white meat highly seasoned.

friction *n* a rubbing together; resistance offered to moving bodies; unpleasantness; conflict between differing opinions, ideas etc.

Friday *n* the sixth day of the week.

fridge *n* a refrigerator.

friend *n* a close companion; one warmly attached to another; a Quaker.

friendly *adj* kind; well-disposed; favourable. * *n* a sporting game played for fun, not in a competition.

friendship *n* mutual attachment.

frieze *n* a decorative band round the upper part of room walls.

frigate *n* a warship smaller than a destroyer used for escort, anti-submarine, and patrol duties.

fright *n* sudden fear; a shock; something unsightly or ridiculous in appearance.

frighten *vt* to strike with fear; to terrify.

frightful *adj* dreadful; fearful; very bad.

frigid *adj* cold; stiff; formal.

frill *n* a ruffle; a fringe; an affectation.

fringe *n* a decorative border of hanging threads; an outer edge; a marginal or minor part. * *vt* to be or make a fringe fore. * *adj* at the outer edge; additional; minor; unconventional.

frisk *vi* to dance, skip, gambol. * *vt* to search (a person) by feeling or looking for concealed weapons etc.

frisky *adj* jumping with gaiety; lively.

fritter *n* fried batter with fruit; a pancake. * *vt* to trifle away; to waste.

frivolity *n* levity; trifling act, thought or action.

frivolous *adj* trivial; trifling; irresponsible.

frizzle *vi* to curl; to grill with hissing noise.

fro *adv* from; back; backward.

frock *n* an outer garment; dress.

frogman *n* a person who wears a rubber suit, flippers, oxygen supply etc and is trained in working underwater.

frolic *adj* joyous; frisky. * *n* a lively party or game; merriment; a merry prank. * *vi* to gambol.

frolicsome *adj* given to pranks.

from *prep* beginning at, starting with; out of; originating with; out of the possibility or use of.

frond *n* the leaf of a fern.

front *n* a outward behaviour; (*inf*) an appearance of social standing etc; the part facing forward; the first part; the promenade of a seaside resort; the advanced battle area in warfare; a person or group used to hid another's activity.

frontage *n* the front of a building.

frontal *adj* of or belonging to the

front; of the forehead. * *n* a decorative covering for the front of an altar.

frontier *n* the border between two countries; the limit of existing knowledge of a subject.

frontispiece *n* picture facing the title page of a book.

frost *n* a temperature at or below freezing point; a coating of powdery ice particles; coldness of manner. * *vt* to cover (as if) with frost or frosting; to give a frostlike opaque surface to (glass).

frostbite *n* injury or deadening of sensation to a part of the body by excessive cold.

froth *n* foam; bubbles; empty talk; frivolity.

frown *vi* to scowl; to concentrate or look displeased by contracting the brow. * *n* a stern look.

frozen *see* **freeze**.

frugal *adj* careful; thrifty; meagre.

frugality *n* thrift.

fruit *n* the produce of plants; offspring; the outcome or result of any action.

fruitful *adj* producing much fruit; very productive.

fruition *n* fulfilment; realization.

frump *n* a dowdy woman.

frustrate *vt* to balk; to foil; to prevent from achieving a goal or gratifying a desire.

frustration *n* disappointment.

fry *vt* to cook over direct heat in hot fat. * *n* young fish.

fuddle *vt* to stupefy with drink.

fudge *n* a soft sweet made of butter,

milk, sugar, flavouring etc. * *vt, vi* to fake; to fail to come to grips with; to refuse to commit oneself; to cheat.

fuel *n* material burned to supply heat and power, or as a source of nuclear energy; anything that serves to intensify strong feelings. * *vt, vi* (*pt* **fuelled**) to supply with fuel.

fugitive *adj* fleeting; transient. * *n* a runaway; a refugee.

fugue *n* a piece of music in which the theme is taken up by the parts in succession.

fulcrum *n* (*pl* **fulcra** *or* **fulcrums**) the point of support of a lever.

fulfil *vt* (*pt* **fulfilled**) to carry into effect; to carry out a promise; to satisfy; to bring to an end, complete.

fulfilment *n* accomplishment.

full *adj* having or holding all that can be contained; having eaten all one wants; having a great number (of); complete; having reached to greatness size, extent etc. * *adv* completely, directly, exactly.

full-blown *adj* fully developed or expanded.

full stop *n* the punctuation mark (.) at the end of a sentence.

full time *n* the finish of a match.

full-time *adj* working or lasting the whole time.

fully *adv* thoroughly, completely; at least.

fulminate *vi, vt* to thunder; to explode.

fulsome *adj* insincere; excessively, flattering.

fumble *vi* to grope; to handle clumsily.

fume *n* (*often pl*) smoke; vapour; rage. * *vi* to emit smoke; to rage.

fumigate *vt* to purify, disinfect by fumes.

fun *n* merriment; sport; amusement.

function *n* office; duty; work; occupation; an official ceremony or social entertainment. * *vi* to perform work; to act; to operate.

functional *adj* of a function or functions; practical, not ornamental.

fund *n* a stock; money set apart for a special object; a supply. * (*pl*) ready money. * *vt* to provide money for; to invest.

fundamental *adj* basic; essential. * *n* an essential part.

funeral *n* the ceremony associated with the burial or cremation of the dead; a procession accompanying a coffin to a burial.

funereal *adj* dark; dismal.

fungus *n* (*pl* **fungi, funguses**) any of a major group of lower plants, as mildews, mushrooms, yeasts, etc, that lack chlorophyll and reproduce by spores.

funicular *adj* made of ropes. * *n* a cable railway.

funnel *n* a utensil for conveying liquids into bottles; an air or smoke shaft; a metal chimney for the escape of smoke, steam etc. * *vt, vi* to (cause to) pour through a funnel.

funny *adj* droll; comical; puzzling; unwell.

fur *n* the short soft hair of certain animals; a coating.

furious *adj* full of rage; violent.

furl *vt* to roll up a sail.

furlong *n* the eighth of a mile.
furlough *n* leave of absence esp for military personnel.
furnace *n* a fire chamber in which a powerful heat can be raised.
furnish *vt* to provide a room with furniture; to supply; to equip.
furnishing *n pl* furniture, carpets etc.
furniture *n* household effects.
furore *n* excitement; stir.
furrow *n* a trench made by a plough; a wrinkle. * *vt* to groove; to wrinkle.
further *adv* besides; farther; in addition. * *adj* more distant; additional. * *vt* to advance; to promote.
furthermore *adv* moreover; besides.
furthermost *adj* most remote.
furthest *adj, adv* farthest.
furtive *adj* sly; stealthy.
fury *n* rage; frenzy.
fuse *n* a tube or wick filled with combustible material for setting off an explosive charge; a piece of thin wire that melts and breaks when an electric current exceeds a certain level. * *vt* to join or become joined by melting.
fuselage *n* the body of an aircraft.
fusillade *n* a general discharge of rifles.
fusion *n* act of melting; a blending; union; partnership; nuclear fusion.
fuss *n* excited activity; bustle; anxious state. * *vt* to worry over.
fusty *n* musty; mildewed.
futile *adj* serving no useful end; ineffective.
futility *n* uselessness.
future *adj* forthcoming. * *n* time to come; future events; likelihood of eventual success.
futuristic *adj* forward-looking in design, appearance, intention etc.
fuzz *n* fluff.
fuzzy *adj* like fuzz; fluffy; blurred.

G

gab *vi* (*pt* **gabbed**) to chatter. * *n* idle talk.
gabble *vt, vi* to talk or utter rapidly or incoherently; to utter inarticulate or animal sounds.
gable *n* the top of end wall of a house.
gadfly *n* a cattle-biting fly.
gadget *n* a small, often ingenious, mechanical or electronic tool or device.
gag *vb* (*pt* **gagged**) *vt* to stop the mouth; to silence. * *vi* to retch; to tell jokes * *n* something thrust into mouth; any restraint.
gaiety *n* mirth; high spirits, liveliness.
gain *vt, vi* to obtain, earn, esp by effort; to win in a contest; to attract; to get as an addition (esp profit or advantage); to make an increase in; to reach. * *vi* to make progress, to

increase in weight. * *n* an increase, esp in profit or advantage; an acquisition.

gainful *adj* profitable. * *adv* **gainfully**.

gainsay *vt* to contradict; to deny; to dispute.

gait *n* a manner of walking.

gala *n* a celebration; a festival; a festive season.

galaxy *n* any of the systems of stars in the universe; any splendid assemblage; the Milky Way.

gale *n* a strong wind; an outburst.

gall *n* bile; rancour; spite; nutlike growth on oaks. * *vt* to fret; annoy intensely.

gallant *adj* brave; courteous; dignified.

gallantry *n* bravery; courtesy.

gall bladder *n* a membranous sac attached to the liver in which bile is stored.

galleon *n* a Spanish warship.

gallery *n* a covered passage for walking; a long narrow outside balcony; a balcony along the inside wall of a building; (the occupants of) an upper area in a theatre; a long narrow room used for a special purpose, e.g. shooting; a room or building where works of art are shown; the spectators at a golf tournament, etc.

galley *n* a long, low vessel with sails and oars; a shallow tray for type; a proof sheet printed from such type; a ship's kitchen.

galling *adj* bitter; provoking.

gallon *n* measure holding 277.42 cubic inches.

gallop *vi* to go at full speed. * *n* a horse's fastest pace.

gallows *n sing* (*pl* **gallows**) a wooden frame for hanging criminals.

gallstone *n* a small solid mass in the gall bladder.

galore *n* abundance; plenty.

galvanize *vt* to electrify; to electroplate; to stimulate into action.

galvanometer *n* an instrument for measuring electric force.

gambit *n* any action to gain an advantage.

gamble *vi* to play games of chance for money.

gambol *vi* (*pt* **gambolled**) to skip; to frisk. * *n* a frolic.

game *n* sport of any kind; a contest; a scheme; animals and birds hunted for sport or food. * *adj* brave; plucky; willing.

gamekeeper *n* a person who breeds and takes care of game birds and animals.

gaming *n* gambling.

gammon *n* a lower part of cured or smoked ham; nonsense.

gamut *n* the musical scale; the entire range of emotions etc.

gander *n* a male goose.

gang *n* a group of persons, esp labourers, working together; a group of person acting or associating together, esp for illegal purposes. * *vt*, *vi* to form into or act as a gang.

ganglion *n* an enlargement in the course of a nerve.

gangrene *n* death of body tissue when the blood supply is obstructed.

gangster *n* a member of a criminal gang.

gangway *n* a passageway, esp an opening in a ship's side for loading etc; a gangplank.

gaol *see* **jail**.

gap *n* an opening; a breach in a wall, fence etc; an interruption in continuity; an interval; a mountain pass; divergence.

gape *vi* to open the mouth wide; to stare wide-eyed and open-mouthed in astonishment; to yawn.

garage *n* an enclosed shelter for motor vehicles; a place where motor vehicles are repaired and services, and fuel sold. * *vt* to put or keep in a garage.

garb *n* dress; clothes.

garbage *n* waste matter; rubbish.

garble *vt* to tell a confused or jumbled story; to tell only part of truth.

garden *n* an area of ground for growing herbs, fruits, flowers, or vegetables, usu attached to a house; a public park or recreation area, usu laidout with plants and trees. * *vi* to make, or work in, a garden.

gardener *n* one who gardens.

gargle *vt, vi* to rinse the throat by breathing air from the lungs through liquid held in the mouth. * *n* a liquid for this purpose; the sound made by gargling.

gargoyle *n* a grotesquely carved face as a gutter spout.

garish *adj* gaudy; showy.

garland *n* a wreath of flowers.

garlic *n* a bulbous strong-smelling herb.

garment *n* any article of clothing.

garner *vt* to store up.

garnet *n* a precious stone.

garnish *vt* to adorn; to decorate (food).

garret *n* an attic.

garrison *n* the soldiers in a fortress. * *vt* to man with troops.

garrotte, garrote *vt* to throttle or strangle.

garrulous *adj* very talkative.

garter *n* an elasticated band to hold up a stocking or sock.

gas *n* (*pl* **gases**) an air-like substance with the capacity to expand indefinitely and not liquefy or solidify at ordinary temperatures; (*inf*) empty talk; gasoline. * *vt* (*pt* **gassed**) to poison or disable with gas; (*inf*) to talk idly.

gash *vt* to slash; to cut. * *n* a deep cut.

gasket *n* a piece or ring of rubber, metal, etc, sandwiched between metal surfaces to act as a seal.

gasp *vi* to labour for breath; to pant. * *vt* to utter breathlessly.

gastric *adj* belonging to the stomach.

gastronomy *n* the art and science of good eating.

gate *n* a movable structure controlling passage through an opening in a fence or wall; a device (as in a computer) that outputs a signal when specified input conditions are met. * *vt* to supply with a gate.

gatecrash *vt* to arrive at a party, etc, uninvited.

gather *vt, vi* to bring together in one place or group; to collect (taxes); to harvest; to draw (parts) together; to come together in a body; to cluster around a focus.

gathering n an assembly; folds made in a garment by gathering; an abscess.

gauche adj socially inept; graceless; tactless.

gaudy adj showy; flashy.

gauge vt to measure. * n a measuring rod; a measure; distance between rails of a railway; calibre.

gaunt adj emaciated; lean.

gauze n a light transparent cloth; a surgical dressing.

gavotte n a sprightly dance.

gay adj merry; frolicsome; colourful; homosexual.

gaze vi to stare; to contemplate. * n a fixed look.

gazebo n a small dwelling in a garden built to command a wide view.

gazette n a newspaper, esp an official one.

gazetteer n a geographical dictionary.

gazpacho n a cold vegetable soup.

gazump vt, vi to force up a price (esp of a house) after a price has been agreed.

gear n clothing; equipment, esp for some task or activity; a toothed wheel for meshing with another; a specific adjustment of such a system. * vt to connect by or furnish with gears; to adapt (one thing) to confirm with another.

gearbox n a metal case enclosing a system of gears.

gear lever n a lever used to engage or change gear, esp in a motor vehicle.

gelatine n a tasteless, odourless substance extracted by boiling bones, hoofs etc and used in food, medicines etc.

gelding n a castrated male horse.

gem n a precious stone.

Gemini npl the Twins, a sign of the zodiac.

gender n sex, male or female; words, masculine or feminine.

genealogy n family descent; lineage.

general adj not local, special, or specialized; of or for a whole genus, relating to or covering all instances or individuals of a class or group; widespread, common to many; not specific or precise; holding superior rank, chief.

general election n a national election to choose parliamentary representatives in every constituency.

generalize vt, vi to form general conclusions from specific instances; to talk (about something) in general terms.

generally adv in general; popularly; usually.

general practitioner n a non-specialist doctor who treats all types of illnesses in the community.

generate vt to beget; to produce.

generation n the act or process of generating; a single succession in natural descent; people of the same period.

generator n one who or that which generates; a machine that changes mechanical energy to electrical energy.

generic adj pertaining to a genus.

generosity n liberality.

generous adj noble; bountiful.

genesis n origin.

genetic adj relating to origin, development or production; of relating to genes.

genial adj cordial; cheerful; pleasing; warm.

genitals, genitalia npl the external sexual organs.

genius n (pl **geniuses**) outstanding capacity; disposition; one gifted with extraordinary mental power.

genius n (pl **genii**) demon; spirit of place.

genre n portrayal of scenes from ordinary life; a sort or category of work esp literary or autistic.

genteel adj affectedly refined or polite.

gentility n refinement; gentle birth.

gentle adj well-born; refined, mild; hot rough or rude.

gentleman n a man of good birth; a courteous, honourable man.

gentry n well-born people.

genuflection, genuflexion n a bending of the knee.

genuine adj real; true; sincere.

genus n (pl **genera**) a kind; race; class containing several species.

geography n the science of the physical nature of the earth, such as land and sea masses, climate, vegetation etc, and their interaction with the human population; the physical features of a region. * n **geographer, geographic, geographical**.

geology n the science relating to the history and the structure of the earth.

geometric, geometrical adj pertaining to geometry.

geometry n the branch of mathematics dealing with the properties, measurement, and relationships of points, lines, planes and solids.

germ n any microscopic, disease-causing organism; an origin or foundation capable of growing and developing.

germane adj closely allied; relevant.

germinate vi to sprout; to start developing.

gerrymander vt to manipulate in one's own or party interests.

gerund n a verbal noun.

gestate vt to carry (young) in the womb during pregnancy; to develop (a plan etc) gradually in the mind.

gestation n pregnancy.

gesticulate vi, vt to make gestures when speaking.

gesture n an expressive movement of the body or limbs.

get vt, vi (pt **got**, pp **got** or **gotten**) to obtain: to gain; to reach; to become; to catch; to persuade; to cause to be; to prepare; to kill; to understand; to come; to go; to arrive; to manage.

geyser n a hot-water spring; a water heater.

ghastly adj deathlike; hideous.

ghetto n (pl **ghettos**) a section of a city in which members of a minority group live, esp because of social, legal or economic pressure.

ghost *n* a spirit; an apparition; a faint trace or suggestion. * *vt* to ghost write; to write on behalf of another who then gets the credit.

ghoul *n* a spirit said to prey on corpses.

giant *n* a huge legendary being of great strength; a person or thing of great size, strength, intellect etc. * *adj* incredibly large.

gibberish *n* inarticulate talk; nonsense.

gibe *vt* to taunt; to sneer. * *n* a taunt.

giddy *adj* dizzy; fickle; frivolous; flighty.

gift *n* a present; talent; natural ability. * *vt* to endow; to present.

gifted *adj* talented.

gigantic *adj* huge; colossal; immense.

giggle *n* to snigger.

gild *vt* (*pt* **gilded**, *pp* **gilded** *or* **gilt**) to cover with gold; to illuminate.

gill[1] *n* the organ of respiration in fishes.

gill[2] *n* a quarter of a pint.

gilt *n* gilding; a substance used for this..

gimlet *n* a boring tool with screw point.

gimmick *n* a trick or device for attracting notice, advertising or promoting a person, product or service. * *n* **gimmickry**.

gin *n* a spirit flavoured with juniper berries; a pile-driving machine; a snare.

ginger *n* a hot spice; vigour; a reddish-brown colour.

gingerbread *n* a cake flavoured with ginger.

gingerly *adv* cautiously.

gingham *n* a striped or checked cotton cloth.

gipsy same as **gypsy**.

girder *n* a large steel beam for supporting joists, the framework of a building etc.

girdle *n* a belt. * *vt* to encompass.

girl *n* a female child.

girlfriend *n* a female friend, esp with whom one is romantically involved.

girth *n* a saddle strap; the thickness round the waist etc.

gist *n* the essence; the substance of anything.

give *vt* (*pt* **gave**, *pp* **given**) to bestow; to hand over; to deliver; to yield; to utter; to pledge; to act as host.

gizzard *n* the muscular stomach of a bird.

glacial *adj* icy, frozen.

glacier *n* a slowly moving mass of ice on a mountain side.

glad *adj* pleased; cheerful.

gladden *vt, vi* to make or become glad.

glade *n* a clear space in wood.

gladiator *n* a combatant in Roman arenas.

glamour *n* charm; allure; attractiveness; beauty.

glance *vi* to strike obliquely and go off at an angle; to flash; to look quickly.

gland *n* an organ that separates substances from the blood and synthesizes them for further use in, or for elimination from, the body.

glare *n* a dazzling light; a fixed,

fierce stare. * vi to shine brightly; to look fiercely and angrily.

glass n a hard brittle substance, usu transparent; glassware; a glass article, as a drinking vessel; (pl) spectacles or binoculars.

glasshouse n a large greenhouse for the commercial cultivation of plants.

glassware n objects made of glass, esp drinking vessels.

glassy adj smooth; expressionless, lifeless.

glaucoma n an eye disease.

glaze vt, vi to provide (windows etc) with glass; to give a hard glossy finish to (pottery etc); to cover (foods, etc) with a glossy surface.

glazier n one whose business is to set window glass.

gleam n a ray. * vi to flash.

glean vt, vi to gather (after reapers); to pick up.

glee n joy and gaiety; a song in parts for three or more male voices.

glen n a narrow valley.

glib adj speaking or spoken smoothly, to the point of insincerity.

glide vt, vi to move smoothly and effortlessly; to descend in an aircraft or glider with little or no engine power.

glider n an engineless aircraft carried along by air currents.

glimmer vi to give a faint, flickering light; to appear faintly.

glimpse n a brief, momentary view. * vt to catch a glimpse of.

glint n a brief flash of light; a brief indication. * vt, vi to (cause to) gleam brightly.

glisten vi to shine, as light reflected from a wet surface.

glitter vi to sparkle; (usu with **with**) to be brilliantly attractive. * n a sparkle; showiness, glamour; tiny pieces of sparkling material used for decoration.

gloaming n twilight.

gloat vi to feast one's eyes on with evil feelings of satisfaction.

globe n a sphere; a planet; a star; the earth.

globule n a small globe-like particle; a droplet of liquid.

gloom n darkness; deep sadness.

gloomy adj dark; dismal; depressed.

glorify vt to extol; to magnify the worth or importance.

glory n praise; honour; renown; splendour. * vi to rejoice; to exult.

gloss n the lustre of a polished surface; a superficially attractive appearance. * vt to give a shiny surface; (with **over**) to hide (error, etc) or make seem right or inconsequential.

glossary n a list of specialized or technical words and their definitions.

glossy adj smooth and shining; highly polished; superficial; (of magazines) lavishly produced.

glove n a cover for the hand.

glow vi to shine (as if) with an intense heat; to emit a steady light without flames; to be full of life and enthusiasm. * n a light emitted due to intense heat; a steady, even light without flames.

glower *vi* to scowl; to stare sullenly or angrily.

glowworm *n* a beetle that units a greenish luminous light.

glucose *n* a crystalline sugar occurring naturally in fruits, honey etc.

glue *n* a sticky substance used as an adhesive. * *vt* to join with glue.

glum *adj* sullen; moody.

glut *vt* to over supply (the market); to stuff; to gorge. * *n* over abundance.

glutinous *adj* gluey; viscous.

glutton *n* a voracious eater; a person with a great capacity for e.g. work.

gluttony *n* excess in eating.

glycerine *n* a colourless sweet liquid obtained from fats.

gnarl *n* a knot in wood.

gnarled *adj* full of knots; rough and weather-beaten (of hands).

gnash *vt* to grind (the teeth).

gnat *n* a biting insect.

gnaw *vt, vi* to nibble; to bite away bit by bit; to torment as by pain or guilt.

gnome *n* a sprite; a dwarf dwelling in the earth.

go *vi, vt* (*pt* **went**, *pp* **gone**) to move on a course; to proceed; to work properly; to act, sound, as specified; to result; to become; to be accepted or valid; to leave, to depart; to die; to be allotted or sold; to be able to pass (through); to fit (into); to be capable of being divided (into); to undertake (duties etc); to fall asleep; to take place as planned.

goad *n* a spiked stick to prick cattle; a spur; a stimulus to action. * *vt* to urge on, prod; to annoy.

goal *n* the winning post; an objective, aim.

gobble *vt* to gulp; to bolt; to read eagerly.

go-between *n* a messenger, an intermediary.

goblet *n* a drinking cup without handle.

goblin *n* a mischievous or evil sprite.

god *n* any of various beings conceived of as supernatural and immortal, esp a male deity; an idol; a person or thing deified; (*with cap*) in monotheistic religions, the creator and ruler of the universe.

godchild *n* the child a godparent sponsors.

goddaughter *n* a female godchild.

goddess *n* a female deity.

godfather *n* a male godparent.

god-forsaken *adj* desolate, wretched.

godliness *n* piety.

godmother *n* a female godparent.

godparent *n* a person who sponsors a godchild, as at baptism etc, taking responsibility for its faith.

godsend *n* anything that comes unexpectedly when needed or desired.

godson *n* a male godchild.

goggle *vi* to roll the eyes; to stare with bulging eyes. * *adj* bulging. * *npl* large spectacles.

gold *n* a precious yellow metal; coins; jewellery made of this, money; wealth.

golden *adj* made of or relating to fold; bright yellow; priceless; flourishing.

gold leaf *n* gold beaten out thin.

goldsmith n a worker in gold.

golf n an outdoor game in which the player attempts to hit a small ball with clubs around a turfed course into a succession of holes in the smallest number of strokes.

golf course n a tract of land laid out for playing golf.

gondola n a long narrow, black boat used on the canals of Venice; an enclosed car suspended from a cable used to transport passengers, esp skiers up a mountain.

gondolier n a person who rows a gondola.

gong n a disk-shaped percussion instrument struck with a usu padded hammer; (sl) a medal.

good adj having the right or proper qualities; valid; healthy or sound; virtuous, honourable; enjoyable, pleasant etc. * n something good; benefit; something that has economic utility.

goodness n quality of being good.

good sense n sound judgment.

good-tempered adj good-natured.

goodwill n benevolence; the established custom and reputation of a business.

gore n (clotted) blood; a gusset in material to shape a garment. * vt to wound with tusk or horn.

gorge n the throat; a very narrow pass. * vt to eat greedily and overmuch.

gorgeous adj splendid; strikingly attractive; brightly coloured.

gory adj bloody.

gospel n the teaching of Jesus Christ; the story of his life as written by Matthew, Mark, Luke or John; any complete system of beliefs; the truth; religious music in a popular style.

gossamer n cobweb-like threads in the air or on bushes; any very flimsy material.

gossip n a tattler; idle talk about others. * vt to tattle.

Gothic adj in the pointed-arch style of architecture of the Middle Ages; dark, supernatural, grotesque.

gouge n a chisel with a grooved blade. * vt to scoop out.

gourd n a general name for melon-like plants; a drinking vessel.

gourmand n a glutton.

gourmet n a fastidious eater.

gout n a disease affecting joints, esp the big toe.

govern vt to rule; to regulate; to influence the action of.

government n the exercise of authority over a state, organization etc; a system of ruling, political administration, etc; those who direct the affairs of a state, etc.

governor n a person appointed to govern a province, etc; the elected head of any state of the US.

gown n a loose outer garment; a woman's formal dress, a night-gown, a long, flowing robe worn by judges, etc; a type of overall worn in the operating room.

grab vt (pt **grabbed**) to seize; to snatch; to catch the interest or attention.

grace n favour; kindness; divine influence; mercy; a title; beauty of form or movement; ease of manner; short prayer before meals. * *vt* to adorn; to dignify.

graceful *adj* elegant.

gracious *adj* having or showing kindness, courtesy etc; compassionate; polite to supposed inferiors.

gradation *n* arrangement step by step.

grade *n* a stage or step in a progression; a group of people of the same rank, merit etc; the degree of slope; a sloping part; a mark or rating in an examination.

gradient *n* degree of ascent or descent, in a road; a sloping road or railway.

gradual *adj* slow and regular.

graduate *vt, vi* to mark off into degrees; to receive a university degree. * *n* a recipient of a degree.

graduation *n* act of marking with degrees; the conferring or receiving of university degrees.

graft *n* a shoot inserted in another plant; the transplanting of skin, bone etc. * *vt* to insert such a shoot; to join organically.

grain *n* the seed of any cereal plant, as wheat, etc; cereal plants; a tiny, solid particle, as of salt or sand; the arrangement of fibres, layers etc of wood, leather, etc.

gram *n* the basic unit of weight in the metric system, equal to one thousandth of a kilogram (one 28th of an ounce).

grammar *n* the study of the correct use of language; the rules for speaking and writing a language; a grammar textbook.

gramophone *n* an instrument that recorded and reproduced sounds; forerunner of the record player.

granary *n* a storehouse for grain.

grand *adj* noble; magnificent; imposing; important; illustrious; comprehensive.

grandeur *n* greatness; splendour.

grandfather *n* a father's or mother's father.

grandiloquence *n* pompous language.

grandiose *adj* imposing; bombastic.

grandmother *n* a mother's or father's mother.

grand piano *n* a large piano with a horizontal harp-shaped case.

granite *n* a hard igneous rock; firmness and endurance.

grant *vt* to bestow; to confer on; to admit as true; to cede. * *n* a gift; money or a gift granted for a particular purpose; a conveyance in writing.

granular *adj* consisting of grains.

granulate *vt, vi* to form into grains.

granule *n* a little grain.

grape *n* the juicy purple or green berry fruit of the vine growing in clusters.

graph *n* a diagram representing successive changes in the value of a variable quantity or quantities.

graphic, graphical *adj* described in realistic detail; pertaining to a graph, lettering, drawing, painting etc.

grapple *vt, vi* to seize; to wrestle.

grasp vt, vi to grip; to lay hold of; to understand. * n a grip; reach; comprehension.

grasping adj avaricious; greedy.

grass n any of a large family of plants with jointed stems and long narrow leaves, including cereals, bamboo etc; such plants grown as lawn; pasture.

grate n a frame of metal bars for holding fuel in a fireplace; a grating * vt to grind into particles by scraping; to rub against (an object) or grind (the teeth) together with a harsh sound; to irritate.

grateful adj pleasing; gratifying; appreciative.

grater n a grinding-down utensil.

gratification n pleasure; enjoyment.

gratify vt to please; delight; to indulge.

grating n a frame of bars. * adj harsh; irritating.

gratis adv without charge.

gratitude n thankfulness for favours, gifts received.

gratuitous adj free of charge; unjustified.

gratuity n a free gift; a tip.

grave[1] adj weighty; serious; solemn; sombre.

grave[2] n a hole dug in the ground for burying the dead; a tomb.

gravel n small pebble; a disease of the kidneys.

gravitate vt, vi to tend towards the centre.

gravity n the force drawing bodies towards the centre of the earth; seriousness.

gravy n meat juice.

graze vt, vi to rub lightly; to scrape (the skin) slightly; to scratch; to eat grass; to supply grass.

grease n fat in a soft state. * vt to smear with grease; to lubricate.

great adj large; eminent; noble; chief; intense; excellent; skilful.

greatness n eminence; grandeur.

greed n avarice; excessive hunger or desire for food, money etc.

greedy adj ravenous; grasping; voracious.

green adj grass-coloured; fresh; not ripe; in experienced; naive; environmentally conscious; jealous. * n a grassy plot; the colour of grass; a mixture of blue and yellow.

greengrocer n a dealer in vegetables and fruit.

greenhouse n a glass house for rearing plants.

greenroom n a theatre retiring room.

greet vt to salute; to welcome; to address in a friendly way.

gregarious adj living in flocks; sociable; fond of company.

grenade n a small bomb thrown manually or projected (as by a rifle or special launcher).

grey n a neutral colour between black and white; something, esp an animal of a grey colour. * adj of a grey colour; grey-haired; dreary; vague; indeterminate.

grid n a grating; an electrode for controlling the flow of electrons in an electron tube; a network of squares on a map used for easy reference; a national network of transmission lines, pipes, etc, for electricity, water, gas, etc.

griddle n a flat iron plate for baking scones etc.

grief n sorrow; deep distress.

grievance n injustice; hardship; a cause for complaint.

grieve vt, vi to deplore; to mourn.

grievous adj heavy; distressing.

grill vt to cook by direct heat using a grill; (inf) to question relentlessly. * n a device on a cooker that radiates heat downward for grilling; grilled food; a grille; a grillroom.

grille n an open grate forming a screen.

grillroom n a restaurant that specializes in grilled food.

grim adj stern; unyielding; forbidding.

grimace n a contortion of the face.

grime n soot, dirt. * vt to dirty; to soil or befoul.

grimy adj foul; dirty.

grin vi to laugh through the teeth. * n a broad, friendly smile.

grind vt (pt, pp **ground**) to reduce to powder or fragments by crushing; to wear down, sharpen, or smooth by friction.

grip n a grasp; a handle. * vt, vi to grasp, clutch.

gripe vt, vi to grasp; to pinch; to complain. * n a clutch.

grisly adj dreadful; terrifying.

gristle n cartilage esp in meat.

grit n coarse particles of sand; stubborn or resolute courage or firmness. * vt to clench the teeth; to spread grit esp on icy roads.

grizzled adj greyish.

groan vi to moan. * n a deep moan.

grocer n a merchant who deals in food and household supplies.

grog n a mixture of spirits and cold water.

groggy adj dazed and unsteady.

groin n the junction of the trunk and thighs in front.

groom n one who tends horses; a bridegroom. * vt to clean and care for animals; to make heat and tidy; to train someone for a specific purpose.

groove n a long hollow; a rut, a spiral track in a gramophone record for the stylus; a settle routine. * vt to furrow or to make a groove in.

grope vi to search about blindly as in the dark; to search uncertainly for a solution to a problem. * vt to find by feeling; (sl) to fondle sexually.

gross adj thick; coarse; obscene; shameful; whole. * n 12 dozen; the whole; the total without deduction.

grotesque adj distorted or fantastic in appearance, shape, etc; absurdly incongruous.

grotto n a picturesque cave.

ground n the solid surface of the earth; soil; the connection of an electrical conductor with the earth.

grounding n basic general knowledge of a subject.

groundwork n basis; foundation.

group n a number of persons or things considered as a collective unit; two or more figures forming one artistic design. * vt, vi to form into a group or groups.

grouse n a game bird. * vt to complain.

grout n coarse meal; mortar.

grove n a small wood.

grovel vi to crawl; to prostrate or abase oneself.

groveller n an abject wretch.

grow vb (pt **grew**, pp **grown**) vi to increase; to make progress; to become; to develop; to accrue. * vt to produce; to raise; to cultivate.

growl vi to snarl; to make a rumbling noise as an angry animal. * vt to speak in a growling voice. * n a growling sound; a grumble.

grown-up adj adult.

growth n the act or process of growing; progressive increase, development; something that grows or has grown; an abnormal formation of tissue, as a tumour.

grub vi, vt to dig; to root out; to work hard. * n the larva of an insect.

grubby adj dirty, soiled.

grudge vi, vt to envy; to give unwillingly. * n ill-will; envy; resentment.

gruel n food made by boiling meal in water.

gruelling adj severely testing; exhausting.

gruesome adj repulsive; causing horror.

gruff adj surly; harsh; hoarse.

grumble vi to mutter with discontent.

grumpy adj surly; gruff; bad-tempered.

grunt vi to make a noise like a hog.

guarantee n a pledge or security for another's debt or obligation; a pledge to replace something substandard etc; an assurance that something will be done as specified.

guarantor n a person who gives a guaranty or guarantee.

guard vt, vi to watch over; to defend. * n defence; protector; sentinel; attention.

guarded adj circumspect; discreet.

guardian n a custodian; a person legally in charge of a minor or someone incapable of taking care of their own affairs.

guerrilla n a member of a force of irregular soldiers, usually biased politically, in conflict with regulars on police etc.

guess vt to form an opinion of or state with little or no factual knowledge; to judge correctly by doing this; to think or suppose. * n an estimate based on guessing.

guest n a person entertained at the home, club etc of another; any paying customer of a hotel, restaurant; a performer appearing by special invitation.

guesthouse n a private home or boarding-house offering accommodation.

guide vt to point out the way for; to lead; to direct the course of; to control. * n a person who leads or directs others.

guidebook n a book containing directions and information for tourists.

guided missile n a military missile whose course is controlled by radar or internal instruments etc.

guide dog *n* a dog trained to guide people who are blind.

guild *n* a society for mutual aid.

guile *n* wiliness; deceit.

guillotine *n* an instrument for beheading persons; a machine for cutting paper. * *vt* to execute by guillotine.

guilt *n* the fact of having done a wrong or committed an offence; a feeling of self-reproach from believing one has done a wrong.

guilty *adj* criminal; wicked; feeling guilt.

guinea pig *n* a person or thing subject to an experiment.

guise *n* an external appearance, aspect; an assumed appearance, pretence.

guitar *n* a musical instrument having six strings and is plucked with the fingers.

gulf *n* an arm of the sea; a bay; a chasm.

gull *n* a long-winged sea bird.

gullet *n* the throat; the food passage from the mouth.

gully *n* watercourse cut out by heavy rain.

gulp *vt* to swallow eagerly. * *n* a mouthful.

gum *n* the firm tissue surrounding the teeth; the sticky substance found in some trees.

gumption *n* shrewd good sense.

gun *n* a weapon with a metal tube from which a projectile is discharged by an explosive.

gunman *n* an armed gangster; a hired killer.

gun-metal *n* an alloy of copper and tin formerly used for cannon.

gunner *n* a soldier etc, who helps fire artillery; a naval warrant officer in charge of a ship's gun.

gunpowder *n* an explosive mixture used for blasting etc.

gunwale, gunnel *n* the upper edge of a ship's side.

gurgle *vi* to flow with a bubbling sound; to utter this sound.

gush *vi* to rush out; to be effusively sentimental in speech or writing.

gushing *adj* rushing forth; effusive.

gusset *n* a triangular piece of cloth inserted in a garment to strengthen or widen.

gust *n* a sudden blast of wind; an outburst.

gut *n* the intestine; (*pl*) entrails; courage; daring * *vt* to remove entrails.

gutter *n* a water channel below eaves or at the roadside. * *vt* (candle) to melt unevenly.

gutter press *n* newspapers that concentrate on the sensational in their coverage.

guttural *adj* throaty. * *n* a throat sound, as g.

guy *n* a rope to steady anything; an effigy of Guy Fawkes; (*inf*) a man or boy; (*inf*) men or women.

guzzle *vi, vt* to swallow greedily.

gymnasium *n* (*pl* **gymnasia, gymnasiums**) a place for athletic exercises.

gymnast *n* a gymnastic expert.

gymnastics *npl* athletic exercises; training in these.

gynaecology *n* the branch of medicine dealing with disorders of the female reproductive system.

gypsy *n* a member of a travelling people, originally from India.

gyrate *vi* to rotate, to whirl.

gyration *n* a whirling round.

gyrfalcon *n* a large northern falcon, often used for hunting.

gyroscope *n* a wheel mounted in a ring so that its axis is free to turn in any direction.

H

haberdasher *n* a seller of cloth, etc.

habit *n* usage; custom; a distinctive costume or dress.

habitable *adj* that may be inhabited.

habitat *n* the natural abode.

habitation *n* abode; residence.

habitual *adj* customary; usual.

habituate *vt* to accustom; to inure.

habitué *n* a regular frequenter.

hack *n* a hired horse; a worn-out horse; a mediocre writer; a coach for hire. * *vt* to gash; to kick; to ride a horse cross-country. * *adj* banal; hackneyed.

hackneyed *adj* much used; trite.

haemorrhage *n* the escape of blood from a blood vessel; heavy bleeding. * *vi* to bleed heavily.

haemorrhoids *npl* piles.

haft *n* the handle of an axe, etc.

hag *n* an ugly old woman.

haggard *adj* wild-looking; gaunt.

haggis *n* a dish of heart, liver, etc, of sheep minced and boiled in the stomach sac.

haggle *vt* to drive a hard bargain; to barter.

hail *n* frozen rain; a call. * *vi*, *vt* to rain hail; to call to; to greet or wel-come with approval; to acclaim; to originate from.

hair *n* a threadlike covering on the skin of mammals; a mass of hair growing on the human head, etc.

hairdresser *n* a person who cuts, styles, colours, etc, hair.

hairpiece *n* an additional piece of hair attached to a person's real hair.

hairpin bend *n* a sharply curving bend in a road, etc.

hair-raising *adj* terrifying, shocking.

hair's-breadth *n* a minute distance.

hair-splitting *n* making fine distinctions.

hairstyle *n* an arrangement of the hair in a certain way.

hairy *adj* covered in hair; difficult; dangerous.

halcyon *adj* calm; peaceful.

hale *adj* sound; robust. * *vt* to drag by force.

half *n* (*pl* **halves**) one of two equal parts.

half-brother *n* a brother by one parent only.

half-caste *n* one born of parents of different races.

half-hearted *adj* lukewarm.

half-sister n a sister by one parent only.

hall n a large public room; the entrance passage of house.

hallmark n a mark used on gold, etc, articles to signify a standard of purity; a characteristic feature. * vt to stamp with a hallmark.

hallucination n the apparent perception of sights, sounds, etc, that are not actually present; something perceived in this manner.

halo n circle of light round sun or moon; a symbolic disc round the head of a saint.

halt vi, vt to hesitate; to stop; to cease marching. * n a limp; stoppage on a march; a minor station on a railway line.

halve vt to divide into two equal parts.

halyard n a line for handling sails.

ham n the thigh of a pig salted and dried; an actor who overacts; a licensed amateur radio operator. * vt (pt **hammed**) to overact; to speak or move in an exaggerated way.

hamburger n ground beef; a cooked patty of such meat, often in a bread roll with pickle, etc.

hamlet n a small village.

hammer n a tool for driving nails, etc. * vt, vi to beat or forge; to defeat utterly.

hammock n a swinging bed of cloth or netting suspended by the ends.

hamper n a large basket. * vt to hinder; to interfere; to encumber.

hamstring n a tendon behind the knee. * vt to lame by cutting.

hand n the part of the arm below the wrist, used for grasping; a side or direction; possession or care; control; an active part; a promise to marry; skill; one having a special skill; handwriting; applause; help; a hired worker; a source; one of a hip's crew; anything like a hand, as a pointer on a clock; the breadth of a hand, four inches when measuring the height of a horse; the cards held by a player at one time; a round of card play.

handbag n a woman's small bag for carrying personal items.

handbook n a textbook; a manual.

handcuff n a fetter; a manacle.

handful n as much as the hand will hold; a small quantity or number; a person difficult to control.

handicap n an allowance in sporting contests to make the chances more equal for the competitors; a mental or physical impairment. * vt to give a handicap to; to hinder.

handicraft n manual skill.

handiwork n product of one's own labour.

handkerchief n a cloth for blowing the nose.

handle vt to feel, use, or hold with the hand; to deal with; to manage; to buy and sell goods. * n the part of anything designed to be held by the hand.

handsome adj good-looking; dignified; genius.

handwriting n manner of writing.

handy adj expert; convenient; ready; near.

hang vt, vi (pt **hung**) to suspend; to attach by hinges to allow to swing freely; to dangle; to fix up; to exhibit works of art; (pt **hanged**) to execute.

hangar n a shelter for aircraft.

hanger n a device on which something is hung, e.g. clothes.

hanger-on n (pl **hangers-on**) a dependent; a parasite.

hang-glider n an unpowered aircraft consisting of a metal frame over which a lightweight material is stretched, with a harness for the pilot suspended below.

hangman n a public executioner.

hangover n the unpleasant after-effects of excessive consumption of alcohol; something surviving from an earlier time.

hang-up n an emotional preoccupation with something.

hank n a skein of yarn, etc.

hanker vi to desire longingly.

hansom n a two-wheeled cab.

haphazard adj chance; random.

hapless adj unlucky; unhappy.

happen vi to take place; to occur.

happy adj pleased; lucky; joyous.

harangue n a speech; a tirade.

harass vt to plague; to vex; to imitate; to trouble an enemy by constant attacks.

harbour n a shelter; a haven; an inlet for anchoring ships. * vt to shelter; to nurse in the mind secretly.

hard adj firm; solid; difficult to understand, accomplish, bear; painful; unfeeling; harsh; grasping; (of drugs) addictive and injurious; (of currency) stable in value; (of news) definite, not speculative; (of drink) alcoholic. * adv fast; with difficulty; earnestly; with concentration.

hardback n a book bound with a stiff cover.

hardboard n a stiff board made of compressed wood chips.

hard cash n payment in coins and notes as opposed to cheque, etc.

harden vt, vi to make hard; to inure; to be unfeeling.

hardhearted adj pitiless.

hardihood n boldness; audacity.

hardly adv scarcely; barely; with difficulty; not to be expected.

hard sell n an aggressive selling technique.

hardship n privation; injustice.

hardware n common metal articles, e.g. tools, etc; the mechanical and electronic components in a computer system.

hardy adj bold; intrepid; able to withstand exposure or emotional hardship.

hare n a long-eared mammal.

harebell n a blue, bell-shaped flower; the Scottish bluebell.

harebrained adj giddy; heedless.

harelip n a congenital deformity of the upper lip in the form of a vertical fissure.

harem n apartments for Muslim women; the women themselves.

haricot n a kidney bean; a stew of meat and vegetables.

hark vi to listen.

harlequin n a well-known comic

pantomime figure; a comic; a buffoon.

harlequinade n buffoonery.

harlot n a prostitute.

harm n hurt; damage; evil. * vt to injure.

harmful adj hurtful.

harmless adj not likely to cause harm.

harmonic adj pertaining to harmony; musical. * n a secondary tone; overtone.

harmonica n a small wind instrument that produces tones when air is blown or sucked across a series of metal reeds; a mouth-organ.

harmonics n the science of harmony.

harmonious adj melodious; friendly.

harmonium n a wind instrument resembling a small organ.

harmonize vi, vt to be in, or bring into, or sing in harmony.

harmony n musical concord; accord; agreement in action, ideas, etc.

harness n the leather straps and metal pieces by which a horse is fastened to a vehicle, plough, etc; any similar fastening or attachment, e.g. for a parachute, hang-glider. * vt to put a harness on; to control so as to use the power of.

harp n a stringed musical instrument.

harpoon n a barbed whaling spear.

harpsichord n a stringed instrument with keyboard resembling a grand piano.

harridan n a bad-tempered hag; a nag.

harrow n a large rake for breaking ploughed ground * vt to draw a harrow over; to cause mental distress to.

harrowing adj distressing.

harry vt to harass; to worry; pillage; to plunder.

harsh adj grating; rough; jarring on the senses or feeling; rigorous, cruel.

hart n a stag or male deer.

harum-scarum adj harebrained.

harvest n the reaping season; the crop reaped; the fruit of labour. * vt to reap; to win; to achieve.

hash vt to chop; to mince. * n a dish of minced meat.

hashish n resin derived from the leaves and shoots of the hemp plant, smoked or chewed as an intoxicant.

hasp n a clasp for a staple.

hassock n a footstool.

haste n speed; hurry. * vt to hurry.

hasten vt, vi to haste; to accelerate.

hasty adj speedy; rash; precipitate.

hat n a head covering.

hatch vt to produce (young) from eggs; to contrive; to devise. * n a brood; a trap door; a door or opening on an aircraft; an opening in a ship's deck.

hatchback n a sloping rear end on a car with a door; a car of this design.

hatchet n a small axe.

hatchment n the coat of arms of a deceased person.

hatchway n an opening in a ship's deck covered with hatches.

hate vt to detest; to abhor. * n great dislike; the person or thing hated.

hateful adj odious.

hatred n great dislike.

hatter n a seller of hats.

haughty adj proud and disdainful; arrogant.

haul vt to pull; to drag. * n a catch (of fish, etc); the distance over which something is transported.

haulage n the transport of commodities; the charge for hauling.

haunch n the hip; the thigh.

haunt vt to frequent; to recur repeatedly to; to appear habitually as a ghost. * n a resort; a place often visited.

haunted adj visited by apparitions.

hauteur n a haughty manner.

have vt (pres t **has**, pres p **having**, pt, pp **had**) to have in one's possession; to possess as an attribute; to hold in the mind; to experience; to give birth to; to allow or tolerate; to arrange or hold; to engage in; to cause, compel or require to be; to be obliged.

haven n a harbour; a shelter.

haversack n a canvas bag similar to a knapsack but worn over ones shoulder.

havoc n widespread destruction or disorder; devastation.

hawk n a bird of prey; an aggressive or ruthless person. * vt to hunt with hawks; to carry about for sale.

hawser n a small cable.

hawthorn n a thorny tree or shrub with pink or white flowers and no berries.

hay n grass cut and dried for fodder.

hay fever n an allergic reaction to pollen causing irritation of the nose and eyes.

hazard n risk; venture; obstacle on the golf course. * vt to risk.

hazardous adj perilous; risky.

haze n vapour; mist; smoke; slight vagueness.

hazel n a tree with edible nuts.

hazy adj obscure; dim; vague.

he pron of the third person. * n a male person.

head n the part of an animal or human body containing the brain, eyes, ears, nose and mouth; the top part of anything; the foremost part; the chief person; (pl) a unit of counting; the striking part of a tool; mind; understanding; the topic of a chapter, etc; crisis, conclusion; pressure of water, steam, etc; the source of a river, etc; froth, as on beer.

headache n pain in the head.

headgear n covering for the head.

heading n something forming the head, top or front; the title, topic, etc, of a chapter, etc; the direction in which a vehicle is moving.

headland n a cape; a promontory.

headlight, headlamp n a light at the front of a vehicle.

headline n printed lines at the top of a newspaper article giving the topic; a brief news summary.

headlong adj with the head first; with uncontrolled speed or force; rashly.

head-on adj with the head or front foremost; without compromise.

headquarters n the centre of operations of one in command, as in an army; the main office in any organization.

headstrong *adj* obstinate; determined to do as one pleases.

headway *n* progress or success.

heady *adj* rash; hasty.

heal *vt* to make sound or healthy; to cure.

health *n* a sound state of body or mind.

healthy *adj* hale; sound; beneficial.

heap *n* a mass; a pile. * *vt* to amass; to pile.

hear *vt, vi* (*pt, pp* **heard**) to perceive by the ear; to listen; to learn; to conduct a legal hearing.

hearing *n* one of the five senses; attention; opportunity to be heard.

hearing aid *n* a small electronic amplifier worn behind the ear to improve hearing.

hearken *vi* to give good heed to.

hearsay *n* report; rumour.

hearse *n* a car for conveying a coffin.

heart *n* the organ that propels the blood; the centre of life; the kernel; the seat of affections and passions; spirit; strength; courage; (*pl*) a suit of playing cards marked with a heart-shaped symbol.

heartache *n* sorrow; anguish.

heartbeat *n* the rhythmic contraction and dilation of the heart.

heartbreak *n* overwhelming sorrow or grief.

heartbroken *adj* overwhelmed by grief.

heartburn *n* a burning sensation in the lower chest.

hearten *vt* to encourage.

heartfelt *adj* sincere.

hearth *n* the floor of the fireplace; the fireside; home.

heartless *adj* unfeeling.

heartsease, heart's-ease *n* the pansy.

hearty *adj* warm; cordial; keen; unrestrained, as laughter; healthy; plentiful.

heat *n* energy produced by molecular agitation; the quality of being hot; the perception of hotness; hot weather or climate; strong feeling, esp anger, etc; a single bout, round, or trial in sports; the period of sexual excitement and readiness for mating in female animals. * *vt, vi* to make or become warm or hot; to make or become excited.

heath *n* a waste or shrub-covered tract of land; heather.

heathen *n* a pagan an irreligious or uncivilized person.

heather *n* an evergreen flowering shrub with purple or white flowers, found on moors or mountains.

heating *n* a system of providing heat, as central heating; the warmth provided.

heat wave *n* a prolonged period of hot weather.

heave *vt, vi* (*pt, pp* **heaved**) to lift; to move upward; to utter; to swell; (*of ship*) (*pt, pp* **hove**) to come to a stop. * *n* an upward throw.

heaven *n* the sky; the abode of God; bliss.

heaviness *n* weight; gloom.

heavy *adj* weighty; sad; drowsy; hard to do; clumsy; dull; serious; grievous; (*of soil*) clayey.

heavyweight *n* a professional boxer weighing more than 175 pounds (29 kg) or wrestler weighing over

209 pound (95 kg); (*inf*) an influential or important individual.

hebdomadal *adj* weekly.

Hebrew *n* a member of an ancient Semitic people; an Israelite; a Jew; the ancient Semitic language of the Hebrews; its modern form.

heckle *n vt* to harass a speaker with questions or taunts.

hectic *adj* feverish; involving intense excitement or activity.

hector *vt* a bully; to bluster.

hedge *n* a fence consisting of a dense line of bushes or small trees; a barrier or means of protection against something, esp financial loss; an evasive or non-committal answer or statement. * *vt* to surround or enclose with a hedge; to place secondary bets as a precaution.

hedgehog *n* a small prickly insectivorous mammal.

hedonism *n* the doctrine that pleasure is the chief good.

heed *vt* to attend to; to notice. * *n* care; attention.

heedless *adj* inattentive; negligent.

heel *n* the hind part of the foot; the part of a sock or shoe covering the heel; a despicable person. * *vt* to add a heel to; (*of ships*) to tilt; (*football*) to strike with the heel.

hefty *adj* heavy; large and strong; big.

Hegira *n* the flight of Mohammed from Mecca, AD 622.

heifer *n* a young cow that has not calved.

height *n* the distance from top to bottom; eminence; elevation; a hill.

heighten *vt* to raise higher or more intense.

heinous *adj* flagrant.

heir *n* one who inherits.

heiress *n* a female heir.

heirloom *n* any possession which descends from generation to generation.

helicopter *n* a kind of aircraft lifted and moved, or kept hovering, by large rotary blades mounted horizontally.

heliograph, heliostat *n* a signalling apparatus for reflecting sun's rays.

heliotrope *n* the bloodstone; a garden plant with blue flowers.

helium *n* a gaseous element.

helix *n* (*pl* **helices**) a wire coil.

hell *n* the abode of the wicked after death; any place or state of extreme misery or pain.

Hellenism *n* a Greek idiom; Greek culture.

hellish *adj* pertaining to hell; very wicked; very unpleasant.

hello *interj* an expression of greeting. * *n* the act of saying 'hello'.

helm *n* a rudder, the steering wheel on a ship; management; authority.

helmet, helm *n* head armour.

helmsman *n* the man who steers a ship.

help *vt* to make things better or easier for; to aid; to assist; to remedy; to keep from; to serve or wait on. * *n* the action of helping; aid; assistance; a remedy; a person that helps, esp a hired person.

helpful *adj* giving help; useful.

helpless *adj* unable to manage alone,

dependent on others; weak and defenceless.

helpmate *n* an assistant; a wife.

helter-skelter *adv* in disorder. * *n* a fairground spiral slide.

hem *n* the border of a garment. * *vt* to form a hem; (*with* **in**) to enclose; to confine.

hemisphere *n* a half sphere; half the earth.

hemlock *n* a poisonous plant.

hemp *n* a widely cultivated Asian herb of the mulberry family; its fibre, used to make rope, sailcloth, etc; a narcotic drug obtained from different varieties of this plant.

hen *n* a female bird (esp the domestic fowl).

henbane *n* a poisonous herb.

hence *adv* from this place; time, reason.

henceforth *adv* from now on.

henceforward *adv* henceforth.

henchman *n* a trusted supporter.

henpecked *adj* ruled by one's wife.

hepatic *adj* pertaining to the liver.

heptagon *n* a seven-sided figure.

heptarchy *n* a government, or parts governed, by seven persons.

Heptateuch *n* the first seven books of the Old Testament.

her *pron* the possessive and objective case of she.

herald *n* a king's messenger; a person who conveys news or messages; a forerunner. * *vt* to proclaim; to usher in.

heraldry *n* the study of genealogies and coats of arms; ceremony; pomp.

herb *n* a plant whose stem dies yearly; any plant used medicinally or as seasoning.

herbaceous *adj* descriptive of fleshy as opposed to woody plants.

herbal *n* a book treating of herbs.

herbalist *n* one skilled in herbs.

herbarium *n* (*pl* **herbariums, herbaria**) a collection of dried plants.

herbivorous *adj* herb-eating.

herd *n* a large number of animals, esp cattle, living and feeding together. * *vt, vi* to assemble or move animals together.

here *adv* in this place; now; on earth.

hereabout, hereabouts *adv* about this place.

hereafter *adv* after this time. * *n* (*with* **the**) the future; life after death.

hereby *adv* by this means; near.

hereditary *adj* descending by inheritance; transmitted to offspring.

heredity *n* the transmission of genetic material that determines physical and mental characteristics from one generation on to another.

heresy *n* a belief contrary to accepted beliefs or doctrines.

heretic *n* one guilty of heresy.

heritable *adj* transmissible.

heritage *n* something inherited at birth; anything deriving from the past or tradition; historical sites, traditions, practices, etc, regarded as the valuable inheritance of contemporary society.

hermaphrodite *adj* being of both sexes. * *n* a flower with both stamens and pistils.

hermetic, hermetical *adj* airtight.

hermit *n* a recluse.

hermitage *n* a hermit's abode.

hernia *n* a rupture esp of part of the intestine.

hero *n* a brave man; the chief character in a play or novel or film.

heroine *n* a woman with the attributes of a hero; the leading female character in a play, novel, etc.

heroism *n* the qualities or conduct of a hero; magnanimity; bravery; valour.

heron *n* a wading bird with long legs and neck.

heronry *n* a place where herons breed.

herring *n* a small migratory sea fish.

hers *pron possessive* used only when no noun follows; belonging to her.

herself *pron* emphatic and reflexive form of she and her.

hesitancy *n* a hesitating.

hesitate *vi* to pause; to be uncertain or undecided; to falter; to stammer.

heterogeneous *adj* mixed; diverse.

hew *vb* (*pp* **hewed** *or* **hewn**) *vt* to cut; chop; hack; to shape. * *vi* to conform.

hexagon *n* a rectilinear figure of six sides.

hexameter *n* a verse of six metrical feet.

hey *interj* an exclamation.

heyday *n* a period of greatest success or happiness; bloom; prime.

hiatus *n* a gap; a break.

hibernate *vt* to pass the winter in sleep; to be inactive.

hiccup *n* a sudden involuntary spasm of the diaphragm followed by inhalation and closure of the glottis producing a characteristic sound; (*inf*) a minor setback.

hickory *n* a tree that yields tough timber.

hide *vt, vi* (*pt* **hid**, *pp* **hidden**) to conceal; to screen; to lie hidden. * *n* the skin of an animal; camouflaged place of concealment used by hunters, bird-watchers, etc.

hidebound *adj* bigoted; narrow-minded.

hideous *adj* frightful; ugly; horrifying.

hiding *n* concealment; a thrashing.

hie *vi* to hasten; to speed.

hierarchy *n* a group of people or things arranged in order of rank, grade, etc.

hieroglyph, hieroglyphic *n* a picture or sign standing for a letter, as in ancient Egyptian writing.

hieroglyphics *n* a system of writing that uses hieroglyphs; writing hard to decipher.

higgledy-piggledy *adv* topsy-turvy.

high *adj* elevated; lofty; strong; (*of price*) dear; sharp; (*of food*) not fresh; intoxicated. * *adv* greatly; in or to a high degree, rank, etc. * *n* a high level, place, etc; a euphoric state induced by drugs or alcohol.

highborn *adj* of noble birth.

highbrow *n, adj* an intellectual.

high-flyer, high-flier *n* an ambitious person; a person of great ability in any profession.

high-handed *adj* overbearing.

highlands *npl* a mountainous region, esp in Scotland.

highlight n the lightest area of a painting, etc; the most interesting or important feature; (pl) lightening of areas of the hair using a bleach. * vt to bring to special attention; to give highlights to.

high-minded adj proud; arrogant; having honourable pride.

highness n a title of honour given to royalty; the state or quality of being high.

high priest n a chief priest.

high-rise adj (n) (a building) with multiple storeys.

highroad n main road.

high school n a secondary school.

high-strung adj sensitive.

highway n a public road; a main thoroughfare.

highwayman n one who robs on the highway.

hike vi to take a long walk. * vt to pull up. * n a long walk; a tramp.

hilarious adj very amusing.

hilarity n laughter; jollity.

hill n a rise in the land lower than a mountain; a slope in a road.

hillock n a small hill.

hilt n a handle, particularly of a sword.

him pron the objective case of **he**.

himself pron the emphatic and re-flexive form of **he** and **him**.

hind n a female stag; a rustic. * adj situated at the back.

hinder vt to prevent; to thwart.

hindmost, hindermost adj farthest behind; last.

hindrance n a check; an obstruction; an obstacle.

hinge n a joint or flexible part on which a door, lid, etc, turns; a natural joint, as of a clam; a small piece of gummed paper for sticking stamps in an album. * vt, vi to attach or hang by a hinge; to depend.

hint vt, vi to suggest indirectly; to insinuate. * n an indirect or subtle suggestion; a slight mention; a little piece of advice or practical help.

hip n the joint of the thigh; the fruit of dog the rose. * adj stylish; up-to-date.

hippopotamus n a large African water-loving mammal with thick, dark skin, short legs and a very large head.

hire vt to engage for wages; to lease out. * n wages; payment for the temporary use of something.

hirsute adj hairy; shaggy.

his pron possessive case of he.

hiss vt to make a sound like that of letters; to show disapproval by hissing.

histology n the study of tissues, animal or vegetable.

historian n a writer of history.

historiographer n an official historian.

history n a record or account of past events; the study, analysis of past events; past events in total; the past events or experiences of a specific person or thing; an unusual or significant past.

histrionic adj theatrical.

histrionics n theatricals; exaggerated behaviour.

hit vt, vi (pt, pp **hit**) to strike; not to

miss; to reach; to affect strongly; to discover by accident or unexpectedly. * n a stroke; a blow; a collision; a successful and popular song, book, etc; a lucky chance.

hit-and-run n a motor vehicle accident in which the driver leaves the scene without stopping or informing the authorities.

hitch vt, vi to move, pull, etc, with jerks; to fasten with a hook, knot, etc; to obtain a ride by hitchhiking.

hitchhike vi to travel by asking for free lifts from motorists along the way.

hither adv to this place.

hitherto adv until now.

HIV abbr human immunodeficiency virus, the virus that causes AIDS.

hive n a shelter for a colony of bees; a beehive; a busy crowded place; a scene of great activity.

hoard n a hidden stock on accumulation of money, food, etc, stored away for future use. * vt, vi to collect; to store secretly.

hoarding n a temporary fence round a building, construction site etc; a large board for pasting advertisements on.

hoar frost n frozen dew.

hoarse adj rough-voiced; grating.

hoary adj white or grey with age.

hoax n a practical joke. * vt to deceive; to trick.

hob n a ledge at the side of a fireplace for keeping kettles, etc, hot; a flat surface on a cooker with hot plates or burners.

hobble vi to limp; to shackle (a horse).

hobbledehoy n a raw gawky youth.

hobby n a favourite spare time pursuit.

hobbyhorse n a wooden horse for children; a favourite or obsessive subject or idea.

hobgoblin n a goblin; an imp.

hobnob vi to get together for friendly conversation; to socialize.

hock¹, **hough** n the joint between the knee and fetlock of a horse, etc.

hock² n a light German wine.

hockey n game played with a ball and curved sticks between two teams of eleven players each.

hocus-pocus n juggling; trickery; deceit.

hod n a trough on a pole for carrying mortar and bricks.

hoe n a garden tool with a long handle for weeding and loosening earth.

hog n a castrated male pig raised for its meat; a selfish, greedy or dirty person. * vt (pt **hogged**) to take more than one's share; to hoard greedily.

hoist vt to heave up. * n an elevator; lift.

hoity-toity adj giddy; petulant.

hold vt, vi (pt, pp **held**) to have in one's grasp; to confine; to keep; to maintain; to contain; to possess; to occupy; to support; to carry on, e.g. a meeting; to regard; to believe; to consider. * n a grasp; possession; a dominance over; the lowermost inside part of a ship.

holdall n a portable bag or container for miscellaneous articles.

holding n a small rented farm with

land; (*often pl*) property, esp land, stocks and bonds.

hole *n* a hollow place; an aperture; cavity; a den; a small dirty place; a difficult situation; a small round hollow to receive a golf ball; a fairway plus tee in golf.

hole-and-corner *adj* underhand.

holiday *n* a day or period away from work, etc; a time for rest or amusement.

holiday-maker *n* a person on holiday.

holiness *n* sanctity; (*with cap*) the Pope.

Hollands *n* Dutch gin.

hollow *adj* not solid; empty; false. * *n* a depression; a cavity; a valley. * *vt* to excavate.

holly *n* a prickly evergreen tree with red berries.

holm oak *n* the evergreen oak.

holocaust *n* a burnt sacrifice; a great slaughter; (*with cap*) the mass murder of Jews in Europe by the Nazis.

holograph *n* a document in one's own handwriting.

holster *n* a leather case attached to a belt for a pistol.

holy *adj* without sin; consecrated.

homage *n* duty; fealty; a demonstration of respect or honour towards someone or something.

home *n* one's own abode; residence; native place; a household; an institution for aged people, orphans, etc.

homeland *n* the country where a person was born.

homely *adj* simple; plain; everyday.

home-made *adj* made or looking as if made at home.

homeopathy *see* **homoeopathy**.

homesick *adj* affected with homesickness; longing for home.

homesickness *n* depression through being away from home.

homespun *adj* coarse; rough; unsophisticated. * *n* a home-made cloth.

homestead *n* a house with the grounds and buildings attached; native seat.

homeward, homewards *adv* towards home.

homework *n* work, esp piecework, done at home; schoolwork to be done outside the classroom; preliminary study for a project.

homicidal *adj* murderous.

homicide *n* manslaughter; a person who kills.

homily *n* a sermon; sound advice.

homoeopathy, homeopathy *n* curing disease by producing similar symptoms, 'like curing like'.

homogeneous *adj* of the same kind; of uniform structure.

homonym *n* a word alike in form or sound, but not in meaning, as here, hear.

homosexual *adj* sexually attracted towards a person of the same sex.

hone *n* a whetstone. * *vt* to sharpen as with a hone.

honest *adj* free from fraud; upright; truthful; trustworthy; frank.

honesty *n* uprightness; truth.

honey *n* a sweet sticky yellowish substance juice collected by bees from flowers and made into a food.

honeycomb *n* the waxy storage cells of bees.

honeymoon *n* the holiday spent together by a newly married couple.

honeysuckle n a sweet-smelling climbing plant.

honorarium n a fee paid for voluntary services.

honorary adj conferring honour; voluntary; unpaid.

honour n glory; good name; fame; integrity; distinction; a title of respect; (pl) university distinctions. * vt to esteem; exalt; to pay (a bill) when due.

honourable adj worthy of honour; distinguished; just.

hood n a cowl; a head covering; anything hood-shaped as the top or bonnet of a car.

hoodwink vt to deceive; to mislead by trickery.

hoof n the horny part of an animal's foot.

hook n a piece of metal bent so as to catch or hold; a sickle. * vt to catch with a hook; to ensnare; (golf) to drive a ball to the left; (rugby) to pass the ball backwards from a scrum. * vi to bend; to be curving.

hookah n a Turkish tobacco pipe.

hooligan n a lawless young person.

hoop n the band of a cask; a ring; anything so shaped.

hoot vi to shout in contempt; to cry as an owl; to blow a whistle, etc. * n the sound an owl makes; a similar sound; (inf) an amusing person.

hooter n something that makes a hooting sound, e.g. a car horn; (inf) a nose.

hop n a leap on one leg; a spring; a short trip by air; a bitter herb. * vi

(pt **hopped**) to leap; to skip.

hope vt to desire and expect. * vi to trust. * n expectation and desire; the object of this; a person or thing who show promise.

hopeful adj filled with hope; inspiring hope or promise of success.

hopeless adj without hope; despondent.

hopper n a contrivance for passing grain into a mill; a barge for dredging.

horde n a crowd; a throng; a rabble.

horizon n the apparent junction of the earth and sky; the limit of a person's knowledge; interest, etc.

horizontal adj level; parallel to the plane of the horizon.

hormone n a product of living cells formed in one part of the organism and carried to another part, where it takes effect; a synthetic compound having the same purpose.

horn n a hard pointed growth on the heads of some animals; the feelers of snails, etc; anything horn-like; a wind instrument esp the French horn; a device blown or sounded as a warning.

hornet n a stinging insect a kin to the wasp.

hornpipe n a sailor's dance.

horology n the science of clockmaking.

horoscope n a chart of the signs and positions of planets, etc, by which astrologers profess to predict future events, esp in the life of an individual.

horrible adj dreadful; frightful; very unpleasant.

horrid adj shocking; hideous.

horrify *vt* to shock; to appal.

horror *n* dread; intense fear; a person or thing inspiring horror.

hors-d'oeuvre *n* a dish served at the beginning of a meal.

horse *n* four-legged, solid-hoofed herbivorous mammal with a flowing mane and a tail, domesticated for carrying loads or riders, etc; cavalry; a vaulting horse; a frame with legs to support something.

horse chestnut *n* a large tree with large palm-shaped leaves and erect clusters of flowers.

horseman *n* a skilful rider.

horsemanship *n* the art of riding horses.

horseplay *n* rough, rude conduct.

horsepower *n* the pulling power of a horse, calculated to be equal to raising 33,000 lb. one foot per minute; the power of a motor or engine measured by this unit.

horseradish *n* a plant with a pungent edible root.

horseshoe *n* a flat U-shaped plate nailed to a horse's hoof; anything shaped like this.

horticulture *n* the art or science of growing flowers, fruit and vegetables.

hosanna *n* a song of praise to God.

hose *n sing or pl* stockings; breeches; a flexible tube for conveying water, etc. * *vt* to spray with a hose.

hosiery *n* stockings and socks.

hospice *n* a nursing home for the care of the terminally ill.

hospitable *adj* generous and welcoming; kind.

hospital *n* an institution for the care of the sick.

hospitality *n* kindness, generosity to guests and strangers.

host[1] *n* a person who receives or entertains a stranger or guest at his house; an animal or plant on or in which another lives; a compere on a television or radio programme.

host[2] *n* a very large number of people or things.

host[3] *n* the wafer of bread used in the Eucharist or Holy Communion.

hostage *n* a person kept as a pledge to secure the performance of conditions.

hostel *n* a lodging house for the homeless; travellers or other groups.

hostess *n* a female host.

hostile *adj* unfriendly.

hostility *n* enmity; (*pl*) warfare.

hot *adj* of high temperature; very warm; giving or feeling heat; causing a burning sensation on the tongue; full of intense feeling; following closely; electrically charged; (*inf*) recent, new; radioactive; stolen.

hot *adj* having heat; burning; passionate; pungent; eager.

hot-blooded *adj* high-spirited.

hotchpotch *n* a confused mixture.

hot dog *n* a sausage esp a frankfurter, served in a long soft roll.

hotel *n* a commercial establishment providing lodging and meals for travellers, etc.

hotelier *n* the owner or manager of a hotel.

hothead n an impetuous person.

hot-headed adj easily excited, rash.

hothouse n a heated greenhouse for raising plants; an environment that encourages rapid growth.

hough see **hock**[1].

hound n a hunting dog. * vt to urge on.

hour n a period of 60 minutes, a 24th part of a day; the time for a specific activity; the time; a special point in time; distance covered in an hour; (pl) customary period for work, etc.

hourglass n a glass containing sand for measuring time.

hourly adj occurring every hour; done during an hour; frequent. * adj at every hour; frequently.

house n a building to live in, esp by one person or family; a household; a family or dynasty including relatives, ancestors and descendants; the audience in a theatre; a business firm; a legislative assembly.

house arrest n detention in one's own house, as opposed to prison.

houseboat n a boat furnished and used as a home.

housebreaker n a burglar; one employed to demolish buildings.

household n inmates of a house. * adj domestic; pertaining to house and family.

housekeeper n a person who runs a home, esp one hired to do so.

housekeeping n the daily running of a household; (inf) money used for domestic expenses; routine maintenance of equipment, records, etc, in an organization.

house warming n a party given to celebrate moving into a new house.

housewife n the woman who keeps house. **housewifery**.

housing n houses collectively; the provision of accommodation; a casing enclosing a piece of machinery, etc; a slot in a piece of wood, etc, to receive an insertion.

hovel n a small mean dwelling.

hover vi (of a bird) to hang in the air; to linger near.

hovercraft n a land or water vehicle that travels supported on a cushion of air.

how adv in what manner.

howdah n a seat on an elephant's back.

however adv in whatever manner. * conj yet; though.

howitzer n a short gun firing shells in curving flight.

howl vt, vi to utter the long, wailing cry of wolves, etc; to utter a similar cry of anger, pain, etc; to shout or laugh in pain, amusement, etc.

hub n the centre part of a wheel; a centre of activity.

hubbub n tumult; noise.

huddle vi, vt to crowd together in a confined space.

hue n colour; tint; an outcry.

huff n a state of smouldering resentment. * vi to blow; to puff.

hug vt to embrace; to keep close to; to squeeze tightly. * n a close embrace.

huge adj immense; enormous.

hulk n the body of an old ship; a large, clumsy person.

hulking adj unwieldy; bulky.

hull n the outer covering of anything, as nut, grain; the framework of a ship. * vt to strip off covering.

hum vt, vi (pt **hummed**) to make a low continuous vibrating sound; to hesitate in speaking and utter an inarticulate sound.

human adj of or relating to human beings; having the qualities of humans as opposed to animals; kind, considerate.

humane adj merciful; compassionate.

humanity n the human race; the state or quality of being human or humane; philanthropy; kindness.

humble adj lowly; modest; meek; servile. * vt to lower in condition or rank; to humiliate.

humbug n a hoax; a fraud; a cheat; an insincere person; a peppermint-flavoured sweet. * vt to impose on; to hoax.

humdrum adj commonplace; dull.

humid adj moist; (of air) damp.

humidifier n a device employed to increase the amount of water vapour in a room.

humidity n moisture; (a measure of) the dampness in the air.

humiliate vt to humble; to mortify; to lower the pride or dignity.

humility n modesty; meekness.

hummingbird n a tropical bird noted for the humming sound made by the wings in flying.

hummock n a rounded knoll.

humorist n a wag; a wit; a humorous writer.

humorous adj jocular; funny; amusing.

humour n disposition; mood; caprice; jocularity; temperament; state of mind. * vt to gratify; to indulge.

hump n a protuberance, especially on the back, e.g. of a camel; a lump.

humpback n a hunchback; a species of whale.

humus n vegetable mould.

hunch n a hump; an intuitive feeling. * vt, vi to arch into a hump; to move forward jerkily.

hunchback n a person with curvature of the spine.

hundred adj ten times ten. * n ten times ten; the symbol for this, X; an old division of a county.

hunger n a craving for food; any strong desire. * vi to feel hunger; to have a strong desire (for).

hungry adj longing for food; craving something.

hunt vt, vi to chase; to search for; to drive away. * n hunting; the chase; a party organised for hunting.

hurdle n a portable frame of bars for temporary fences or for jumping over by horses or runners; an obstacle.

hurdy-gurdy n a barrel organ.

hurl vt to throw with force.

hurly-burly n tumult; bustle.

hurrah interj an exclamation of joy.

hurricane n a violent tropical cyclone with winds of at least 74 miles per hour.

hurried adj hasty; performed quickly.

hurry vt, vi to act; move; drive with haste. * n rush; urgency; haste.

hurt n a wound; an injury; harm. * vt,

vi (*pt, pp* **hurt**) to pain; to bruise; to harm; to injure; to damage; to offend.

hurtful *adj* harmful.

hurtle *vi* to move or throw with great speed and force.

husband *n* a man who has a wife. * *vt* to manage frugally; to conserve.

hush *n* stillness. * *vt, vi* to silence.

husk *n* the outer dry covering of certain fruits and seeds.

husky *adj* dry; hoarse; harsh; hefty; strong. * *n* an Arctic sledge dog.

hussy *n* a shameless girl.

hustle *vt, vi* to jostle; to push or force hurriedly; to obtain by rough or illegal means.

hut *n* a small crude house or cabin.

hutch *n* a pen or coop for small animals.

hyacinth *n* a plant with spikes of bell-like flowers; a colour ranging from pale violet to mid-purple.

hybrid *n* the offspring of two plants or animals of different species; a mongrel. * *adj* crossbred.

hydra *n* a many-headed monster.

hydrangea *n* a garden plant with a large beautiful head of flowers.

hydrant *n* a large pipe with a valve for drawing water from a main.

hydraulic *adj* operated by water or other liquid, esp by moving through pipes under pressure; of hydraulics.

hydraulics *n* the science dealing with the mechanical properties of liquids.

hydrogen *n* a flammable, colourless, odourless, tasteless, gaseous chemical element, the lightest sub-stance known.

hydrometer *n* an instrument for finding specific gravity of liquids.

hydrophobia *n* a disease caused by the bite of an infected animal and marked by dread of water; rabies.

hydrostatic *adj* relating to hydrostatics.

hydrostatics *n* the science that treats of the reactions of fluids at rest.

hyena *n* a dog-like animal that feeds on carrion.

hygiene *n* principles and practice of health and cleanliness.

hygrometer *n* an instrument for measuring humidity of air.

hymn *n* a song of praise.

hymnal *n* a collection of hymns to God.

hyperbola *n* one of the curves formed by the section of a cone.

hyperbole *n* an exaggeration in speech or writing for effect or emphasis.

hypercritical *adj* overcritical.

hypertext *n* computer software/hardware that allows the user to pick up on one area of a document as a route to a different document.

hyphen *n* a mark (-) joining syllables or words.

hypnosis *n* (*pl* **hypnoses**) a relaxed state resembling sleep in which the mind responds to external suggestion.

hypnotism *n* the inducing of hypnosis; the study and use of hypnosis.

hypnotize *vt* to put in a state of hypnosis; to fascinate.

hypochondria *n* chronic depression; needless anxiety about one's health.

hypochondriac *n* a person suffering

from hypochondria.

hypocrisy *n* a falsely pretending to possess virtues, beliefs, etc; an example of this.

hypocrite *n* a person who pretends to be what he or she is not.

hypocritical *adj* not sincere, false.

hypodermic *adj* (*injection*) introduced beneath the skin.

hypotenuse *n* the side opposite the right angle of a right-angled triangle.

hypothesis *n* (*pl* **hypotheses**) something assumed as correct for the purpose of argument; a theory to explain some fact that may or not prove to be true; supposition; conjecture.

hypothetical *adj* based on hypothesis, conjectural. * *adv* **hypothetically**.

hysteria *n* a mental disorder marked by excitability, anxiety, imaginary organic disorders, etc; frenzied emotion or excitement.

hysteric *n* a hysterical person; (*pl*) fits of hysteria.

hysterical *adj* caused by hysteria; suffering from hysteria; (*inf*) extremely funny.

I

I *pron* the first person who is speaking or writing, used in referring to himself or herself.

ice *n* frozen water; ice cream or water ice. * *vt*, *vi* to freeze; to cool with ice; to cover with icing.

iceberg *n* a floating mass of ice.

icebound *adj* surrounded with ice.

ice cream *n* a sweet frozen food.

ice floe *n* a sheet of floating ice.

icicle *n* a hanging taper of ice formed by frozen dripping water.

icy *adj* like ice; chilling.

idea *n* a mental impression or notion; an opinion or belief.

ideal *adj* perfect. * *n* perfect type; a standard for attainment or imitation; an aim or principle.

idealism *n* the pursuit of high ideals; the doctrine that ideas are the sole reality.

idealist *n* a visionary.

idealize *vt* to represent as ideal.

identical *adj* exactly the same.

identification *n* act of identifying.

identify *vt* to consider to be the same; to establish the identity of; to associate closely.

identity *n* the state of being exactly alike; the distinguishing characteristics of a person, personality; the state of being the same as a specified person or thing.

ideology *n* the doctrines, opinions or beliefs of an individual, class, political party, etc.

idiocy *n* mental deficiency; stupidity.

idiom *n* an accepted expression with a different meaning from the literal.

idiosyncrasy *n* a personal peculiarity; a quirk; eccentricity.

idiot *n* (*inf*) a foolish person.

idiotic *adj* stupid; senseless.

idle *adj* doing nothing; lazy; not occupied; out of work; useless; worthless * *vt* to waste or spend time uselessly * *vi* to move aimlessly; (*of an engine*) to operate without transmitting power.

idleness *n* inaction; sloth.

idly *adv* lazily; carelessly.

idol *n* an image or object worshipped as a god; a person who is intensely admired.

idolatry *n* the worship of idols.

idolize *vt* to love excessively.

idyll *n* a romantic or a pastoral poem.

idyllic *adj* describing an idyll; charmingly picturesque.

if *conj* on condition that; in the event that; supposing that; even though; whenever.

igneous *adj* descriptive of rocks formed from solidified magma or lava.

ignite *vt, vi* to kindle; to set fire to; to burn or cause to burn.

ignition *n* an act or instance of igniting; the starting of an internal combustion engine.

ignoble *adj* mean; base.

ignominious *adj* shameful; base.

ignominy *n* public disgrace; shame.

ignoramus *n* an ignorant person.

ignorance *n* lack of knowledge.

ignorant *adj* uninformed; uneducated.

ignore *vt* to disregard.

ill *adj* bad or evil; crabbed; sick; ugly. * *n* evil; pain. * *adv* not well; badly.

ill-bred *adj* not polite; rude.

illegal *adj* contrary to law.

illegible *adj* unreadable.

illegitimate *adj* born out of wedlock.

illicit *adj* improper; unlawful.

illiterate *adj* not able to read or write; ignorant, uneducated.

ill-judged *adj* injudicious; unwise.

ill-mannered *adj* rude; boorish.

ill-natured *adj* bad-tempered; spiteful.

illness *n* sickness.

illogical *adj* not logical.

ill-tempered *adj* cross; morose.

ill-treat *vt* to treat unkindly, unfairly, etc.

illuminate *vt* to light up; to adorn; to enlighten.

illumination *n* a supply of light; a brightening up with colours or lights.

illuminative *adj* enlightening.

illusion *n* a false notion; an unreal or misleading image or appearance; deception.

illusionist *n* a conjuror; a magician.

illusive *adj* deceptive.

illusory *adj* fallacious.

illustrate *vt* to make clear by explanation or drawing.

illustration *n* an example, a picture or drawing, esp in a book.

illustrative *adj* explanatory.

illustrious *adj* renowned; distinguished.

ill-will *n* hatred; malice.

image *n* a likeness; an idol; a mental picture; the visual impression of something in a lens, mirror, etc.

imagery *n* picturesque language.

imaginary *adj* not real; visionary.

imagination n fancy; the creative faculty.

imagine vt, vi to fancy; to conceive; to believe falsely.

imbecile adj weak-minded; foolish. * n an adult with a mental age of a three- to eight-year-old child; a silly person.

imbibe vt to drink in; to absorb.

imitate vt to copy; to mimic; to impersonate.

imitation n a counterfeit; a copy; an act of impersonation or mimicking.

imitative adj given to imitation.

immaculate adj spotless; pure; morally unblemished.

immaterial adj unimportant.

immature adj unripe; not mature.

immeasurable adj immense.

immediate adj acting or occurring without delay; next, nearest, without intervening agency; next in relationship; in close proximity, near to.

immediately adv instantly; directly; near.

immemorial adj ancient beyond memory.

immense adj immeasurable; huge; vast.

immensity n infinity; vastness.

immerse vt to plunge into (esp water).

immersion heater n an electric element for heating liquids.

immigrant n one who settles in a country not his or her own.

immigrate vi to enter a country as a settler.

imminent adj impending; about to happen; threatening.

immobile adj fixed; stable.

immoderate adj excessive; intemperate.

immodest adj indelicate.

immoral adj depraved; wicked; corrupt.

immortal adj living forever; having lasting fame. * n an immortal being or person.

immortality n endless life or fame.

immortalize vt to make famous for ever.

immovable adj steadfast; unalterable.

immune adj not susceptible to a specified disease through inoculation or natural resistance; conferring immunity.

immunity n freedom from (disease, service, etc); exemption.

immunize vt to make immune, esp against infection.

immutable adj unchangeable.

imp n a mischievous child.

impact n the force with which one thing strikes another; a collision; a strong effect or impression.

impair vt to make worse; to weaken.

impale vt to transfix with a sharp point.

impalpable adj intangible; not easily understood.

impart vt to give; to bestow; to confer.

impartial adj just; fair; unbiased.

impartiality n freedom from bias.

impassable adj incapable of being travelled over or through.

impasse n a deadlock.

impassioned adj moved by passion.

impassive *adj* unmoved; apathetic.

impatience *n* intolerance of delay; restlessness; short temper.

impatient *adj* fretful; intolerant; restless.

impeach *vt* to question a person's honesty; to charge with a crime.

impeachment *n* an indictment.

impeccable *adj* faultless.

impecunious *adj* penniless.

impede *vt* to hamper; to obstruct.

impediment *n* an obstruction; a physical defect, e.g. a stammer.

impel *vt* (*pt* **impelled**) to drive or urge forward.

impend *vi* to hang over; to threaten.

impenetrable *adj* impervious; unable to be passed through.

impenitent *adj* unrepentant; obdurate.

imperative *adj* commanding; obligatory; designating or of the mood of a verb that expresses a command, entreaty, etc.

imperceptible *adj* minute; not easily grasped or detected by the senses.

imperfect *adj* incomplete; faulty; designating a verb tense that indicates a past action or state as incomplete or continuous.

imperfection *n* the state or quality of being imperfect; a defect, fault.

imperial *adj* pertaining to an empire.

imperil *vt* to endanger.

imperious *adj* commanding; arrogant.

imperishable *adj* indestructible.

impermeable *adj* impervious; impenetrable by liquids.

impersonal *adj* without reference to a particular person; cold; unfeeling; (*of a verb*) occurring only in the third person singular

impersonate *vt* to assume the character of another for entertainment or for fraud.

impertinence *n* insolence; irrelevance.

impertinent *adj* pert; rude; irrelevant.

imperturbable *adj* serene; unmoved.

impervious *adj* impassable; not receptive to or affected by.

impetuous *adj* hasty; thoughtless.

impetus *n* the force with which a body moves against resistance; driving force or motive.

impinge *vi* to collide; to clash; to encroach.

impish *adj* mischievous.

implacable *adj* not to be appeased; inexorable; unrelenting.

implant *vt* to plant; to instil.

implement *n* a tool, utensil or instrument. * *vt* to fulfil; to carry out.

implicate *vt* to involve; to incriminate.

implication *n* entanglement; deduction.

implicit *adj* implied; not stated; unquestioning.

implore *vt, vi* to beseech, to entreat.

imply *vt* to suggest; to suggest indirectly.

impolite *adj* rude, uncivil.

impolitic *adj* inexpedient.

imponderable *adj* without weight. * *n* something difficult to measure or assess.

import¹ vt to bring in goods from abroad. * n something brought in from abroad.

import² n meaning; importance. * vt to mean; to signify. * vi to matter.

importance n significance; a high place in public estimation; high self-esteem.

important adj momentous; serious; powerful and authoritative.

importunate adj urgent; persistent.

importune vt to press urgently; to crave.

impose vt to lay on as a tax; to inflict oneself on others; to cheat; to lay pages of type or film and secure them.

imposing adj impressive; stately.

imposition vt, vi an unfair obligation.

impossibility n state or character of being impossible; that which cannot be, or cannot be done.

impossible adj not possible; inconceivable; unendurable.

impostor, imposter n a deceiver.

impotence, impotency n powerlessness; inability to engage in sexual intercourse.

impotent adj feeble; incompetent; sexually impotent.

impound vt to confine; to seize legally.

impoverish vt to make poor; to exhaust.

impracticable adj not feasible; unmanageable; unattainable.

impractical adj not practical; not competent in practical skills.

impregnable adj invincible; secure.

impregnate vt to cause to become pregnant; to fertilize; to saturate; to pervade.

impresario n the manager of an opera, concert series, etc.

impress vt to press into; to stamp; to fix deeply and favourably (on the mind).

impression n the effect produced in the mind by an experience; a mark produced by imprinting; a vague idea, notion; the number of copies of a book printed at one time; an impersonation.

impressionable adj susceptible; easily influenced.

impressionism n a movement in art giving more attention to general effect and impressions than to details.

impressionist n an artist who aims at broad effects; a mimic or impersonator.

impressive adj imposing; striking; arousing admiration.

imprint vt to impress; to stamp. * n a publisher's name, address, etc.

imprison vt to confine in prison.

improbable adj unlikely to be true or to happen.

impromptu n an unprepared remark, poem, etc; a short, unrehearsed musical composition. * adj extempore.

improper adj lacking propriety; indecent; erroneous; unsuitable.

impropriety n an unbecoming act.

improve vt, vi to better; to grow better; to use to good purpose.

improvement n advance; betterment; an alteration that enhances value.

improvidence n wastefulness.

improvident *adj* thriftless; careless.

improvise *vt* to compose and recite, etc, without preparation; to do or use whatever is at hand.

imprudence *n* rashness, indiscretion.

imprudent *adj* indiscreet; heedless.

impudent *adj* impertinent; saucy.

impugn *vt* to challenge; to contradict.

impulse *n* a thrust; a motive; a sudden determination to act.

impulsive *adj* impetuous; hasty.

impunity *n* freedom from punishment.

impure *adj* foul; obscene; adulterated.

impute *vt* to attribute; ascribe.

in *prep, adv* within; not out; during; being a member of; wearing.

inability *n* lack of ability.

inaccuracy *n* incorrectness; error.

inaccurate *adj* incorrect; not exact.

inaction *n* idleness; rest.

inactive *adj* idle; indolent.

inadequacy *n* insufficiency.

inadequate *adj* defective; not capable.

inadmissible *adj* not allowable.

inadvertent *adj* heedless; careless.

inadvisable *adj* not advisable; inexpedient.

inalienable *adj* incapable of being transferred.

inane *adj* silly; senseless.

inanimate *adj* lifeless; spiritless.

inanity *n* silliness.

inapplicable *adj* inappropriate.

inapposite *adj* not to the point.

inappropriate *adj* unsuitable.

inapt *adj* not apt; unfit.

inarticulate *adj* not expressed in words; incapable of coherent or effective expression of ideas, feelings, etc.

inattention *n* want of attention; neglect.

inattentive *adj* not attending; thoughtless.

inaugural *adj* introductory.

inaugurate *vt* to introduce, to install into office; to open a building, etc, formally to the public; to initiate.

inauspicious *adj* ill-omened.

inborn *adj* innate; inherent.

inbred *adj* innate; produced by inbreeding

inbreed *vt, vi* to breed by continual mating of individuals or related stocks.

incalculable *adj* numberless; very great; uncertain.

incandescent *adj* white or glowing with heat.

incantation *n* recital of words containing a magic spell.

incapable *adj* unfit to perform.

incapacitate *vt* to render unfit; to disable.

incapacity *n* unfitness; disqualification.

incarceration *n* imprisonment.

incarnate *vt* to embody in flesh. * *adj* endowed with a human body.

incarnation *n* embodiment in human form.

incautious *adj* unwary; imprudent.

incendiary *n* an arsonist. * *adj* inflammatory; seditious; (*of bomb*) designed to start fires.

incense[1] *n* perfume of spices burnt in religious rites.

incense² vt to inflame; to provoke.

incentive adj inciting. * n an inducement.

inception n the initial stage.

incessant adj unceasing; constant.

incessantly adv continually.

incest n intercourse between close blood relations.

incestuous adj guilty of incest.

inch n the twelfth part of a foot in length. * vt, vi to move very slowly or by degrees.

incidence n the degree or range of occurrence or effect.

incident n a distinct event; a minor event.

incidental adj casual; occasional; happening by the way; (pl) miscellaneous items.

incidentally adv in passing; as an aside.

incinerate vt to burn to ashes.

incinerator n a furnace for burning.

incipient adj beginning to be or appear.

incise vt to cut in or into; to carve.

incision n a cut, esp by a surgeon into a body.

incisive adj sharp; biting; trenchant.

incisor n a front cutting tooth.

incite vt to urge on; to stir up.

incitement n a motive; encouragement.

inclemency n harshness; severity (of the weather).

inclement adj not clement; stormy.

inclination n a propensity or disposition, esp a liking; a deviation from the horizontal or vertical; a slope.

incline vi to lean, to slope; to be disposed towards an opinion or action. * vt to cause to bend forwards; to cause to deviate. * n a slope

inclined adj sloping; disposed.

include vt to enclose; to comprise; to contain.

inclusive adj including; comprising; including the limits specified.

incoherent adj confused; unintelligible.

incombustible adj not able to be burned.

income n all moneys coming in for work or investments, etc.

incoming adj coming; accruing. * n the act of coming in; that which comes in; income.

incomparable adj matchless.

incompatible adj irreconcilable; unable to exist together in harmony.

incompetence, incompetency n unfitness; incapacity; lack of skill or ability.

incompetent adj not competent; incapable; unskilful; an incompetent person.

incomplete adj imperfect; defective; unfinished.

incomprehensible adj unintelligible; inconceivable.

inconceivable adj unimaginable.

inconclusive adj indecisive; uncertain as to result or outcome.

incongruity n inconsistency; absurdity.

incongruous adj discordant; inconsistent; lacking harmony or agreement of parts.

inconsequential, inconsequent adj not following logically; irrelevant.

inconsiderable *adj* unimportant; insignificant.

inconsiderate *adj* thoughtless; unkind.

inconsistency *n* incongruity; want of agreement; irregularity; fickleness.

inconsistent *adj* not consistent; variable.

inconspicuous *adj* not easily noticed; undistinguished.

incontinence *n* lack of self-restraint; inability to control excretion of bodily wastes.

incontinent *adj* unable to control one's bladder and/or bowels.

incontrovertible *adj* certain; indisputable.

inconvenience *n* annoyance; awkwardness; that which incommodes.

inconvenient *adj* awkward.

incorporate *vt* to unite in one body.

incorrect *adj* faulty; untrue; improper.

incorrigible *adj* incurable; hopeless.

incorruptible *adj* incapable of physical corruption, decay or dissolution; incapable of being bribed.

increase *vi* to become greater; to augment. * *vt* to add to. * *n* a growing larger; addition; profit; interest.

incredible *adj* unbelievable.

incredulity *n* doubt; scepticism.

incredulous *adj* sceptical; doubting.

increment *n* the amount of an increase.

incriminate *vt* to involve in an accusation; to accuse.

incubate *vi* to sit on eggs; to hatch.

incubator *n* an apparatus in which eggs are hatched by artificial heat;

an apparatus for nurturing premature babies.

inculcate *vt* to teach; to implant.

incumbent *n* holder of a church living.

incur *vt* to bring upon oneself.

incurable *adj* hopeless; past cure.

incursion *n* a raid; an inroad.

indebted *n* beholden; obliged; owing.

indecency *n* immodesty; impurity.

indecent *adj* unseemly; obscene.

indecipherable *adj* incapable of being deciphered.

indecision *n* inability to take a decision.

indecisive *adj* wavering; vacillating.

indecorous *adj* unseemly; improper.

indeed *adv* truly; certainly. * *interj* expressing irony, disbelief, surprise, etc.

indefatigable *adj* untiring; unremitting.

indefensible *adj* untenable; inexcusable.

indefinable *adj* vague; difficult to explain clearly.

indefinite *adj* uncertain; unlimited; vague.

indelible *adj* not able to be erased.

indelicacy *n* immodesty; coarseness.

indelicate *adj* improper; coarse.

indemnify *vt* to make good a loss; to insure against loss, damage, etc.

indemnity *n* compensation for loss.

indent *vt* to notch; to indicate a paragraph by leaving a space at the margin. * *n* an order for supplies.

indentation *n* a notch; a small bay.

indenture *n* a written contract between two parties; a contract binding one person to work for another. * vt to bind by indenture.

independence n the state of being independent.

independent adj free; unrestrained.

indescribable adj unutterable; inexpressible; too beautiful, etc, for words.

indestructible adj imperishable.

indeterminate adj uncertain.

index n an alphabetical list of names, subjects, items, etc, at the end of a text; any indication or sign.

index finger n the forefinger.

index-linked adj anything linked directly to changes in the cost of living index.

indicate vt to point out; to show; to be a sign or symptom of; to state briefly; to suggest.

indicative adj pointing out; affirming; serving as a sign of.

indicator n a thing that indicates or points; an instrument showing the operating condition of a piece of machinery.

indict vt to charge with a crime.

indictment n a formal charge or accusation of a crime.

indifference n unconcern; apathy.

indifferent adj unconcerned; heedless; uninterested; average; mediocre.

indigenous adj native; existing naturally in a particular place or environment.

indigestible adj not easily digested.

indigestion n pain caused by difficulty in digesting food.

indignant adj angry; scornful.

indignation n wrath and scorn; annoyance; esp at an injustice.

indignity n humiliation; an insult.

indigo n a blue vegetable dye.

indirect adj roundabout.

indiscreet adj tactless; imprudent.

indiscretion n imprudence; a thoughtless act; rashness.

indiscriminate adj not making any distinction; general; confused; random.

indispensable adj necessary; vital.

indisposed adj disinclined; unwell.

indisposition n a slight ailment.

indisputable adj unquestionable.

indistinct adj faint; confused.

indistinguishable adj incapable of being distinguished.

individual adj existing as a separate thing or being; of, by, for, or relating to a single person. * n a single thing or being.

individualist n a person who thinks or behaves with marked independence.

individuality n separate or distinct existence; personality.

indivisible adj not able to be divided.

indoctrinate vt to instruct systematically in a doctrine, idea or belief.

indolence n laziness; idleness.

indolent adj lazy; idle.

indomitable adj unyielding; invincible.

indoors adv within house.

indubitable adj certain; evident.

induce vt to persuade; to draw (a conclusion) from particular facts; to bring on.

inducement *n* an incentive; a motive.

induct *vt* to install; to introduce.

induction *n* introduction to office; a prologue; magnetic influence.

indulge *vt* to gratify; to humour. * *vi* to give way to one's desire.

indulgence *n* favour; intemperance; tolerance.

indulgent *adj* forbearing; yielding; lenient.

industrial *adj* pertaining to industry.

industrialist *n* a person who owns or manages an industrial enterprise.

industrious *adj* diligent; active.

industry *n* organised production or manufacture of goods.

inebriated *adj* drunken.

ineffective *adj* useless; impotent.

ineffectual *adj* fruitless; futile.

inefficient *adj* incapable; ineffective.

inelegant *adj* plain; ungraceful; uncouth.

ineligible *adj* not qualified; unsuitable.

inept *adj* unsuitable; awkward; clumsy.

inequality *n* lack of equality; unevenness of surface.

inequitable *adj* unfair; unjust.

inert *adj* lifeless; sluggish; inactive; dull with few or no properties.

inertia *n* inactivity; tendency of matter to remain in existing state of rest (or continue in a fixed direction) unless acted on by an outside force.

inestimable *adj* invaluable; priceless.

inevitable *adj* unavoidable.

inexact *adj* not exactly true or correct.

inexcusable *adj* indefensible.

inexhaustible *adj* unfailing.

inexorable *adj* inflexible; relentless.

inexpensive *adj* cheap.

inexperienced *adj* unskilled; raw.

inexplicable *adj* unaccountable.

inexpressible *adj* unspeakable.

inextricable *adj* that cannot be disentangled, solved, or escaped from.

infallibility *n* freedom from liability to error; perfection.

infallible *adj* incapable of errors; reliable.

infamous *adj* scandalous; notorious.

infamy *n* public disgrace; ignominy.

infancy *n* early childhood; the early stages of anything.

infant *n* a very young child.

infanticide *n* child murder.

infantile *adj* childish; weak.

infantry *n* foot soldiers.

infatuate *vt* to inspire with foolish or short-lived passion.

infect *vt* to taint with disease; to corrupt.

infection *n* an infecting or being infected; an infectious disease; a diseased condition.

infectious *adj* able to be transmitted.

infer *vt* (*pt* **inferred**) to conclude, to deduce.

inference *n* conclusion; deduction.

inferior *adj* subordinate. * *n* a person lower in rank, degree, quality.

infernal *adj* diabolical; fiendish; extremely irritating.

inferno *n* hell; intense heat; a devastating fire.

infertility *n* barrenness.

infest *vt* to overrun in large numbers,

usu to be harmful; to be parasitic in or on.

infidelity n want of faith; dishonesty; unfaithfulness esp in marriage.

infighting n intense competition within an organisation.

infiltrate vt, vi to filter or pass gradually through or into; to permeate; to penetrate gradually or stealthily, e.g. as spies.

infinite adj limitless; vast.

infinitesimal adj microscopic; minute.

infinitive n the form of a verb without reference to person, number or tense.

infinity n immensity; a countless number, quantity or time period.

infirm adj weak; sickly.

infirmary n a hospital.

infirmity n physical weakness; fault; disease.

inflame vt to kindle; to excite; to incense. * vi to grow hot.

inflammable adj combustible.

inflammation n a condition of the body marked by heat, swelling and pain.

inflammatory adj tending to excite passion.

inflate vt to fill up with air or gas; distend; to increase beyond what is normal, esp the supply of money or credit.

inflation n an increase in the currency in circulation or a marked expansion of credit, resulting in a fall in currency value and a sharp rise in prices.

inflection n modulation of voice; changes in word forms.

inflexible adj unbending; rigid.

inflict vt to impose as a penalty.

inflorescence n a flowering.

influence n moving or directing power; sway; effect. * vt to move; to persuade.

influential adj exerting influence; possessing power.

influenza n contagious, feverish viral disease marked by muscular pain and inflammation of the respiratory system.

influx n a flowing in of people or things to a place.

inform vt to tell; to enlighten; to teach; to give information to the police, etc, in accusing another.

informal adj without ceremony; unofficial; casual.

information n intelligence; news; data stored in, or retrieved from a computer.

informative adj instructive.

informer n one who informs; a spy.

infraction n a violation; a breach.

infrequent adj uncommon; rare.

infringe vt to break; to transgress.

infringement n a breach, esp of the law.

infuriate vt to madden; to enrage.

infuse vt to pour in; to instil; to steep.

infusion n process of infusion; liquor (as tea) so obtained.

ingenious adj inventive, original; resourceful.

ingenuity n inventiveness.

ingenuous adj open, original or candid.

ingot n a bar of metal got from a mould.

ingratiate vt to get into another's favour.

ingratitude n thanklessness.

ingredient n something included with others in a mixture; a component.

ingress n entrance.

inhabit vt, vi to live in; to dwell; to reside.

inhabitable adj habitable.

inhabitant n a resident.

inhale vt to draw into the lungs.

inhaler n a respirator; an apparatus for inhaling vapours.

inharmonious adj discordant.

inherent adj inborn; ingrained.

inherit vt, vi to come into possession of as an heir.

inheritance n a heritage; something inherited.

inhibit vt to restrain; to forbid.

inhibition n restraint; embargo.

inhospitable adj unfriendly; barren.

inhuman adj cruel; merciless.

inhumanity n cruelty.

inimical adj unfriendly; hostile.

inimitable adj matchless; peerless.

iniquitous adj wicked; criminal.

iniquity n wickedness; injustice.

initial adj primary; of or at the beginning. * n the first letters of a person's name(s). * vt to mark or sign with initials.

initiate vt to begin; to originate; to admit as a member of a club, etc.

initiation n formal introduction or admittance.

initiative n first step; lead; power of originating.

inject vt to force (fluid into the body), esp with a syringe.

injunction n a command; exhortation; advice; a legal writ restraining or ordering.

injure vt to hurt; to damage.

injurious adj harmful; wrongful.

injury n physical damage; harm.

injustice n wrong; unfairness.

ink n a coloured liquid used for writing, printing, etc. * vt to cover, mark, or colour with ink.

inkling n a vague notion; a hint.

inland adj interior; remote from the sea; domestic. *n an inland region.

inlay vt to decorate a surface by inserting pieces of metal, wood, etc.

inlet n a narrow strip of water extending into a body of land; an opening.

inmate n a resident; an occupant, esp of a prison or other institution.

inn n a small hotel; a public house.

innate adj inborn; natural; instinctive.

inner adj interior. * n the part of a target adjoining the bull's eye.

innings n sing (pl innings) (cricket) the batting period of each side.

innocence n purity; simplicity; without guilt or guile.

innocent adj not guilty of a particular crime; free from sin; blameless.

innocuous adj harmless.

innovate vi to introduce new methods, ideas, etc; to make changes.

innovation n novelty; change.

innuendo n an indirect hint; a sly remark, often derogatory.

innumerable adj countless.

inoculate vt to inject a serum or a

vaccine into, esp in order to create an immunity; to protect as if by inoculation.

inoculation *n* the act of inoculating.

inopportune *adj* untimely; inconvenient.

inordinate *adj* excessive; extravagant.

inorganic *adj* not having the structure or characteristics of living organisms.

inpatient *n* a patient being treated while remaining in hospital.

inquest *n* a judicial inquiry held by a coroner.

inquire *vi* to ask about; to question; to investigate.

inquiry, enquiry *n* research; a question; an investigation.

inquisition *n* an inquiry; a formal search; a tribunal for trial.

inquisitive *adj* prying; inquiring; curious.

inroad *n* a raid; a foray; an encroachment or advance.

insane *adj* not sane; mentally ill.

insanity *n* lunacy; derangement of the mind; mania.

insatiable *adj* rapacious; greedy.

inscribe *vt* to mark or engrave on a surface; to add (a person's name) to a list; to dedicate (a book) to someone.

inscription *n* words engraved on stone or metal.

inscrutable *adj* hard to understand; incomprehensible; enigmatic.

insect *n* a tiny creature with a body divided into sections, usu with three pairs of legs, a head, thorax and abdomen and two or four wings.

insecticide *n* an insect killer.

insectivorous *adj* insect-eating.

insecure *adj* unsafe; risky; feeling anxiety; not dependable.

insecurity *n* unsteadiness; peril; risk; lack of confidence; instability; something insecure.

insensible *adj* unconscious; unaware; indifferent; imperceptible.

insensitive *adj* not sensitive; callous.

inseparable *adj* never apart; closely attached, as romantically.

insert *vt* to put, fit, or set in.

insertion *n* a thing inserted (as advertisement); lace, etc, worked into cloth.

inset *vt* to set in; to implant. * *n* an insertion.

inshore *adj, adv* near or towards the shore.

inside *n* the inner side, surface, or part. * *adj* internal; known only to insiders; secret. * *adv* on or in the inside; within; indoors. * *prep* in or within.

insider *n* a person within a place or group; one with access to secret information.

insidious *adj* treacherous; stealthy.

insight *n* discernment; penetration.

insignia *npl* badges of office or honour.

insignificance *n* littleness; triviality.

insignificant *adj* trifling; mean.

insincere *adj* faithless; deceitful.

insincerity *n* hypocrisy.

insinuate *vt* to introduce slowly, by degrees, etc; to hint.

insipid *adj* tasteless; flat; uninteresting.

insist *vi* to urge or press strongly.

insistence *n* urgency.

insobriety *n* intemperance.

insolence *n* rudeness; impudence.

insolent *adj* overbearing; insulting.

insoluble *adj* incapable of being dissolved; impossible to solve or explain.

insolvency *n* bankruptcy.

insolvent *adj* not able to pay debts.

insomnia *n* abnormal sleeplessness.

inspect *vt* to examine; to scan carefully.

inspection *n* careful survey; examination.

inspector *n* one who inspects to ensure compliance with regulations, etc.

inspiration *n* an inspiring; any stimulus to creative thought.

inspire *vt* to stimulate, as to creative effort; to motivate by divine influence; to arouse (a feeling) in; to cause.

instability *n* inconstancy; fickleness.

install *vt* to invest with office; to settle in a position or state.

installation *n* machinery, equipment, etc, that has been installed.

instalment *n* a sum of money to be paid at regular specified times.

instance *n* an example; a step in proceeding. * *vt* to give as an example

instant *adj* immediate; (*food*) concentrated or pre-cooked for quick preparation. * *n* a moment; a particular moment.

instantaneous *adj* done in an instant.

instead *adv* in place of.

instep *n* the upper part or arch of the foot.

instigate *vt* to spur on; to urge; to initiate.

instigation *n* incitement; prompting.

instil *vt* (*pt* **instilled**) to put (an idea, etc) in or into (the mind) gradually.

instinct *n* a natural impulse; a knack.

instinctive *adj* spontaneous.

institute *vt* to set up; to found; to begin; to originate. * *n* an organization for the promotion of science, art, etc.

institution *n* an established law, custom, etc; an organization with a special purpose; the building housing it; (*inf*) a long-established person or thing.

instruct *vt* to teach; to advise; to give instruction.

instruction *n* information; education; knowledge imparted; (*pl*) orders, directions; detailed guidance.

instructive *adj* educational; informative.

instrument *n* a thing by means of which something is done; a device for indicating, controlling, measuring, etc; a device producing musical sound; a formal document.

instrumental *adj* serving as a means of doing something; helpful; of, performed on, or written for musical instruments.

instrumentalist *n* a person who plays a musical instrument.

insubordinate *adj* disobedient; mutinous.

insubordination *n* revolt; disobedience.

insufferable *adj* intolerable.

insufficiency *n* inadequacy; unfitness.

insufficient *adj* not enough; inadequate.

insular *adj* pertaining to an island; narrow-minded.

insulate *vt* to set apart; to isolate; to cover with a non-conducting material in order to prevent the escape of, heat, sound, etc.

insulin *n* a hormone that controls absorption of sugar by the body.

insult *n* a gross affront; indignity. * *vt, vi* to treat with insolence; to offend.

insuperable *adj* incapable of being overcome; insurmountable.

insupportable *adj* intolerable.

insurance *n* a contract purchased to guarantee compensation for a specified loss by fire, death, etc.

insure *vt* to contract against damage, etc.

insurgent *adj* rebellious. * *n* a rebel.

insurmountable *adj* incapable of being overcome; insuperable.

insurrection *n* a revolt; a rebellion.

intact *adj* untouched; unimpaired; whole.

intangible *adj* that cannot be touched, incorporeal; indefinable. * *n* something that is intangible.

integer *n* a whole; a whole number.

integral *adj* necessary for completeness; whole or complete; made up of parts forming a whole.

integrate *vt* to make up a whole; to complete; to bring together into a whole.

integrity *n* uprightness; honesty.

intellect *n* the ability to reason or understand; high intelligence; a very intelligent person.

intellectual *adj* of, involving, or appealing to the intellect; requiring intelligence. * *n* an intellectual person.

intelligence *n* the ability to learn or understand; the ability to cope with information; those involved with gathering secret, esp military, information.

intelligent *adj* quick of mind; acute; well informed.

intelligible *adj* comprehensible; clear.

intemperate *adj* immoderate; unrestrained; (*weather*) extreme.

intend *vt* to design; to have in mind as an aim or purpose.

intense *adj* strained; extreme; severe; passionate; emotional.

intensify *vt* to deepen; to augment.

intensity *n* vehemence; keenness; ardour; strength; the force or energy of any physical agent.

intensive *adj* strained; concentrated; describing the special and extensive care give to patients after serious surgery.

intent *adj* set; bent. * *n* purpose.

intention *n* purpose; design.

intentionally *adv* on purpose.

inter *vt* to bury.

interact *vi* to act reciprocally.

interactive *adj* interacting; allowing two-way communication between a device such as a computer or a compact video disc, and its user.

intercede *vi* to mediate; to plead for.

intercept *vt* to take or stop in its course; to obstruct; to cut off.

intercession *n* mediation.

interchange *vt* to give and receive one thing for another; to alternate.

* *n* an interchanging; a junction on a motorway designed to prevent traffic interesecting.

intercom *n* (*inf*) a system of intercommunication, as in an aircraft.

intercommunication *n* interchange of ideas and means for securing it.

intercourse *n* communion; fellowship; sexual intercourse.

interdict *vt* to forbid; to veto.

interest *n* concern about something; anything in which one has a share; benefit; money paid for the use of money. * *vt* to excite the attention of; to cause to have a share in; to concern oneself with.

interfere *vi* to clash; to interpose; to meddle; to obstruct.

interference *n* intermeddling; clashing; (*radio*, *TV*) the interruption of reception by atmospherics or unwanted signals.

interim *n* the meantime; an intervening period of time. * *adj* temporary.

interior *adj* internal; inland.

interject *vt* to throw in between; to insert; to interrupt

interjection *n* a word thrown in abruptly.

interlock *vi*, *vt* to clasp together.

interloper *n* an intruder; a meddler.

interlude *n* an interval.

intermediary *n* a go-between; a mediator.

intermediate *adj* intervening; middle.

interment *n* burial.

interminable *adj* endless; boundless.

intermission *n* a pause between parts of a performance; a rest.

intermittent *adj* coming and going; ebbing and flowing; periodic.

intern *vt* to confine prisoners, etc, in a prescribed area.

internal *adj* of or on the inside; inward.

international *adj* between or among nations; concerned with the relationship between nations; for the use of all nations; of or for people in various nations.

internecine *adj* deadly; bloody; mutually destructive.

Internet *n* the worldwide system of linked computer networks.

interpolate *vt* to interrupt speech, etc, with comments; to insert a passage into a text.

interpose *vt* to place between.

interpret *vt* to explain; to translate; to construe; to give one's own conception of. * *vi* to translate between speakers of different languages.

interpretation *n* an explanation.

interpreter *n* one who interprets.

interrogate *vt* to question.

interrogation *n* a questioning; a mark of questioning (?).

interrogative *adj* denoting a question.

interrupt *vi* to break in upon.

interruption *n* a hindrance; a stoppage; a break in continuity, by passing through or crossing.

intersect *vt* to divide; to cross mutually.

intersection *n* a cutting; crossing of two lines; the point of crossing.

intersperse to scatter; to mingle.

interval *n* time or distance between; the difference of pitch between two sounds.

intervene vi to interpose or interfere; to settle or hinder a matter, etc.

intervention n a coming between; interference; mediation.

interview n a meeting in which a person is asked about his or her views, etc; a meeting at which a candidate for a job is questioned and assessed for a job.

intestate adj dying without having made a will.

intestinal adj pertaining to the intestines.

intestine n the part of the alimentary canal between the stomach and the anus.

intimacy n close friendship; familiarity.

intimate adj most private or personal; very close or familiar, esp sexually. * n a close friend. * vt to make known.

intimation n a hint; an announcement.

intimidate vt to overawe; to cow.

into prep expressing motion towards the inside; to a particular condition.

intolerable adj insufferable; unbearable.

intolerance n bigotry; narrow-mindedness; inability to endure.

intolerant adj illiberal; bigoted.

intonation n a modulation of the voice.

intone vi to chant in a slow monotone.

intoxicate vt to make drunk; to stir up.

intractable adj ungovernable; headstrong; difficult to solve or alleviate.

intransigent adj irreconcilable; unwilling to compromise.

intransitive adj of a verb whose action is limited to its subject.

intrepid adj undaunted; fearless.

intricacy n entanglement; complexity.

intricate adj involved; detailed.

intrigue n an underhand plot. * vi to plot secretly; to rouse curiosity.

intriguing adj scheming; crafty; interesting; attractive.

intrinsic adj in itself; belonging to the real nature of a person or thing; inherent.

introduce vt to present; to insert; to begin; to make known; to bring into use.

introduction n an introducing or being introduced; the presentation of one person to another; preliminary statement; preface; presentation.

introductory adj prefatory; preliminary.

introspection n self-examination.

introvert n a person who is more interested in his or her own thoughts, feelings, etc, than in external objects or events. * adj characterized by introversion (also **introverted**).

intrude vi to trespass; meddle. * vt to thrust in; to force oneself on others.

intrusion n encroachment; trespass.

intrusive adj jutting in; forward.

intuition n insight; instinctive perception apprehension of the truth of something.

intuitive adj natural; apprehended instinctively.

inundate vt to flow over; to flood.

inure vt to harden by use.

invade vt to enter as an enemy; to attack; to encroach upon.

invalid[1] adj void; illegal.

invalid[2] n a person who is ill or disabled. * vt to cause to become an invalid; to disable; to cause to retire.

invalidate vt to render of no effect.

invalidity n ineffectiveness.

invaluable adj priceless.

invariable adj constant; unchangeable.

invasion n hostile entrance; encroachment; intrusion.

invective n a tirade; vituperation.

inveigh vi to rail against.

inveigle vt to beguile; to decoy.

invent vt to originate; to devise; to concoct; to fabricate (a lie, etc).

invention n a new contrivance; ingenuity.

inventive adj ingenious; skilled in invention.

inventory n an itemized list of goods, property, etc. * vt to make an inventory of; to enter in an inventory.

inverse adj opposite; reversed; contrary.

inversion n reversal; complete turn about.

invert vt to turn upside down; to reverse in order, position or relationship.

invertebrate adj without backbone. * n an animal without a backbone.

invest vt to commit (money) to property, shares, etc, for profit; to devote effort, time, etc, on a an activity; to install in office with ceremony; to furnish with power, authority, etc. * vi to invest money.

investigate vt to search into; to examine; to inquire into.

investiture n the act or right of giving legal possession; the ceremony of investing a person with an office, robes, etc.

investment n the act of investing; the amount invested.

inveterate adj deep-rooted; confirmed.

invidious adj envious; causing ill-will.

invigorate vt to strengthen; to enliven; to refresh.

invincible adj unconquerable.

inviolable adj sacred; not to be broken.

inviolate adj virgin; stainless; intact.

invisible adj unseen; imperceptible.; hidden.

invitation n a bidding to come or do something.

invite vt to ask to come somewhere or do something; to ask for; to give reason for; to tempt; to entice.

invocation n a prayer to God for help; an appeal to muse for aid; a summons.

invoice n a list of goods supplied; a bill. * vt to make out a bill (for goods).

invoke vt to call upon (God, etc); to address in prayer; to resort to (law, etc) as pertinent; to implore.

involuntary adj done without power to choose; instinctive.

involve vt to roll up; to include; to implicate; to complicate; to make busy.

invulnerable *adj* not able to be hurt; secure.

inward *adj* situated within or directed to the inside; relating to or in the mind or spirit. * *adv* inwards.

inwardly *adv* within; in the mind or spirit; towards the inside or centre.

inwards *adv* towards the inside or interior; in the mind or spirit.

iodine *n* a nonmetallic element got from seaweed.

iota *n* a jot; a very small quantity.

irascibility *n* anger; testiness.

irascible *adj* easily angered; irritable.

irate *adj* angry; enraged.

ire *n* anger; wrath; rage.

iridescent *adj* shimmering with rainbow colours.

iris *n* (*pl* **irises, irides**) the pigmented membrane surrounding the pupil of the eye; a plant with sword-shaped leaves and bright flowers.

irk *vt* to weary; to vex; to annoy.

irksome *adj* wearisome; tedious.

iron *n* a metallic element, the most common of all metals; a tool of this metal; a heavy implement with a heated flat undersurface for pressing cloth; (*pl*) shackles of iron; firm strength; power; a golf club with an angled metal head. * *adj* of iron; like iron, strong and firm. * *vt, vi* to press with a hot iron.

ironic, ironical *adj* satirical; sarcastic.

ironmonger *n* a dealer in hardware.

irony *n* a form of sarcasm in which the sense is opposite to the words.

irradiate *vt* to illuminate; to enlighten.

irradiation *n* illumination.

irrational *adj* void of reason; senseless; absurd.

irreconcilable *adj* inconsistent; implacable; incompatible.

irregular *adj* not regular; crooked; not conforming to the rules; imperfect; not belonging to the regular armed forces.

irrelevance, irrelevancy *n* inaptness; lack of point.

irrelevant *adj* not to the point.

irreparable *adj* not able to be repaired, rectified or made good.

irreproachable *adj* faultless.

irresistible *adj* overwhelming; resistless; fascinating.

irresolute *adj* undecided; wavering.

irrespective *adj* making no exceptions; regardless of.

irresponsible *adj* lacking a sense of responsibility; flighty.

irretrievable *adj* irreparable; hopeless.

irreverence *n* disrespect; impiety.

irreverent *adj* not paying due respect.

irrevocable *adj* unalterable.

irrigate *vt* to water land artificially; (*med*) to wash out a cavity, wound, etc.

irrigation *n* supplying land with water.

irritable *adj* short-tempered; touchy.

irritant *adj* irritating; galling. * *n* an irritating agent; a stimulant.

irritate *vt* to provoke; to inflame.

irritation *n* annoyance.

irruption *n* an invasion; inroad.

is *third person sing pres indicative of verb* to **be**.

Islam *n* the religion of Mohammed; the Muslim world.

island *n* land surrounded by water.

isle *n* an island.

islet *n* a little isle.

isobar *n* a line on a map joining places with equal atmospheric pressure.

isolate *vt* to cut off; to set apart from others; to quarantine.

isolation *n* detachment; loneliness.

isometric *adj* pertaining to equality of measure or dimension.

isosceles *adj* having two sides equal.

isotherm *n* a line on a map joining places with equal temperature.

isotope *n* any of two or more forms of an element having the same atomic number but different atomic weights.

issue *n* an outgoing; an outlet; a result; offspring; a point under dispute; a sending or giving out; all that is put forth at one time. * *vi* to go or flow out; to result (from) or end (in); to be published. * *vt* to let out; to discharge; to give or deal out, as supplies; to publish.

isthmus *n* a narrow neck of land connecting two larger bodies of land.

it *pron third person neuter*.

italic *n* (*adj*) (of) a printing type in which the letters slant upwards to the right.

italicize *vt* to print in italics.

itch *n* an irritating sensation on the surface of the skin causing a need to scratch; an insistent desire. * *vt* to have or feel an itch.

item *n* an article; a unit; a separate thing; a bit of news or information; (*inf*) a couple having an affair.

itemize *vt* to specify the terms of; to set down by items.

iterate *vt* to repeat.

itinerant *adj* travelling from place to place. * *n* a traveller.

itinerary *n* a travel route; a record or detailed plan of a journey.

its *pron third person possessive of* it.

itself *n* the neuter reflexive pronoun.

ivory *n* a hard bony substance forming tusks of elephants, etc; a creamy white colour. * *adj* of or like ivory.

ivy *n* a climbing or creeping plant with a woody stem and evergreen leaves.

J

jab *vt, vi* to poke or thrust roughly; to punch with short, straight blows.

jabber *vi* to gabble; to speak or say rapidly, incoherently, or foolishly.

jack *n* a device used to lift something heavy; the small white ball aimed at in the game of bowls; the knave in cards; a young pike; a flag. * *vt* to raise by means of a jack.

jackal *n* a dog-like wild animal.

jacket *n* a short outer garment; an outer covering of a book.

jack-knife n a pocket-knife. * vi (of articulated lorry) to lose control so that the cab and trailer swing against each other.

jackpot n the accumulated stakes in certain games, as poker.

jade n a hard, semiprecious stone; its light green colour.

jaded adj tired, exhausted; satiated.

jag vt to notch; to prick. * n a point.

jagged adj ragged; notched.

jail n a prison; a gaol.

jam n a preserve made of boiled fruit and sugar. * vt to press into a confined space; to crowd full of people or things; to cause interference to a radio signal.

jangle vi to make a harsh or discordant sound, as bells. * vt to cause to jangle.

janitor n a caretaker.

January n the first month of the year.

jar vi to clash; to grate. * n a harsh sound; a vase or jug; a jolt.

jargon n the specialized or technical vocabulary of a science, profession, etc; obscure and usu pretentious language.

jaundice n a disease marked by yellowness of the eyes and skin.

jaundiced adj disillusioned.

jaunt vi to go from place to place.

jaunty adj sprightly.

javelin n a spear for throwing.

jaw n one of the bones which hold the teeth.

jaywalk vi to walk across a street carelessly without obeying traffic rules.

jazz n American popular music, characterized by syncopated rhythms.

jealous adj suspicious of a rival; envious.

jealousy n suspicion; envy.

jeans npl trousers made from denim.

jeep n a small robust vehicle with heavy duty tyres and four-wheel drive.

jeer vi to laugh derisively; to mock.

jehad see jihad.

jelly n the juice of fruit boiled with sugar to a glutinous state.

jemmy n a burglar's crowbar.

jeopardize vt to hazard.

jeopardy n hazard; risk.

jerk vt, vi to give a sudden pull, thrust or push to. * n a sudden thrust; a quick pull.

jerky adj moving by jerks.

jersey n a knitted woollen garment; a sweater.

jest n a joke; pleasantry. * vi to joke.

jet n a spouting forth; a nozzle for emission of fluid or gas; a hard black mineral used for jewellery.

jet-black adj of the deepest black.

jetsam, jetson n cargo thrown overboard to lighten a ship; this cargo washed ashore.

jettison vt to throw goods overboard.

jetty n a small pier.

jewel n a precious stone; a highly prized thing.

jeweller n a dealer in jewels.

jewellery n jewels in general.

jib n the triangular foremost sail of a ship; the arm of a crane. * vt, vi to shift a sail; to turn aside.

jibe vt to taunt; to scoff at; gibe. * n a taunt; a sneer.

jig n a lively dance or tune. * vi (pt **jigged**) to dance.

jigsaw *n* a saw with a narrow fine-toothed blade for cutting irregular shapes.

jigsaw (puzzle) *n* a picture on wood or board cut into irregular shapes for re-assembling.

jihad, jehad *n* a holy war waged by Muslims against non-believers; a crusade for or agains a cause.

jilt *vt* to discard a lover.

jingle *vi, vt* to clink, or tinkle. * *n* a tinkling sound, as of bells; a catchy verse.

jingoism *n* belligerent patriotism.

jinx *n* someone or something thought to bring bad luck.

jitter *vi* to feel nervous. * *npl* a nervous feeling of panic.

job *n* a piece of work done for pay; a task; a duty; the thing or material being worked on; work; employment.

jobber *n* a person who buys goods and then sells them; a broker.

jockey *n* a professional racehorse rider. * *vt* to manoeuvre for a better position.

jocular *adj* joking; full of jokes.

jog *vb* (*pt* **jogged**) *vt* to give a slight shake or nudge to; to rouse, as the memory. * *vi* to run at a slow pace for exercise. * *n* a slight shake or push; a nudge; a slow walk or trot.

join *vt, vi* to bring and come together (with); to connect; to unite; to become a part or member of; to participate in. * *n* a joining; a place of joining.

joiner *n* a worker in wood.

joint *n* a place where, or way in which, two things are joined; the part where two bones move on one another in an animal. * *adj* common to two or more; sharing with another. * *vt* to connect by a joint or joints; to divide (an animal carcass) into parts for cooking.

jointly *adv* together; in common.

joist *n* a beam supporting floorboards.

joke *n* something said or done in fun or to cause laughter. * *vi* to make jokes

jolly *adj* merry; jovial; full of fun.

jolt *vi, vt* to shake with sudden jerks; to surprise or shock suddenly.

jostle *vt, vi* to knock against; to hustle; to elbow for position.

jot *n* an iota. * *vt* to note down briefly.

jotter *n* a notebook.

jotting *n* a memorandum.

journal *n* a daily record of happenings, as a diary; a newspaper or periodical.

journalism *n* the work of gathering news for, or producing a newspaper, etc.

journalist *n* a newspaper contributor.

journey *n* a travelling; the distance travelled; a tour * *vi* to travel.

jovial *adj* gay; merry; jolly.

jowl *n* the jaw. **cheek by jowl** side by side.

joy *n* delight; gladness.

joyful *adj* filled with, expressing, or causing joy.

joyous *adj* full of joy.

jubilant *adj* rejoicing greatly; triumphant.

jubilation *n* the joy of triumph.

jubilee *n* a 25th or 50th anniversary of an event.

Judaism *n* the religion of the Jews; Jewish modes of thought.

judge *n* a public official with authority to hear and decide cases in a court of law. * *vt*, *vi* to hear and pass judgment on the relative worth of anything.

judgment *or* **judgement** *n* act of judging; a legal decision; an opinion; good sense; discernment; censure.

judicial *adj* pertaining to judges or courts of justice; impartial.

judiciary *adj* relating to courts of justice. * *n* judges collectively.

judicious *adj* possessing prudence; characterized by sound judgment.

judo *n* a Japanese system of unarmed combat, adapted as a competitive sport from jujitsu.

jug *n* a vessel for holding and pouring liquids; a pitcher.

juggernaut *n* a terrible, irresistible force; a large heavy truck.

juggle *vi* to conjure; to manipulate.

juggler *n* a conjuror.

jugular *adj* pertaining to the throat.

juice *n* fluid of fruits, vegetables and meat.

July *n* the seventh month of the year.

jumble *vt*, *vi* to mix in a confused mass * *n* a muddle; articles for a jumble sale.

jumbo *n* something very large of its kind.

jump *vi* to spring or leap from the ground, a height, etc; to jerk; a sudden transition; an obstacle; a nervous start.

jumper *n* a knitted pullover.

junction *n* a point of union; a railway centre.

juncture *n* where lines meet, link or cross each other.

June *n* the sixth month of the year.

jungle *n* an area overgrown with dense tropical trees and other vegetation, etc.

junior *adj* younger in age; of more recent or lower status.

junk *n* useless articles; any narcotic drug; a Chinese floating vessel.

junk food *n* a snack or fast food with little nutritional value.

junk mail *n* unsolicited mail, e.g. advertising leaflets.

jurisdiction *n* judicial authority, its range or extent.

jurisprudence *n* the science or philosophy of law; a division of the law.

jurist *n* one versed in law.

juror *n* one who serves on a jury.

jury *n* people sworn to hear evidence and deliver a verdict on a case; a panel.

just *adj* fair, impartial; deserved, merited; proper, exact; conforming strictly with the facts. * *adv* exactly; nearly; only.

justice *n* justness, fairness; the use of authority to maintain what is just; the administration of law; a judge.

justiciary, justiciar *n* an administrator of justice.

justifiable *adj* that may be justified.

justification *n* a defence; vindication; remission of sin.

justify *vt* to prove right; to vindicate.

justly *adv* rightly; properly.

jut *vi* to project.

juvenile *adj* young; youthful; immature.

juxtaposition *n* a placing near or side by side.

K

kail, kale n a kind of cabbage.

kaleidoscope n a tube containing bits of glass reflected by mirrors to form symmetrical patterns when rotated.

karate n a Japanese system of unarmed combat using sharp blows of the feet and hands.

karaoke n a CD music system that plays recordings of popular songs with the vocal part removed to allow amateurs to sing.

keel n the backbone of a ship. * vt, vi to (cause to) turn over.

keen adj shrewd; sharp; eager; (of prices) low so as to be competitive.

keep vt (pt, pp **kept**) to hold; to preserve; to guard; to detain; to continue any state, course, or action; to obey; to perform * vi to endure; not to perish or be impaired * n care; guard; a strong tower.

keeper n one who guards.

keeping n care, charge; observance.

keepsake n a gift treasured because of the giver.

keg n a small cask or barrel.

kennel n a small shelter for dogs; (pl) a place where dogs are bred or kept.

kerb n stone edging to pavement.

kernel n the core (esp of a nut).

kerosene n a fuel oil distilled from petrol.

kettle n a metal vessel with a spout for boiling water.

kettledrum n a drum made of a hollow metal body with a parchment head.

key n a device for locking and unlocking something; a thing that explains or solves, as the legend of a map, etc.

keyboard n a set of levers on which the fingers press on a piano, computer, etc.

keynote n the basic note of a musical scale; the basic idea or ruling principle.

keystone n the top stone of an arch.

khaki adj dull yellowish-brown.

kick vt, vi to strike with the foot; to recoil * n a blow with the foot or feet; recoil; a thrill; an intoxicating effect.

kidnap vt to carry off a person by force and hold to ransom.

kidney n one of two glands that excrete waste products from the blood as urine; an animal's kidney as food.

kill vt to cause the death of; to destroy. * n the act of killing; the animals killed.

kiln n a stone furnace for baking or hardening lime, bricks, pottery, etc.

kilogram, kilogramme n a measure of weight (2.204 pounds).

kilometre n a measure of length, 1000 metres or 0.62 mile.

kin n family; kindred; relatives.

kind n race; genus; variety; nature * adj humane; friendly; sympathetic.

kindle vt, vi to set on fire; to light; to arouse.

kindly adj friendly; genial; kind; gracious.

kindred n kinship; blood relations * adj related; akin; similar.

kinetic adj causing motion; of motion in relation to force.

kinetics n the science of motion in relation to force.

king n the man who rules a country and its people; a man with the title of ruler, but with limited power to rule.

kingdom n a country headed by a king; any of the three divisions of the natural world: animal, vegetable, mineral.

kink n a tight twist or curl in a piece of string, rope, hair, etc; a painful cramp in the neck, back, etc; an eccentricity of personality. * vt, vi to form or cause to form a kink or kinks.

kiosk n a light open structure for sale of papers, sweets, etc; a public telephone booth.

kipper n a herring split open, salted, and dried.

kirk n a church.

kiss vt, vi to touch with the lips as an expression of love, affection or in greeting. * n an act of kissing; a light, gentle touch.

kit n an outfit; equipment e.g. tools, etc; a set of parts for assembly.

kitchen n a place where food is prepared.

kite n a light paper-covered frame for flying in air.

kiwi n a flightless bird of New Zealand.

kiwi fruit n a fruit of an Asian vine.

kleptomania n an irresistible impulse to steal.

knack n dexterity; a trick; a habit.

knapsack n a backpack.

knead vt to work dough; to squeeze and press with the hands.

knee n the joint between the thigh and the lower part of the human leg. * vt (pt **kneed**) to hit or touch with the knee.

kneel vi (pt, pp **knelt** or **kneeled**) to go down and remain on the knees.

knell n the sound of a bell (esp funeral bell). * vi to toll.

knickers npl an undergarment covering the lower body and having separate leg holes, worn by women and girls.

knife n a cutting instrument. * vt to cut or stab with a knife.

knight n a rank conferring title Sir; a chessman shaped like a horse's head.

knighthood n the rank or dignity of a knight.

knit vt, vi (pt **knitted** or **knit**) to form (fabric) by interlooping yarn using knitting needles or a machine.

knob n a rounded lump or protuberance; a boss or stud or handle (of a door).

knock vt, vi to strike; to rap on a door; to criticize. * n a blow; a rap.

knocker n the device hinged against a door for knocking.

knockout n a punch or blow that produces unconsciousness.

knoll n a little round hill.

knot n a lump in a thread, etc, formed by a tightened loop or tangling; a fastening made by tying lengths of rope, etc. * vt, vi (pt **knotted**) to make or form a knot (in); to entangle or become entangled.

know vt, vi (pt **knew**, pp **known**) to be aware that; to be sure that; to understand; to be acquainted with; to have knowledge.

knowing adj well informed; shrewd; implying a secret understanding.

knowledge n acquaintance with; learning; information.

knuckle n the joint of a finger.

Koran n the sacred book of Muslims.

krill n the tiny shrimp-like plankton eaten by many whales.

kudos n glory; fame; renown.

L

label n a slip of paper, cloth, metal, etc, attached to anything to provide information about its nature, contents. * vt (pt **labelled**) to provide with a label.

laboratory n a building where scientific work and research is carried out.

laborious adj arduous; laboured; hard-working.

labour n exertion; toil; workers collectively; the process of childbirth * vi to work; to be burdened; to give unnecessary details.

labourer n a worker; esp doing heavy or manual work.

labyrinth n a place full of winding paths; a maze.

lac n a resin yielding shellac.

lace n a cord, etc, used to draw together and fasten parts of a shoe, a corset, etc.

lacerate vt to tear to torture.

lack vt to want; to need. * vi to be in want. * n want; failure deficiency.

lackadaisical adj languid; showing lack of energy or interest.

lackey n a servant.

laconic adj concise; using few words.

lacquer n varnish; lacquered ware * vt to varnish; to gloss.

lactic adj related to or procured from milk.

lad n a boy; a young man.

ladder n a portable metal or wooden framework for climbing up and down.

laden adj loaded; burdened.

lading n cargo; freight.

ladle n a large long-handled spoon.

lady n a woman of rank; a title.

lag vi to loiter; to fall behind. * vt (pt **lagged**) to insulate pipes with insulating material.

lager n a light beer.

laggard adj slow. * n one who dawdles.

lagging n insulating material.

lagoon n a shallow saltwater lake cut off from the sea by a coral reef.

laisser faire n non-interference; freedom of action (esp in commerce, etc).

laity n lay people, as distinguished from the clergy.

lake n water wholly surrounded by land; a purplish-red pigment.

lame adj crippled; limping.

lament vi to weep; to grieve * vt to bewail * n a mournful song or tune.

lamentable adj distressing; deplorable.

lamentation n mourning; sorrow.

lamp n any device producing light, either by electricity, gas or by burning oil, etc.

lance n a long spear * vt to cut or pierce with a lancet.

land n the solid part of the earth's surface; ground, soil; a country and its people; property in land. * vt, vi to go ashore from a ship; to come to port; to arrive at a specified place; to come to rest.

landing n act or place of disembarking; a flat area at the top of a flight of stairs; the floor between flights of stairs.

landlady n the mistress of an inn or boarding house; a woman who rents property.

landlocked adj enclosed by land.

landlord n owner of land or houses; owner or host of an inn, etc.

landlubber n one with little experience of the sea and sailing.

landmark n a prominent feature that serves as a guide or distinguishes a locality; an important event.

landowner n a person who owns land.

landscape n an expanse of natural scenery seen in one view; a picture of natural, inland scenery. * vt to make (a plot of ground) more attractive.

landslip, landslide n the sliding of a mass of soil or rocks down a slope; an overwhelming victory esp in an election.

lane n a narrow road, path, etc; a path or strip specifically designated for ships, aircraft, cars, etc.

language n human speech; speech peculiar to a nation.

languid adj faint; listless; weak.

languish vi to be or become faint; to droop; to pine.

languor n faintness; listlessness.

lank adj tall and thin; long an limp.

lanky adj lean, tall and ungainly.

lanoline n a soothing ointment.

lantern n a portable transparent case for holding a light.

lap n the flat area formed by the knees and thighs in sitting posture; one round of a course in a race. * vt, vi (pt **lapped**) to fold (over or on); to wrap; to overlap; to extend over something in space or time.

lapel n the folded back part of coat, etc, continuous with the collar.

lapse n a small error; a decline or drop to a lower condition, degree, or state; a moral decline. * vi to depart from the accepted standard, esp in morals; to pass out of use; to become void; (time) to slip away.

larceny n theft of goods.

lard n melted and clarified pig fat. * vt to embellish.

larder n a store cupboard for provisions.

large *adj* great in size, number; big; bulky.

largely *adv* widely; copiously; mainly.

largess *n* a present; bounty.

largo *adv* (*mus*) slow and dignified. * *n* a passage played in this way.

lark *n* a frolic; a prank.

larva *n* (*pl* **larvae**) the form of an insect on coming out of the egg, a grub.

larynx *n* the upper part of the windpipe containing the vocal cords.

lascivious *adj* lewd; lecherous.

lash *n* the thong of a whip; a stroke with a whip * *vt* to whip; to bind.

lassitude *n* faintness; weariness.

last *adj* coming after all the others; latest; final. * *adv* the last time. * *vi* to endure; to continue. * *n* a shaped block on which shoes are made; a foot mould.

lasting *adj* durable; permanent.

latch *n* the catch of a door, gate, etc. * *vt*, *vi* to fasten with a latch.

late *adj* behind time; long delayed; deceased * *adv* at a late time; recently.

latent *adj* not yet apparent; dormant.

lateral *adj* of, at, from, towards; on the side.

lath *n* a long narrow slip of wood to support plaster, etc.

lathe *n* a machine for shaping wood or iron.

lather *n* froth of soap and water; frothy. * *vt*, *vi* to cover with or form lather.

Latin *adj* of ancient Rome, its people, their language, etc.

latitude *n* breadth; width; scope; freedom from restriction on action or opinions; distance north or south of the equator.

latter *adj* later; coming after; modern; being the last mentioned of two.

lattice *n* a network of crossed laths; a trellis; a window so formed.

laudable *adj* praiseworthy.

laudatory *adj* expressing praise.

laugh *vi* to make the sound expressive of mirth; to be mirthful * *n* the sound or act of laughing.

laughable *adj* amusing; comical.

laughing stock *n* an object of ridicule.

laughter *n* the act or sound of laughing.

launch *vt* to throw; to propel and slide (into water). * *vi* to initiate; to put into action. * *n* the act of launching; a large open motorboat.

launder *vt*, *vi* to wash and iron clothes.

launderette *n* an establishment equipped with coin-operated washing machines.

laundry *n* place where clothes are washed and ironed.

laureate *adj* decked with laurel leaves as a mark of honour. * *a poet laureate*, the official court poet.

lava *n* molten volcanic rocks.

lavatory *n* a place for washing hands, urinating, etc.

lavish *adj* profuse; generous; abundant; extravagant * *vt* to give or spend generously.

law *n* all the rules of conduct in an

organized community as upheld by authority.

law-abiding adj obeying the law.

lawbreaker n a person who violates the law.

lawful adj legal; rightful.

lawgiver n a legislator.

lawless adj not regulated by law; not in conformity with law, illegal.

lawn n a smooth grass plot; a fine linen.

lawsuit n a suit between private parties in a law court.

lawyer n a person whose profession is advising others in matters of law or representing them in a court of law.

lax adj loose; slack; vague; not strict.

laxative adj purging * n a gentle purgative.

laxity n slackness; carelessness.

lay vt (pt, pp **laid**) to cause to lie; to place; to impose; to allay, to bring forth eggs; to wager. * n a song; a poem. * adj not clerical or expert.

layer n a stratum; a single thickness; a coat, as of paint. * vt to separate into layers.

layman n one not a clergyman; a non-specialist or professional.

layout n the manner in which anything is laid out.

laziness n indolence; sloth.

lazy adj slothful; indolent.

lea n a meadow.

lead[1] n a soft and heavy metal; a stick of graphite.

lead[2] vt, vi (pt, pp **led**) to guide or conduct; to direct; to precede; to entice; to influence; to be first * n guidance; the role of a leader; the amount or distance ahead; a clue; the leading role in a play, etc.

leaden adj heavy; dull; like lead; gloomy.

leader n a guide; a captain; an editorial article; the first violin in an orchestra.

leading adj chief; principal.

leaf n (pl **leaves**) one of the thin parts of a plant growing from the skin; a sheet of paper or metal; two pages of a book. * vi to bear leaves; (with **through**) to turn the pages of.

leaflet n a little leaf; a sheet of printed information or advertising matter.

league n a union for mutual help; an alliance; a treaty; an association of sports club that organizes matches between members.

leak n a hole which admits water or gas; confidential information made public deliberately or accidentally * vi to let water in or out; to disclose.

leakage n a leaking.

lean[1] vt, vi (pt, pp **leant** or **leaned**) to slope; to incline; to rest against; to rely on.

lean[2] adj thin; barren; meagre.

leaning n inclination, tendency.

leap vi, vt (pt, pp **leapt** or **leaped**) to jump; to bound * n a spring.

learn vt, vi (pt, pp **learnt** or **learned**) to gain knowledge or skill; to find out; to realize.

learning n knowledge; scholarship.

lease n a letting for a term of years * vt to let or lease.

leasehold *adj* held by lease * *n* tenure by lease.

leaseholder *n* a tenant under a lease.

leash *n* a thong or strap for leading animals. * *vt* to hold or restrain on a leash.

least *adj* smallest. * *adv* in the smallest degree. * *n* the smallest amount.

leather *n* tanned and dressed hide.

leave *n* permission; farewell; the period allowed for absence. * *vt* (*pt*, *pp* **left**) to let remain; to bequeath; to quit; to deposit.

leaves *pl of* **leaf**.

lecherous *adj* lustful; lewd.

lectern *n* a reading desk in a church.

lecture *n* a discourse; a reprimand * *vi* to deliver a lecture * *vt* to reprove.

ledge *n* a narrow shelf; a ridge; a layer.

ledger *n* an account book.

leech *n* a bloodsucking worm; a person who clings to or uses another.

leer *n* a sly or lewd glance. * *vi* to give a leer.

lees *npl* dregs; sediment.

leeward *adj* pertaining to the lee. * *adv* towards the lee.

leeway *n* the drift of a ship to leeward.

left *adj* denoting opposite to the right; towards the west when facing north. * *n* the left side; the left hand; the left wing in politics.

left-wing *adj* of or relating to the liberal faction of a political party.

leg *n* one of the limbs on which humans and animals support themselves and walk; any of a series of games or matches in a competition.

legacy *n* money, property, etc, left to someone in a will.

legal *adj* of or based on law; permitted by law; of or for lawyers. * *vt* to make lawful.

legality *n* conformity to law.

legalize *vt* to make lawful; to sanction.

legatee *n* one to whom a legacy is left.

legend *n* a story handed down from the past; a notable person or the stories of his or her exploits.

legendary *adj* fabulous; mythical.

leggings *npl* protective outer covering for the lower leg; a leg-hugging fashion garment for women.

legible *adj* able to be read.

legion *n* a great number.

legislate *vi* to make or pass laws.

legislative *adj* capable of enacting laws.

legislator *n* one who makes laws.

legislature *n* the lawmaking body in a state.

legitimate *adj* legal; born in wedlock; genuine; valid.

leguminous *adj* pertaining to pod-bearing plants, e.g. peas, pulse, beans, etc.

leisure *n* spare time; freedom from business; relaxation.

leisurely *adj* not hasty; relaxed. * *adv* slowly.

lend *vt* (*pt*, *pp* **lent**) to grant use of a thing temporarily; to provide money at interest.

length *n* extent from end to end; duration; extension; a long expanse; a piece of specified length cut from a longer piece.

lengthen vt to make long; to extend.

lengthways adv in the direction of the length.

lenience, leniency n quality of being lenient; mildness.

lenient adj merciful; forbearing; not harsh.

lens n (pl **lenses**) a curved piece of transparent glass, plastic, etc, used in optical instruments to form an image; a similar transparent part of the eye that focuses light rays on the retina.

Leo n the Lion, fifth sign of zodiac.

leotard n a skin-tight one-piece garment worn by dancers and others engaged in strenuous exercise.

leper n one affected with leprosy.

leprosy n disease of the skin.

lesbian n a female homosexual. * adj of or characteristic of lesbians.

lesion n an injury; a wound.

less adj smaller. * adv in a lower degree; to a smaller extent. * n a smaller quantity.

lessee n the holder of a lease.

lessen vt, vi to make or become less.

lesser adj less; smaller.

lesson n something to be learned or studied; an example.

lest conj for fear that.

let vt (pres p **letting**, pt, pp **let**) to permit; to allow; to lease; to rent.

let-down n a disappointment.

lethal adj deadly; fatal.

lethargic adj drowsy; dull.

lethargy n a drowsy state.

letter n a symbol representing a pho-

netic value in a written language; a character of the alphabet; a written or printed message.

letter box n a slit in the doorway of a house or building through which letters are delivered; a postbox.

lettering n the act or process of inscribing with letters; letters collectively; a title; an inscription.

lettuce n a leafy plant used in salads.

leukaemia n a chronic disease characterized by an abnormal increase in the number of white blood cells.

level n an instrument for determining the horizontal; a horizontal line or surface; an even surface. * adj horizontal; even; flat * vt, vi to make level; to flatten.

level-headed adj having an even temper and sound judgment.

lever n a bar for raising weights; a means to an end; a device used to operate machinery.

leverage n power gained by use of a lever; power; influence.

levity n lightness; frivolity; lack of seriousness.

levy vt to collect (taxes) by the force or authority. * n the amount levied.

lewd adj lustful; sensual; obscene.

lexicographer n a dictionary compiler.

lexicon n a dictionary.

liability n an obligation; debt; a handicap; a disadvantage; (pl) debts; obligations.

liable adj responsible; subject to; likely to do.

liaison n intercommunication as between units of a military force; an illicit love affair.

liar n one who tells lies.

libel n a defamatory or damaging writing.

libellous adj slanderous; defamatory.

liberal adj generous; ample; profuse; not too strict; free; of education, contributing to a general broadening of the mind.

liberality n generosity; breadth of view.

liberate vt to free; to deliver.

liberator n one who liberates.

libertine n a profligate; a rake * adj licentious.

libertinism n depravity.

liberty n state of being free, esp from slavery; captivity; etc; privilege; licence; undue familiarity; impertinence.

libidinous adj lustful.

Libra n the Balance, the seventh sign in the zodiac.

librarian n the keeper of a library.

library n a collection of books or the place in which they are kept.

lice npl of **louse**.

licence n authority given to do something specified; a certificate or document giving permission; excess of liberty.

license vt to grant a licence to.

licensee n one to whom a licence is granted.

licentious adj profligate; morally unrestrained.

lichen n a kind of moss, alga or fungus.

licit adj lawful; legal.

lick vt to pass the tongue over; to lap; to flicker round of flames; to thrash; to defeat. * n a licking with the tongue; (inf) a sharp blow; (inf) a short, rapid burst of activity.

lid n a removable cover of a box, vessel, etc, an eyelid.

lido n (pl **lidos**) an open-air swimming pool and recreational complex for public use.

lie[1] vi (pres p **lying**, pp, pt **lied**) to speak untruthfully. * n an untrue statement.

lie[2] vi (pres p **lying**, pp **lain**, pt **lay**) to stretch out or rest in a horizontal position; to be in a specified condition; to be situated; to exist. * n relative position of objects.

lied n (pl **lieder**) a German song or ballad.

lieu n place; stead.

lieutenant n a deputy; a chief assistant; an army officer ranking below a captain.

life n the state of living or being alive; existence; spirit; vigour; vivacity.

lifeboat n a small rescue boat carried by a ship; a specially designed and equipped rescue vessel that helps those in distress along the coastline.

life buoy n a buoyant object for keeping persons afloat.

lifeguard n an expert swimmer employed to prevent drownings.

lifeless adj dead; dull; heavy.

lifelike adj true to life in appearance.

lifelong adj lasting through life.

lift vt, vi to raise up; to hoist; to cheer; to steal; (of fog) to disperse; to rise * n a hoist; an elevation of mood; a ride in a vehicle.

liftoff *n* the vertical thrust of a spacecraft, etc, at launching; the time of this.

ligament *n* band of tough tissue joining bones at joints.

ligature *n* a tie for blood vessels in operations.

light *n* the agent by which objects are made visible to the eye; day; that which gives or admits light; illumination of mind. * *adj* bright; clear; not heavy; active; slight. * *vt, vi* (*pt, pp* **lit** *or* **lighted**) to give light to; to enlighten; to ignite; to brighten; to alight.

lighten *vi* to shine; to flash * *vt* to illuminate; to make less heavy; to alleviate; to cheer.

lighter *n* a flat-bottomed boat for loading and unloading ships; a small device producing a flame.

light-footed *adj* nimble; active.

light-headed *adj* giddy.

light-hearted *adj* merry; carefree.

lighthouse *n* a tower with a light to guide ships.

lightly *adv* easily; nimbly.

lightning *n* the vivid flash of electricity that precedes thunder.

lightweight *adj* of less than average weight; trivial, unimportant. * *n* a person or thing of less than average weight; a professional boxer of a specific weight; a person of little importance or influence.

light year *n* the distance light travels in one year.

lignite *n* a soft brownish-black coal with the texture of the original wood.

like *adj* equal; similar; resembling * *adv, prep* similarly. * *vt, vi* to be fond of; to be pleased; to approve. * *n* a like; a counterpart.

likelihood *n* probability.

likely *adj* probable; suitable. * *adv* probably.

liken *vt* to compare.

likewise *adv* in like manner; also.

liking *n* inclination; fondness; affection.

limb *n* the arm or leg; a large branch of a tree.

limber *adj* flexible * *n* the detachable front of a gun carriage.

limbo *n* a kind of purgatory; an intermediate stage between extremes.

lime *n* a substance got by heating limestone, and with sand and water forming cement.

limelight *n* intense publicity.

limerick *n* a humorous doggerel verse of five lines.

limestone *n* a rock composed mainly of calcium carbonate of lime.

limit *n* boundary; utmost extent; restraint. * *vt* to bound; to restrict.

limited *adj* narrow; restricted; lacking imagination.

limp *vi* to walk lamely * *n* a lameness in walking. * *adj* not firm; flabby; lethargic.

limpid *adj* clear; crystal.

linchpin *n* a pin fastening a wheel to the axle; a person or thing vital to the success of an enterprise.

line *n* a length of cord, rope or wire; a cord for measuring, making level; a system of conducting fluid, electricity, etc; edge, limit, boundary;

border, outline, contour; a row of persons or things, as printed letters across a page; (*inf*) glib, persuasive talk; a verse; the forward combat position in warfare; a short letter, note; (*pl*) all the speeches of a character in a play. * *vt* to mark or cover with lines; to form a line along; to arrange in a line; to cover on the inside. * *vi* to align.

lineage *n* race; descent.

lineal *adj* straight; direct; hereditary.

lineament *n* a facial feature; form.

linear *adj* of, made of, or using a line or lines; narrow and long.

linen *n* cloth made of flax; household articles made of linen, e.g. sheets.

liner *n* a large passenger ship or aircraft.

linesman *n* an assistant referee.

linger *vi* to delay; to loiter; to remain in the mind.

linguist *n* one skilled in languages.

linguistics *adj* the science of language.

lining *n* an inner covering of a garment, etc.

link *n* a single loop or ring of a chain; a person or thing acting as a connection, as in a communication system. * *vt, vi* to connect or become connected.

links *npl* flat sandy ground; a golf course, esp by the seaside.

linoleum *n* a floor covering of coarse fabric backing with a smooth, hard decorative coating.

linseed *n* flaxseed.

lint *n* linen specially prepared as a dressing for wounds; fluff.

lintel *n* the upper bar of a doorway or a window.

lion *n* a beast of prey; king of the beasts; sign in zodiac (Leo); a celebrity.

lion-hearted *adj* courageous.

lip *n* either of the front edges of the mouth; the edge or rim of a jug, etc; insolent talk.

lipstick *n* a small stick of cosmetic for colouring the lips.

liquefy *vt* to melt; to dissolve.

liqueur *n* a sweet and variously flavoured alcoholic drink.

liquid *n* a substance that, unlike a gas, does not expand indefinitely and, unlike a solid, flows readily. * *adj* in liquid form; clear; limpid; flowing smoothly and musically (*of assets*) readily convertible into cash.

liquidate *vt* to settle the accounts of; to wind up a bankrupt business; to convert into cash; to kill; to eliminate.

liquidation *n* the winding up of a bankrupt estate.

liquor *n* a drink (esp alcoholic).

liquorice *n* a black extract from the root of a plant, used in medicine and confectionery; a liquorice flavoured sweet.

lisp *vi* to pronounce imperfectly (esp 's'). * *n* lisping speech.

lissom *adj* supple.

list *n* a series of names, numbers written in order.

listen *vi* to try to hear; to give heed.

listener *n* a person who listens.

listless *adj* languid; weary; unenthusiastic.

litany *n* a series of petitions in a prayer book; any tedious recital.

literacy *n* the ability to read and write.

literal *adj* exact; word for word.

literary *adj* versed in letters and literature.

literate *adj* able to read and write; educated.

literature *n* the writings of a period or country.

lithe *adj* pliant; flexible.

lithesome *adj* supple; nimble.

lithograph *vt* to imprint on stone and transfer to paper.

litigant *n* one engaged in a lawsuit.

litigate *vt, vi* to go to law; to contest points of law.

litigious *adj* contentious.

litre *n* a unit of capacity in metric system, 1.76 pints.

litter *n* a portable bed; scattered rubbish; young produced at one birth. * *vt, vi* to strew carelessly; to make tidy.

little *adj* small; short * *adv* in a small degree; less; slightly; not in the least. * *n* small in amount, degree, etc.

liturgy *n* a ritual for public worship.

live[1] *vi* to exist; to dwell; to conduct one's self in life; to subsist; to gain a livelihood. * *vt* to lead; to spend; to pass.

live[2] *adj* alive; having life; not exploded; carrying electric current.

livelihood *n* means of living.

lively *adj* vivacious; spirited.

liver *n* the organ which secretes bile; animal liver as food.

livestock *n* (farm) animals raised for use or sale.

livid *adj* of a leaden colour; very angry.

living *n* livelihood; benefice of a clergyman; a way of living.

living room *n* a room in a house used for general entertainment and relaxation.

load *vt* to charge with a load; to burden; to oppress; to put film in a camera; to install a program in a computer memory; to charge, as a gun. * *n* a burden; cargo; a large amount.

loaf *n* a shaped mass of bread. * *vi* to idle about.

loam *n* a rich clayey soil.

loan *n* lending; something lent, esp money. * *vt, vi* to lend.

loath, loth *adj* reluctant.

loathe *vt, vi* to hate; abhor.

loathsome *adj* disgusting.

lob *n* (*cricket, etc*) a slow, high-pitched ball. * *vt* to bowl slowly.

lobby *n* an entrance hall; a person or group who try to influence (legislators) to support a cause, etc.

lobe *n* the lower part of the ear; a division of the brain, lungs, etc.

local *adj* pertaining to or serving the interests of a particular place; of or for a particular part of the body. * *n* an inhabitant of a specific place; a local pub.

locale *n* a locality.

locality *n* a place; a neighbourhood.

locate *vt* to place the position of something.

loch *n* a Scottish lake.

lock¹ *n* a fastening device operated by a key; the part of a canal dock in which the level of the water can be changed by the operation of gates; a a controlling hold as used in wrestling. * *vt* to fasten with a lock; to shut; to fit, link; to jam together so as to make immovable. * *vi* to become locked.

lock² *n* a curl of hair; a tuft of wool, etc.

locker *n* a small cupboard, chest, etc.

locket *n* a small gold case worn round the neck.

locksmith *n* a maker of locks.

locomotive *n* a railway engine.

locum (tenens) *n* a temporary deputy.

locust *n* a type of destructive grasshopper; a hardwood tree.

lode *n* a vein of mineral ore.

lodge *n* a small house at the entrance to a park or stately home. * *vt, vi* to live in a place for a time; to live as a paying guest.

lodger *n* a person who lives in a rented room in another's home.

lodging *n* a temporary abode; rented accommodation.

loft *n* the space or room under the rafters; a gallery. * *vt* to lift into the air.

lofty *adj* high; haughty; stately.

log *n* a section cut from a felled tree; a device for measuring the speed of ships; a written record, esp one kept on a ship's voyage or aircraft's flight. * *vt, vi* (*pt* **logged**) to record in a log; to fell trees; to sail or fly (a specified distance); (*with* **on, off**) to establish or disestablish communication with a computer.

logarithms *n* a mathematical system for facilitating calculations.

logbook *n* an official record of a ship's or aircraft's voyage or flight; an official document containing details of a vehicle's registration.

logic *n* the science of reasoning; a particular way of thinking; (*inf*) good sense.

logical *adj* conforming to the rules of logic; capable of reasoning; consistent.

logistics *n* the planning and organization of any complex activity.

loin *n* the lower part of the back.

loiter *vi* to hang about; to linger.

loll *vi* to lean idly; (*of tongue*) to hang out.

lone *adj* solitary; single; isolated.

lonesome *adj* solitary.

long *adj* not short; protracted; late; tedious; slow; far-reaching; well supplied. * *vt* to desire earnestly. * *adv* for a long time; from start to finish.

long-distance *adj* travelling or communicating over long distances.

longevity *n* great length of life.

longhand *n* ordinary handwriting, as opposed to shorthand.

longing *n* an intense desire.

longitude *n* length; distance east or west of fixed meridian.

longitudinal *adj* running lengthways.

long-suffering *adj* patient.

long-term *adj* of or extending over a long time.

long-winded *adj* tedious.

look *vi* to direct the eye so as to see;

to gaze; to consider; to expect; to heed; to appear. * *n* gaze; a glance; aspect; appearance.

lookout *n* a place for keeping watch; a person assigned to watch.

loom[1] *vi* to come into view indistinctly, large or threateningly.

loom[2] *n* a machine or frame for weaving. * *vt* to weave on a loom.

loop *n* a line that curves back and crosses itself; a similar rounded shape in cord, rope, etc, crossed on itself; a set of instructions in a computer program that are executed repeatedly; a segment of film or magnetic tape. * *vt, vi* to make a loop of; to fasten with a loop; to form a loop or loops.

loophole *n* a narrow slit for outlook, etc; a way of escape or evading obligation, etc.

loose *adj* untied; free; vague; careless; not firm, tight or compact. * *vt* to untie; to set free; to discharge a bullet.

loosen *vt* to make loose. * *vi* to become loose.

loot *n* booty; plunder; money.

lop *vt* to cut off.

lopsided *adj* leaning to one side.

loquacious *adj* talkative.

lord *n* a master; a ruler; a nobleman.

lordly *adj* proud; haughty.

lore *n* learning, esp of a traditional kind, e.g. folklore.

lose *vt, vi* (*pt, pp* lost) to have taken from one by death, accident, removal, etc; to be unable to find.

loss *n* a losing or being lost; the damage, trouble caused by losing; the person, thing, or amount lost.

lot *n* a part or share; fate which falls to one; a considerable quantity; the thing drawn at random to decide something.

loth *see* loath.

lotion *n* a healing or cleansing or cosmetic liquid.

lottery *n* a system of raising money by selling numbered tickets that offer the chance of winning a prize.

lotus *n* a legendary plant causing forgetfulness to the eater; a kind of lily.

loud *adj* easily audible; noisy; showy; obtrusive.

lounge *vi* to loiter; to loll; to spend time idly. * *n* a comfortable room.

louse *n* (*pl* lice) a parasitic insect.

lousy *adj* infested with lice.

lout *n* an awkward, rude fellow.

love *vt* to regard with affection; to like; to delight in. * *vi* to be in love. * *n* warm affection; the passionate affection for another; a word of endearment.

lovely *adj* beautiful; charming.

lover *n* a person in love with another; a person having an extramarital sexual relationship.

loving *adj* fond; kind.

low[1] *adj* situated below any given surface; not high; less in size, degree, etc, than usual; deep in pitch; depressed in spirits; humble; vulgar; not loud. * *adv* in or to a low degree, level, etc. * *n* a low level, degree, etc; a region of low barometric pressure.

low[2] *vi* to bellow, as an ox; to moo like a cow.

lower[1] vt to let down; to abase.

lower[2] vi to frown; to threaten a storm.

lowering adj threatening a storm.

lowland n comparatively low or level country.

lowly adj humble; meek.

loyal adj faithful; true.

loyalist n one who is true to his or her country.

loyalty n fidelity; constancy.

lozenge n a four-sided, diamond-shaped figure; a cough drop or sweet, originall of this shape.

LSD n a powerful hallucinatory drug (lysergic acid diethylamide).

lubber n a clumsy fellow.

lubricant n a substance for oiling or greasing.

lubricate vt to smear with oil to lessen friction; to make smooth, slippery, greasy.

lucent adj shining; resplendent.

lucid adj easily understood; sane.

luck n chance; fortune; success.

lucky adj fortunate; auspicious.

lucrative adj paying; gainful.

ludicrous adj laughable; droll; absurd.

lug vt to haul. * n the ear.

luggage n a traveller's baggage.

lugubrious adj sad; doleful.

lukewarm adj moderately warm; indifferent.

lull vt to calm; to send to sleep; to allay (fears, etc), usu by deception. * n a calm interval.

lullaby n a cradle song.

lumbago n rheumatism in the lower back.

lumbar n pertaining to the lower back.

lumber n useless articles; rubbish; felled timber.

luminary n an enlightening, influential or famous person.

luminous adj shining; clear.

lump n a small shapeless mass; an abnormal swelling; a stupid or boring person.

lunacy n mental derangement; utter folly.

lunar adj pertaining to the moon.

lunatic adj insane. * n a madman.

lunch, luncheon n a midday meal.

lung n either of the two organs of respiration.

lunge n a sword thrust; a plunge forward. * vt, vi to (cause to) move with a lunge.

lurch vi to roll or sway to one side. * n a sudden roll.

lure n a bright fishing bait; something that tempts or entices. * vt to entice.

lurid adj vivid; glaring; sensational; ghastly pale; wan.

lurk vi to lie hidden in wait; to loiter furtively.

luscious adj very sweet; delicious.

lush adj luxuriant; juicy.

lust n longing desire; sensual appetite. * vi to desire eagerly; to feel lust.

lustily adv stoutly; vigorously.

lustre n brightness; renown; a glossy surface.

lustrous adj bright; shining.

lusty adj vigorous; robust.

luxuriant adj profuse; abundant.

luxuriate vi to give oneself up to luxury.

luxurious *adj* given to luxury.

luxury *n* indulgence in sumptuous things; (*pl*) something costly and enjoyable but not a necessity.

lymph *n* colourless fluid in the body contained in and collected from the tissues.

lynch *vt* to put to death by mob law.

lyre *n* an ancient stringed instrument related to the harp.

lyric *adj* of the nature of a song or poem, expressing emotion; of or having a high voice with light flexible quality. * *n* a lyric poem; (*pl*) the words of a popular song.

lyrical *adj* lyric; expressing enthusiasm or rapture.

lyricism n lyrical quality or expression.

lyricist *n* a person who writes lyrics.

M

macaroni *n* pasta rolled into tubes.

macaroon *n* a cake or biscuit of ground almonds.

mace *n* a spiked club; an ensign of office; an aromatic spice made from the outside covering of the nutmeg.

machine *n* a structure of fixed and moving parts, for doing useful work; an organization functioning like a machine; the controlling group in a political party.

machine gun *n* an automatic gun.

machinery *n* machines in general; mechanism.

machinist *n* one who works a machine.

machismo *n* excessive masculine pride.

macrocosm *n* great world or the universe regarded as a whole.

mad *adj* insane; crazy; frantic; angry.

madam *n* a polite form of address a woman; a woman in charge of a brothel.

madcap *adj* reckless, lively. * *n* a frolicsome person.

madden *vt* to make mad.

madman, madwoman *n* an insane person.

madness *n* insanity; folly.

maelstrom *n* a whirlpool.

magazine *n* a storehouse; a munitions depot; a periodical publication containing feature articles, fiction, etc; a supply chamber as in a camera, a rifle, etc.

magenta *n* a bright purplish-crimson dye or colour.

maggot *n* a worm-like grub.

magic *n* the use of charms, spells, etc, supposedly to influence events by supernatural means; any mysterious power; the art of producing illusions by sleight of hand, etc. * *vt* (*pt* **magicked**) to influence, produce or take (away) by or as if by magic.

magical *adj* marvellous.

magician n a conjurer.

magistrate n a public officer who administrates justice.

magnanimity n greatness of soul or mind; noble and generous conduct.

magnanimous adj noble and generous; unselfish.

magnate n a man of rank, wealth or influence.

magnesium n a white malleable metal.

magnet n a piece of iron or steel that has the property of attracting iron.

magnetic adj of magnetism or a magnet.

magnetism n the science which treats of magnetic phenomena; personal charm.

magnificence n grandeur; pomp.

magnificent adj imposing; splendid; superb.

magnify vt to enlarge; to extol; to glorify; to exaggerate.

magnitude n greatness; importance.

mahogany n a hard reddish wood much used for furniture; a reddish-brown colour.

maid n a young girl; a female servant.

maiden n a young unmarried woman; a runless over in cricket.

mail n letters, etc, conveyed and delivered by the post office; a postal system.

maim vt to mutilate; to disable.

main adj chief; leading. * n strength; the greater part; the ocean.

mainland n the land, other than islands.

mainstay n the chief support.

maintain vt, vi to keep up; to sustain.

maintenance n upkeep; the support (esp financial) given to a spouse after divorce.

maize n corn; a light yellow colour.

majestic adj august; stately.

majesty n grandeur; nobility; dignity.

major adj the greater in number, quantity, or extent; very serious; life-threatening; (mus) higher than the corresponding minor by half a tone. * n an army officer below lieutenant colonel.

majority n the greater number.

make vt, vi (pt, pp **made**) to create; to construct; to produce; to cause to be; to perform; to force; to act or do; to earn; to reach. * n style; brand or origin; manner of production.

make-believe n pretence; sham.

makeshift n a temporary substitute.

maladjustment n poor adaptation, esp to social environment.

maladministration n bad management.

malady n illness; disease.

malaise n a feeling of discomfort.

malaria n an infectious disease.

malcontent n a discontented person.

male n a man or boy; an animal or plant of that sex. * adj of the sex of a man.

malefactor n a criminal; a felon.

malevolent adj spiteful; malicious.

malformation n deformity.

malfunction n faulty functioning.

malice n spite; ill will.

malicious adj spiteful; intentionally destructive.

malign adj harmful; evil; malignant.

malignant adj malevolent; virulent.

malinger vi to feign illness.

mall n an avenue; an area of shops.

malleable adj capable of being beaten out by hammering; pliable.

mallet n a wooden hammer.

malnutrition n lack of nutrition.

malpractice n evil practice; misconduct.

malt n barley prepared by various processes for brewing and distilling.

maltreat vt to abuse.

mammal n any member of a class of warm-blooded vertebrates that suckle their young.

mammoth n an extinct species of elephant. * adj gigantic.

man n a human being; a male adult; mankind; a male servant; a husband; an ordinary soldier; a member of a team.

manacle n a handcuff * vt to fetter.

manage vt to wield; to conduct or direct.

manageable adj able to be managed; tractable.

management n direction; the directors of a business, organization, etc.

manager n a person who manages a company, organization, etc; an agent who looks after the business affairs of an actor, writer, etc.

mandarin n any high-ranking official; (with cap) the Beijing dialect that is the official pronunciation of the Chinese language.

mandate n a command; written authority to act for another.

mandatory adj compulsory.

mandible n an animal's jaw.

mandolin n a stringed instrument.

mane n the long hair on the neck of the horse, lion, etc.

manful adj bold; energetic.

mange n a skin disease of dogs, etc.

mangle vt to mutilate; to smooth; to press.

manhole n a hole giving entrance.

manhood n virility; manliness.

mania n great enthusiasm; a craze.

maniac n a madman; an enthusiast.

manicure n the fingernails and care of the hands.

manifest adj clearly visible; evident. * vt to display. * n a list of a ship's or aircraft's cargo.

manifestation n evidence; revelation.

manifestly adv evidently.

manifesto n a public declaration of policy issued by a government or a party.

manifold adj numerous and various.

manipulate vt to handle; to manage skilfully or craftily.

mankind n the human race.

manly adj brave; hardy.

man-made adj manufactured or created by man; artificial, synthetic.

mannequin n a woman who models fashion clothes.

manner n the mode in which anything is done; bearing or conduct; (pl) behaviour.

mannerism n a personal peculiarity.

manoeuvre n a planned and controlled movement of troops, ships, etc; a skilful or shrewd move; a stratagem. * vt, vi to (cause to) perform manoeuvres; to manage or plan skilfully; to move get, make, etc, by some scheme.

manor n the land or house belonging to a lord; a police district.

mansion n a large imposing house.

manslaughter n the killing of a person without malice.

mantel, mantelpiece n the ornamental work round a fireplace; the shelf above.

mantle n a loose sleeveless cloak.

manual adj done by the hand. * n a textbook; a book of instructions.

manufacture vt to make, esp on a large scale, using machinery; to invent, fabricate. * n the production of goods by manufacturing.

manure n dung or other substance for fertilizing soil. * vt to treat with manure.

manuscript n a paper written with the hand.

many adj numerous.

map n a plan of any part of the earth's surface. * vt (pt **mapped**) to make a map; to plan.

mar vt to injure; to impair; to spoil.

marauder n a robber; a rover.

marble n a valuable building and monumental stone; a small ball of stone, etc.

march vi to walk in step * vt to cause to march. * n a measured or military walk; a distance walked; a musical composition for marching to; a boundary.

March n the third month of a year.

mare n the female of the horse.

margarine n a butter substitute made from vegetable and animal fats, etc.

margin n an edge; the blank border of a printed page; surplus; the difference between the cost and the selling price.

marginal adj written in the margin; situated at the margin or border; close to the lower limit of acceptability; very slight, insignificant.

marginalize vt to transfer someone away from the centre of affairs in order to render them powerless.

marina n a harbour for pleasure craft.

marine adj pertaining to the sea; naval.

mariner n a seaman.

marionette n a puppet.

marital adj pertaining to marriage.

maritime adj relating to the sea or ships; bordering on or living near the sea.

marjoram n a herb used in cooking.

mark n a visible sign or stamp; eminence; token; aim; a cross made instead of a signature; a symbol, e.g. a punctuation mark; a grade for academic work; impression; influence; formerly the monetary unit of Germany.

marked adj pre-eminent; obvious.

market n a meeting of people for buying and selling merchandise; a space or building in which a market is held; the chance to sell or buy; demand for (goods, etc); a region where goods can be sold.

marketable adj fit for sale.

marketing n all the processes involved in moving goods from the producer to the consumer.

marksman *n* one skilled at shooting.

marmalade *n* a preserve made from oranges, sugar and water.

maroon *n* a brownish-crimson colour; a distress rocket. * *vt* to abandon esp on a desert island.

marquee *n* a large tent used for entertainment.

marquetry *n* inlaid work.

marriage *n* wedlock; a wedding; a union.

marrow *n* a soft substance in cavities of bones; a kind of gourd eaten as a vegetable.

marry *vt*, *vi* to unite in wedlock.

marsh *n* a swamp; boggy land.

marshal *n* one who is in charge of ceremonies, etc; a military officer of the highest rank. * *vt* to arrange in order.

marsupial *adj* (*n*) (an animal) carrying its young in a pouch.

martial *adj* warlike; military.

martyr *n* one who is tortured and suffers death for his or her faith; a person who suffers from an illness. * *vt* to kill as a martyr; to make a martyr of.

martyrdom *n* the death of a martyr; torture.

marvel *n* a wonder. * *vi* (*pt* **marvelled**) to feel astonishment; to be filled with wonder.

marvellous *adj* wonderful; miraculous; astonishing.

mascot *n* a charm; someone or something thought to bring good luck.

masculine *adj* male; manly; robust.

mash *n* a soft thick mixture of ingredients, esp as food for horses and cattle; mashed potatoes.

mask *n* a covering to conceal or protect the face; a moulded likeness of the face; anything that conceals or disguises; a respirator placed over the nose and mouth to aid or prevent inhalation of a gas; (*photog*) a screen used to cover part of a sensitive surface to prevent exposure.

mason *n* a worker or builder in stone; (*with cap*) a Freemason.

masonry *n* stonework; the craft of masons.

masquerade *n* a fancy-dress ball at which masks are worn; a pretence.

mass *n* a lump; magnitude; a large quantity; bulk; size; the main part; in physics, the property of a body expressed as a measure of the amount of material contained in it; (*pl*) the common people; (*with cap*) the celebration of the Eucharist. * *adj* of or for the masses. * *vt*, *vi* to gather or form into a mass.

massacre *n* ruthless slaughter. * *vt* to slaughter.

massage *n* the rubbing and kneading of parts of body.

masseur (*m*), **masseuse** (*f*) *n* one who gives massage professionally.

massive *adj* bulky and heavy; solid.

mast *n* an upright on which a ship's sails are set.

mastectomy *n* the removal of a breast by surgery.

master *n* one who rules or directs; an employer; an owner; a ship's captain; a teacher; an expert of craftsman; a writer, painter, etc, regarded as pre-eminent; an original from which copies are made; a holder of an advanced academic degree. * *vt* to be or become master of.

masterful *adj* imperious; headstrong.

masterly *adj* skilful; expert.

masterpiece *n* an artist's greatest work; any extraordinary piece of work.

masterstroke *n* a supremely able act.

mastery *n* command; ascendancy.

masticate *vt* to chew and prepare for swallowing.

masturbate *vi* to manually stimulate one's sexual organs to achieve orgasm without sexual intercourse.

mat *n* a fabric of plaited fibre, straw, etc, for protection purpose.

match *n* any person or thing which goes with another; an equal; a contest; a marriage; a strip of wood or cardboard tipped with a chemical that ignites when struck.

matchless *adj* unrivalled.

mate *n* an associate; an animal's sexual partner; a companion; a husband or wife; four as a pair; a ship's officer.

material *n* consisting of matter; important; not spiritual; essential. * *n* the substance of which anything is made; a person suitable for a task, a position, etc.

materialism *n* the doctrine of materialists.

materialist *n* one whose interest lies in acquiring possessions.

materialize *vt* to give concrete form to.

maternal *adj* of, like a mother.

maternity *n* motherhood. * *adj* relating to pregnancy.

mathematician *n* one concerned with mathematics.

mathematics *n* the science dealing with quantities, forms, space, etc, and their relationships by use of numbers and symbols.

matins *npl* morning prayers.

matinée *n* an afternoon performance.

matriarch *n* a woman who rules.

matricide *n* the killing of a mother; the person guilty of it.

matriculate *vt, vi* to enrol or be enrolled.

matrimonial *adj* pertaining to marriage.

matrimony *n* marriage.

matrix *n* a mould.

matron *n* a woman in charge of domestic and nursing arrangements.

matted *adj* entangled.

matter *n* what a thing is made of; material; whatever occupies space and is perceptible to the senses.

matting *n* a course material, such as woven straw or hemp.

mattress *n* a casing of strong cloth filled with cotton, foam rubber, springs, etc.

mature *adj* ripe; fully developed; due payable. * *vt, vi* to make or become ripe.

maturity *n* ripeness; perfection.

maul *vt* to handle roughly; to paw.

mausoleum *n* a large tomb.

mauve *n* a shade of pale purple.

maxim *n* an established principle.

maximum *n* the greatest quantity.

May *n* the fifth month of the year.

may[1] *vb aux* (*pt* **might**) used to imply possibility, desire, etc.

may[2] hawthorn blossom.

maybe adv perhaps.

mayhem n violent destruction, confusion.

mayonnaise n a salad dressing.

mayor, mayoress n the chief administrative officer of a municipality.

maze n a labyrinth; a perplexity.

me personal pron the objective case of I.

meadow n a piece of land where grass is grown for hay.

meagre adj thin; scanty.

meal n the food taken at one time; any edible ground grain.

mean[1] adj middle; moderate. * n the middle; average; (pl) resources; measures.

mean[2] vt, vi (pt, pp meant) to have in mind; to intend; to signify.

mean[3] adj selfish; ungenerous; despicable.

meander n a winding course. * vi to wind about; to wander aimlessly.

meaning adj significant. * n significance.

meantime adv during the intervening time; at the same time. * n the intervening time.

meanwhile adv, n meantime.

measles n an acute, contagious viral disease.

measurable adj that may be measured.

measure n the extent, capacity or magnitude of a thing; a standard; an instrument for measuring; just degree; a course of action; a legislative proposal; a musical time, metre.

measured adj set, marked off by a standard; rhythmical; regular; deliberate; stately.

measurement n dimensions.

meat n food in general; animal flesh as food; the essence of something.

mechanic n a person skilled in operating, maintaining or repairing machines.

mechanical adj of or using machinery or tools; produced or operated by machinery; done as if by a machine, lacking thought or emotion.

mechanics n the science of motion and force; knowledge of machinery; the technical aspects of something.

mechanism n the working parts of a machine; any system of interrelated parts.

medal n a piece of metal struck to celebrate an event; a reward of merit.

medallist n a winner of a medal.

meddle vi to interfere in another's affairs.

meddlesome adj interfering.

mediate vi to try to reconcile; to intercede.

mediation n intercession for another.

mediator n an intercessor; an advocate.

medical adj pertaining to medicine.

medicament, medication n a medicine.

medicinal adj healing.

medicine n the science of preventing, treating or curing disease; any healing substance.

medieval, mediaeval adj pertaining to the Middle Ages.

mediocre adj of moderate quality.

mediocrity n moderate skill, ability, etc.

meditate vi to think deeply; to reflect.

meditation n reflection; contemplation of spiritual, etc, matters.

meditative adj thoughtful.

medium n (pl **media** or **mediums**) the middle state or condition; a substance for transmitting an effect; any intervening means, instrument, or agency; (pl **media**) a means of communicating information (e.g. newspapers, television, radio); (pl **mediums**) a person claiming to act as an intermediary between the living and the dead.

medley n a miscellany; a musical piece made up of various tunes.

meek adj patient; submissive.

meet vt, vi (pt, pp **met**) to come face to face; to encounter; to light on; to receive; to satisfy; to assemble.

meeting n an assembly; an encounter.

melancholy n mental depression; dejection; sadness. * adj dejected.

mellifluent, mellifluous adj sweet; honeyed.

mellow adj soft and ripe; (of wine) matured; genial; kind-hearted.

melodious adj tuneful; pleasing to the ear.

melodrama n a thrilling or sensational play, etc, usu with an improbable plot.

melodramatic adj over-emotional.

melody n a tuneful composition.

melon n a large juicy fruit.

melt vt, vi to liquefy; to soften; to dissolve; to fade; to disappear.

member n a limb; one of a society or company; a representative in parliament, etc.

membership n the members of a body.

membrane n a thin flexible sheet or film.

memento n a souvenir.

memoir n a biography or autobiography.

memorabilia npl things worthy of record; objects, souvenirs of famous people.

memorable adj worthy to be remembered; easy to remember; famous.

memorandum n (pl **memorandums** an informal written communication as within an office; (pl **memoranda**) a note to help the memory.

memorial adj bringing to memory. * n a monument; a remembrance.

memorize vt to commit to memory.

memory n the faculty of remembering; the sum of the things remembered; an individual recollection.

menace n a threat. * vt to threaten.

mend vt to repair; to improve.

mendacious adj lying; false.

mendacity n deceit.

menial adj low; servile descriptive of work of little skill.

meningitis n inflammation of the membranes enveloping the brain.

menopause n the time of life during which a woman's menstrual cycle ceases.

menstrual adj monthly.

menstruation n the monthly discharge of blood from the uterus.

mental adj pertaining to the mind; occurring or performed in the mind; having a psychiatric disorder; crazy; stupid.

mention n a brief reference or notice;

an official recognition or citation. * vt to refer to briefly; to remark; to honour officially.

mentor n a wise adviser.

menu n a bill of fare; a list of options.

mercantile adj relating to trade.

mercenary adj hired; grasping. * n a soldier hired for service in a foreign army.

merchandise n goods; trade.

merchant n a trader on a large scale; a retailer.

merchant navy n commercial shipping.

merciful adj compassionate; tender.

merciless adj pitiless; cruel.

mercurial adj volatile; sprightly.

mercury n a heavy silvery liquid metallic element used in thermometers, etc.

mercy n pity; compassion; pardon.

mere adj sole; simple; nothing more than.

meretricious adj gaudy; insincere.

merge vt to absorb; to blend.

merit n excellence; worth; (pl) the rights and wrongs (of a case). * vt to deserve; to be worthy of.

meritorious adj praiseworthy.

merriment n mirth; noisy gaiety.

merry adj joyous; jovial; cheerful.

mesh n the wires of a screen, etc; engagement of geared wheels.

mesmeric adj hypnotic.

mesmerism n the power by exercise of will to control the actions of another.

mesmerize vt to subject to mesmerism; to hypnotize; to hold spellbound.

Mesozoic adj belonging to one of the geological periods or formations.

mess n a state of disorder or untidiness, esp if dirty; a building where service personnel dine.

message n a communication; an errand; the chief idea a writer, artist, etc, seeks to communicate in a work.

messenger n one who bears a message.

messy adj dirty; confused; untidy.

metabolism n the total processes in living organisms by which tissue is formed, energy produced and waste product eliminated.

metal n any of a class of chemical elements which are often lustrous, ductile solids, and are good conductors of heat, electricity, etc, such as gold, iron, copper, etc.

metallurgy n the science of extracting metals from their ores.

metamorphic adj altered in structure.

metamorphosis n (pl **metamorphoses**) a complete change of form.

metaphor n a figure of speech in which a word or phrase is used for another of which it is an image.

metaphoric, metaphorical adj figurative.

metaphysical adj pertaining to metaphysics; abstract.

metaphysics n the branch of philosophy dealing with the nature of being and reality.

mete vt to dole out or distribute.

meteor n a small particle of matter that travels at great speeds through space.

meteoric *adj* brilliant but transitory.

meteorite *n* a spent meteor.

meteorology *n* the study of the atmosphere and of weather-forecasting.

meter *n* an instrument for registering consumption of gas, water, time, etc.

method *n* mode of procedure; system; orderliness of thought or arrangement.

methodical *adj* systematic; orderly.

methylated spirit *n* a form of alcohol, used as a solvent.

meticulous *adj* over careful; precise about small details.

metre[1] *n* pattern in verse or music.

metre[2] *n* the basic unit of length in the metric system (39.37 inches).

metric *adj* pertaining to the decimal system.

metrication *n* conversion of an existent system of units into the metric system.

metric system *n* a decimal system of weights and measures.

metronome *n* an instrument that beats musical tempo.

metropolitan *adj* belonging to a metropolis.

mettle *n* spirit; courage.

mezzanine *n* an intermediate storey between others; a theatre balcony.

mezzo *adj* in music, middle; mean.

mezzo-soprano *n* a female voice, singer with a range between soprano and contralto.

mice *npl* of mouse.

microbe *n* a germ; a bacillus.

microcosm *n* man as an epitome of the universe or macrocosm; a very small copy.

microfilm *n* film on which documents, etc, are recorded in reduced scale.

microphone *n* an instrument for transforming sound waves into electric signals, esp for transmission, or recording.

microscope *n* an optical instrument for magnifying.

microscopic *adj* minute; visible only through a microscope.

mid *adj* middle; intervening.

midday *n* the middle of the day; noon.

middle *adj* equally distant from the extremes.

middle age *n* the time between youth and old age.

Middle Ages *npl* the period of European history between about AD 500 and 1500.

middle class *n* people between the working classes and the aristocracy.

midnight *n* twelve o'clock at night.

midriff *n* the diaphragm.

midst *n* the middle. * *prep* amidst; among.

midsummer *n* the middle of summer.

midway *n* halfway.

midwife *n* a woman that assists women in childbirth.

might *n* power; strength.

mighty *adj* strong; powerful; large.

migrant *n* a person or animal who migrates.

migrate *vi* to remove from one region or country to another.

migratory *adj* roving; wandering.

mild *adj* gentle; merciful; soft.

mildew *n* a mouldy deposit or coating caused by fungus.

mile *n* 1760 yards or 1.61 km.

mileage *n* distance in miles.

milestone *n* a stone or post marking each mile of a road; an important event in life.

militancy *n* aggressiveness.

militant *adj* warring; combative.

militarism *n* military spirit; reliance on force.

military *adj* pertaining to soldiers.

militate *vi* (*with* **against**) to influence, to have an adverse effect on.

militia *n* an army composed of civilians.

milk *n* a fluid secreted by female mammals to feed their young. * *vt* to draw milk from; to extract money, etc, from; to exploit.

mill *n* a machine for grinding corn, etc; a factory. * *vt* to grind.

millennium *n* a period of 1000 years.

milligram *n* the thousandth part of a gram.

millimetre *n* the thousandth part of a metre.

million *n* a thousand thousands, 1,000,000.

millionaire *n* a person worth a million pounds; one who is extremely rich.

millstone *n* a stone used in grinding corn.

mime *n* a drama enacted through gestures. * *vi* to act without words.

mimic *adj* imitative. * *n* one who imitates; an actor skilled in mimicry.

mimicry *n* imitation.

mince *vt, vi* to chop into small pieces; to act or walk affectedly; to clip (words).

mincemeat *n* a mixture of chopped apples, raisins, etc, used as a pie filling.

mind *n* the intellectual faculty or power; intellect; reason; understanding; inclination; opinion; memory. * *vt* to heed; to pay attention to; to obey; to take care of; to care about; to object.

mindful *adj* attentive; heedful.

mine[1] *poss pron* my; belonging to me.

mine[2] *n* an excavation from which minerals are dug; an explosive device concealed in the water or ground to destroy enemy ships, personnel, or vehicles that pass over or near them; a rich supply or source. * *vt* to dig or work a mine.

minefield *n* an area in which explosive mines are laid; a situation containing hidden problems.

miner *n* a person who works in a mine.

mineral *n* an inorganic substance found in or on the earth.

mineralogist *n* an expert on mineralogy.

mineralogy *n* the science of minerals.

mingle *vt* to mix together; to blend.

miniature *n* a small-scale portrait; a reduced copy.

minim *n* a note in music; the smallest liquid measure; a single drop.

minimize *vt* to estimate at the lowest; to disparage.

minimum *n* the smallest amount.

minister *n* a member of a government heading a department; a diplomat; a clergyman serving a church. * *vt, vi* to give help to; to perform a service.

ministration *n* service; a giving of aid; the work of a minister of the church.

ministry *n* service; office of a minister; clergy; a government department headed by a minister.

minor *adj* lesser; smaller; petty. * *n* a person under full legal age.

minority *n* the state of a minor; the smaller of two parties voting; any smaller group.

minstrel *n* a bard; a travelling musician of the Middle Ages.

mint *n* the place where money is coined; a large amount of money; an aromatic plant with leaves used for flavouring. * *vt* to coin. * *adj* in perfect condition.

minuet *n* a slow graceful dance; the music played for it.

minus *adj* less. * *n* the sign of subtraction (-).

minute¹ *adj* very small; precise: exact.

minute² *n* the sixtieth part of an hour or a degree; (*pl*) a summary of proceedings; an official record of a meeting. * *vt* to record, summarize the proceedings (of).

minutiae *npl* small details.

miracle *n* a marvel; a supernatural event.

miraculous *adj* marvellous; supernatural.

mirage *n* an optical illusion caused by light reflection from hot air.

mire *n* wet, muddy soil; mud.

mirror *n* a looking glass; a faithful depiction.

misadventure *n* a mishap; bad luck.

misalliance *n* an unsuitable marriage.

misanthrope, misanthropist *n* a hater of mankind.

misapply *vt* to apply wrongly.

misapprehend *vt* to misunderstand.

misapprehension *n* a mistake.

misappropriate *vt* to appropriate dishonestly; to embezzle.

misbehave *vi* to behave badly.

miscalculate *vt* to reckon wrongly.

miscarriage *n* a failure; mismanagement; the premature expulsion of a foetus.

miscellaneous *adj* mixed; diverse.

mischance *n* ill luck; mishap.

mischief *n* wayward, prankish behaviour.

mischievous *adj* troublesome; hurtful.

misconduct *n* immoral or bad behaviour.

misconstrue *vt* to interpret wrongly.

miscount *vt, vi* to make an error in counting; a wrong counting.

misdeed *n* an evil action.

misdemeanour *n* a minor offence.

miser *n* a skinflint; a hoarder of money.

miserable *adj* wretched; despicable.

misery *n* wretchedness; sorrow; poverty.

misfit *n* a bad fit; a maladjusted person.

misfortune n ill fortune; calamity.

misgiving n a doubt; mistrust.

misguided adj foolish; mistaken.

mishap n a slight or unfortunate accident.

misinform vt to give wrong information to.

misinterpret vt to interpret wrongly.

misjudge vt to judge erroneously.

mislay vt to lose temporarily; to put down in the wrong place.

mislead vt to deceive; to misinform.

mismanage vt to manage badly.

misnomer n an incorrect or unsuitable name for someone or something.

misogynist n a woman-hater.

misplace vt to put out of place.

misprint n a mistake in printing.

mispronounce vt, vi to pronounce wrongly.

misquote vt to quote incorrectly.

misrepresent vt to represent falsely.

misrule n misgovernment.

miss[1] vt to fail to hit, find, meet, etc; to lose; to omit; to fail to take advantage of; to feel the loss of. * n a failure to hit; loss; want.

miss[2] n an unmarried woman; a girl.

misshapen adj ill-formed.

missile n an object, as a rock, spear, rocket, to be thrown, fired or launched.

missing adj lost; absent.

mission n a group of people sent by a church, government, etc, to carry out a special duty or task.

missionary n one sent to a foreign country to propagate religion.

missive n an official letter.

misspell vt to spell wrongly.

misspend vt to squander; to waste.

mist n a mass of visible water vapour.

mistake vb (pt **mistook**, pp **mistaken**) vt to misunderstand or misinterpret. * vi to err. * n a blunder, an error of judgment; a misunderstanding.

mistaken adj erroneous; ill-judged.

mistress n the feminine of master; a woman with whom a man is having an affair.

mistrust n suspicion. * vt to suspect; to doubt.

misunderstand vt to take the wrong meaning from.

misuse vt to use for wrong purpose; to abuse. * n improper use.

mite n a minute parasitic animal; a very small object or person.

mitigate vt to lessen, to abate, to moderate.

mitre n the headdress of a bishop; a diagonal joint between two pieces of wood to form a corner.

mitten n a fingerless glove.

mix vt, vi to unite or blend; to mingle; to join; to combine (ingredients, etc).

mixed adj blended; assorted; of different kinds, classes, races, etc; confused.

mixture n a compound; a medley.

mix-up n a mistake; confusion, muddle.

mnemonics n art of memory; rules for assisting memory.

moan vi to utter a mournful sound.

moat n a ditch round a castle or fort.

mob n a crowd; a rabble; a gang of animals. * vt (pt **mobbed**) to attack in a disorderly group; to surround.

mobile adj movable, not fixed; easily changing; characterized by ease in change of social status; capable of moving freely and quickly; having transport. * n a suspended structure of wood, etc, with parts that move.

mobilize vt to organize troops in readiness for service.

moccasin n a deerskin shoe; any soft flexible shoe.

mock vt to imitate or ridicule; to behave with scorn; to defy; (with **up**) to make a model of. * n ridicule; an object of scorn. * adj false, sham, counterfeit.

mockery n derision; a sham.

mock-up n a full-scale working model of a machine, etc.

mode n way of acting, doing, existing; manner; fashion; (mus) any of the scales used in composition; (statistics) the predominant item in a series of items; a mood in grammar.

model n a pattern; an ideal; a standard worth imitating; a representation on a smaller scale, usu three-dimensional; a person who sits for an artist or photographer; a person who displays clothes by wearing them.

moderate vt to restrain from excess; to temper, to lessen. * vi to preside over.

moderation n temperance; restraint.

modern adj of the present or recent times; contemporary; up-to-date.

modernism n modern thought or practice.

modernize vt to make modern.

modest adj retiring; bashful; diffident; moderate.

modesty n bashful reserve; chastity.

modicum n a small quantity.

modification n the act of modifying.

modify vt to change slightly; to lessen the severity of; to limit in meaning.

modulate vt to measure; to vary (the voice) in tone.

module n a unit of measurement; a self-contained unit, esp in a spacecraft; one of a set of learning units making up a course of study.

moist adj slightly wet; damp.

moisten vt to make damp or moist.

moisture n dampness; humidity.

moisturize vt to add moisture to the skin, air, etc, with various preparations.

mole n a dark spot on human skin; a breakwater; a spy within an organization.

molecular adj belonging to or consisting of molecules.

molecule n the simplest unit of a substance; a small particle.

molest vt to annoy; to vex; to assault esp sexually.

mollify vt to soften; to appease; to tone down.

mollusc n a soft-bodied invertebrate animal with a hard shell (e.g. oyster, etc).

molten adj melted by heat.

moment n an indefinitely brief period of time; importance; gravity.

momentary *adj* lasting only for a moment.

momentous *adj* important; weighty.

momentum *n* (*pl* **momenta**) the force possessed by a moving body.

monarch *n* a sovereign ruling by hereditary right.

monarchy *n* government headed by a monarch; a kingdom.

monastery *n* the residence of monks.

monastic *adj* of monks or monasteries.

monasticism *n* the monastic life or system.

Monday *n* the second day of the week.

monetary *adj* relating to money.

money *n* current coin or its equivalent in bank notes, etc.

moneyed *adj* wealthy.

mongrel *adj* of mixed or unknown breed.

monitor *n* a prefect; any device for regulating the performance of a machine, aircraft, etc. * *vt, vi* to check on; to regulate, control a machine, etc.

monk *n* a male member of a religious order in a monastery.

monkey *n* any of the primates except man and the lemurs, esp the smaller, long-tailed primates; a mischievous child.

monocle *n* a single eyeglass.

monogamy *n* marriage to one wife or husband only.

monogram *n* letters (esp initials) interwoven in one design.

monograph *n* an essay on one subject.

monolith *n* a standing stone or pillar.

monologue *n* a soliloquy.

monopolize *vt* to obtain entire control of.

monopoly *n* an exclusive trading privilege; exclusive use or possession.

monosyllable *n* a word of one syllable.

monotone *n* speaking without inflection; a sameness of style, colour, etc.

monotonous *adj* unvarying; tedious.

monotony *n* an irksome sameness.

monsoon *n* a seasonal wind of Southern Asia.

monster *n* a huge frightening creature.

monstrosity *n* an unnatural, misshapen creature or thing.

monstrous *adj* unnatural; horrible.

montage *n* the art or technique or assembling various elements.

month *n* any of the twelve divisions of the year; a calendar month; a period corresponding to the moon's revolution.

monthly *adj* continuing for a month; done, happening, payable, etc, every month. * *n* a monthly periodical. * *adv* one a month, every month.

monument *n* a tomb, pillar, statue, etc, erected as a memorial.

monumental *adj* of, like, or serving as a monument; colossal; lasting.

moo *n* the long deep sound made by a cow. * *vi* (*cattle*) to low.

mood *n* a temporary state of mind; (*gram*) the form of the verb indicating mode of action.

moody *adj* in low spirits; temperamental.

moon *n* the natural satellite that revolves around the earth and shines by reflected sunlight; any natural satellite of another planet; something shaped like the moon.

moonbeam *n* a ray of light from the moon.

moonlight *n* the light of the moon. * *vi* to have a secondary (usu nighttime) job.

moor *n* a heath; wasteland. * *vt* to secure a ship by cable or anchor.

mooring *n* the anchors, buoys, etc, by which or to which a boat is moored.

moose *n* a large North American deer.

moot *adj* debatable; hypothetical.

mop *n* a rag, sponge, etc, fixed to a handle for washing floors or dishes; a thick, unruly head of hair. * (*pt* **mopped**) to wash with a mop.

mope *vi* to be downcast and uninterested.

moral *adj* of or relating to character and human behaviour, particularly as regards right and wrong; virtuous, esp in sexual conduct; capable of distinguishing right from wrong.

morale *n* the tone, spirit, or mental condition prevailing with regard to courage, discipline, confidence, etc.

morality *n* the doctrine of moral duties; ethics; virtue; an old form of drama.

moralize *vt, vi* to reflect on, moral questions.

morass *n* a marsh; a bog; a fen.

moratorium *n* legal permission to defer payments due; a temporary stoppage.

morbid *adj* diseased; sickly; gruesome.

more *adj* *comp* of much and many greater in amount, extent, etc. * *adv* in a greater degree.

moribund *adj* in a dying state.

morning *n* the first part of the day.

morose *adj* surly; sullen; glum.

morphia, morphine *n* an alkaloid derived from opium.

morsel *n* a bite; a small piece.

mortal *adj* subject to death; deadly; fatal; human. * *n* a human being.

mortality *n* the state of being mortal; the death rate.

mortar *n* a bowl in which substances are pounded with a pestle; an artillery piece that fires shells at low velocities and high trajectories; a cement.

mortgage *n* a conveyance of property as security for loan; the deed of conveyance. * *vt* to pledge as security.

mortification *n* gangrene; humiliation.

mortify *vt, vi* to affect with gangrene; to shame.

mortifying *adj* humiliating.

mortise *n* a hole cut in a piece of wood, etc, so that part of another piece (the tenon) may fit into it.

mortise lock *n* a lock set into a mortise in a door.

mortuary *n* a place for temporary storage of dead bodies; a morgue.

mosaic *n* inlaid work of marble, precious stones, etc.

Moslem same as **Muslim**.

mosque n a Moslem place of worship.

moss n a very small green plant that grows in clusters on rocks, moist ground, etc.

mossy adj overgrown with moss.

most adj superl of **more** greatest in any way. * adv in the greatest degree.

motel n an hotel for motorists with adjacent parking.

moth n a nocturnal insect allied to the butterfly.

mother n a female parent; source or origin; the head of a nunnery, etc. * adj of, like a mother; native. * vt to be or care for as a mother.

mother-in-law n the mother of one's spouse.

motherly adj of, proper to a mother.

motion n activity, movement; a formal suggestion made in a meeting, law court, or legislative assembly; evacuation of the bowels. * vt, vi to signal or direct by a gesture.

motionless adj not moving; still.

motion picture n a film, movie.

motive n something (as a need or desire) that causes a person to act.

motley adj composed of diverse element.

motor n anything that produces motion; a machine for converting electrical energy into mechanical energy; a motor car. * adj producing motion; of or powered by a motor; of, by or for motor vehicles. * vi to travel by car.

motorbike n a motorcycle.

motorboat n a boat propelled by an engine or motor.

motorcycle n a two-wheeled motor vehicle.

motorist n a person who drives a car.

motorway n a road with controlled access for fast-moving traffic.

mottled adj marked with blotches of various colours.

motto n (pl **mottoes**) a short saying adopted as a maxim or ideal.

mould n a fungus producing a furry growth on the surface of organic matter; a hollow form in which something is cast. * vt to make in or on a mould; to form, to shape, to guide.

moulder vt, vi to decay; to crumble.

moulding n anything cast in a mould; ornamental contour along an edge.

moult vi to shed or cast the hair, horns, skin, etc.

mound n an artificial elevation of earth or stones; a rampart; a hillock.

mount n a hill; a mountain; a setting for photographs, etc; a backing; a horse. * vi to rise; to get on horseback; to provide with horses; to amount. * vt to climb; to fix, place in position.

mountain n a high hill, a vast number.

mountaineer n a mountain climber.

mourn vi to sorrow. * vt to grieve for.

mournful adj expressing grief or sorrow.

mourning n lamentation; clothes worn by mourners.

mouse n (pl **mice**) a small rodent

with a pointed snout, long body and slender tail; a timid person; a hand-held device used to position the cursor and control software on a computer screen.

mousse *n* a chilled dessert; a substance applied to hair to keep its style.

moustache *n* the hair on the upper lip.

mouth *n* the opening in the head through which food is eaten, sound uttered or words spoken; the lips; opening, entrance, as of a bottle, etc. * *vt* to say, esp insincerely; to form words with the mouth without uttering sound. * *vi* to utter pompously; to grimace.

mouthpiece *n* the part of a musical instrument or tobacco pipe placed between the lips; a spokesperson for others.

mouth-watering *adj* appetizing; tasty.

movable *adj* portable. * *npl* furniture; belongings; personal property.

move *vt* to cause to change place; to set in motion; to affect; to rouse; to prevail on; to make a motion. * *vi* to stir; to go from one place to another; to walk; to change residence. * *n* the act of moving; a movement, esp in board games; one's turn to move; a premeditated action.

movement *n* motion; change of position; a gesture; joint action; the policy of a group; a trend; a division of a musical work.

movies *npl* the cinema.

moving *adj* touching; pathetic.

mow *vt*, *vi* (*pp* **mown** *or* **mowed**) to cut down; to cut grass.

much *adj* (*comp* **more**, *superl* **most**) great in quantity. * *adv* considerably.

mucous, mucose *adj* slimy, sticky; like mucus.

mucous membrane *n* a membrane lining the nose and other cavities of the body.

mucus *n* a viscid fluid secreted by mucous membranes.

mud *n* moist soft earth; mire.

muddle *vt* to make a mess of; to mix up; to confuse. * *n* a mess; confusion.

muddy *adj* like, covered in mud; confused; not bright; unclear.

muff *n* a fur cover for both hands.

muffin *n* a baked roll.

muffle *vt* to wrap up close; to conceal; to deaden sound.

muffler *n* a long scarf; the silencer of a motor vehicle.

mug *n* a large cup. * *vt* (*pt* **mugged**) to assault (and rob).

mule[1] *n* the offspring of a male donkey and a female horse; an obstinate person.

mule[2] *n* (*inf*) someone used to smuggle drugs.

mull *vt* to heat, sweeten, and spice (as wine, etc); to ponder.

multifarious *adj* many and varied.

multilateral *adj* many-sided.

multiple *adj* manifold; various; complex. * *n* a number which contains another an exact number of times.

multiplication *n* the act or process of multiplying.

multiplicity *n* great number or variety.

multiply *vt*, *vi* to make or become many; to increase; to find the product of by multiplication.

multipurpose adj able to be used for many tasks or functions.

multi-storey adj (n) (building) with many storeys.

multitude n a crowd; a throng; the populace.

mumble vi, vt to mutter; to speak indistinctly.

mummify vi to embalm as a mummy.

mummy n an embalmed human body, esp an embalmed corpse of ancient Egypt.

mumps n a contagious disease.

munch vt, vi to chew steadily.

mundane adj routine; everyday; banal.

municipal adj of or concerning a city, town, etc, or its local government.

municipality n the corporation or governing body of a town.

munificent adj bountiful; generous.

munitions npl war supplies, esp weapons and ammunition.

mural adj pertaining to a wall. * n a picture or design painted onto a wall.

murder n unlawful and intentional manslaughter. * vt to kill (with malice aforethought); to mar.

murderous adj cruel; savage.

murky adj dark; gloomy; obscure.

murmur n a low continuous, indistinct sound; an abnormal sound made by the heart.

muscle n fibrous tissue that contracts and relaxes, producing body movement; strength; power.

muscular adj brawny; sinewy.

muse n poetic inspiration. * vi, vt to ponder; to meditate.

museum n a building housing a collection of curios, works of art, etc.

mushroom n an edible fungus. * vi to gather mushrooms; to spread rapidly.

music n melody or harmony; the art of producing musical compositions featuring vocal or instrumental sounds having rhythm, harmony, melody.

musical adj melodious; harmonious; having an interest in or talent for music. * n a play or film incorporating story, song and dance.

musician n one skilled in music.

musing n meditation.

Muslim n an adherent of Islam. * adj of Islam, its adherents and culture.

muslin n a fine cotton cloth.

must vb aux (pt **had to**) expressing necessity or certainty. * n something that must be done or possessed.

mustard n a plant with pungent seeds; the condiment got from them; a brownish-yellow colour.

muster vt to collect, as troops. * vi to assemble. * n an assembling of troops.

musty adj mouldy; stale; damp.

mutable adj changeable; unstable.

mutation n change; alteration.

mute adj silent; dumb; not pronounced. * n a person who cannot speak.

mutilate vt to cut off a part; to maim.

mutineer n one guilty of mutiny.

mutinous adj rebellious.

mutiny n a revolt against authority in military service. * vi to rise in revolt.

mutter vi to mumble; to murmur to grumble. * n indistinct speech.

mutual adj reciprocal; shared alike; having the same feelings one for the other.

muzzle n the projecting mouth and nose of an animal; the open end of a gun; a strap fitted over an animal's jaws to prevent biting. * vt to gag.

muzzy adj bewildered; tipsy.

my pron the possessive case sing of I.

myopia n short-sightedness.

myriad n a countless number.

myself pron emphatic and reflexive form of I; in my normal state.

mysterious adj very obscure; incomprehensible; secret.

mystery n something beyond human intelligence; something unexplained; a secret; an old form of drama.

mystic n one who seeks direct knowledge of God or spiritual truths by self-surrender. * adj mystical.

mystical adj having a meaning beyond normal human understanding; magical.

mysticism n the beliefs or practices of a mystic.

mystify vt to perplex; to bewilder.

myth n a tradition or fable embodying the primitive ideas of a people.

mythology n the study of myths; a collection of myths.

N

nab vt (pt **nabbed**) to catch; to seize or arrest.

nadir n the lowest point.

nag n a horse; a person who nags. * vt, vi (pt **nagged**) to plague; to pester; to scold constantly.

nail n a horny substance covering the tip of the finger or toe; a metal spike. * vt to fasten, secure or hang with nails.

naïve adj ingenuous; unsophisticated.

naïveté n lack of sophistication.

naked adj bare; nude; destitute.

name n the word by which a person or thing is designated; title; reputation; a family. * vt to give a name to.

nameless adj unknown; unspeakable.

namely adv that is to say.

namesake n one named after, or with the same name as another.

nap n the woolly substance on the surface of cloth, etc; a short sleep.

napalm n a substance added to petrol to form a jellylike compound used in fire bombs and flame-throwers.

nape n the back of the neck.

napery n table and household linen.

naphtha n a volatile oil distilled from coal.

napkin n a serviette; a small square

of cloth or paper used at table to protect clothes or wipe the mouth and fingers.

nappy n a piece of absorbent material wrapped around a baby to absorb or retain its urine, etc.

narcotic n a sedative; a drug often addictive used to induce sleep or relieve pain.

narrate vt to tell or relate.

narration n a narrative; a story.

narrative adj pertaining to narration. * n a history or tale spoken or written.

narrow adj of little breadth; very limited; not liberal; near. * vt, vi to make or become narrow.

narrow-minded adj illiberal; prejudiced.

nasal adj pertaining to or sounded through the nose. * n a sound made through the nose.

nascent adj budding; dawning; opening.

nasty adj filthy; indecent; disagreeable.

natal adj pertaining to birth.

nation n people living under the same government and of common descent, culture, language and history.

nationalist n one who supports a policy of independence or home rule.

nationality n national character; patriotism; a nation or national group.

nationalize vt to convert land, mines, etc, into state property.

native adj pertaining to the place of one's birth; indigenous; inborn. * n a person born in the place indicated; a local inhabitant; an indigenous plant or animal; an indigenous inhabitant.

nativity n birth; time, place, manner of birth.

natural adj pertaining to nature; native; inborn; normal; unaffected; simple; naïve; (mus) not sharp or flat.

natural history n the study of nature, esp the animal, mineral and vegetable world.

naturalist n a person who studies natural history.

naturalization n the giving of citizen's rights to one of foreign birth.

naturalize vt to acclimatize; to confer citizenship on.

naturally adv in a natural manner, by nature; of course.

nature n the phenomena of physical like not dominated by man; the entire material world as a whole, or forces observable in it; the essential character of anything.

naught n nought; nothing.

naughty adj bad; mischievous; titillating.

nausea n sickness; disgust.

nauseate vt, vi to arouse feelings of disgust or revulsion.

nauseous adj loathsome; disgusting.

nautical adj pertaining to ships.

naval adj pertaining to ships or to a navy.

nave n the central part of a church.

navel n a depression in the centre of the abdomen.

navigable adj affording passage to ships.

navigate *vi, vt* to guide the course of a ship, aeroplane, etc; to sail.

navigation *n* the method of calculating the position of a ship, aircraft, etc.

navvy *n* a labourer, who works on roads.

navy *n* the warships of a nation with their crews and equipment.

near *adj* not distant; intimate; closely related; approximate; (*of escape, etc*) narrow. * *prep* close to. * *adv* almost; close by. * *vt, vi* to approach.

nearly *adv* almost; closely.

near-sighted *adj* short-sighted.

neat *adj* trim; (*of alcohol*) undiluted.

nebula *n* (*pl* **nebulae**) celestial objects like white clouds, generally clusters of stars.

nebulous *adj* cloudy; hazy; indistinct.

necessary *adj* indispensable; essential. * *n* a proved need, (*pl*) essential needs.

necessitate *vt* to compel; to constrain.

necessity *n* urgent need; compulsion.

neck *n* the part of body connecting the head and shoulders; an isthmus; the narrowest part of a bottle.

necklace *n* a string of beads worn round the neck.

necropolis *n* cemetery.

nectar *n* the fabled drink of the gods; a delicious drink; the honey of flowers.

need *n* want; necessity; poverty. * *vt, vi* to lack; to require; to be obliged.

needful *adj* needy; necessary.

needle *n* a small steel instrument for sewing; an indicator on a dial; the thin, short leaf of trees such as the pine or spruce.

needy *adj* indigent; very poor.

negation *n* a denial; a saying no.

negative *adj* expressing denial or refusal; the opposite of positive. * *n* a photographic print from which positive prints are taken. * *vt* to veto; to contradict.

neglect *vt* to disregard; to slight; to pay no attention to; to leave uncared for; to omit. * *n* lack of care.

neglectful *adj* heedless; careless.

negligée *n* a woman's loose dressing gown.

negligence *n* carelessness.

negotiable *adj* capable of being negotiated or transferred.

negotiate *vi* to treat; to bargain in order to reach an agreement or settlement.

negotiation *n* bargaining.

neigh *vi* to whinny. * *n* the cry of a horse.

neighbour *n* a person living near; a fellow human being. * *vt* to adjoin.

neighbourhood *n* a particular area, district or community; the vicinity.

neighbouring *adj* adjoining.

neighbourly *adj* friendly.

neither *pron, adj* not either. * *conj* not either; also not.

nephew *n* the son of a brother or sister.

nepotism *n* favouritism to relatives or friends shown by influential people.

nerve n one of the fibrous threads that convey messages to and from the brain; courage; (*inf*) audacity; (*pl*) anxiety. * *vt* to strengthen.

nervous *adj* timid; excitable; forcible.

nest n a bird's hatching place; a cosy place. * *vi* to make or occupy a nest.

nestle *vi* to lie close and snug.

net[1] n a meshwork of cord, twine, etc; a piece of this used to catch fish, divide a tennis court, etc; a snare. * *vt* to snare; to twine.

net[2], **nett** *adj* clear of deductions, allowances or changes, the opposite ofgross. * *vt* (*pt* **netted**) to bring in as a profit.

netball n a game for two teams, in which points are scored by putting a ball through an elevated horizontal ring.

nether *adj* lower.

netting n a piece of network.

nettle n a weed with stinging hairs. * *vt* to irritate.

network n an interconnecting arrangement of lines; a group cooperating with each other; a chain of interconnected operations, computers, etc.

neuralgia n pain in a nerve.

neuritis n inflammation of nerve.

neurology n the study of nerves.

neurosis n (*pl* **neuroses**) a mental disorder with symptoms such as anxiety.

neurotic *adj* suffering from neurosis; highly strung.

neuter *adj* (*of nouns*) neither masculine nor feminine; (*biol*) having no sex organs. * *vt* to remove the testicles of (an animal).

neutral *adj* non-aligned; not taking sides with either party in a dispute or war; having no distinctive characteristics; (*chem*) neither acid nor alkaline. * n a position of a gear mechanism in which power is not transmitted.

neutralize *vt* to render neutral.

never *adv* at no time; in no case.

nevertheless *adv* for all that; notwithstanding.

new *adj* recent; novel; fresh; unused. * *adv* again; newly; recently.

news *npl* current events; recent happenings; the mass media's coverage of such events.

newsagent n a retailer of newspapers.

newspaper n a printed periodical containing new, published daily or weekly.

next *adj* nearest; immediately preceding or following; adjacent. * *adv* in the nearest time, place, rank, etc; on the first subsequent occasion.

nexus n (*pl* **nexus** *or* **nexuses**) a connecting principle or link.

nibble *vt, vi* to bite little by little.

nice *adj* fastidious; pleasant; dainty.

nicety n precision; exactness.

niche n a recess in a wall for a statue, etc.

nick n a notch; a score; a critical moment; a police station. * *vt* to make a small cut in; to wound superficially.

nickname n a name given to an individual in jest or ridicule. * vt to give a nickname to.

nicotine n a poisonous alkaloid present in tobacco.

niece n the daughter of one's brother or sister.

nigh adj near. * prep near to.

night n the period from sunset to sunrise.

nightcap n a cap worn in bed; an alcoholic drink taken just before bedtime.

nightclub n a place of entertainment for drinking, dancing, etc, at night.

nightdress n a loose garment worn in bed by women and girls.

nightfall n evening.

nightly adj done or happening by night or every night; nocturnal.

nightmare n a frightening dream; any horrible experience.

nil n nothing.

nimble adj active; agile.

nine adj, n one more than eight. * n the symbol for this (9 or IX).

nineteen adj, n nine and ten. * n the symbol for this (19 or XIX).

ninety adj, n nine times ten. * n the symbol for this (90 or XC).

ninth adj, n next after eighth; one of nine equal parts of a thing.

nip vt (pt **nipped**) to pinch; to snip. * n a pinch; a small bite from a dog; frost or cold.

nipper n a person or thing that nips; the pincer of a crab; (pl) pliers; (inf) a child.

nipple n the small protuberance on a breast or udder through which the milk passes, a teat; something resembling this, e.g. a rubber part on the cap of a baby's bottle.

nitrogen n a gaseous element forming nearly 78 per cent of air.

nitrogenous adj pertaining to nitrogen.

nitroglycerine n a powerful explosive.

no adv expressing negation. * n a denial; a refusal; a negative vote or voter. * adj none.

noble adj of high rank; famous; lofty in character; stately. * n a peer; a person of high rank.

nobleman n a noble; a peer.

nobody n no one; a person of no importance.

nocturnal adj nightly; by night.

nod vi, vt to make a slight bow, to incline the head quickly in assent or greeting.

node n a knot; a knob; the joint of a stem.

nodule n a little knot or lump.

noise n a din; clamour; a harsh sound. * vt to make public.

noisome adj noxious; offensive.

nomad n a wanderer; one of a people or tribe who travel in search of pasture.

nomenclature n a system of names; vocabulary of scientific terms.

nominal adj formal; existing in name only; having only token worth.

nominate vt to name; to designate; to appoint to an office or post; to propose someone as a candidate (for election).

nominee n a person nominated for office, etc.

nonchalance n indifference; coolness.

noncommittal adj not revealing one's opinion.

nonconductor n a substance that does not conduct heat, electricity, etc.

nonconformist n one who does not conform to the established church.

nondescript adj hard to classify, indeterminate; lacking individual characteristics. * n a nondescript person of thing.

none n, pron not one; not any.

nonentity n a person of no significance.

nonsense n words without meaning.

nonstop adj (of train, etc) making no intermediate stops. * adv never ceasing; never stopping or pausing.

noodles npl pasta in thin strips.

noon n twelve o'clock in the day.

noose n a loop on a running knot; a lasso.

nor conj and not; not either.

norm n a rule; a pattern; a standard.

normal adj according to a rule; regular.

north n the cardinal point opposite the midday sun. * adj in, of, to- wards, from the north. * adv in or towards the north.

northeast n the point midway between north and east.

northward adv, adj towards the north.

northwest n the point midway between the north and west.

nose n the part of the face above the mouth, used for breathing and smelling, having two nostrils; the sense of smell. * vt to discover as by smell. * vi to sniff for; to inch forwards; to pry.

nostalgia n yearning for past times or places.

nostalgic adj feeling or expressing nostalgia; longing for one's youth.

nostril n one of the two apertures of the nose for breathing and smelling.

not adv expressing denial, refusal or negation.

notable adj worthy of being noted or remembered; distinguished; memorable.

notation n act of recording anything by symbols.

notch n an incision; nick. * vt to indent.

note n a mark, a sign or token; an explanation; an epistle; a musical sound or its symbol; the sound of a bird's call. * vt to mark down; to observe.

noted adj famous; celebrated.

notepaper n paper for writing down notes.

nothing n not anything; a trifle; a zero; thing of no importance or value. * adv in no way; not at all.

notice n heed; regard; intimation; warning; information. * vt to observe.

noticeable adj worthy of notice; remarkable; easily seen or noticed.

notice board n a board on which notices are pinned for public information.

notification n intimation; warning.

notify vt to make known; to inform.

notion n a concept; an idea; an opinion.

notoriety n publicity (esp discreditable).

notorious adj widely known, esp unfavourably.

notwithstanding prep, conj in spite of; nevertheless; although.

nougat n a chewy sweet consisting of sugar paste and nuts.

nought n not anything; a zero.

noun n (gram) a word that names a person, a living being, an objection, action, etc.

nourish vt to feed; to foster; to encourage the growth of; to raise.

nourishment n food, nutriment.

novel adj new and striking. * n a fictitious story or narrative in book form.

novelty n a new or strange thing; (pl) cheap, small objects for sale.

November n the eleventh month of the year.

novice n a beginner; a person in a religious order before taking vows.

now adv, at the present time. * conj since; seeing that.

nowhere adv not in, at, or to anywhere.

noxious adj hurtful; pernicious.

nozzle n the projecting spout of something, e.g. a nose or pipe.

nuance n a subtle distinction of meaning, colour, etc.

nub n a lump or small piece; (inf) the central point or gist of a matter.

nuclear adj of or relating to a nucleus; using nuclear energy.

nuclear energy n energy released as a result of nuclear fission or fusion.

nuclear fission n the splitting of a nucleus of an atom either spontaneously or by bombarding it with particles.

nuclear fusion n the combining of two nuclei into a heavier nucleus.

nuclear power n electrical or motive power produced by a nuclear reactor.

nuclear reactor n a device in which nuclear fission is maintained and harnessed to produce energy.

nucleus n (pl **nuclei, nucleuses**) the central part or core around which something may develop or be grouped or concentrated; the central, positively charged portion of an atom.

nude adj naked; bare. * n a naked human figure, esp in a work of art; nakedness.

nudge n a light jog with the elbow. * vt to jog with the elbow; to remind.

nugget n a lump, as of gold.

nuisance n that which annoys.

null adj of no force; void; invalid.

nullify vt to render null; to cancel out.

numb adj benumbed; having no feeling through shock or cold. * vt to deaden.

number n a symbol or word indicating how many; a numeral identifying a person or thing by its position in a series. * vt, vi to count; to give a number to; to include or be included as one of a group; to limit the number of; to total.

numberplate *n* a plate on the front or rear of a motor vehicle that displays its registration number.

numeral *adj* pertaining to number. * *n* a figure or symbol representing a number.

numerate *adj* able to use and understand numbers and arithmetic.

numerical *adj* denoting number; consisting of numbers.

numerous *adj* many.

numismatics *n* the study of coins and medals.

nun *n* a woman belonging to a religious order.

nuncio *n* an ambassador of the Pope.

nunnery *n* a house in which the nuns of a religious order live.

nuptials *npl* marriage.

nurse *n* one trained to care for the sick or infirm. * *vt* to tend; to suckle; to foster.

nursery *n* a place where children may be left in temporary care; a place where young plants are raised for transplanting.

nursery rhyme *n* a short traditional poem or song for children.

nursery school *n* a school for young children, usu under five.

nursery slope *n* a gently inclined slope for novice skiers.

nursing *n* the profession of a nurse.

nursing home *n* an establishment providing care for convalescent, chronically ill or disabled people.

nurture *n* upbringing; education; nourishment. * *vt* to nourish; to educate.

nut *n* a fruit containing a kernel in a hard covering; a screw fastening a bolt; (*sl*) a mad person; (*sl*) a fan.

nutcracker *n* an instrument for cracking nuts; a bird with speckled plumage.

nutmeg *n* the aromatic kernel produced by an eastern tree, grated and used as a spice.

nutriment *n* food; nourishment.

nutritious *adj* nourishing; health-giving.

nylon *n* any of numerous tough, synthetic materials used esp in plastics.

nymph *n* the larva of the dragonfly, mayfly, etc; in legend, a goddess of forests, rivers, etc.

O

oaf *n* a lout; a stupid clumsy person.

oak *n* a tree with a hard durable wood, having acorns as fruits.

oar *n* a pole with a flat blade for rowing a boat.

oarsman *n* one who rows at the oar.

oasis *n* (*pl* **oases**) a fertile tract in a desert.

oast *n* a kiln to dry hops or malt.

oats *npl* a cereal grass widely cultivated for its edible grain; the seeds.

oath *n* a solemn declaration to a god

or higher authority that one will speak the truth; a swear word.

oatmeal n ground oats; porridge or this.

obdurate adj unrelenting.

obedience n the doing of what is commanded.

obedient adj submissive; dutiful; complaint.

obeisance n a bow or curtsy; an act of respect.

obese adj very stout; corpulent.

obesity n excessive fatness.

obey vt, vi to do as commanded; to yield to; to comply with.

obfuscate vt to darken; to confuse.

obituary n an announcement of a person's death, often with a short biography.

object n the end aimed at; a purpose; anything present to the senses. * vt, vi to oppose; to disapprove.

objection n the act of objecting; a ground for, or expression of, disapproval.

objectionable adj causing an objection; disagreeable.

objective adj not influenced by opinions or feelings; impartial; having an independent existence of its own. * n a thing or place aimed at.

obligation n the binding power of a promise, contract or law.

obligatory adj binding; compulsory.

oblige vt to constrain; to compel by moral, legal or physical force; to do or favour; to gratify.

obliging adj civil; kind; agreeable.

oblique adj slanting; indirect; allusive.

obliterate vt to blot out; to destroy.

oblivion n the state of forgetting or being utterly forgotten.

oblivious adj forgetful; unaware.

oblong adj rectangular and longer than broad. * n an oblong figure.

obnoxious adj odious; unpopular.

oboe n a wind instrument of wood with a mouthpiece with a double reed.

obscene adj indecent; vile; offensive to a moral standard.

obscenity n the state of being obscene; an obscene act, word, etc.

obscure adj darkened; dim; abstruse; unimportant; humble. * vt to darken; to hide from view; to confuse; to make unclear.

obscurity n darkness; dimness; an obscure thing or person.

obsequious adj cringing; fawning.

observance n the observing of a rule or practice; the performance of rites, etc.

observant adj attentive; watchful.

observation n the act or faculty of observing; a comment or remark.

observatory n a place from which astronomers study the stars, planets, etc.

observe vt, vi to take notice of; to remark; to keep religiously; to celebrate.

observer n a person who observes; a delegate who attends a formal meeting but may not take part; an expert analyst and commentator in a particular field.

obsess vt to possess or haunt the mind of.

obsession *n* the complete capture of the mind by some idea; a persistent preoccupation.

obsolescent *adj* going out of date.

obsolete *adj* antiquated; out of date.

obstacle *n* an obstruction; a hindrance.

obstetrics *n* the branch of medicine concerned with the care and treatment of women during pregnancy and childbirth.

obstinate *adj* stubborn; self-willed.

obstreperous *adj* unruly; disorderly.

obstruct *vt* to block up; to impede; to hinder; to keep light from.

obstructive *adj* causing delay; preventing.

obtain *vt* to acquire; to gain; to earn. * *vi* to prevail; to hold good.

obtrusive *adj* forward; interfering; pushy.

obtuse *adj* stupid; (*geom*) greater than a right angle.

obvious *adj* plain; evident.

obverse *n* the 'head' side of a coin.

occasion *n* an occurrence; an incident; an opportunity; a cause; a juncture.

occasional *adj* casual; happening now and then; incidental.

occult *adj* hidden; mysterious; belonging to the supernatural arts, mystic. * *n* (*with* **the**) supernatural arts, magic, etc.

occupancy *n* tenancy.

occupation *n* possession; tenure; business; vocation; employment.

occupy *vt* to take possession of; to fill; to employ; to engage; to engross.

occur *vi* (*pt* **occurred**) to happen; to exist; to come into the mind of.

occurrence *n* an event, an incident.

ocean *n* the vast body of water surrounding the land or one of its divisions.

OCR *abbr* optical character recognition, an information processing technology that can convert readable text into computer data.

octagon *n* a plane figure having eight angles and sides.

octave *n* (*mus*) a scale of eight notes beginning and ending with a note of the same tone but different pitch; a stanza of eight lines.

October *n* the tenth month of the year.

ocular *adj* pertaining to the eye; visual.

oculist *n* one skilled in eye diseases.

odd *adj* eccentric; peculiar; occasional; not divisible by two; extra or left over.

oddity *n* the state of being odd; an odd thing or person; peculiarity.

oddment *n* a remnant esp of fabric.

odds *npl* inequality; excess; difference in favour of one; advantage.

ode *n* a lyric poem of exalted tone.

odious *adj* hateful; offensive; disgusting.

odium *n* hatred; dislike; blame.

odorous *adj* fragrant.

odour *n* any scent or smell; reputation.

oesophagus *n* the gullet.

of *prep* denoting source, cause, etc.

off *adv* away; distant; detached; out of condition. * *adj* cancelled; (*of food*) having gone bad. * *prep* away from; not on.

offence *n* injury; insult; displeasure; crime; law; misdemeanour.

offend vt to displease; to affront; to shock. * vi to break the law.

offensive adj causing offence; disgusting; impertinent; aggressive. * n an attack.

offer vt to present for acceptance or rejection; to tender; to bid. * vi to present itself * n a bid; a proposal.

offering n a gift; a sacrifice.

offhand adv without thinking. * adj inconsiderate; curt; brusque.

office n duty; public employment; function; service; place of business.

officer n the holder of an office; one who has a commission in the army or navy.

official adj pertaining to an office properly authorized; formal. * n an officer; one holding public office.

officious adj fussy; meddling; interfering.

offing n the near or foreseeable future.

off-licence n a licence to sell alcohol for consumption off the premises.

off-peak adj denoting use of a service, etc, in a period of lesser demand.

offset n a method of printing in which an image is transferred from a plate to a rubber surface and then to paper.

offshoot n a shoot; a sprout.

offshore adv at sea some distance from the shore.

offside adj, adv illegally in advance of the ball.

offspring n, sing, pl children; progeny.

offstage adj, adv out of sight of the audience; behind the scenes.

often adv frequently; many times.

ogle vt, vi to gape at; to look at lustfully.

ohm n the unit of electric resistance.

oil n a greasy liquid, often inflammable, got from animal, vegetable and mineral sources; (pl) paint mixed by grinding a pigment in oil. * vt to smear with oil, lubricate.

oilskin n waterproof cloth; a garment of this.

oil slick n a mass of oil floating on the surface of water.

oil well n a well from which petroleum is extracted.

oily adj like or covered with oil; greasy; too suave or smooth, unctuous.

ointment n a fatty substance for applying to skin for healing or cosmetic purposes.

old adj aged; not new or fresh; out of date; former; not modern; worn out.

old-fashioned adj out of date.

olfactory adj pertaining to sense of smell.

oligarchy n rule by a small select body of people; a state ruled in this way.

olive n an evergreen tree; its edible fruit yielding oil; a greenish colour.

Olympiad n a four-year period, being the term between successive Olympic games.

omega n the last letter of the Greek alphabet.

omelette n eggs beaten with water and cooked flat in a pan.

omen n a sign of a future event.

ominous adj foreboding; ill-omened.

omission n a failure to do something; a leaving out of something.

omit vt to neglect; to leave out.

omnibus see bus.

omnipotence n unlimited power.

omnipotent adj all-powerful.

omniscience n the faculty of knowing all things; universal knowledge.

omniscient adj all-knowing.

omnivorous adj all-devouring.

on prep in contact with the upper surface of; supported by, attached to, or covering; at the time of; concerning, about; immediately after; using. * adv (so as to be) covering or in contact with something; forward; (device) switched on; continuously in progress; due to take place; (actor) on stage; on duty.

once adv on the occasion only; formerly; at some time. * conj a soon as. * n one time.

oncoming adj approaching.

one adj single; undivided; united; the same; of a certain unspecified time. * n the figure I; unity; unit. * pron any single person; any individual; anything.

onerous adj burdensome; heavy.

one-sided adj partial; unfair.

one-way adj requiring no reciprocal action or obligation.

ongoing adj progressing, continuing.

onion n an edible bulb with a pungent taste and odour.

onlooker n a spectator.

only adj single; sole. * adv for one purpose; merely; just; not more than. * conj but; except that.

onomatopoeia n forming words by imitation of sounds, as hiss.

onrush n a rapid onset.

onset n an attack; an assault; a beginning.

onslaught n a fierce attack.

onus n a burden; a duty; a responsibility.

onward adj advancing.

onwards adv forward; ahead.

ooze n soft mud or slime. * vi to issue gently; to percolate; to seep.

opal n a precious stone, remarkable for its changing colours.

opaque adj not transparent.

open adj not shut; uncovered; accessible; unfenced; treeless; public; candid; clear. * vt, vi to begin; to declare open. * n a sporting competition that any player can enter.

open-hearted adj frank; generous.

opening adj beginning. * n a way in or out; a breach; a vacancy; a chance.

opera n a musical drama.

operate vt, vi to work; to act; to produce an effect; to treat surgically; to control.

operation n action; process; procedure; surgical treatment; military action.

operative adj effective; functioning; in force. * n a workman; factory hand.

operetta n a light musical drama.

ophthalmology n the branch of medicine dealing with the eyes.

opiate n a narcotic drug containing opium.

opinion n a belief; a notion; a judgment; an evaluation; expert advice.

opium *n* a drug obtained from poppies.

opponent *n* an adversary.

opportune *adj* timely; convenient.

opportunist *n* a person who seizes opportunities for his or her benefit.

opportunity *n* a fit or convenient time.

oppose *vt, vi* to act against; to resist; to obstruct; to bar.

opposed *adj* adverse; hostile.

opposite *adj* facing; adverse; contrary.

opposition *n* the act of opposing; contradiction; antagonism; contrast; the party opposing the government.

oppress *vt* to treat harshly; to subjugate; to weigh down in the mind.

oppression *n* cruelty; severity; persecution; physical or mental distress.

oppressive *adj* burdensome; tyrannical; sultry, close of weather.

opt *vi* to chose or exercise an option.

optical *adj* of or relating to the eye or light; optic; aiding or correcting vision; visual.

optician *n* one who makes or sells optical aids.

optics *n* the science of light and sight.

optimism *n* the tendency to take the most hopeful and cheerful view.

optimist *n* a sanguine person.

option *n* choice; free choice; the right to buy, sell or lease at a fixed price within a specified time.

optional *adj* voluntary; left to choice.

opulence *n* wealth; riches; luxury.

opulent *adj* wealthy, rich.

or *conj* denoting an alternative and the last in a series of choices.

oracle *n* a very wise person.

oral *adj* spoken; of the mouth; taken by mouth. * *n* a spoken examination.

orange *n* a juicy, a trees fruit; its tree; its colour, reddish-yellow.

oration *n* a public speech.

oratory *n* eloquence in public speaking.

orb *n* a sphere, esp one ornamented and surmounted by a cross as part of royal insignia.

orbit *n* the path of a planet; the eye socket; the path of an electron around the nucleus of an atom. * *vt, vi* to put (a satellite) into orbit; to circle round.

orchard *n* an area planted with fruit trees.

orchestra *n* a group of musicians playing together under a conductor.

orchestral *adj* suitable for or performed by an orchestra.

ordain *vt* to consecrate (for ministry).

ordeal *n* a severe trial or test.

order *n* arrangement; method; relative position; sequence; tidiness; rules of procedure; a religious fraternity; an honour of decoration; an instruction or command. * *vt, vi* to arrange; to command.

orderly *adj* in good order; well-behaved; methodical. * *n* a hospital attendant; a soldier attending an officer.

ordinal *adj, n* a number showing position in a series.

ordinance *n* a statute; an edict.

ordinary *adj* regular; usual; normal; commonplace; unexceptional.

ordination *n* the act of ordaining or being ordained; admission to the ministry.

ordnance *n* military stores; artillery.

ore *n* rock substance containing metal.

organ *n* a complex musical wind instrument with pipes, stops, and a keyboard; a part of an animal or plant that performs a vital or natural function.

organic *adj* pertaining to or affecting a bodily organ; of the class of compounds that are formed from carbon; (*vegetables, etc*) grown without the use of artificial fertilizers or pesticides.

organism *n* anything living; an organized body.

organization *n* suitable arrangements for effective work; system; structure.

organize *vt* to put in working order; to establish; to institute; to arrange for.

orgasm *n* the climax of sexual excitement.

orgy *n* a wild party, with excessive drinking and indiscriminate sexual activity.

orient, orientate *vt, vi* to adjust (oneself) to a particular situation.

oriental *adj* of the Orient.

orifice *n* an opening or mouth of a cavity.

origin *n* a source; a beginning; ancestry or parentage.

original *adj* relating to the origin or beginning; novel; unusual; inventive, creative. * *n* an original work, as of art; something from which copies are made.

originality *n* initiative; freshness and independence of thought.

originate *vt, vi* to bring into being.

ornament *n* decoration. * *vt* to beautify.

ornamental *adj* decorative, not useful.

ornate *adj* richly ornamented; (*style*) highly elaborate.

ornithology *n* the study of birds.

orphan *n, adj* a child without parents.

orphanage *n* an institution for the care of orphans.

orthodox *adj* conforming with established behaviour or opinions; not heretical.

orthopaedics *n* the study and surgical treatment of bone and joint disorders.

oscillate *vi* to swing back and forth as a pendulum.

ossification *n* the formation of bone.

ossify *vt, vi* to change into bone; (*of habits, etc*) to become rigid and inflexible.

ostensible *adj* apparent; pretended.

ostentation *n* a showing off.

ostentatious *adj* showy; pretentious.

osteopathy *n* the treatment of disease by manipulation of the bones and muscles.

ostracize *vt* to exclude; to banish from society.

other *adj, pron* not the same.

ought *vi* to be bound; to be obliged.

ounce *n* a unit of weight, equal to one

sixteenth of a pound or 28.34 grams.

our *adj, pron* pertaining or belonging to us.

ourselves *pron* emphatic and reflexive form of we.

oust *vt* to eject, expel, esp by underhand means; to remove forcibly.

out *adv* not in; outside; in the open air; beyond bounds; ruled out, no longer considered; on strike; at an end; extinguished; into the open; published. * *prep* out of; out through; outside. * *adj* external; outward. * *n* means of escape.

outbid *vt* to bid more than another.

outboard *n* an engine attached to the outside of a boat.

outbreak *n* a sudden eruption of anger, war, disease, etc.

outburst *n* an explosion of anger, etc.

outcast *n* a person rejected by society.

outclass *vt* to surpass or excel greatly.

outcome *n* the issue; the result.

outcrop *n* the exposure of strata at the surface.

outcry *n* clamour; protest.

outdistance *vt* to get ahead of.

outdo *vt* to excel; to surpass.

outdoors *adv* in or into the open air.

outer *adj* external.

outer space *n* any region of space beyond the earth's atmosphere.

outfit *n* the equipment used in an activity; clothes worn together, an ensemble.

outfitter *n* a supplier of clothes.

outgoing *adj* departing; sociable;

forthcoming. * *n* an outlay; (*pl*) expenditure.

outgrow *vt* to surpass in growth; to grow too large for (clothes); to change one's ideas, habits, etc, as one develops.

outhouse *n* a small building.

outing *n* a short excursion for pleasure.

outlandish *adj* strange; unconventional.

outlaw *vt* to declare illegal. * *n* an outlawed person; a notorious criminal.

outlay *n* expenditure.

outlet *n* an opening.

outline *n* a profile; a draft.

outlive *vt* to live longer than; to outlast.

outlook *n* a view; a prospect; a viewpoint.

outlying *adj* detached; remote, distant.

outmanoeuvre *vt* to surpass in strategy.

outmoded *adj* old-fashioned.

outnumber *vt* to exceed in number.

outpatient *n* a non-resident hospital patient.

outpost *n* a military post or detachment at a distance from a main force.

output *n* the quantity (of goods, etc) produced, esp over a given period; information delivered by a computer; esp to a printer.

outrage *vt* to injure; to ravish. * *n* a gross offence, injury or insult.

outright *adv* completely; utterly.

outset *n* the beginning.

outside *n* the external surface; the

exterior. * adj outer; outdoor; (of a chance) slight. * adv on or to the outside.

outsider n a person or thing not included in a set, group, etc, a nonmember; a contestant not thought to have a chance in a race.

outsize adj of a larger than usual size.

outskirts npl districts remote from the centre, as of a city.

outspoken adj frank; candid; blunt.

outstanding adj excellent; distinguished, prominent; unpaid; unresolved.

outstrip vt to outrun; to excel.

outward adj directed towards the outside; external.

outweigh vt to count for more than, to exceed in value, weight, or importance.

outwit vt to defeat by cunning.

oval adj egg-shaped.

ovary n one of the two female reproductive organs producing eggs.

ovation n enthusiastic applause.

oven n an enclosed cooking or baking compartment.

over prep higher than; on top of; across; to the other side of; above; more than; concerning. * adv above; across; in every part; completed; up and down; in addition; too. * adj upper; excessive; surplus; finished; remaining.

overact vt, vi to act in an exaggerated manner, to overdo a part.

overall adj including everything. * adv as a whole; generally. * n a loose protective garment.

overawe vt to restrain by awe; to daunt.

overbalance vt to lose balance and fall.

overbearing adj haughty; domineering.

overboard adv over the side of a ship; to extremes of enthusiasm.

overburden vt to overload; to oppress.

overcast adj clouded over.

overcharge vt to charge too much; of battery, to overload; to fill to excess.

overcoat n a warm topcoat.

overcome vt to subdue; to conquer; to get the better of; to render helpless or powerless, as by tears, laughter, etc.

overdo vt to do to excess; to overcook.

overdose n too great a dose. * vt, vi to take too much, esp of a drug.

overdraft n an amount overdrawn at a bank.

overdraw vt, vi to take more from a bank than one has in an account; to exaggerate.

overdue adj past the time fixed or due.

overestimate vt to set too high an estimate on or for.

overflow vt, vi to flood; to abound (with emotion, etc). * n surplus; excess; an outlet for surplus water, etc.

overflowing adj abundant, copious.

overgrown adj grown beyond the normal size; rank; ungainly.

overhang vt, vi to project over.

overhaul vt to examine thoroughly with a view to repairs; to overtake.

overhead adj, adv above the head; in the sky. * n (often pl) the continuing costs of a business, as of rent, light, etc.

overhear vt to hear by accident.

overjoyed adj highly delighted.

overland adj, adv by, on or across land.

overlap vt to extend over so as to coincide in part.

overlay vt to coat; to smother. * n a coating.

overleaf adv on the other side of the leaf of a book.

overload vt to overburden.

overlook vt to superintend; to pardon; to fail to notice.

overlord n an absolute or supreme ruler.

overnight adv for, through or during the night.

overpass n a road crossing another road, path, etc, at a higher level.

overpower vt to overcome; to subdue.

overpowering adj overwhelming.

overrate vt to rate or assess too highly.

overreach vt to fail by attempting too much or going too far.

override vt to nullify; to prevail.

overrule vt prevail over.

overrun vt to ravage; to outrun, to swarm over. * vi to overflow.

overseas adj, adv across or beyond the sea; abroad.

overseer n an inspector; a superintendent.

overshadow vt to throw a shadow over; to cast into the shade; to outdo.

overshoot vt to shoot or send beyond (a target, etc); (aircraft) to fly or taxi beyond the end of a runway when landing or taking off.

oversight n a mistake; an omission.

oversleep vi to sleep beyond the intended time.

overstate vt to exaggerate.

overstep vt to exceed.

overt adj public; openly done; unconcealed; deliberate.

overtake vt to come up with and pass; to catch.

overtax vt to overstrain oneself.

overthrow vt to overturn; to defeat. * n ruin; defeat.

overtime n time beyond the regular hours; (payment for) extra time work.

overtone n an additional subtle meaning; an implicit quality; the colour of light reflected (as by a paint).

overture n a proposal; an offer; a musical introduction to an opera, etc.

overturn vt to capsize; to overthrow.

overweight adj weighing more than the proper amount. * n excess weight.

overwhelm vt to submerge; overpower.

overwhelming adj irresistible; uncontrollable; vast; vastly superior; extreme.

overwork vt to work beyond one's strength or too long.

overwrought *adj* too nervous.

owe *vt* to be indebted to; to feel the need to do or give out of gratitude.

own[1] *adj* belonging to oneself or itself.

own[2] *vt* to possess by right; to avow; to concede.

owner *n* one who owns or possesses, a proprietor.

oxide *n* a compound of oxygen with another element.

oxtail *n* the tail of an ox, esp skinned and used for stews, soups, etc.

oxygen *n* a colourless, odourless, tasteless, highly reactive gaseous element forming part of air, water, etc, and essential to life and combustion.

oxygen mask *n* an apparatus worn over the nose and mouth through which oxygen passes from a storage tank.

oxygen tent *n* a canopy over a hospital bed, etc, within which a supply of oxygen is maintained.

ozone *n* a condensed form of oxygen; (*inf*) bracing sea air.

ozone layer *n* a layer of ozone in the upper atmosphere that absorbs ultraviolet rays from the sun.

P

pace *n* the measure of a single stride; gait; rate of progress. * *vi* to step; to walk slowly. * *vt* to walk up and down; to determine the pace in a race.

pacific *adj* peaceable; calm.

pacifier *n* one who pacifies; a baby's dummy.

pacifism *n* opposition to the use of force.

pacify *vt* to calm; to restore peace to.

pack *n* a set of cards; a set of hounds; a gang. * *vt* to make up into a bundle; to fill; to stuff; to crowd; to dismiss. * *vi* to form into a hard mass; to assemble.

package *n* a parcel; a wrapped bundle.

packet *n* a small parcel; a mailboat; (*inf*) a considerable sum.

pack ice *n* ice masses packed together.

packing *n* wrapping material; stuffing.

pact *n* a contract; an agreement.

pad *n* a piece of stuffing, esp absorbent material; a block of writing paper.

padding *n* anything added to achieve length or amount, esp in a book.

paddle *vi* to wade in shallow water; to row. * *vt* to propel by an oar or paddle. * *n* a broad short oar.

paddock *n* a grassy enclosure for horses.

paddy *n* threshed, unmilled rice; a rice field.

padlock *n* a detachable lock. * *vt* to secure with a padlock.

pagan *n* a person who has no religion.

page[1] *n* an attendant at a formal function; a uniformed boy employed to run errands. * vt to summon by messenger, etc.

page² n a sheet of paper in a book, newspaper, etc.

pageant n a procession in which historical scenes are acted; a fine display or show.

pageantry n splendid display, pomp.

pager n a device carried on a person for summoning or communicating with.

pagoda n an Eastern temple.

pail n a bucket.

pain n bodily suffering; distress; ; labour; effort. * vt to cause pain to.

painstaking adj laborious and careful.

paint vt to coat with colour; to portray. * vi to make a picture. * n a pigment.

painter n one whose occupation is to paint (houses, etc); an artist; a rope for fastening a small boat.

painting n the act or art of painting.

pair n two things of like kind; a couple; a man and his wife. * vi to join in pairs.

palace n a royal residence.

palaeography n the art of deciphering ancient writing.

palaeontology n the science of fossils.

palatable adj having a pleasant taste; pleasant and acceptable.

palate n the roof of the mouth; taste.

palatial adj spacious; magnificent.

pale¹ n a pointed stake; a boundary.

pale² vi to grow pale. * adj light in colour.

palette n an artist's mixing board.

paling n a fence formed with stakes.

pall n a mantle, as of smoke; a covering on a coffin. * vi to shroud.

pallet n a portable platform used in bulk storage.

palliate vt to alleviate; to excuse.

palliative adj mitigating. * n something that eases pain, sorrow, etc.

pallid adj pale; wan.

pallor n paleness.

palm¹ n the underside of the hand. * vt to conceal in the palm; (with **off**) to pass off by fraud.

palm² n a tropical tree; a symbol of victory.

palmistry n fortune-telling by reading the lines on the palm of the hand.

palpable adj perceptible by the touch; plain; obvious.

palpitate vi to throb; to tremble.

palpitation n violent pulsation of the heart.

paltry adj mean; trifling.

pamper vt to indulge to excess; to spoil.

pamphlet n a small unbound book.

pan n a broad shallow vessel for cooking; the bowl of a lavatory.

panacea n a remedy for all ills.

panache n stylish behaviour.

pancake n a thin cake of cooked batter.

pancreas n a fleshy gland secreting digestive juice.

panda n a large black and white animal of China.

pandemonium n chaos; scene of disorder and noise.

pander vi to gratify or exploit the

weaknesses of others. * *n* one who panders.

pane *n* a plate of glass in a window.

panegyric *n* a eulogy.

panel *n* a rectangular section of door, ceiling, etc; a group of selected persons; a board for instruments or controls. * *vt* (*pt* **pannelled**) to decorate with panels.

pang *n* a sudden pain or feeling.

panic *n* a sudden blind fear. * *vt*, *vi* (*pt* **panicked**) to affect or be affected by panic.

panoply *n* splendid display.

panorama *n* a complete view.

pant *vi* to gasp; to long for. * *vt* to speak while gasping.

pantomime *n* a drama without words; a Christmas theatrical show.

pantry *n* a small cupboard for provisions.

papacy *n* the office of the pope.

paper *n* thin sheets used for writing, printing, etc; a newspaper; an essay. * *adj* made of paper. * *vt* to cover with paper.

papyrus *n* (*pl* **papyri**) a reed from which paper was made in ancient times.

par *n* state of equality; the face value of shares; (*golf*) the score for a hole required by an expert player.

parable *n* a religious allegory; a story with a moral lesson.

parachute *n* a fabric canopy to retard speed of fall from an aircraft. * *vt*, *vi* to drop or descend by parachute.

parade *n* display; show; muster; a promenade. * *vt*, *vi* to show off; to marshal; to walk up and down.

paradise *n* the garden of Eden; heaven; supreme bliss.

paradox *n* something containing seeming contradictory qualities or phrases.

paraffin *n* a distilled oil used as fuel.

paragon *n* a model of excellence.

paragraph *n* a subdivision in a piece of writing, marked by a new line.

parallax *n* the apparent change of position of an object when viewed from different points.

parallel *adj* equidistant at all points; corresponding. * *n* a circle of latitude.

parallelogram *n* a quadrilateral whose opposite sides are parallel and of equal length.

paralyse *vt* to affect with paralysis; to render helpless.

paralysis *n* the loss of sensation and movement in any part of the body.

parapet *n* a wall breast-high.

paraphernalia *npl* belongings; trappings.

paraphrase *n* an interpretation of a passage for the sake of clarity. * *vt* to restate.

parasite *n* a hanger-on; a plant or animal that lives on another.

parasol *n* a sun shade.

parboil *vt* to boil partly.

parcel *n* a small bundle or packet. * *vt* (*pt* **parcelled**) to wrap up into a parcel; (*with* **out**) to divide into portions.

parch *vt*, *vi* to become hot, dry or thirsty; to scorch.

parchment *n* a skin prepared for writing on.

pardon *vt* to forgive; to excuse. * *n* forgiveness; remission of penalty.

pardonable *adj* excusable.

pare *vt* to trim by cutting; to peel.

parent *n* a father or mother; a source.

parentage *n* extraction; birth.

parenthesis *n* (*pl* **parentheses**) a written explanatory 'aside', usu in brackets, thus ().

parenting *n* the act of being a parent; the role of a parent in relation to a child.

pariah *n* an outcast.

parish *n* a district served by one clergyman. * *adj* parochial.

parity *n* equality; a likeness.

park *n* land kept as a game preserve or recreation area; a large enclosed space of open ground round a country house; an enclosed stadium; a stance for cars. * *vt* to leave (a car, etc) in a certain place temporarily; to manoeuvre (a car, etc) into a space.

parlance *n* conversation; talk.

parley *vi* to confer, to discuss. * *n* conference, esp with an enemy during cessation of hostilities.

parliament *n* a legislative assembly made up of representatives of a nation.

parlour *n* a sitting room.

parochial *adj* of or relating to a parish; narrow-minded.

parody *n* a humorous imitation of a literary or musical work or style. * *vt* to make a parody of.

parole *n* word of honour; conditional release of a prisoner.

paroxysm *n* a fit (of rage, grief, etc).

parquet *n* wood flooring.

parse *vt* to tell the parts of speech and their relations in a sentence.

parsimonious *adj* miserly.

parsimony *n* excessive economy.

parson *n* a parish minister; a clergyman.

part *n* a portion; a section; a share; a role; (*pl*) ability; a region. * *vi* to divide; share; break; separate; depart.

partake *vi, vt* to get a share of; to have or take a share in a meal.

partial *adj* only; incomplete; biased.

participate *vi, vt* to share in.

participle *n* a word that is partly verb and partly adjective.

particle *n* an atom; a word that cannot be used alone; a prefix; a suffix.

particular *adj* single; special; careful; fastidious. * *n* a detail; a single item.

parting *adj* separating; final. * *n* departure; a division; a shed of the hair.

partisan *adj* biased; one-sided. * *n* a strong supporter of a person, party or cause.

partition *n* division; a dividing wall or screen. * *vt* to divide up.

partner *n* a sharer in business, etc; either of a couple, married or unmarried.

partnership *n* fellowship; joint interest; the state of being a partner.

party *n* a social gathering; a person involved in a contract or lawsuit; a political group; an accessory. * *vt, vi* to give or attend social parties. * *adj* of or for a party.

pass *vt, vi* to go past; to go beyond or

exceed; to move from one place, etc, to another; to die; to elapse; to be enacted; to succeed at examination; to cross; to utter; to become law. * *n* an approval; passport; a narrow passage or road; transfer (of a ball) to another player; an uninvited sexual approach.

passable *adj* allowable; fairly good.

passage *n* a way through; transit; road; channel; journey; part of book.

passenger *n* a traveller in a conveyance.

passing *adj* current; fleeting.

passion *n* strong feeling, such as love, hate, envy; ardent love or desire; the object of any strong desire; (*with cap*) the suffering of Christ on the cross.

passionate *adj* moved by passion; hasty.

passive *adj* submissive; acted on, not acting; (*gram*) denoting the voice of a verb whose subject receives the action.

passive resistance *n* nonviolent noncooperation with the authorities.

passive smoking *n* involuntary inhalation of smoke from others' cigarettes.

passport *n* a licence to travel abroad; ticket of admission or acceptance.

password *n* a secret word that gives ready entrance.

past *adj* gone by; spent; ended. * *n* former time. * *prep* beyond. * *adv* by.

paste *n* a plastic mass of varied materials.

pastel *n* a crayon drawing.

pasteurize *vt* to inoculate; to sterilize (milk, etc).

pastime *n* recreation; play.

pastor *n* a minister of a church.

pastoral *adj* rustic; rural; relating to a pastor.

pastry *n* crust of pies, tarts, etc.

pasture *n* grass for cattle; grass land. * *vi* to graze.

pasty *adj* like paste; of a pallid appearance.

pat *n* a tap; a small lump. * *vt* to tap. * *adj* apt; glib.

patch *n* a repair piece; a small piece of ground. * *vt* to mend.

patchwork *n* something made of various bits, esp in needlework.

patella *n* the kneecap.

patent *n* grant of sole right to make or sell patented article. * *adj* open; obvious; secured by patent. * *vt* to obtain patent for.

paternal *adj* fatherly; hereditary.

paternity *n* fatherhood; origin; descent.

path *n* a footpath; a track; a course; a direction.

pathetic *adj* inspiring pity.

pathologist *n* a medical specialist in pathology.

pathology *n* the study of diseases.

pathos *n* a quality that excites pity; an expression of deep feeling.

patience *n* endurance; composure under trial; a card game.

patient *adj* uncomplaining; calm * *n* an invalid.

patriarch *n* the male chief of a family, etc.

patrician *adj* high-born; aristocratic. * *n* a noble person.

patriot *n* a lover of his or her country.

patriotism *n* love of country.

patrol *n* a unit of persons, esp employed for security; their going of the rounds. * *vt, vi* (*pt* **patrolled**) to go the rounds, inspect, etc.

patron *n* one who encourages, helps or protects.

patronage *n* support; conferring of favours or benefits.

patronize *vt* to act as patron of; to favour; to treat with condescension.

patter *vi* to make a sound like that of rain or hail, or feet; to mumble. * *n* chatter.

pattern *n* a model; a design.

paucity *n* fewness; poverty.

paunch *n* the belly, esp a potbelly.

pauper *n* a very poor person.

pause *n* a temporary stop; suspense. * *vi* to stop; hesitate.

pave *vt* to make a smooth roadway with blocks, flags, etc.

pavement *n* paved path for walkers.

pavilion *n* a large tent; a clubhouse; temporary building for exhibitions.

paw *n* the foot of animals with claws. * *vt* to scrape with the forefoot.

pawn *n* a security; pledge; (*chess*) piece of least value. * *vt* to give in pledge.

pawnbroker *n* a person licensed to lend money on pledged goods.

pay *vt, vi* (*pt, pp* **paid**) to give money for goods, service, etc; to reward; to bestow (attention, etc). * *n* wages; salary; reward.

payable *adj* due on a certain date.

payee *n* one to whom money is to be paid.

payment *n* act of paying; what is paid.

peace *n* quiet; calm; freedom from war or disorder; a treaty ending a war.

peaceable *adj* disposed to peace.

peaceful *adj* quiet; calm; mild.

peacemaker *n* one who restores good feeling; a reconciler.

peak *n* pointed top of hill; projection on cap; highest point.

peal *n* a loud clash; a clang; chime; loud laughter. * *vi* to ring out.

pearl *n* a lustrous gem found in oyster.

peasant *n* a rural labourer.

peasantry *n* peasants; country people.

peat *n* partly carbonized turf used as fuel.

pebble *n* small water-worn stone.

peccable *adj* liable to sin.

peccadillo *n* a petty fault or sin.

peck *n* a quick kiss. * *vi, vt* to strike or pick up with the beak.

peckish *adj* hungry.

pectoral *adj* pertaining to the breast.

peculiar *adj* one's own; particular; special; odd.

peculiarity *n* a characteristic; an oddity.

pecuniary *adj* financial; relating to money.

pedal *adj* pertaining to a foot. * *n* foot lever in cycle, etc. * *vt, vi* (*pt* **pedalled**) to work a pedal; to cycle.

pedant *n* one who parades his or

knowledge, esp of insignificant details.

pedantry *n* a vain display of learning.

peddle *vi*, *vt* to sell small items from place to place.

peddler same as **pedlar**.

pedestal *n* the base of a column, etc.

pedestrian *adj* going on foot; commonplace. * *n* a person who walks.

pedigree *n* lineage; ancestry.

pedlar, peddler *n* one who sells small goods from place to place.

peel *vt* to strip off skin, esp of fruit; to bare. * *vi* to lose the skin, bark or rind. * *n* the skin or rind.

peep[1] *vi* to make shrill noises, as a young bird. * *n* a peeping sound.

peep[2] *vi* to begin to appear; to look through a slit. * *n* a furtive or hurried glance.

peer[1] *n* an equal; a nobleman.

peer[2] *vi* to look closely or with difficulty.

peerage *n* the rank or title of a peer.

peerless *adj* matchless.

peevish *adj* fretful; querulous.

peg *n* a wooden nail, pin or bolt.

pellet *n* a little ball; a pill; small shot.

pelt *n* a raw hide; a blow. * *vt*, *vi* to assault (with stones, etc); (*rain*) to fall heavily; to hurry; to rush.

pelvis *n* the bony framework that joins the lower limbs to the body.

pen *n* an instrument for writing, drawing, etc; an enclosure for livestock. * *vt* (*pt* **penned**) to write; to coop up.

penal *adj* involving punishment.

penalty *n* due punishment; a fine.

penance *n* punishment imposed for sin.

pence *n* plural of **penny**.

penchant *n* bias; liking.

pencil *n* an instrument for drawing; a fine paintbrush.

pendant *n* a hanging ornament.

pendent *adj* hanging; pendulous.

pending *adj* in suspense. * *prep* during.

pendulous *adj* hanging; swinging.

pendulum *n* a weight suspended and swinging (as in clock).

penetrate *vt*, *vi* to enter or pierce; to discern.

penetrating *adj* sharp; discerning.

peninsula *n* land almost surrounded by water.

penis *n* the male copulative and urinary organ in mammals and humans.

penitence *n* repentance; sorrow.

penitent *adj* repentant; contrite.

pennant *n* a long pointed flag at masthead.

penny *n* (*pl* **pennies** *or* **pence**: pennies denotes the number of coins; pence the value) a low-value coin.

pension *n* a periodic payment for past services or old age; a boarding house.

pensioner *n* one in receipt of a pension.

pensive *adj* thoughtful; grave.

pentagon *n* a plane figure having five sides.

pentameter *n* a verse of five feet.

penthouse *n* a top floor apartment.

penultimate *adj* the last but one.

penury *n* poverty; want.

people *n* human beings; a nation; a race; a person's family; (*pl*) persons; the masses. * *vt* to populate.

pepper *n* a seasoning; fruit of the pepper plant.

peptic *adj* promoting digestion.

perambulate *vt* to walk up and down.

perceive *vt* to apprehend; understand.

percentage *n* the duty, rate, etc, on each hundred.

perceptible *adj* discernible.

perch *n* a freshwater fish; a roost for fowls; an elevated position.

percolate *vt* to filter through.

percolator *n* a strainer or filter.

percussion *n* collision; impact; (*med*) sounding; musical instruments usu played with sticks or hammers.

perdition *n* entire ruin; eternal death.

peremptory *adj* urgent; insistent; dictatorial.

perennial *adj* lasting through the year; never-ending.

perfect *adj* finished; complete; faultless. * *vt* to make perfect.

perfection *n* great excellence; flawlessness.

perfidious *adj* treacherous.

perfidy *n* treachery.

perforate *vt* to bore through; to pierce.

perform *vt* to accomplish; to do. * *vi* to act a part; to play a musical instrument.

performance *n* achievement; deed; entertainment (musical, etc).

performer *n* an actor, musician, etc.

perfume *n* a pleasant scent; fragrance. * *vt* to scent.

perfunctory *adj* careless; indifferent.

perhaps *adv* it may be; possibly.

peril *n* risk; danger.

perimeter *n* the total measurement round any figure; a boundary around.

perineum *n* the area between the genitals and the anus.

period *n* a portion of time; an age; full stop (.); menstruation; a stage in life.

periodic *adj* relating to a period; recurring at regular intervals; intermittent.

periodical *adj* periodic. * *n* a publication issued weekly, monthly, etc.

periphery *n* the boundary line of a figure.

periscope *n* an instrument by which an underwater observer can see objects on the surface.

perish *vi* to die; to decay.

perjure *vt* to commit perjury.

perjury *n* false evidence given on oath.

permanence *n* duration; fixedness.

permanent *adj* lasting; abiding.

permeable *adj* allowing the passage of fluid, gases, etc.

permeate *vt* to pass through; to pervade.

permissible *adj* allowable.

permission *n* leave; consent.

permissive *adj* allowing but not compelling.

permit *vt, vi* to allow; to grant; to concede. * *n* a written permission.

permutation *n* interchange; (*math*) all the possible variations of a series.

pernicious *adj* injurious; deadly; noxious.

perpendicular *adj* upright; at right

angles. * *n* a line at right angles to another.

perpetrate *vt* to commit.

perpetration *n* commission.

perpetual *adj* unending; eternal.

perpetuate *vt* to make lasting.

perpetuity *n* endless duration.

perplex *vt* to confuse; to puzzle.

perplexity *n* bewilderment.

perquisite *n* a reward or benefit, other than salary, attaching to an office; a gratuity.

persecute *vt* to harass with unjust punishment; to ill-treat; to oppress, esp minority group, race, etc.

persevere *vi* to pursue steadily any design.

persevering *adj* constant in purpose.

persist *vi* to persevere; to stand firm.

persistence, persistency *n* steadfastness; obstinacy.

persistent *adj* persisting; steady.

person *n* a human being; the body; (*gram*) a verb inflexion.

personal *adj* individual; private; one's own; (*remarks*) unkind.

personality *n* one's individual characteristics; a celebrity; a person with distinct qualities.

personification *n* embodiment; a metaphor ascribing life to inanimate objects.

personify *vt* to embody; to endow with human qualities.

personnel *n* the staff of an organization, etc.

perspective *n* the art of representing objects on a flat surface as they are to the eye; objectivity.

perspicacity *n* acuteness of mind.

perspicuity *n* clearness; lucidity.

perspiration *n* sweat.

perspire *vi* to sweat.

persuade *vt* to influence by argument, etc.

persuasive *adj* convincing; winning.

pert *adj* lively; saucy; forward.

pertain *vi* to belong; to concern.

pertinent *adj* to the point.

perturb *vt* to disturb; to disquiet.

perturbation *n* uneasiness; disquiet.

perusal *n* reading; study.

peruse *vt* to read through; to examine carefully.

pervade *vt* to permeate; to spread throughout.

perverse *adj* obstinate in being wrong; stubborn; contrary.

perversion *n* corruption; misuse; an abnormal way of obtaining sexual satisfaction.

perversity *n* obstinacy; wickedness; a perverse act.

pervert *vt* to corrupt; to misapply. * *n* a person who is sexually perverted.

pervious *adj* penetrable.

pessimism *n* tendency to make or expect the worst of everything.

pessimist *n* one who takes a gloomy view of life.

pest *n* a plague; a nuisance.

pestilence *n* a deadly epidemic.

pestilential *adj* destructive; hurtful.

pestle *n* an instrument for grinding material.

pet *n* a darling; a favourite; a domestic animal kept as a companion. * *adj* cherished. * *vt* (*pt* **petted**) to fondle.

petal n a flower leaf.

petite adj tiny; dainty.

petition n an entreaty; a written demand for government action, etc, signed by many. * vt to ask humbly for; to present a petition.

petrify vt to turn into stone; to paralyse or stupefy with terror.

petrol n refined petroleum.

petroleum n natural mineral oil.

petrology n the study of rocks.

petty adj small; trivial; small-minded.

petulance n peevishness; ill-humour.

petulant adj irritable; fretful.

pew n a seat in a church.

pewter n an alloy of tin and lead.

phantom n an apparition; a spectre.

pharmaceutical adj of or relating to pharmacy or drugs.

pharmacist n a person trained to practise pharmacy.

pharmacy n the preparation and dispensing of drugs; a shop where drugs are sold.

phase n a stage; an aspect; apparent shape (of the moon).

phenomenal adj astounding.

phenomenon n (pl **phenomena**) an appearance; anything visible; a remarkable thing or person.

phial same as **vial**.

philander vi to flirt.

philanthropic, philanthropical adj benevolent.

philanthropy n the love of mankind; benevolence; charitable actions.

philatelist n a collector of postage stamps.

philately n stamp collecting.

philologist n one versed in philology.

philology n the study of language.

philosopher n a person who studies philosophy.

philosophically adv calmly; wisely; serenely.

philosophy n the science of mind, conduct, and phenomena; a particular system of ethics.

phlegm n the secretion of the mucous membrane discharged in coughing, etc; lack of emotion.

phlegmatic adj sluggish; unemotional.

phoenix n a fabled bird, said to burn itself and rise again from its own ashes; emblem of immortality.

phone n contraction for telephone.

phonetic adj pertaining to vocal sound.

phonetics npl the science of the sounds of the human voice and their representation.

phonograph n an instrument for reproducing sounds.

phosphate n a salt of phosphoric acid.

phosphorescence n emission of light without heat as from fish in the dark.

phosphorescent adj luminous.

phosphorus n a nonmetallic element, luminous in dark.

photograph n a picture obtained by photography. * vt to take or produce a photograph.

photography n the art of recording images permanently and visibly by action of light on prepared plates.

phrase n a related group of words; diction; style.

phrenetic *adj* frantic.

phrenology *n* theory that intelligence is related to shape of skull.

phylloxera *n* an insect that attacks vines.

physical *adj* relating to matter and energy, the human body, or natural science. * *n* a general medical examination.

physician *n* a doctor of medicine.

physicist *n* a specialist in physics.

physics *n* the science of matter in relation to force.

physiognomy *n* reading character from study of facial expression.

physiology *n* the science of bodily structures, organs, and functions.

physique *n* physical frame.

pianist *n* a performer on the piano.

piano *n* a large stringed keyboard instrument.

piazza *n* a square surrounded by colonnades.

pica *n* a standard printing type, equal to twelve points.

picaresque *adj* describing the fortunes of adventurers.

piccolo *n* a small flute.

pick *vt, vi* to strike with something sharp; to pick at; to pluck; to choose; to nibble. * *n* an excavating axe; choice.

pickaxe *n* a pick.

picket *n* a pointed stake; a military guard; a preventive guard against strike-breakers. * *vt* to post (soldiers, etc); to tether.

pickle *n* brine; vegetables preserved in vinegar; plight. * *vt* to preserve in pickle.

picnic *n* an informal meal taken on an outing and eaten outdoors.

pictorial *adj* illustrated by pictures.

picture *n* a painting, drawing, likeness, etc; mental image; vivid description; motion picture * *vt* to portray.

picturesque *adj* striking, vivid, usually pleasing.

pie *n* meat or fruit with paste covering baked; unsorted type.

piece *n* a portion; a distinct part; a short composition or writing; a picture; a coin.

piecemeal *adv* in or by pieces.

piecework *n* work paid by quantity, not by time.

pied *adj* of various colours.

pier *n* stone column supporting arch, etc; a wharf or landing stage.

pierce *vt* to thrust through; to perforate.

piercing *adj* penetrating; cutting.

pierrot *n* a humorous entertainer in clown-like dress.

piety *n* religious devoutness.

pig *n* a hog; a bar of smelted iron.

pigeon *n* a bird with a small head and a large body.

pigeonhole *n* a compartment in a desk for papers.

pig-headed *adj* stupidly obstinate.

pigment *n* colouring matter.

pigtail *n* a plait of hair hanging down back.

pile *n* a heap; a large amount; a massive building; a supporting pillar driven into the ground. * *vt* to heap.

piles *npl* a swelling of the rectum veins.

pilfer *vi* to steal on a small scale.

pilgrim *n* a person who makes a pilgrimage.

pilgrimage *n* a journey, esp to a holy place.

pill *n* a medicine in a tablet form; an oral contraceptive.

pillage *n* plunder; spoil. * *vt* to plunder.

pillar *n* a supporting column.

pillion *n* a cushion on back of saddle for second rider.

pillory *n* the stocks or frame once used for punishment of offenders. * *vt* to expose to ridicule.

pillow *n* a cushion for the head while sleeping; something which supports and distributes pressure.

pilot *n* a person who operates a ship or an aircraft; a guide. * *vt* to direct the course of; to act as a pilot; to guide.

pimp *n* a prostitute's agent

pimple *n* a small red swelling on skin.

pin *n* a short pointed piece of metal for fastening clothes; a peg; a bolt. * *vt* (*pt* **pinned**) to fasten.

pinafore *n* a sleeveless garment worn over a dress, blouse, etc.

pincer *n* the claw of a crab; (*pl*) nippers.

pinch *vt* to cramp; to be sparing. * *n* a nip; distress; need; small portion.

pine *n* a coniferous tree. * *vi* to languish.

pinion *n* the outer joint of a bird's wing. * *vt* to restrain; to bind the arms to the sides.

pink *n* a garden flower; a pale red colour; excellence. * *vt* to stab.

pinnace *n* a boat with oars and sails.

pinnacle *n* a turret; pointed peak; the highest point; climax.

pint *n* a liquid measure equal to one eighth of a gallon.

pioneer *n* a person who initiates or explores new areas of enterprise, research, etc; an explorer; an early settler. * *vt* to initiate; to explore; to act as a pioneer.

pious *adj* devout; religious; sanctimonious.

pip *n* the seed of a fleshy fruit; spot on cards, dice, etc.

pipe *n* a musical instrument; long tube conveying gas, water, etc; shrill voice; tobacco-smoking apparatus. * *vt* (*mus*) to play on a pipe.

piping *adj* giving out a whistling sound. * *n* sound of pipes; system of pipes.

piquant *adj* sharp; pungent.

pique *n* irritation; resentment. * *vt, vi* to cause resentment in; to offend.

piracy *n* robbery committed at sea; infringement of copyright.

pirate *n* a sea robber; one who infringes copyright.

pirouette *n* spinning round on toe in ballet.

piscatorial *adj* of or relating to fish or fishing.

Pisces *npl* the Fishes, a sign in the zodiac.

pistil *n* the seed-bearing organ of a flower.

pistol *n* a small firearm fired with one hand.

piston *n* a metal plug that slides to

and fro in the hollow cylinder of an engine, pump, etc.

pit *n* a hollow in the earth; shaft of a mine; a depression in skin; orchestra space in a theatre. * *vt* (*pt* **pitted**) to mark with little hollows; to set in competition.

pitch *vt* to fix in ground; to set; to throw; to set the keynote of; to set in array. * *vi* to fall headlong; to encamp; to rise and fall, as a ship. * *n* a throw; highest rise; elevation of a note; a thick dark substance obtained from tar.

pitcher *n* a vessel for carrying liquids.

pitchfork *n* a fork for pitching hay.

piteous *adj* arousing pity.

pitfall *n* concealed danger; a trap.

pith *n* the soft centre of stem of plant; marrow; essence.

pitiable *adj* deserving pity.

pittance *n* a small quantity or allowance of money.

pity *n* sympathy or compassion. * *vt* to grieve for.

pivot *n* that on which something turns or depends.

placard *n* a poster or notice for public display.

placate *vt* to appease.

place *n* an open space in a town; a locality; position; room; passage in book; rank; office. * *vt* to put or set; to locate.

placid *adj* calm; tranquil.

plagiarism *n* the stealing words or ideas of another.

plague *n* a deadly epidemic; pestilence; nuisance.

plaid *n* a large woollen shawl-like wrap; cloth with a tartan or chequered pattern.

plain *adj* smooth; level; clear; simple; evident; not flavoured. * *n* a tract of level land.

plaint *n* a lamentation; formal statement of grievance.

plaintiff *n* a person who brings a lawsuit against another.

plaintive *adj* mournful.

plait *n* a fold; a braid, as of hair, etc. * *vt* to fold; to braid.

plan *n* the ground shape of an object; scheme; process; method. * *vt* (*pt* **planned**) to scheme; to design.

plane[1] *adj* level; flat; (*figure*) having all the points in one surface or plane. * *n* a smooth surface; a joiner's smoothing tool; an aeroplane. * *vt*, *vi* to make smooth; to skim across water; to travel by aeroplane.

plane[2] *n* a tall tree with large broad leaves.

planet *n* a celestial body moving around the sun or another star.

planetary *adj* under the influence of one of the planets; wandering.

plank *n* a flat broad piece of timber.

plant *n* a vegetable organism; an herb; a shoot; industrial machinery and equipment. * *vt* to set in ground; to implant; to establish.

plantation *n* a cultivated planting of trees; a tropical estate.

plaque *n* an ornamental plate; a film of mucus on the teeth that harbours bacteria.

plasma *n* the colourless liquid part of blood, milk or lymph.

plaster *n* a cement for covering walls; a preparation for casts, etc; adhesive dressing for wounds or relief of pain.

plastic *adj* easily shaped or moulded. * *n* any of various non-metallic compounds, synthetically produced.

plasticine *n* a modelling clay.

plate *n* a flat piece of metal, glass, etc; a shallow dish for meals. * *vt* to coat with gold, etc.

plateau *n* (*pl* **plateaux** *or* **plateaus**) a flat, elevated piece of land; a stable period.

platform *n* a raised structure for speaking from, entering trains, etc; a statement of political policy.

platinum *n* a heavy metal very difficult to fuse.

platitude *n* a dull truism; a commonplace remark.

platonic *adj* free from physical desire.

platoon *n* a military unit divided into squads or sections.

platter *n* a large, oval serving dish.

plaudit *n* (*usu pl*) a commendation.

plausibility *n* quality of being plausible; speciousness.

plausible *adj* apparently truthful or reasonable.

play *vi*, *vt* to sport; frolic; gamble; act; engage in games; perform upon. * *n* free movement; a game; sport; gaming; a drama.

player *n* an actor; musician; sportsman, sportswoman.

playful *adj* full of fun, humorous, sportive.

playhouse *n* a theatre; a small house for children to play in.

playschool *n* a nursery for preschool children.

plaything *n* a toy; a thing or person treated as a toy.

playwright *n* a writer of plays.

plea *n* an answer to a charge; an entreaty; a request.

plead *vi*, *vt* to argue for or against; to answer to a charge; to urge; to beg earnestly; to urge in excuse.

pleading *n* statement of facts for or against a claim.

pleasance *n* pleasure; a shady grove.

pleasant *adj* pleasing; agreeable.

pleasantry *n* a polite or amusing remark.

please *vt*, *vi* to satisfy; to give pleasure to; to be willing. * *adv* a word to express politeness or emphasis in a request; an expression of polite affirmation.

pleasing *adj* agreeable; giving pleasure.

pleasure *n* enjoyment; recreation; preference.

plebeian *adj*, *n* relating to the common people; base; vulgar.

plebiscite *n* a vote of the whole electorate on a political issue.

plectrum *n* a thin piece of metal, etc, for plucking strings of guitar, etc.

pledge *n* something given in security; a surety; a toast. * *vt* to pawn; to toast; to bind by solemn promise.

plenary *adj* full; complete; attended by all members.

plenitude *n* fullness; abundance.

plentiful *adj* ample; abundant.

plenty n abundance; more than enough. * adj plentiful.

plethora n overabundance; a glut; (med) an excess of red corpuscles in the blood.

pleura n (pl **pleurae**) membrane enveloping the lungs.

pleurisy n an inflammation of the pleura.

pliable adj supple; easily persuaded; pliant.

pliant adj pliable; flexible.

pliers npl a hand tool for cutting, shaping wire.

plight vt to pledge (word, honour, etc). * n a pledge; predicament.

plinth n square slab forming base of column.

plod vi to work or walk laboriously.

plot n a small piece of ground; a plan; a conspiracy; the story of a novel, etc. * vt (pt **plotted**) to devise; to conspire; to mark on a map.

plough n an implement for turning up the soil. * vt, vi to furrow; to work at laboriously; (inf) to fail an examination.

pluck vt to pick or gather; to snatch; to strip off feathers. * n courage or spirit.

plug n a stopper used for filling a hole; a device for connecting an appliance to an electrical supply; a cake of tobacco. * vt (pt **plugged**) to stop with a plug.

plumage n the feathers of a bird.

plumb n a lead weight attached to a line, used to determine depth or true vertical. * adj true; vertical * adv vertically. * vt to supply or install

as plumbing; to test with a plumb.

plumber n a person who installs and repairs water or gas pipes.

plumbing n the system of pipes used in water or gas supply, or drainage.

plume n a bird's feather; an ornament of feathers in hat, etc. * vt to preen.

plummet n a plumb. * vt to fall in a perpendicular manner; to drop abruptly.

plump adj rounded; chubby * vt, vi to make plump; to favour or give support. * adv straight down; straight ahead; suddenly.

plunder vt to steal goods by force; to loot. * n plundering; booty.

plunge vt to thrust into water; to immerse; to penetrate quickly. * vi to dive into water, etc; to rush into. * n a dive.

plunger n a large rubber suction cup used to free clogged drains.

plural adj denoting more than one. * n (gram) the form referring to more than one person or thing.

plurality n a majority; a large number.

plus prep added to; in addition to. * n the sign of addition (+).

plush n a velvety fabric. * adj (inf) luxurious.

plutocracy n the power or rule of wealth.

ply vt, vi to work at; to wield skilfully; to press hard; to voyage or journey regularly; to sell (goods). * n a layer or thickness of cloth, etc.

pneumatic adj concerning wind, air or gas; operated by or filled with compressed air.

pneumonia *n* an acute inflammation of the lungs.

poach *vt* to cook (eggs) by breaking into boiling water. * *vi* to take game illegally; to trespass; to encroach upon.

pocket *n* a small pouch in a garment, etc; a deposit, as of gas, minerals, etc; an isolated or closed area. * *vt* to put in one's pocket; to take dishonestly.

pod *n* the seed vessel of plants; a detachable compartment on a spacecraft; a protective container.

poem *n* an imaginative arrangement of words, esp in metre, often rhymed.

poet *n* the author of a poem.

poetry *n* the art of writing poems; poems collectively; poetic spirt or quality.

pogrom *n* an organized extermination of a minority group.

poignant *adj* incisive; deeply moving.

point *n* the sharp end of anything; a headland; a dot; a moment in time; exact spot; purpose; a place in a cy-.cle, scale or course; essence; feature; railway switch; a unit in printing equal to one seventy-second of an inch * *vt, vi* to indicate; to sharpen; to aim.

point-blank *adj* aimed straight at a mark; direct, blunt.

pointed *adj* sharp; personal.

pointer *n* an indicator; a rod for pointing with; a dog trained to point out game.

poise *n* a balanced state; bearing; carriage * *vt* to balance; to put into readiness. * *vi* to hover.

poison *n* a substance which when absorbed is fatal or injurious to an organism; any corrupt influence. * *vt* to give poison to; to taint; to corrupt.

poke *n* a bag or sack; a prod or nudge. * *vt* to prod; to hit. * *vi* to pry or search (about or around).

poker *n* an iron rod for poking a fire; a card game.

polar *adj* of or near the North or South pole; of a pole; having positive and negative electricity; directly opposite.

polarity *n* the condition of being polar; the magnet's property of pointing north; diametrical opposition.

pole *n* a long slender piece of wood, metal, etc; either end of an axis, esp of the earth; either of two opposed forces, parts, etc, as the ends of a magnet.

polemic *n* a controversy or argument over doctrine; strong criticism. * *adj* polemical.

polemical *adj* involving dispute; controversial.

police *n* the government department for maintaining public order, detecting crime, law enforcement, etc. * *vt* to control, protect, etc, with police or similar body.

policy *n* system or manner of government; principle or course of action; an insurance contract.

polish *vt, vi* to make smooth and glossy; to refine. * *n* gloss; elegance.

polite *adj* polished in manners; refined; elegant.

politic *adj* prudent; astute.

political *adj* relating to politics or government.

politician *n* a person engaged in politics.

politics *n* the science and art of government; political activities; factional scheming for power.

polka *n* a lively dance.

poll *n* a counting, listing, etc, of persons; the number of votes recorded; an opinion survey. * *vt* to cast a vote.

pollen *n* the fine, powder-like material found in the anthers of flowers.

pollinate *vt* to fertilize by uniting pollen with seed.

pollute *vt* to contaminate with harmful substances; to make corrupt; to profane.

pollution *n* the act of polluting; contamination by chemicals, noise, etc.

polo *n* a game resembling hockey, played on horseback.

polygamy *n* the practice of being married to more than one person at a time.

polyglot *adj* having command of many languages; composed of several languages. * *n* a person who speaks several languages.

polygon *n* a plane figure of three or more sides.

polygraph *n* an instrument for measuring involuntary changes in blood pressure, etc, used as a lie detector.

polystyrene *n* a rigid plastic material used for packing insulating, etc.

polysyllable *n* a word of more syllables than three.

polytechnic *n* an institution that provides instruction in many applied sciences and technical subjects.

polyurethane *n* any of various polymers that are used esp in flexible and rigid foams, resins, etc.

pommel *n* a knob or ball, as on sword hilt, saddle bow. * *vt* to pummel.

pomposity *n* the state of being pompous; a pompous act or utterance.

pompous *adj* pretentious; self-important.

pond *n* a body of standing water smaller than a lake.

ponder *vt* to consider carefully.

ponderous *adj* heavy; awkward; dull.

pontiff *n* the Pope; a bishop.

pontifical *adj* of a pontiff; pompous.

pontoon *n* a boat or float forming a support for a bridge.

pony *n* a small horse.

pool *n* a small pond; a swimming pool; a puddle; a combination of resources for a common purpose; a form of billiards.

poop *n* the stern of a ship.

poor *adj* having little money; needy; unfortunate; deficient; inferior; disappointing. * *n* those who have little.

pop *n* a short, explosive sound; any carbonated beverage; a shot. * *adj* in a popular modern style.

pope *n* the head of the Roman Catholic church.

populace *n* the common people; all the people in a country, region, etc.

popular *adj* well-liked; common; prevalent.

population *n* the inhabitants; total number of people in an area.

populous *adj* densely inhabited.

porcelain *n* the variety of ceramic ware.

porch *n* a covered entry to a building.

pore *n* a minute opening in the skin; a small interstice. * *vi* to examine or study with care.

pork *n* the flesh of a pig, as food.

pornography *n* pictures, films, etc, intended primarily to arouse sexual desire and usu considered obscene.

porridge *n* a food made from oatmeal boiled in water or milk.

port *n* a harbour; a gate; a porthole; the left side of a ship; a circuit in a computer for the transferring of data

port *n* a fortified red wine.

portable *adj* able to be carried; not heavy.

portal *n* a door or gate; the main entrance.

portcullis *n* a sliding or falling grating at portal of a castle.

portend *vt* to give warning of; to foreshadow.

portent *n* an omen; a warning.

porter *n* a doorkeeper; a carrier; a dark brown beer.

portfolio *n* a case for drawings, papers, etc; office of minister of state; a list of stocks, shares, etc.

portico *n* a covered walkway.

portion *n* a part; a share; fate. * *vt* to divide.

portly *adj* dignified; stout.

portrait *n* a picture of a person; a vivid description.

portray *vt* to make a portrait of; to depict.

pose *n* attitude or position. * *vi, vt* to strike an attitude; to assert; to sit for a painting, photograph, etc.

poser *n* a difficult problem; a person who poses.

position *n* place; situation; posture; rank; a job; point of view. * *vt* to place or locate.

positive *adj* explicit; absolute; confident; affirmative; (*gram*) noting the simple form of an adjective; a form of electricity; greater than zero; (*photog*) having light, colour, etc, as in the original. * *n* a positive quality or quantity; a photographic print made from a negative.

possess *vt* to have and hold; to own.

possession *n* ownership; occupancy.

possessive *adj* denoting possession. * *n* (*gram*) the possessive case.

possible *adj* that may be or may happen; practicable.

post[1] *n* a piece of timber, etc, set upright to support a building, sign, etc; the starting or finishing point of a race. * *vt* to put up (a poster); to put (a name) on a list.

post[2] *n* a place assigned; a military or other station; office or employment; a trading post. * *vt* to station in a given place.

post[3] *n* the official conveyance of letters, parcels, etc; the items so conveyed; collection or delivery of post, mail. * *vt* to send a letter or parcel; to keep informed.

postage n a charge for conveyance by post.

postal adj relating to the carrying of post.

postcard n a card, usu decorative, for sending messages by post.

poster n a large printed bill for advertising.

posterior adj later or subsequent. * n the buttocks.

posterity n descendants; future generations.

postern n a back or private entrance.

postgraduate n a person pursuing further study after a degree.

posthaste adv with all speed.

posthumous adj (child) born after the father's death; occurring after one's death.

postman n a mail carrier.

post-mortem adj (autopsy) held after death.

post office n a place where postal business is conducted; the public department in charge of postal services.

postpone vt to delay; defer.

postscript n an addition to a letter after signature.

postulate n self-evident truth; assumption. * vt to state; assume.

posture n an attitude; a body position; a stand.

pot n a vessel for holding or boiling liquids; vessel for holding plants; frame for catching fish, lobsters, etc. * vt (pt **potted**) to plant in a pot; to shoot.

potash n potassium carbonate.

potassium n the metallic element.

potato n a tuber eaten as a vegetable.

potbelly n a protruding belly.

potency n power; force.

potentate n one who possesses great power; a monarch.

potential adj possible. * n unrealized ability.

potion n a mixture of liquids.

potpourri n a mixture of scented, dried flowers; a medley.

pottery n earthenware; a workshop where this is made.

pouch n a pocket; a small bag.

poultice n a moist dressing applied to sore parts of the body.

poultry n domestic birds kept for meat or eggs.

pounce n to fall on suddenly.

pound[1] n a British monetary unit equal to 100 pence; a unit of weight equal to 16 ounces or 0.454 kilogram.

pound[2] vt, vi to beat; to pulverize; to strike repeatedly; to throb; to work hard; to walk heavily.

pound[3] n an enclosure for lost cattle; a place where property is held until claimed.

pour vi to flow continuously; to rain heavily; to serve liquid refreshment.

pout vi to thrust out the lips; to look sulky. * n a sullen look.

poverty n want; the condition of being poor.

powder n any substance in fine particles; dust; gunpowder. * vt, vi to reduce to or sprinkle with powder.

powdery adj dusty; friable.

power n ability to act or do; strength;

influence; talent; command; authority; a state or government; warrant; a mechanical advantage or effect. * *adj* operated by electricity, a fuel engine, etc; carrying electricity. * *vt* to supply with a source of power.

practicable *adj* feasible; possible.

practical *adj* skilful in work; useful; handy.

practice *n* custom; habit; exercise of any profession; training; drill.

practise *vt*, *vi* to do frequently or habitually; to exercise, as any profession; to commit; to form a habit.

practitioner *n* one who practises a profession (esp medicine).

pragmatic *adj* practical; testing all concepts by their practical results.

prairie *n* an extensive tract of grassy land.

praise *vt* to express approval of; to commend; to worship. * *n* commendation.

pram *n* carriage for a baby.

prance *vi* to spring on the hind legs; to swagger.

prank *n* a mischievous trick or joke.

prattle *vi* to talk much and idly; to prate. * *n* trifling talk.

pray *vi*, *vt* to beg or implore; to ask reverently.

prayer *n* supplication; entreaty; praise or thanks to God.

preach *vi* to deliver a sermon; to give earnest advice. * *vt* to proclaim.

preamble *n* introductory part of a story, speech, etc.

precarious *adj* uncertain; insecure.

precaution *n* a preventative measure; careful foresight.

precede *vt* to go before; to preface.

precedence *n* priority; order according to rank.

precedent *n* a parallel case serving as example.

precept *n* rule of conduct; maxim; mandate.

precinct *n* a bounding line; an urban area where traffic is prohibited; (*pl*) neighbourhood; environs.

precious *adj* of great worth or value; very fastidious; affected.

precipice *n* a cliff or overhanging rock face.

precipitate *vt*, *vi* to hurl headlong; to hasten rashly; to sink to the bottom of a vessel; to bring down (moisture). * *adj* headlong; overhasty. * *n* a deposit from a liquid.

precipitation *n* rash haste; rain, snow, etc.

precipitous *adj* very steep.

précis *n* a summary; abstract.

precise *adj* exact; definite; punctilious; particular.

precision *n* exactness; accuracy.

preclude *vt* to shut out; to prevent; to make impossible.

precocious *adj* prematurely ripe; forward.

precocity *n* too early development.

preconceive *vt* to form an opinion beforehand.

preconcerted *adj* pre-arranged.

precursor *n* a forerunner; omen.

precursory *adj* forerunning.

predator *n* a person who preys, plunders or devours.

predecessor *n* one who was in office before another.

predestinate vt to foreordain. * adj foreordained.

predetermine vt, vi to determine beforehand.

predicament n a quandary; critical position.

predicate vt, vi to affirm one thing of another. * n that which is affirmed.

predict vt to foretell.

prediction n a prophecy.

predilection n a previous preference.

predispose vt to incline beforehand.

predominant adj outstanding; superior.

preen vt (of birds) to clean and trim the feathers; to groom oneself.

preface n an introduction; foreword. * vt to introduce by preliminary remarks.

prefect n person placed in authority over others; a student monitor in a school.

prefer vt to like better; to promote or advance.

preferable adj more desirable.

preference n choice; favour; prior claim.

preferential adj implying preference.

preferment n promotion.

prefix vt to put at the beginning. * n a letter or syllable put at beginning of a word.

pregnant adj having a foetus in the womb; significant; filled with.

prehistoric adj prior to the time of written records.

prejudge vt to condemn beforehand.

prejudice n bias; intolerance. * vt to affect or injure through prejudice.

preliminary adj preparatory; introductory. * n an event preceding another; a preliminary step or measure.

prelude vt to preface. * n a musical introduction.

premature adj too early; untimely; hasty.

premeditate vt, vi to plan beforehand.

premier adj first; principal * n the prime minister.

premiere n the first public performance of a play, film, etc.

premise n a proposition on which reasoning is based; something assumed.

premises n a building and its adjuncts.

premium n a reward; a bonus; sum paid for insurance; increase in value.

premonition n a foreboding; a feeling that something is about to happen.

preoccupied adj engrossed; lost on thought.

preparatory adj introductory.

prepare vt, vi to make ready.

preponderance n superiority of weight, influence, etc; ascendancy.

preponderant adj superior in power, influence, etc.

preposition n a word used before a noun or pronoun to show its relation to another part of the sentence.

prepossess vt to influence in advance; to prejudice.

prepossessing adj attractive.

prepossession n preconceived opinion; prejudice.

preposterous *adj* absurd; utterly ridiculous.

prerogative *n* a prior claim; an exclusive privilege; hereditary right.

presage *n* a presentiment; omen. * *vt*, *vi* to forebode.

prescience *n* foreknowledge.

prescribe *vt*, *vi* to lay down authoritatively; to direct medically; to appoint.

prescription *n* a written direction for preparing a medicine; a claim or title based on long use.

prescriptive *adj* based on and acquired by long use.

presence *n* state of being visible; appearance; personality; something (as a spirit) felt or believed to be present.

present *adj* now existing or happening; ready at hand; in the place required or mentioned. * *n* the time in which we live.

present *vt* to introduce (one person to another); to show; to give or bestow; to nominate to a benefice; to point or aim; (*law*) to lay a charge before a court.

presentable *adj* suitable for presenting.

presentation *n* act of presenting; thing presented; a gift; a display or exhibition.

presently *adv* in a short while; soon; now.

preservation *n* the act of preserving.

preservative *adj* tending to preserve. * *n* something that preserves, esp a food additive.

preserve *vt* to save from injury; to keep in a sound state; to maintain; to restrict the hunting of. * *n* fruit, vegetables, etc, treated with a preservative; jam; a restricted area.

preside *vi* to direct or control (a meeting); to take the chair.

presidency *n* office of president.

president *n* highest officer in a republic; chairman.

press *vt* to weigh down; to urge; to enforce; to emphasize; to embrace. * *vi* to push with force. * *n* a pressing; a crowd; a machine for crushing or squeezing; a printing machine; printing; newspapers.

pressing *adj* urgent.

pressure *n* a weighing down; force; influence; urgency.

prestige *n* influence based on character or conduct.

presume *vt*, *vi* to take for granted; to infer; to act in a forward way.

presumption *n* arrogance; supposition.

presumptuous *adj* over-confident; arrogant.

presuppose *vt* to take for granted.

pretence *n* act of pretending; pretext; false claim.

pretend *vt*, *vi* to claim, represent, or assert falsely; to feign.

pretentious *adj* claiming great importance; ostentatious.

pretext *n* a pretence; excuse.

pretty *adj* attractive; pleasing. * *adv* moderately; fairly.

prevail *vi* to overcome; to be in force; to succeed; to persuade.

prevalence *n* superior strength or influence; general diffusion.

prevalent *adj* prevailing; dominant; widespread.

prevaricate *vi* to make evasive or misleading statements.

prevent *vt* to stop or impede.

prevention *n* hindrance; obstruction.

previous *adj* antecedent; prior.

prey *n* a victim; animal killed for food by another. * *vi* to victimize.

price *n* the value of a commodity; cost; worth.

priceless *adj* invaluable.

prick *n* a sharp point; puncture or piercing. * *vt* to puncture.

pride *n* self-esteem; conceit; delight. * *vt* to be proud of.

priest *n* in various churches, a person authorized to perform sacred rites.

priesthood *n* the office of a priest; the order of priests.

priggish *adj* conceited; affected.

prim *adj* formal; demure.

primacy *n* the office of primate or archbishop.

prima donna *n* the chief female singer in an opera; (*inf*) a temperamental person.

primal *adj* primary; primitive; fundamental.

primary *adj* first; chief; elementary; first in order of time.

primate *n* any of the highest order of mammals, including man.

prime *adj* original; not divisible by any smaller number; best quality.

primer *n* child's first reader; first coat of paint; a detonating device.

primeval *adj* primitive; original.

primitive *adj* original; antiquated; primary.

primordial *adj* first of all; original.

prince *n* the son of a king or emperor.

princely *adj* noble; august; magnificent.

principal *adj* first; chief; most important. * *n* head of a school, firm, etc; chief in authority; capital sum lent at interest.

principality *n* sovereignty; territory of a prince.

principally *adv* chiefly; mainly.

principle *n* cause or origin; a general truth; a fundamental law; a rule of conduct; uprightness.

print *vt* to mark by pressure; to stamp; to copy by pressure. * *vi* to publish. * *n* a mark made by pressure; an engraving, etc; a newspaper; printed calico.

printing *n* the art or process of making impressions on paper, cloth, etc; typography.

prior *adj* preceding; earlier. * *n* a monk next in dignity to an abbot.

priority *n* precedence; first claim.

priory *n* a religious house ruled by a prior.

prise *vt* to force up.

prism *n* a solid whose ends are any similar, equal, and parallel plane figures; a kind of lens for decomposing light.

prison *n* a place of confinement; a jail. * *vt* to imprison.

pristine *adj* original; first.

privacy *n* seclusion; secrecy.

private *adj* separate from others; solitary; personal; secret. * *n* a common soldier.

privation *n* destitution; hardship.

privilege n a prerogative, benefit, or right. * vt to authorize; to exempt.

privy adj private; clandestine; (with to) admitted to the knowledge of.

prize n that which is seized from an enemy; a reward of merit. * vt to value highly.

prize-fight n a boxing match for a prize.

probability n likelihood.

probable adj likely; credible.

probate n the official proof of a will; confirmation.

probation n proof; trial; period of trial.

probe n a surgeon's instrument for examining a wound. * vt to explore; to examine carefully.

probity n uprightness; honesty.

problem n a question for solution; a knotty point.

proboscis n the trunk of an elephant, etc; the sucking tube of insects.

procedure n mode of conducting business; conduct.

proceed vi to go forward; to issue; to take legal action.

proceeding n transaction; procedure.

proceeds npl money brought in by a transaction.

process n progressive course; method of operation; lapse; legal proceedings; a writ.

procession n a body of people on the march.

processional adj relating to a procession. * n a service book as guide for religious processions.

proclaim vt to announce publicly; to publish.

proclamation n an official public announcement.

proclivity n inclination; tendency.

procrastinate vt, vi to put off; to postpone unduly.

procreation n the begetting of young.

procurator n the manager of another's affairs; legal agent or prosecutor.

procure vt to obtain; to cause.

prod n a goad; a nudge; a stab. * vt to goad.

prodigal adj lavish; wasteful. * n a waster; a spendthrift.

prodigious adj portentous; enormous.

prodigy n a gifted child; an extraordinary person, thing or act.

produce vt, vi to bring forward; to exhibit; to bear, yield; to cause; to extend. * n outcome; yield.

product n result; effect.

production n fruit; product; performance.

productive adj fertile; fruitful.

profane adj not sacred; secular; blasphemous; impure. * vt to treat with irreverence; to pollute.

profanity n profane language or conduct.

profess vt to declare openly; to acknowledge; to pretend.

profession n open avowal; vocation; calling; members of a profession.

professional adj pertaining to a profession. * n one who makes his living by arts, sports, etc, as distinguished from an amateur.

professor n a university teacher of highest rank.

professorship *n* the office of a professor.

proffer *vt* to offer for acceptance.

proficiency *n* expertness; degree of advancement.

proficient *adj* fully versed; competent. * *n* an adept or expert.

profile *n* an outline; the side face or outline of it.

profit *n* any advantage, benefit, or gain. * *vt* to benefit. * *vi* to derive profit; to improve.

profitable *adj* yielding profit; lucrative; useful.

profligacy *n* depravity; vicious course of life.

profligate *adj* dissolute; openly vicious. * *n* a depraved man.

profound *adj* deep; deep in skill or knowledge; far-reaching.

profundity *n* depth.

profuse *adj* lavish; exuberant.

progeny *n* offspring; descendants.

prognosis *n* a forecast of the course of a disease.

prognosticate *vt* to foretell, predict.

program *n* a sequence of instructions fed into a computer. * *vt*, *vi* to write a program.

programme *n* a plan of proceedings; list of items at concert, etc; a radio or television broadcast; policy of political party.

progress *n* a going forward; a journey of state; advance. * *vi* to advance; to improve.

progressive *adj* forward; liberal; increasing by degrees; relating to whist drive where some players move forward.

prohibit *vt* to forbid; to prevent.

prohibition *n* an interdict; veto on sale of intoxicants.

prohibitive *adj* excessive.

project *vt*, *vi* to hurl; to scheme; to delineate; to jut. * *n* a scheme, plan.

projectile *adj* throwing forward. * *n* a missile; a bullet or shell.

projection *n* a prominence; plan or outline on a plane surface.

projector *n* an instrument that projects images from transparencies or film; a person who promotes enterprise.

prolapse *n* displacement of an internal organ.

proletariat *n* the lower classes.

prolific *adj* fruitful.

prologue *n* introduction; a speech, usu in verse, introducing a drama.

prolong *vt* to lengthen out.

promenade *n* a walk for pleasure; a public walkway. * *vi* to walk up and down.

prominence *n* a projection; distinction.

prominent *adj* jutting out; eminent.

promiscuous *adj* indiscriminate, esp in sexual relations.

promise *n* an undertaking to do or not do something; pledge. * *vt*, *vi* to give one's word; to show promise of.

promissory *adj* containing a promise. * *a* signed promise to pay.

promontory *n* a headland.

promote *vt* to forward; to encourage; to exalt; to form (a company).

promotion *n* advancement; furtherance.

prompt *adj* ready; unhesitating. * *vt* to incite to action; to whisper (words to actor, etc).

promulgate *vt* to publish.

prone *adj* lying face-downwards; inclined; apt.

prong *n* a spike, as of a fork.

pronominal *adj* of the nature of a pronoun.

pronoun *n* a word used instead of a noun.

pronounce *vt*, *vi* to articulate; to utter; to affirm.

pronouncement *n* a definite statement of policy.

pronunciation *n* articulation.

proof *n* trial; convincing evidence; argument; test; standard strength of alcohol; a printed copy for revision. * *adj* impenetrable; able to resist.

prop *n* a support. * *vt* to hold up; to sustain.

propaganda *n* methods or system of spreading beliefs, doctrines, etc.

propagandist *n* a popularizer of special doctrines; a missionary.

propagate *vt* to multiply; to diffuse. * *vi* to have young.

propel *vt* to drive or thrust forward.

propeller *n* a screw for propelling steamboats, etc.

propensity *n* natural tendency.

proper *adj* one's own; peculiar; correct; real.

property *n* a quality or attribute; characteristic; ownership; goods; estate; a stage requisite.

prophecy *n* a prediction; inspired utterance.

prophet *n* a seer; inspired preacher.

prophylactic *adj*, *n* preventive of disease.

propitious *adj* favourable; merciful.

proportion *n* comparative relation; symmetry; equal share; lot; ratio.

proposal *n* proposition; offer (esp of marriage).

propose *vt* to offer for consideration. * *vi* to make a proposal; to purpose.

proposition *n* a proposal; offer of terms; a statement or assertion; a problem or theorem for solution.

propound *vt* to propose; to put, as a question.

proprietary *adj* belonging to a proprietor.

proprietor *n* an owner.

propriety *n* fitness; justness.

propulsion *n* the driving forward (as of an engine).

prosaic *adj* like prose; commonplace.

proscribe *vt* to outlaw; to forbid.

proscription *n* the act of proscribing.

prose *n* ordinary speech.

prosecute *vt*, *vi* to carry on; to pursue at law.

prosecution *n* a suit at law; the party prosecuting.

prosecutor *n* one who prosecutes.

proselyte *n* a convert.

proselytize *vt*, *vi* to make or seek to make converts.

prospect *n* a distant view; scene; outlook; expectation. * *vt*, *vi* to search, explore (for metals, oil, etc).

prospective *adj* looking forward; probable.

prospectus *n* a statement or outline of some enterprise.

prosper *vi, vt* to thrive or cause to thrive.

prosperity *n* success; a thriving state; good fortune.

prostitute *n* a person who performs sex acts for money.

prostitution *n* the act or activity of being a prostitute; to corrupt for unworthy purposes.

prostrate *adj* lying flat; lying at mercy. * *vt* to lie flat, to humble oneself.

protagonist *n* chief actor in a drama; the principal leader in an affair.

protean *adj* assuming different shapes; changeable.

protect *vt* to shield from danger, loss, etc.

protection *n* defence; shelter; taxation of foreign goods to protect home products.

protégé (*m*), **protégée** (*f*) *n* one under the care of another.

protein *n* an essential element in food of animals.

protest *vi* to affirm with solemnity. * *vt* to assert; to mark for nonpayment, as a bill. * *n* a formal declaration of dissent.

protestation *n* a solemn affirmation; a strong protest.

protocol *n* first draft of a treaty; ceremonial etiquette.

protoplasm *n* a semi-viscous fluid that is the essential living matter of all animal and plant cells.

prototype *n* model; pattern.

protozoa *npl* the lowest class of animal life.

protract *vt* to prolong; to delay.

protractor *n* an instrument for measuring or plotting angles.

protrude *vt, vi* to thrust forward; to project.

protrusion *n* a sticking out.

protuberance *n* a prominence; a knob.

proud *adj* haughty; arrogant; high-spirited.

prove *vt, vi* to test; to establish the truth of; to demonstrate; to obtain probate of; to turn out to be.

proverb *n* a popular saying; an adage; a maxim.

proverbial *adj* well-known; notorious.

provide *vt, vi* to make ready beforehand; to prepare; to supply.

provided *conj* on condition.

providence *n* foresight; divine foresight and care.

provident *adj* foreseeing; prudent; frugal.

providential *adj* due to divine providence.

province *n* a division of a country; sphere of action.

provincial *adj* rustic; countrified.

provision *n* preparation; stores provided; proviso; (*pl*) food.

provisional *adj* temporary.

proviso *n* a stipulation; condition.

provisory *adj* conditional.

provocation *n* cause of resentment.

provocative *adj* inciting; rousing.

provoke *vt, vi* to incite; to irritate.

prow *n* the forepart of a ship.

prowess *n* bravery; skill.

prowl *vi, vt* to sneak around.

proximate *adj* nearest; next.

proximity n nearness.

proxy n agency of a substitute; a deputy; a warrant to act or vote for another.

prude n an excessively modest person.

prudence n caution; discretion.

prudent adj provident; cautious; discreet.

prune vt to trim; to lop off * n a dried plum.

prurience, pruriency n a lustful craving.

prurient adj lustful; filthy-minded.

pry vi to scan closely; to peer.

psalm n a sacred song or hymn.

pseudo prefix signifying false or spurious.

pseudonym n a false name, as assumed by a writer.

psyche n the spirit, soul; the mind.

psychedelic adj of or causing extreme chances in the conscious mind.

psychiatry n the branch of medicine dealing with disorders of the mind.

psychic adj belonging to the soul; spiritualistic.

psychology n the science concerned with the human mind and behaviour.

puberty n beginning of manhood and womanhood; sexual maturity.

pubescent adj arriving at puberty.

public adj not private; pertaining to a whole community; open to all; common. * n the people. * In public, in open view.

publican n keeper of a public house.

publication n act of publishing; a published book, etc.

publicity n any information or action that brings a person or cause to public notice; work concerned with such matters.

publish vt to make public; to proclaim; to print and offer for sale.

pucker vt, vi to wrinkle. * n a fold or wrinkle.

pudding n a dessert dish.

puddle n a small pool of dirty water; clay impervious to water.

puddling n process of working clay so as to be impervious or of converting cast iron into wrought iron.

puerile adj boyish; childish.

puff n whiff of wind or breath; light pastry; undeserved praise. * vt, vi to breathe hard; to praise overmuch.

pugilism n the practice of boxing.

pugnacious adj quarrelsome.

pugnacity n aggressiveness; quarrelsomeness.

pull vt, vi to draw towards one; to tug; to rend; to pluck; to gather. * n act of pulling; an effort.

pulley n a grooved wheel with running cord for raising weights.

pulmonary adj pertaining to the lungs.

pulp n the fleshy part of fruit, etc; soft substance obtained by mashing down cloth, wood, etc.

pulpit n preacher's raised desk or platform.

pulsate vi to beat or throb.

pulse n the beating of heart or artery; vibration; beans, etc.

pulverize vi to reduce to dust.

pumice n a porous stone, used for polishing.

pummel vt (pt **pummelled**) to strike with the fists.

pump n a machine for raising water or extracting air; a shoe used in dancing. * vi to work a pump. * vt to raise with a pump; to quiz.

pun n a play upon words. * vi to make puns.

punch n a tool for perforating; a blow; a spirituous beverage; a puppet show figure. * vt to stamp or perforate; to strike.

punctilious adj formal; precise.

punctual adj exact; prompt.

punctuality n scrupulous exactness.

punctuate vt to mark with points or stops.

punctuation n the art of inserting stops in sentence.

puncture n hole made by sharp point. * vt to pierce.

pungent adj biting; acrid; caustic.

punish vt to inflict pain as a penalty; to chastise.

punishment n pain, loss, or penalty.

punitive adj penal; designed to punish.

punt n a flat-bottomed boat.

puny adj small and weak.

pup n a young dog, seal, fox, etc.

pupa n (pl **pupae**) the chrysalis form of an insect.

pupil n a learner; a scholar; opening in the centre of the eye.

puppet n a mechanical figure moved by strings; a person who is a mere tool.

purchase vt to buy; to acquire. * n buying; thing bought; leverage.

pure adj clean; clear; unmixed; chaste.

purgative adj cleansing. * n a purging medicine.

purge vt, vi to make pure or clean; to clear from accusation.

purification n a cleansing from guilt.

purify vt to make pure or clear.

puritan n one very strict in religious and moral matters.

purity n cleanness; innocence; chastity; freedom from adulteration.

purl n gentle murmur of a stream; a stitch in knitting. * vi to ripple.

purloin vt to steal or pilfer.

purple n a colour; red and blue blended; purple robe or the imperial rank denoted by it; regal power. * adj blood-red; royal.

purport n meaning. * vt to signify.

purpose n end or aim; design; intention. * vt to propose.

purse n a small pouch for money; funds. * vt to pucker.

purser n the ship's officer in charge of accounts.

pursuance n the carrying out (of a design).

pursuant adj agreeable; conformable to.

pursue vt, vi to follow for some end; to chase.

pursuit n chase; quest; business occupation.

purvey vt, vi to provide; to supply provisions.

purveyor n a caterer.

purview n the scope; limit; sphere.

pus n yellow matter of a sore.

push vt, vi to press against with force; to shove; to urge. * n vigorous effort; emergency.

pusillanimous adj cowardly; timid.

pustule n a small blister or pimple.

put vt (pt, pp **put**) to place or set; to ask; to apply; to state.

putative adj supposed; reputed.

putrefaction n decay; rottenness.

putrefy vt to render putrid. * vi to decay, rot.

putrescence n a putrid state.

putrid adj rotten; corrupt.

putt vt, vi to throw (a stone) from the shoulder; (golf) to play the ball into the hole.

putter n a kind of golfing club.

putty n a paste made of whiting and linseed oil. * vt to cement with putty.

puzzle vt to perplex. * vi to be bewildered. * n perplexity.

pyjamas npl sleeping clothes.

pylon n a tower-like structure supporting electric power lines.

pyramid n a solid body having triangular sides meeting in a point at the top.

pyre n a funeral pile.

pyrotechnics n the art of making or the use of fireworks.

Q

qua adv in the quality of; as.

quack vi to cry like a duck. * n the cry of a duck; an untrained person who practises medicine fraudulently. * adj sham.

quad n a quadrangle or court.

quadrangle n a plane figure, having four angles and sides; an inner square of a building.

quadrant n the fourth part of a circle or its circumference; an instrument for taking altitudes; a sextant.

quadratic adj in algebra, involving the square of an unknown quantity.

quadrennial adj lasting or occurring once in four years.

quadrilateral n a plane figure having four sides and angles.

quadrille n a dance for four couples, each forming side of a square.

quadruped n an animal with four feet.

quadruple adj fourfold. * vt, vi to make or become fourfold.

quaff vt, vi to drink deep.

quagmire n wet bog-like ground.

quaich n a silver or wooden drinking cup.

quail vi to flinch; to cower. * n a bird allied to partridge.

quaint adj attractive or pleasant in an old-fashioned style.

quaintly adv oddly; whimsically.

quake vi to shake; to tremble, esp with fear or cold.

Quaker n a member of the Society of Friends.

qualification n quality which fits a person for office or occupation; ability; capability; restriction.

qualified *adj* competent; limited.

qualify *vt* to render or to become fit for office, etc; to modify or limit.

qualitative *adj* determining the nature of the component parts of bodies.

quality *n* sort, kind, or character; attribute; high rank.

qualm *n* a sudden fit of nausea; a scruple.

quandary *n* a state of perplexity; a predicament.

quantitative *adj* relating to the size or amount.

quantity *n* bulk; measure; amount; large portion.

quantum *n* a quantity; a sufficient amount.

quarantine *n* isolation period imposed to prevent the spread of disease.

quarrel *n* an angry dispute; a brawl. * *vi* to dispute violently.

quarrelsome *adj* apt to quarrel; contentious.

quarry *n* an excavation for the extraction of stone, slate, etc; a place from which stone is excavated; a source of information, etc. * *vt, vi* to excavate (from) a quarry; to research.

quart *n* two pints or one-fourth of a gallon.

quarter *n* the fourth part of anything; any point of the compass; a district; locality; one of four divisions of heraldic shield; proper position; mercy to a beaten foe; (*pl*) shelter or lodging. * *vt* to divide into four equal parts; to cut to pieces; lodge.

quarterly *adj* recurring each quarter. * *adv* once in a quarter. * *n* a periodical published quarterly.

quartermaster *n* (*navy*) a petty officer in charge of steering, signals, etc; (*army*) an officer in charge of stores, rations, etc.

quartet *n* a musical composition in four parts; the four performers.

quarto *n* a page size, approximately 9 by 12 inches (23 by 30.5 mm).

quartz *n* silica in crystalline form.

quash *vt* to quell; to suppress; to make void.

quasi- *prefix* meaning sort of, sham, almost, as quasi-religious.

quassia *n* a medicinal bark with bitter taste.

quatercentenary *n* a four-hundredth anniversary.

quatrain *n* a stanza of four lines rhyming alternately.

quaver *vi, vt* to shake; to tremble; to quiver. * *n* a voice tremor; half a crotchet.

quay *n* a landing stage for vessels; wharf.

queasy *adj* squeamish.

queen *n* the wife of a king; a female sovereign.

queenly *adj* royal; gracious.

queer *adj* odd; droll; peculiar.

quell *vt* to subdue; to allay.

quench *vt* to put out, as fire; to slake, as thirst.

querulous *adj* complaining; peevish.

query *n* a question; the mark of interrogation (?). * *vi* to ask questions. * *vt* to question.

quest *n* search; pursuit; inquiry.

question *n* an interrogation; inquiry; discussion. * *vi* to ask a question; to doubt. * *vt* to interrogate.

questionable *adj* doubtful.

question mark *n* a punctuation mark (?) used at the end of a sentence to indicate a question or to express doubt; something unknown.

questionnaire *n* a series of questions designed to collect statistical information.

queue *n* a line of people, vehicles, etc, awaiting entry, a turn, etc.

quibble *n* a minor objection or criticism. * *vi* to evade the question by play on words; to prevaricate.

quick *adj* alive; brisk; swift; keen; living. * *n* the living flesh.

quicken *vt, vi* to give life to; to vivify; to cheer; to speed up.

quicklime *n* lime burned but not slaked.

quicksand *n* a bank of sand yielding under pressure, therefore dangerous.

quicksilver *n* mercury.

quickstep *n* a ballroom dance in quick time.

quidnunc *n* one always on the alert for news; a gossip.

quiescent *adj* resting; still; tranquil.

quiet *adj* at rest; calm; peaceful; secluded. * *n* rest; peace. * *vt* to calm; to lull; to allay.

quietism *n* tranquillity; resignation; a form of mysticism.

quill *n* the hollow stem of a feather; anything made of this as a pen; the spine of a porcupine. * *vt* to plait.

quilt *n* a padded bedcover.

quince *n* pear-shaped fruit used for preserves.

quincentenary *n* a five-hundredth anniversary.

quinine *n* a bitter drug from bark of cinchona tree, used as an anti-malarial.

quinquennial *adj* lasting for or occurring once every five years.

quinquennium *n* the space of five years.

quinsy *n* inflammation of tonsils or throat.

quintessence *n* purest form of a substance; vital part.

quintet *n* a musical composition in five parts.

quintuple *adj* fivefold.

quintuplet *adj* one of five offspring produced at one birth.

quip *n* a gibe; retort. * *vt* (*pt* **quipped**) to make a clever or sarcastic remark.

quire *n* twenty-four sheets of paper.

quirk *n* an unexpected turn or twist; a peculiarity of mannerism.

quit *adj* discharged; free. * *vt, vi* (*pt, pp* **quit** *or* **quitted**) to discharge; to depart; to acquit.

quite *adv* completely; wholly.

quiver *n* a sheath for arrows. * *vi* to shake; to shiver.

quixotic *adj* romantic or chivalrous to extravagance.

quiz *n* a short written or oral test; a form of entertainment where players are asked questions of general knowledge. * *vt* (*pt* **quizzed**) to examine by questioning; to make fun of.

quoit *n* a flattish ring of metal, plastic, etc, thrown at a mark in quoits; (*pl*) a game in which rings are thrown at or over a peg.

quondam *adj* former.

quorum *n* minimum number needed that must be present at a meeting or assembly to make its proceedings valid.

quota *n* share assigned to each.

quotation *n* passage quoted; estimated price.

quotation mark *n* a punctuation mark to indicate the beginning (" or ') and the end (" or ') of a quoted passage.

quote *vt* to cite (from writings or speeches); to repeat the words of a poem, speech, etc, exactly; to give prices of articles. * *n* (*inf*) something quoted.

quotient *n* the answer to a division sum.

R

rabbi *n* (*pl* **rabbis**) the religious and spiritual leader of a Jewish congregation.

rabbit *n* a small burrowing animal of the hare family.

rabble *n* a noisy crowd; a mob.

rabid *adj* infected with rabies; fanatical.

rabies *n* an acute viral disease transmitted by the bite of an infected animal.

race *n* any of the divisions of human kind; a contest in speed; a course or career; a rapid current. * *vt* to run swiftly; to compete in speed.

racecourse *n* a track on which races are run.

racehorse *n* a horse bred for racing.

raceme *n* a flower cluster on a common stem.

racial *adj* characteristic of race.

racism, **racialism** *n* a belief in the superiority of some races over others; prejudice against or hatred of other races.

rack *vt* to stretch unduly; to torture. * *n* a frame for holding or stretching articles; a frame for setting up snooker balls for play, anguish; instrument of torture.

racket *n* a din, clamour; the bat in tennis, etc; (*pl*) a game like tennis.

radial *adj* branching from a common centre.

radiance *n* brilliancy; lustre.

radiant *adj* emitting rays; brilliant; beaming.

radiate *vi*, *vt* to emit rays; to broadcast; to spread; to shine.

radiation *n* emission of rays.

radiator *n* an apparatus for warming a room; a cooling device for a vehicle engine.

radical *adj* pertaining to the root;

original; fundamental; inherent. * *n* a root; a political reformer.

radically *adv* fundamentally; thoroughly.

radicle *n* the first little root of a seed; a root-like subdivision of a nerve or vein.

radii *see* **radius**.

radioactive *adj* giving off radiant energy in the form of particles or rays caused by the disintegration of atomic nuclei.

radiograph *n* an image given by X-rays.

radiography *n* the process of taking pictures by X-rays for use in medicine.

radium *n* a metallic element that is highly radioactive.

radius *n* (*pl* **radii, radiuses**) the distance from the centre of a circle to the circumference; a bone of the forearm.

raffle *n* a kind of lottery. * *vi* to engage in a raffle. * *vt* to dispose of by raffle.

raft *n* logs fastened together and floated; a floating structure.

rafter *n* one of several sloping beams supporting a roof.

rag *n* a tattered cloth; a shred; a sensational newspaper.

rage *n* violent anger; fury. * *vi* to be furious with anger.

ragged *adj* tattered.

ragwort *n* a common weed.

raid *n* a hostile incursion; a sudden foray. * *vt* to make a raid on.

rail *n* a bar of wood or metal; a connected series of posts; a railway.

* *vt, vi* to enclose with rails; to scold; to jeer.

railing *n* a fence.

raillery *n* banter; chaff.

railroad *n* a railway.

railway *n* a road or track with parallel lines of rails along which vehicles travel.

rain *n* moisture falling in drops. * *vi* to fall in drops.

rainbow *n* a many-coloured bow that often appears in the sky during sunshine and showers, containing the colours of the spectrum.

rainfall *n* the quantity of rain that falls.

raise *vt* to cause to rise; to lift upwards; to excite; to stir up; to levy; to breed; to abandon (siege).

rajah *n* an Indian prince or ruler.

rake *n* a toothed implement for scraping the ground or for gleaning; a dissolute person. * *vt* to glean; to gather.

rakish *adj* dissolute; sloping, as masts; jaunty.

rally *vt* to reunite, as disordered troops; to collect; a large gathering of people. * *vi* to recover strength. * *n* a stand; recovery of health, morale, etc.

ram *n* a male sheep; the sign (Aries) of the zodiac; a battering engine; a pile-driving machine. * *vt* to batter; to charge.

ramble *vi* to roam about; to talk incoherently. * *n* an aimless walk.

rambler *n* a climbing plant; a person who rambles.

rambling *adj* unsettled; disconnected.

ramification *n* a branching; a network of parts; a consequence.

ramify *vt, vi* to subdivide; to branch out.

ramp n a sloping walk or runway.

rampage vi to prance; to rage and storm.

rampant adj in heraldry, standing on hind legs; unchecked; unrestrained.

rampart n a defensive earthwork.

ramshackle adj broken-down; shaky.

ranch n a large cattle or sheep farm.

rancid adj rank; tainted.

rancorous adj spiteful; virulent.

rancour n deep-seated hatred.

random n chance; **at random** without aim * adj haphazard.

range vt, vi to set in a row; to place in order; to roam over; to rank. * n a row; a series of mountains; compass or extent; a place for gun or golf practice.

ranger n a park warden.

rank n a row; a line; a social class; dignity. * vt, vi to classify; to place in line. * adj overgrown; tainted.

rankle vi, vt to grow bitter; to irritate.

ransack vt to plunder; to search thoroughly.

ransom n release from captivity by payment; the price paid for release. * vt to redeem.

rant vi to rave, declaim * n bombast.

ranter n a voluble speaker.

ranunculus n any of a genus of plants, including buttercups.

rap n a smart blow; a knock; (inf) talk, conversation. * vi, vt to strike smartly.

rapacious adj greedy of plunder; grasping.

rapacity n excessive greed; extortion.

rape n the act of forcing a person to have sexual intercourse against his or her will; a plundering. * vt to commit rape (upon).

rapid adj very swift; speedy. * n a swift current.

rapier n a long narrow sword.

rapt adj transported; enraptured.

rapture n extreme joy; ecstasy.

rapturous adj ecstatic; enthusiastic; intensely joyful.

rare adj sparse; uncommon; infrequent; precious; underdone.

rarefy vt, vi to make or become less dense.

rarity n scarceness; thinness; a rare article.

rascal n a scoundrel; a rogue.

rase vt to wipe out; to destroy; to level to the ground.

rash adj precipitate; hasty. * n an eruption on the skin.

rasher n a thin slice of bacon.

rasp vt to rub with something rough; to grate. * n a coarse file; a raspberry.

raspberry n a shrub with red berry fruits.

rat n a small rodent.

rat race n hectic, competitive activity.

ratchet n a catch which checks a toothed wheel and moves only one way.

rate n proportion; standard; degree of speed; price; a tax; assessment. * vt to fix the value, rank, etc, of; to reprove. * vi to classify.

rather adv more readily; preferably.

ratification n sanction; confirmation.

ratify vt to approve and sanction.

ratio n proportion of two classes of objects to each other.

ration n a fixed amount allowed.

rational adj endowed with reason; wise; judicious.

rationale n exposition of reasons for any opinion or action.

rattan n a walking stick or cane.

rattle vi, vt to clatter; to chatter. * n a clattering noise; a toy which makes a clatter.

rattlesnake n a venomous snake with scaly rattling tail.

raucous adj hoarse; harsh; loud.

ravage n havoc; devastation. * vt to lay waste.

rave vi to be delirious; to dote.

raven n a large crow-like bird with glossy black feathers. *adj of the colour or sheen of a raven.

ravenous adj excessively hungry.

ravine n a gorge or pass.

ravioli n small cases of pasta filled with highly seasoned chopped meat or vegetables.

ravish vt to carry off by force; to captivate; to rape.

ravishing adj enchanting.

raw adj uncooked; in natural state; crude; unripe; cold and damp; sore.

ray n a line of light; a gleam of intelligence; a radius; a flatfish.

rayon n a textile fibre made from a cellulose solution; a fabric of such fibres.

raze vt to blot out; to demolish.

razor n an instrument for shaving off hair.

reach vt to extend; to hand; to stretch out; to arrive at; to gain. * vi to extend. * n extent; scope.

react vi, vt to act in return; to return an impulse.

reaction n an action in response to a stimulus; (chem) an action set up by one substance in another.

reactionary adj retrograde. * n one who opposes progress.

read vb (pt, pp read) vt to peruse; to utter aloud; to explain. * vi to peruse; to study; to stand written or printed; to make sense. * red adj well-informed.

reader n a person who reads; a proof corrector; a university lecturer.

readily adv promptly; cheerfully.

reading adj bookish; studious. * n perusal; study of books; interpretation; rendering.

ready adj prepared; prompt; willing.

ready-made adj kept in stock; not made to order.

reagent n a substance employed chemically to detect the presence of other bodies.

real adj actual; true; genuine; in law, applied to things fixed as land, houses, etc.

real estate n property; land.

realism n doctrine that the things of sense are the only reality; truth to nature in art; the practical as opposed to the ideal.

realist n one who believes in realism.

realistic adj lifelike; vivid.

reality n fact; truth.

realize vt to make real; to convert into money; to make tangible; to gain.

really adv actually; in truth; positively.

realm *n* kingdom; domain; sphere.

realty *n* real property.

ream *n* 20 quires or 480 sheets of paper.

reanimate *vt* to inspire afresh; to revive.

reap *vt, vi* to harvest; to gather in; to receive as a reward.

reappear *vi* to appear anew.

reappoint *vt* to appoint again.

rear *n* the part behind; the part of army or fleet behind van. * *vt, vi* to raise; to educate; to breed; to stand on the hind legs.

rearguard *n* troops guarding the rear.

rearmost *adj* last of all.

reason *n* mental faculty; power of thinking; a motive or cause; justice; moderation. * *vi, vt* to use reason; to argue.

reasonable *adj* rational; just; moderate.

reasoning *n* the exercise of faculty of reason; arguments used.

reassurance *n* act of reassuring; a second assurance against loss.

reassure *vt* to give confidence.

rebate[1] *vt* to blunt; to diminish; to make a discount from.

rebate[2] *n* abatement in price; deduction; discount.

rebeck *n* an early form of fiddle.

rebel *n* one who refuses to cooperate with lawful authority. *adj* rebellious. * *vi* to revolt; to act as rebel.

rebellion *n* a rising up against authority.

rebound *n* a recoil. * *vi* to spring back; to bounce back.

rebuff *n* a check; a repulse. * *vt* to check; snub.

rebuke *vt* to reprimand. * *n* a reproof.

rebut *vt* to repel; to refute by argument.

recalcitrant *adj* obstinate.

recall *vt* to call back; to revive in the memory.

recant *vt, vi* to withdraw or retract; to abjure.

recantation *n* withdrawal of previous statements or beliefs.

recapitulate *vt* to summarize; to go over chief points.

recapitulation *n* a summary.

recast *vt* to mould anew.

recede *vi* to go back; to grow less. * *vt* to give back.

receipt *n* a written acknowledgment of something received. * *vt* to discharge, as an account.

receive *vt* to take, as a thing offered; to accept; to welcome; to take in.

receiver *n* a person who receives; one who knowingly takes stolen goods from a thief; equipment that receives electronic signals; (*law*) a person appointed to manage or hold in trust property in bankruptcy or lawsuit.

recent *adj* new; late; fresh.

receptacle *n* a place or vessel for holding articles.

reception *n* welcome; a formal receiving of guests; admission.

receptionist *n* a person employed to receive visitors in an office, hospital, hotel, etc.

receptive *adj* quick to absorb knowledge.

receptivity *n* the power of absorbing ideas or knowledge.

recess *n* withdrawal; a nook or alcove; a holiday.

recession *n* a time of severe economic downturn.

recipe *n* a list of ingredients and directions for preparing food; a method for achieving an end.

recipient *n* a person who receives.

reciprocal *adj* mutual; alternating.

reciprocate *vi* to move backward and forward; to give in return. * *vt* to interchange.

reciprocity *n* an interchange on even terms; equality of tariffs; fair trade.

recital *n* a narration; musical entertainment, esp by one performer.

recite *vt, vi* to repeat aloud from memory; to relate.

reckless *adj* heedless; rash; incaution.

reckon *vt, vi* to count; consider; to calculate.

reckoning *n* calculation; a statement of accounts.

reclaim *vt* to claim back; to reform; to bring under cultivation.

recline *vt, vi* to lean backwards; to lean down on one side.

recluse *adj* retired; solitary. * *n* a hermit.

recognition *n* the act of recognizing; identification; acknowledgement; admission.

recognizable *adj* that may be recognized.

recognize *vt* to know again; to acknowledge.

recoil *vi* to start back; to shrink; to rebound. * *n* a rebound, as of gun.

recollect *vt* to remember.

recollection *n* remembrance.

recommend *vt* to praise to another; to advise.

recommendation *n* a favourable notice; repute.

recompense *vt* to compensate; to reward. * *n* compensation; amends.

reconcile *vt* to make friendly again; to harmonize; to settle.

reconciliation *n* act of reconciling; renewal of friendship.

recondite *adj* abstruse; profound.

recondition *vt* to repair and restore to good working order.

reconnaissance *n* a survey for military purposes.

reconnoitre *vt, vi* to survey or spy out an area or position.

reconsider *vt* to consider again.

reconstruct *vt* to rebuild.

record *vt* to preserve in writing; to chronicle. * *n* a written memorial; a register; best result in contests; gramophone disc.

recorder *n* an official registrar; a device that records; a tape recorder.

recount *vt* to relate in detail; to count again.

recoup *vt* to make good; to indemnify.

recourse *n* a going to for help or protection.

recover *vt* to get back; to regain; to revive; to obtain as compensation. * *vi* to grow well.

recovery *n* restoration from sickness, etc; a winning back.

recreant *adj* craven; cowardly. * *n* a coward; renegade.

recreate vt to revive; to amuse.

re-create vt to create anew.

recreation n relaxation after toil; amusement or sport.

recrimination n mutual accusations.

recrudescence n renewed outbreak.

recruit vt to enlist new soldiers. * vi to gain new supplies. * n a soldier newly enlisted; a beginner.

rectangle n a four sided geometric figure having all its angles right angles.

rectangular adj right-angled.

rectification n refining by distillation; adjustment.

rectify vt to set right; to correct or redress.

rectitude n uprightness; honesty.

rector n a ruler; a clergyman in charge of a parish; a headmaster.

rectory n a clergyman's house.

recumbent adj leaning; reclining.

recuperate vt, vi to recover health.

recuperative adj healing; strengthening.

recur vi to return; to happen again and again.

recurrence n a happening occurring again and again.

recurrent adj returning repeatedly.

red adj blood-coloured. * n a primary colour.

Red Cross n a red cross on a white ground; the symbol of the International Red Cross, a society for the relief of suffering in time of war and disaster.

redden vt to make red. * vi to blush.

reddition n a giving back; explanation.

redeem vt to buy back; to ransom; to save; to atone for; to perform (a promise).

redemption n ransom; release.

red-handed adj in the very act of crime.

red-herring n a herring cured to a dark brown colour; something that diverts attention from the real issue.

red lead n a red oxide of lead; a pigment.

red-letter adj marked in calendar by red letters; notable.

redolent adj fragrant; reminiscent.

redoubtable adj formidable; valiant.

redress vt to set right; to adjust; to relieve. * n relief; compensation.

red tape n excessive official formality.

reduce vt to bring down; to decrease; to degrade; to subdue.

reduction n act of reducing; diminution; conversion into another state or form; subjugation.

redundant adj superfluous to requirements; deprived of one's job as being no longer necessary.

reduplicate vt, vi to double again; to repeat.

re-echo vt, vi to echo back; to reverberate.

reed n a tall grass with jointed hollow stem; a pastoral pipe.

reedy adj harsh and thin, as a voice.

reef n a fold in a sail; a low line of rocks in sea; a vein of ore * vt to reduce sail.

reefer n a short thick jacket worn by sailors; (inf) a cigarette containing cannabis.

reek n vapour; smoke. * vi to smoke; to exhale.

reel n a bobbin; an appliance for winding a fishing line; a lively Scottish dance; a length of film. * vt to wind upon a reel; to stagger.

re-entry n the resuming possession of lost lands.

re-examine vt to examine anew.

refectory n a dining hall of a college.

refer vt to trace back; to submit (a matter) to another person; to assign. * vi to appeal; to allude.

referee n an umpire; a judge.

reference n allusion; relation; scope.

referendum n the settling of a national question by a direct vote of the people.

refill vt to fill again.

refine vt, vi to purify; to polish; to become purer.

refinement n fineness of manners or taste; an improvement; a fine distinction.

refinery n a place for refining sugar, metals, oil, etc.

refit vt, vi to fit anew; to repair. * n repair.

reflect vt, vi to throw back, esp rays of light or heat; to mirror; to meditate; to consider; to cast reproaches on.

reflection n act of reflecting; meditation; reproach; a reflected image.

reflective adj thoughtful; meditating.

reflector n a polished surface for reflecting light, etc.

reflex adj bent or directed back; involuntary response to a stimulus. * n a reflex action.

reflexive adj in grammar, referring back to subject.

refold vt to fold again.

reform vt, vi to improve; to better; to amend; to form anew. * n a beneficial change; amendment.

reformation n improvement; the Protestant revolution of the 16th century.

reformed adj amended; improved.

reformer n one who effects reforms in religion, politics, etc.

refract vt to bend back sharply; to deflect (a ray of light).

refraction n deflection of rays on passing from one medium to another.

refrain vt to restrain. * vi to forbear. * n the recurring phrase or chorus of a song.

refresh vt to revive; to freshen.

refreshment n that which refreshes, as food and drink.

refrigerate vt to cool.

refrigerator n an apparatus for keeping things cool or for making ice.

refuge n protection from danger or distress; a retreat; a shelter; a plea.

refugee n one who seeks refuge in another land; to escape persecution.

refund vt to repay.

refusal n rejection; option.

refuse[1] vt, vi to deny what is asked; to say 'no'.

refuse[2] adj worthless. * n waste matter; rubbish.

refutation n disproof.

refute vt to disprove; to rebut.

regain vt to recover possession of; to reach again.

regal adj royal; relating to a king or queen.

regale vt, vi to entertain sumptuously.

regalia npl ensigns of royalty, as crown, sceptre, etc.

regard vt to notice carefully; to observe; to heed; to consider; to value. * n look or gaze; respect; deference; attention; (pl) good wishes.

regarding prep respecting; concerning.

regardless adj heedless; careless.

regatta n a yacht (or boat) race.

regency n government of a regent.

regenerate vt to produce anew; to produce again in the original form.

regent adj ruling. * n a ruler; one who governs during minority, illness, or absence of king.

regicide n the murder, or murderer, of a king.

regime n mode or system of government; administration.

regimen n orderly government; regulation of diet, exercise, etc.

regiment n a military unit smaller than a division. * vt to organize in a strict manner.

region n a tract of land; country.

register n an official record; a roll of voters; a recording machine; a meter.

registered adj enrolled; insured.

registrar n official keeper of records.

registration n act of registering; enrolment.

registry n place where a register is kept.

registry office n an office where civil marriages are held, and births and deaths recorded.

regret n grief; remorse; penitence. * vt to grieve at; lament.

regretful adj full of regret.

regrettable adj deplorable; unwelcome.

regular adj according to rule, law, etc; normal; constant; uniform * n a soldier.

regularity n evenness; uniformity.

regulate vt to adjust by rule; to direct.

regulation n a rule; order.

regurgitate vt, vi to pour or cause to surge back.

rehabilitate vt to put back in good condition.

rehearsal n a trial performance.

rehearse vt to repeat; to recite; to perform (by way of practice).

reign vi to be sovereign; to rule; to prevail. * n royal authority; duration of kingship.

reimburse vt to refund.

reimbursement n repayment.

rein n the strap of a bridle; restraint. * vt to govern by a bridle. * vi to obey the reins.

reindeer n a deer of northern parts with branched antlers.

reinforce vt to supply with fresh strength or assistance.

reinstate vt to restore to a former position.

reinvest vt to invest anew.

reissue vt to issue a second time. * n a second issue.

reiterate vt to repeat again and again.

reject vt to cast off; to discard; to forsake; to decline; to refuse to accept.

rejoice vi, vt to be glad; to exult; to cheer.

rejoin vt to join again; to answer.

rejoinder n an answer to a reply.

rejuvenate vt to make young again.

relapse vi to fall back into a worse state. * n a falling back into bad health; a backsliding.

relate vt to tell; to narrate. * vi to refer.

related adj connected by blood or by some common bond.

relation n act of relating; account; connection; kindred; a relative; proportion.

relationship n kinship.

relative adj comparative; pertinent; relating to a word, clause, etc. * n a kinsman; a relating word, esp relative pronoun.

relatively adv comparatively.

relax vt to slacken; to unbend. * vi to become feeble or languid.

relaxation n recreation; the condition of being relaxed.

relay n supply of horses to relieve jaded ones; fresh supply of men or materials; a relayed broadcast. * vt to broadcast signals.

release vt to set free; to deliver from; to allow cinema film to be shown. * n liberation from; discharge from.

relegate vt to send away; to move to an inferior position; to demote.

relent vi to relax severity; to grow milder.

relentless adj unmerciful; pitiless.

relevance, relevancy n pertinence; pointedness; applicability.

relevant adj applicable; to the purpose.

reliable adj trustworthy; dependable.

reliance n trust; confidence.

reliant adj confident; self-reliant.

relic n something treasured for connection with a saint or hero; a memento; (pl) bones of saints.

relief n ease of pain; remedy; redress; assistance given to the needy or victims of a disaster; raised design in sculpture; prominence; relief from duty by another person.

relieve vt to ease or lessen pain; to succour; to release from duty; to give variety to.

religion n a system of faith or worship; a belief in God or gods.

relinquish vt to give up; to renounce.

relish vt to enjoy the taste of; to have a taste for. * vi to have a pleasing taste. * n taste; flavour; savour.

reluctance n unwillingness.

reluctant adj loath; averse.

rely vt to depend upon; to trust in.

remain vi to continue in a place; to survive; to be left; to last. * npl a dead body.

remainder n residue; remnant.

remand vt to recommit to jail for further enquiries.

remark n notice; a comment * vt to observe; to note; to utter.

remarkable adj noteworthy; uncommon; striking.

remediable adj curable; correcting.

remedy n a cure; redress; a specific. * vt to cure; to repair; to put right.

remember vt, vi to recollect; recall; observe; bear in mind.

remembrance *n* memory; recollection; memorial; keepsake.

remind *vt* to put in mind.

reminder *n* a jog to memory.

reminisce *vi* to write, think or talk about past events.

reminiscence *n* recollections; what is recalled to mind; (*pl*) personal recollections.

reminiscent *adj* recalling the past.

remiss *adj* careless; heedless.

remission *n* pardon; abatement.

remit *vt* to send payment; to relinquish; to forgive; to transmit. * *vi* to slacken.

remittance *n* sum of money remitted.

remnant *n* a scrap; fragment.

remonstrance *n* a protest against something; expostulation.

remonstrate *vi* to protest against; to warn.

remorse *n* sorrow for a fault; compunction; bitter regret.

remorseless *adj* ruthless; merciless.

remote *adj* distant; foreign; slight; inconsiderable.

remount *vt, vi* to mount again. * *n* a fresh horse.

removable *adj* able to be removed.

removal *n* change of place; dismissal.

remove *vt, vi* to move from its place; to take away; to dismiss. * *n* a removal; departure; a stage in gradation.

remunerate *vt* to reward for service; to recompense.

remuneration *n* pay for service; reward.

remunerative *adj* profitable; lucrative.

renaissance *n* revival; the revival of learning in 15th century.

renal *adj* pertaining to the kidneys.

renascent *adj* becoming active again.

rend *vt, vi* (*pt, pp* **rent**) to tear away and apart; to split.

render *vt* to give in return; to give back; to afford; to furnish; to translate; to interpret; to boil down.

rendering *n* translation; interpretation.

rendezvous *n* appointed meeting place.

renegade *n* a deserter; a person who is faithless to a principle, party, religion, or cause.

renew *vt, vi* to make new again; to restore; to repair; to grant anew; to begin again.

renewal *n* a revival; a repetition.

reniform *adj* kidney-shaped.

rennet *n* a preparation for curdling milk in cheese-making.

renounce *vt* to disown; to forsake. * *vi* to revoke.

renovate *vt* to renew; to make like new.

renovation *n* act of renovating; renewal.

renown *n* fame; glory; celebrity.

renowned *adj* famous; eminent.

rent *n* money paid for use of lands or houses; a tear; a schism * *vt, vi* to let or hire for rent.

rental *n* rent; rent roll.

renunciation *n* act of disowning or rejecting; disavowal.

reorganize *vt* to organize anew.

repair *vt* to restore; to mend; to re-

trieve. * vi to take oneself to; to resort. * n return to good condition;
renovation.

reparation n amends; compensation.

repartee n a witty retort.

repast n a meal; food.

repatriate vt to restore to one's own
country.

repay vt to pay back; to refund; to requite.

repayment n act of repaying; money
repaid.

repeal vt to revoke; to annul; to abrogate. * n a cancelling; revocation.

repeat vt to do or utter again; to recite; to recapitulate. * n repetition.

repeatedly adv again and again.

repeating adj recurring again and
again indefinitely.

repel vt, vi to drive back; to repulse;
to shock.

repellent adj repulsive; unattractive.

repent vi, vt to feel regret for one's
conduct; to be penitent.

repentance n penitence; sorrow for
wrongdoing.

repentant adj feeling or showing
sorrow.

repercussion n reverberation; echo;
a far-reaching, often indirect reaction to an event.

repertoire n actor's or company's
stock of plays, etc.

repertory n a treasury; a storehouse.

repetition n repeating; saying from
memory; recitation.

replace vt to put back in place; substitute; supersede.

replenish vt to fill again; to stock
anew.

replete adj filled up; stuffed; gorged.

repletion n surfeit; plethora.

replica n an exact copy; a reproduction.

replication n an answer; echo; plaintiff's answer to defendant's plea.

reply vt, vi to answer; to respond. * n
an answer; a rejoinder.

report vt, vi to bring back as answer;
to relate; to take down a speaker's
exact words; to give an account of;
to inform against. * n an official
statement; an account of progress;
an account of something said or
done, esp for a newspaper; a rumour; a loud noise.

reporter n one who reports for newspaper, radio or television.

repose vt to lay at rest. * vi to lie at
rest; to rely. * n sleep; quiet; composure; serenity.

repository n a storehouse, warehouse.

reprehend vt to reprove; to censure.

reprehensible adj deserving censure; culpable.

reprehension n reproof; blame.

represent vt to show; to typify; to describe; to act part of; to stand for; to
be entitled to speak for (constituency).

representation n an image or likeness; dramatic performance; a remonstrance; the representing of a
constituency.

representative adj typical; representing; acting as delegate. * n a
member of parliament; an agent,
delegate.

repress vt to check; to quell; to keep
under control.

repression n check; restraint.

repressive adj tending to repress.

reprieve vt to grant a respite to; suspension of punishment of a criminal; respite.

reprimand n a severe reproof * vt to rebuke sharply.

reprint vt to print again. * n a new edition.

reprisal n something done by way of retaliation.

reproach vt to reprove, rebuke. * n censure; blame; disgrace.

reproachful adj abusive; upbraiding.

reprobate adj dissolute; profligate. * n a hardened sinner. * vt to condemn strongly; to cast off.

reproduce vt to generate, as offspring; to multiply; to make a copy, duplicate or likeness of.

reproduction n the act of reproducing; a copy; a facsimile.

reproductive adj generative; producing again (as seed).

reproof n rebuke; censure.

reprove vt to censure; to reprimand.

reptile adj creeping; grovelling. * n any of a class of cold-blooded, airbreathing vertebrates with horny scales or plates; a grovelling or despised person.

reptilian adj like reptiles.

republic n a state governed by rulers popularly elected.

republican adj pertaining to a republic. * n one who favours republican government.

repudiate vt to reject; to disown; to deny.

repudiation n rejection; disavowal.

repugnance n aversion; reluctance.

repugnant adj offensive; highly distasteful.

repulse n a check or defeat; a refusal; a rebuff * vt to repel.

repulsion n aversion; the tendency of certain bodies to repel each other.

repulsive adj forbidding; disgusting.

reputable adj held in esteem; respectable.

reputation n good name; repute; character.

repute vt to estimate; to deem * n reputation; character.

reputed adj supposed; seeming.

request n an expressed desire; a petition. * vt to ask; to beg.

requiem n a mass for the dead; music for this mass.

require vt to ask as of right; to demand; to exact.

requirement n demand; an essential condition.

requisite adj necessary; essential.

requisition n a demand, esp for supplies.

requite vt to repay; to reward; to avenge.

rescind vt to annul; to revoke.

rescue vt to free from danger or harm. * n deliverance.

research n careful investigation; a scientific study.

resemblance n likeness.

resemble vt to be like; to compare.

resent vt to be indignant about; to begrudge; to take badly.

resentment n deep sense of injury; indignation.

reservation n something kept back;

doubt; scepticism; land reserved for special purpose, as big game, etc; a proviso.

reserve vt to keep in store; to retain. * n that which is retained; stiffness of manner; caution; limitation; shyness; (pl) emergency troops.

reserved adj shy; distant.

reservoir n a place where water is stored for use.

reside vi to dwell; to live.

residence n abode; dwelling.

residential adj pertaining to or suitable for residence.

residual adj left after part is taken.

residue n remainder; part of estate left after paying all charges.

resign vt to give up; to renounce; to submit calmly.

resignation n calm submission; giving up of office.

resigned adj submissive; patient.

resile vt to leap back; to withdraw.

resilience n springiness; elasticity.

resilient adj rebounding; elastic.

resin n a sticky substance that oozes from trees and plants etc.

resinous adj of or obtained from resin.

resist vt, vi to withstand; to oppose.

resistance n opposition; stopping power or effect.

resolute adj determined; bold.

resolution n firmness of purpose; formal decision; the picture definition on a television screen, computer monitor, etc.

resolve vt, vi to split up into elements; to analyse; to solve; to determine. * n fixed purpose; resolution; courage.

resonance n power of sending back or intensifying sound.

resonant adj resounding; ringing.

resort vi to have recourse; to go. * n recourse; a popular holiday destination.

resource n any source of aid; an expedient; (pl) funds; means.

respect vt to regard; to esteem; to concern. * n regard; deference; reference to.

respectable adj worthy of respect; decent; moderate.

respectably adv worthily; pretty well.

respectful adj civil; courteous.

respective adj relating severally each to each.

respiration n act of breathing.

respiratory adj pertaining to breathing.

respite n temporary intermission; a delay; interval; reprieve. * vt to reprieve.

resplendent adj very bright; glittering.

respond vi to answer.

respondent adj answering; corresponding. * n defendant in a lawsuit, esp in divorce.

response n an answer; to reply.

responsibility n liability; charge; trust.

responsible adj answerable; liable; important.

responsive adj responding; sensitive to influence or stimulus; sympathetic.

rest n cessation of action; peace; sleep; a pause; remainder. * vi to cease from action; to repose; to die; to remain. * vt to lean or place for support.

restaurant n a place where meals can be bought or eaten.

restaurateur n the keeper of a restaurant.

restful adj giving rest; quiet; peaceful.

restitution n a giving back; reparation; amends.

restive adj fidgety; restless; impatient under control.

restless adj always on the move; uneasy; anxious.

restoration n act of restoring; renewal; repair; (with cap) the re-establishment of monarchy in Britain, 1660.

restorative adj having power to renew strength.

restore vt to make strong again; to cure; to give back.

restrain vt to hold back; to curb; to check.

restraint n the ability to hold back; something that restrains; control of emotions, impulses, etc.

restrict vt to limit; to curb.

restrictive adj imposing restraint.

result vi to follow as a consequence; to ensue; to end. * n consequence; outcome.

resultant adj following as a result or consequence.

resume vt to begin again; to continue after stopping.

resumé n a recapitulation; a summary.

resumption n act of resuming.

resurgent adj rising again.

resurrection n a rising again; the rising of the dead at the general Judgment.

resuscitate vt, vi to revive.

resuscitation n recovering from seeming death.

retail vt to sell directly to the consumer in small quantities. * n the sale of goods in small quantities; used also as adj.

retain vt to hold back; to keep in possession; to engage (a barrister) for a law case.

retainer n a follower; a dependant; a retaining or preliminary fee paid to barrister for his services.

retaliate vi, vt to return like for like; to take revenge.

retaliation n the return of like for like.

retard vt to render slower; to impede; to delay.

retardation n delay; a slowing down; obstruction.

retch vi to strain in vomiting.

retention n a holding back; power of retaining (ideas); memory.

retentive adj good at remembering.

reticence n silence; reserve.

reticent adj uncommunicative; reserved.

retina n inner part of eye where visual nerves are.

retinue n a body of attendants.

retiral n act of retiring.

retire vi, vt to go back; to withdraw from active working life; to go to bed.

retired adj (place) secluded, private;

(*person*) withdrawn from business.

retirement *n* retired life; seclusion.

retiring *adj* reserved; unobtrusive; shy.

retort *vt* to retaliate; to make a smart reply. * *n* a ready answer; a repartee; a vessel used in distilling.

retouch *vt* to improve by new touches, as a picture.

retrace *vt* to trace back; to trace over again.

retract *vt, vi* to take back; to recant; to unsay.

retraction *n* act of drawing back; recantation.

retreat *n* seclusion; a shelter; the retiring of an army from an enemy. * *vi* to draw back; to retire from an enemy.

retrench *vt* to cut down. * *vi* to economize.

retrial *n* a second trial.

retribution *n* just punishment; requital for evil done.

retrievable *adj* that may be retrieved or recovered.

retrieve *vt* to recover; to regain.

retriever *n* a dog trained to fetch game when shot.

retrocession *n* act of going or of ceding back.

retrograde *adj* going backwards; declining morally.

retrogressive *adj* declining; backward.

retrospect *n* a review of the past.

retrospective *adj* looking back; affecting things past.

retroussé *adj* turned up (esp of the nose).

return *vi* to come or go back. * *vt* to send back; to report officially; to elect. * *n* repayment; yield on investment; election of representative; official report; (*pl*) tabulated statistics.

returning officer *n* the presiding officer at an election.

reunion *n* a social gathering, esp of old associates.

reunite *vt, vi* to bring together again after separation.

rev *vt* to increase the speed of an engine.

reveal *vt* to disclose; to divulge.

reveille *n* the bugle call to get up (army).

revel *n* a noisy feast. * *vi* to carouse; to make merry.

revelation *n* act of making known; an illuminating experience.

revelry *n* noisy festivity; jollity.

revenge *vt, vi* to take vengeance for; to avenge. * *n* retaliation; vindictive feeling.

revenue *n* income from lands, etc; yearly income of a state; produced by taxation.

reverberate *vt, vi* to return, as sound; to echo.

reverberation *n* echoing; resounding.

revere *vt* to regard with awe and respect.

reverence *n* awe combined with respect; veneration; a title of the clergy. * *vt* to revere; to pay reverence to.

reverend *adj* worthy of reverence; a title given to clergymen.

reverent adj expressing reverence.

reverie n a daydream.

reversal n the act of reversing.

reverse vt to alter to the opposite; to annul; to move backwards. * n a defeat; a set back; a check; the back surface (of coin, medal, etc). * adj opposite.

reversible adj able to be reversed, turned outside in, etc.

reversion n a return to a former condition or type; right to future possession.

revert vt to go back; * vi to return to a former position, habit, etc.

review vt to re-examine; reconsider; inspect. * vi to write reviews. * n a survey; retrospect; a criticism; a magazine which reviews books; official inspection of troops.

reviewer n one who writes reviews.

revile vi to vilify; to abuse.

revise vt to go over carefully and correct. * n a second proof sheet in printing.

revival n a reawakening; a religious awakening.

revive vi to recover new vigour. * vt to refresh; to reproduce (a play, etc).

revocation n annulment; repeal.

revoke vt to repeal; to annul. * vi in card playing, to neglect to follow suit.

revolt vi to rebel; to be disgusted; with at * vt to shock. * n rebellion; mutiny.

revolting adj exciting extreme disgust; shocking.

revolution n act of revolving; rotation; circuit; a radical change in government, as from a monarchy to a republic.

revolutionary adj involving radical changes. * n one in favour of revolution.

revolutionize vt to bring about a complete change in.

revolve vi to turn round an axis or centre; to consider attentively.

revolver n a pistol capable of firing several shots without reloading.

revue n a topical play usually interspersed with music.

revulsion n disgust; aversion.

reward n recompense. * vt to repay.

rhapsody n an enthusiastic speech or writing; (mus) an irregular instrumental composition of an epic.

rhetoric n the art of speaking or writing correctly and effectively; eloquence; declamation.

rhetorical question n a question asked for effect to which no answer is expected.

rhetorician n one who teaches or is versed in rhetoric; an orator.

rheum n watery fluid secreted by mucous glands of the nose, eyes, etc.

rheumatic adj subject to rheumatism.

rheumatism n a painful disease of the muscles and joints.

rhinoceros n a large thick-skinned animal with horn or two horns on the nose.

rhizome n a prostrate stem that throws out roots.

rhododendron n an evergreen shrub with brilliant flowers.

rhomb, rhombus n a parallelogram with equal sides but angles not right angles.

rhomboid n a quadrilateral whose opposite sides only are equal and whose angles are not right angles.

rhubarb n a plant whose stalks are edible when cooked.

rhyme n the repetition of like endings in words or verse lines; poetry; verse. * vt to make rhymes; to put into rhyme.

rhythm n regular recurrence of accent in music and poetry.

rib n one of the curved bones springing from the backbone; something resembling a rib, as in an umbrella.

ribald adj irreverent; humorously vulgar.

ribbon n a narrow band of silk, satin, etc.

rice n a cereal extensively cultivated in hot countries.

rich adj wealthy; costly; fertile; plentiful; bright; mellow; highly flavoured.

rickets npl a disease of children marked by softening and distortion of the bones.

rickety adj ramshackle; shaky.

ricochet n a rebounding from a surface.

rid vt (pt, pp **rid**) to free (from something objectionable); to disencumber. * adj free; clear.

riddance n deliverance; clearance.

riddle n a puzzling question; an enigma; a coarse sieve. * vt ; to sift; to perforate with shot.

ride vb (pt **rode**, pp **ridden**) vi to be borne on horseback, in a vehicle, etc; to practise horsemanship; to be at anchor. * vt to sit on, so as to be carried; to domineer over. * n an excursion on horseback or in a vehicle.

ridge n a narrow elevation as the crest of a hill or edge of a roof.

ridicule n laughter with contempt; mockery. * vt to make sport of.

ridiculous adj absurd; laughable.

riding habit adj the clothes used in riding.

rife adj abundant; prevalent; widespread.

rifle n a shoulder gun with a grooved barrel. * vt to plunder; to groove a gun barrel.

rift n an opening; a cleft; a split.

rig vt (pt **rigged**) to manipulate fraudulently; to fit with tackling. * n style of masts and cut of sails of a ship.

rigging n a ship's spars, ropes, etc.

right adj straight; upright; just; correct; opposite of left; perpendicular. * adv justly; very; to the right hand. * n uprightness; truth; justice. * vt, vi to put right; to do justice; to make erect.

righteous adj moral; virtuous; just.

rightful adj lawful.

rightly adv properly; justly.

right-wing adj of or relating to the conservative faction of a political party, organization, etc.

rigid adj stiff; unyielding; stern.

rigidity n stiffness; harshness.

rigmarole n confused or disconnected talk.

rigor *n* a sudden chill attended with severe shivering.

rigorous *adj* severe; stringent.

rigour *n* stiffness; austerity; severity.

rilievo *n* relief, in carving, etc.

rim *n* border; edge; margin.

rind *n* outer coat of fruits, trees, etc; bark.

ring *n* anything in the form of a circle; a gold hoop for finger; a circular area for contests, a group with mutual interests; sound of bell. * *vb* (*pt* **rang**, *pp* **rung**) *vt* to encircle; to cause to sound. * *vi* to sound.

ringleader *n* the leader of a faction.

ringlet *n* a small ring; a curl.

ringworm *n* a skin disease characterized by circular patches.

rink *n* a space on the ice reserved for curling; a place for roller-skating.

rinse *vt* to wash lightly; to flush under clean water to remove soap. * *n* the act of rinsing; a preparation for tinting the hair.

riot *n* an uproar; a tumult; noisy revelry. * *vi* to engage in a riot; to revel.

riotous *adj* noisy; turbulent; disorderly.

rip *vt* to tear or cut open. * *n* a rent; a scamp.

riparian *adj* pertaining to a river bank.

ripe *adj* ready for harvest; mature.

ripple *n* a little wave on the surface of water.

rise *vi* (*pt* **rose**, *pp* **risen**) to ascend; to stand up; to swell; to slope upwards; to rebel. * *n* ascent; elevation; source; increase (in price).

risible *adj* prone to laugh; laughable.

rising *adj* increasing in power, etc; approaching. * *n* a mounting up; an insurrection; a prominence.

risk *n* hazard; jeopardy. * *vt* to hazard; to venture.

risky *adj* dangerous; full of risk.

rite *n* a solemn religious act; form; ceremony.

ritual *n* a fixed (religious) ceremony.

rival *n* a competitor for the same goal. * *adj* competing. * *vt* to emulate; to strive to excel.

rivalry *n* competition; emulation.

river *n* a large running stream of water.

rivet *n* a fastening bolt clinched by hammering. * *vt* to clinch; to fasten firmly.

rivulet *n* a small stream.

road *n* a public way for travellers, vehicles, etc; a highway; a surfaced track for travelling.

road block *n* a barrier erected across a road to halt traffic.

roam *vi* to wander; to travel.

roan *adj* of mixed colour, red predominating. * *n* a horse of roan colour.

roar *vi* to cry with a loud voice; to bellow. * *n* the full loud cry of large animal; a shout.

roaring *adj* boisterous; noisy; brisk.

roast *vt* to cook with little or no moisture; to expose to great heat. * *n* roasted meat, or meat for roasting.

rob *vt* to take by force; to steal from.

robbery *n* theft with violence.

robe *n* a gown, or long, loose garment. * *vt* to invest with robes.

robot n a mechanical device that acts in a seemingly human manner; a mechanism guided by automatic controls.

robust adj sturdy; healthy and strong.

rock vt to move to and fro; to swing. * vi to reel. * n a large mass of stone; a reef; a sweetmeat.

rockery n an artificial mound of earth and stones for growing ferns, etc, on.

rocket n any device driven forward by gases escaping through a rear vent. * vi to move in or like a rocket; to soar.

rococo n, adj (of) a florid style of decoration prevalent in the 18th century.

rod n a straight slender stick; a wand; a fishing rod.

rodent adj gnawing. * n an animal that gnaws, as the rat.

rodeo n the rounding up of cattle; a display of cowboy skill.

roe n the spawn of fishes.

rogue n a knave; a rascal.

roguery n trickery; fraud; mischievousness.

roister vt to bluster; to swagger.

roll n a scroll; anything wound into cylindrical form; a list or register; a rolling movement; a small cake of bread; an undulation; the sound of thunder; the beating of drumsticks. *vt, vi to move by turning over or from side to side; to move like a wheel; to press with a roller.

roll call n the calling over a list of names.

roller n a cylinder for smoothing, crushing, etc; a long, swelling wave.

roller skate n a skate mounted on small wheels.

rolling adj revolving; undulating.

rolling pin n a roller for kneading dough.

rolling stock n the carriages, engines, etc, of a railway.

Roman adj of or relating to the city of Rome or its ancient empire, or the Latin alphabet; Roman Catholic. * n an inhabitant or citizen of Rome; a Roman Catholic.

Roman Catholic adj belonging to the Christian church that is headed by the pope. * n a member of the Roman Catholic church.

romance n a tale in prose or verse; a novel of adventures; a love story; a love affair; a picturesque falsehood.

Romanesque adj, n (of) the style of architecture of the later Roman Empire.

romantic adj imaginative; fanciful; picturesque.

romanticism n a literary movement of the 19th century opposed to the prevailing classicism.

romp n a noisy game; a frolic. * vi to play boisterously.

rood n a cross or crucifix.

roof n the cover of any building; a canopy; an upper limit.

rook n a kind of crow; a cheat; a piece in chess. * vi, vt to cheat; to rob.

rookery n a nesting place for crows.

room n space; scope; opportunity; stead; apartment in a house.

roomy adj spacious; wide.

roost *n* a bird's perch or sleeping place; a place for resting. * *vi* to rest or sleep on a roost.

rooster *n* the male of the domestic fowl; a cockerel.

root *n* that part of a plant that fixes itself in the ground; foundation; origin; a form from which words are derived; (*math*) the factor of a quantity that, multiplied by itself, gives the quantity; (*pl*) plants with edible roots. * *vt, vi* (*pt* **rooted**) to take root; to become established; to dig up with the snout; to search about, rummage; (*with* **out**) to tear up; to eradicate; (*with* **for**) to encourage a team by cheering.

rooted *adj* fixed; deep; radical.

rope *n* a stout cord; a series of things connected; a cable. * *vi, vt* to fasten with a rope; to curb.

rosary *n* a string of beads for keeping count of prayers.

rose *n* a plant and its flower, of many species; knot of ribbons; a perforated nozzle. * *adj* rose colour.

roseate *adj* rosy; blooming.

rosemary *n* an evergreen fragrant shrub.

rosette *n* an ornamental knot of ribbons.

rosewood *n* the wood (rose-scented) of a tree much used as a veneer.

rosin *n* resin in the solid state.

roster *n* a list showing order in which officers, etc, are to take up certain duties (army).

rostrum *n* a platform for public speaking.

rosy *adj* red; blooming; hopeful.

rot *vi, vt* to decompose; to decay. * *n* putrid decay; a fatal sheep disease; nonsense.

rota *n* a turn in succession; a list or roster of duties.

rotary *adj* turning on an axle.

rotate *vi* to revolve round a centre or axis; to act in turn.

rotation *n* motion round a centre or axis; regular succession (as of crops).

rote *n* repetition without understanding.

rotten *adj* decomposed; decayed.

rotund *adj* round; spherical; plump.

rotunda *n* a round building.

rouble *n* a Russian monetary unit.

rouge *n* a red cosmetic for tinting cheeks and lips.

rough *adj* not smooth; rugged; harsh; rude; uneven; ill-mannered.

roughcast *vt* to cover with a coarse plaster.

roughen *vt* to make rough. * *vi* to become rough.

rough-hew *vt* to shape crudely.

roulette *n* a game of chance played with a revolving disc and a ball.

round *adj* circular; spherical; plump; curved; (*number, etc*) not minutely accurate. * *n* rung of a ladder; a circular course; a circuit made by one on duty; a song in parts; ammunition for firing once; a turn or bout. * *vt* to make round; to encircle. * *vi* to make a circuit. * *adv* in a circle; around. * *prep* about; around.

roundabout *adj* indirect; circuitous. * *n* a merry-go-round.

rounders *n* a ball game played by two sides.

Roundhead n a member of the Puritan or parliamentary party in the English Civil War.

roundly adv openly; plainly.

round robin n a written petition, having signatures circle-wise so as not to show who signed it first.

rouse vt to arouse; to awaken. * vi to awake.

rout n a noisy crowd; a disorderly retreat. *vt, vi to grub up, as a pig; to make a furrow.

route n a course or way.

routine n regular habit or practice.

rove vi to roam; to wander.

row[1] n a line of objects; a rank; a line of seats.* vt to impel by oars, as a boat.

row[2] n a noisy disturbance; a riot.

rowdy n a turbulent fellow; a rough. * adj disreputable.

rowlock n the support for the oar of a boat.

royal adj regal; relating to a king or queen.

royalist n an adherent of a king or queen.

royalty n state of being royal; a royal personage; share paid to a superior, inventor, or author.

rub vt, vi (pt **rubbed**) to move one thing along surface of another with pressure or friction; to scour; to chafe. * n an impediment; friction; pinch; gibe.

rubber n that which rubs; an eraser; in card playing, winning two out of three games.

rubbish n refuse; debris; trash; nonsense.

rubble n broken stones of irregular shapes.

rubicund adj ruddy; red-faced.

rubric n headings entered on margin of page, worked out in red.

ruby n a valuable gem of various shades of red.

ruche vt to pleat or gather fabric to use as a trimming.

rucksack n a bag worn on the back by hikers.

rudder n the steering apparatus of a ship.

ruddy adj reddish; a healthy red.

rude adj rough-hewn; uncivilized; ill-mannered; vulgar.

rudiments npl the origin, first principle, or germ of anything, esp learning, art, etc.

rudimentary adj undeveloped; primitive.

rue vt to feel remorse for.

rueful adj woeful; piteous; remorseful.

ruff n a plaited collar or frill; a ruffle; act of trumping at cards. * vt to trump at cards.

ruffian n a brutal lawless person.

ruffle vt to rumple; to derange. * vi to bluster. * n a frill for the neck or wrist; agitation.

rug n a heavy fabric used as a mat or coverlet.

rugged adj rough; uncouth; rocky.

rugby n a football game for two teams of 15 players played with an oval ball.

ruin n destruction; fall; overthrow; (pl) remains of old buildings. * vt to destroy; to impoverish.

ruinous adj fallen to ruin; disastrous.

rule n a ruler or measure; a guiding principle; a precept, law, maxim; government; method. * vt, vi to govern; to manage; to mark with lines; to decide; to reign.

ruling adj reigning; predominant. * n a point settled by a judge, chairman, etc.

rum n spirit distilled from molasses.

rumble vi to make a dull, continued sound. * n a low, continued sound; a seat for servants behind a carriage.

ruminant n an animal that chews the cud.

ruminate vi to regurgitate food after it has been swallowed; to meditate.

rummage vt to search narrowly but roughly; to ransack. * n a careful search.

rumour n an unconfirmed report. * vt to spread abroad.

rump n end of an animal's backbone; buttocks.

rumple vt to wrinkle; to ruffle.

rumpus n a great disturbance; a din.

run vb (pt **ran**, pp **run**) vi to move rapidly; to take part in a race, election, etc; to flee; to spread or flow. * vt to incur; to smuggle; to melt. * n act of running; course run; trip; general demand; distance sailed or travelled.

runaway n a deserter; fugitive. * adj effected by running away or eloping.

rune n letter of the old Teutonic alphabet; (pl) inscriptions in these letters.

rung n the round or step of a ladder.

runner n a messenger; an athlete; a creeping plant; that on which anything slides.

runner-up n (pl **runners-up**) the competitor who finishes second in a race, contest, etc.

running adj continuous; moving swiftly; discharging pus.

runway n a landing strip for aircraft.

rupee n the unit of currency in India.

rupture n a break; fracture; breach; disagreement; quarrel; hernia. * vt, vi to cause or suffer a rupture.

rural adj pertaining to the country; rustic.

ruse n artifice; trick; deception.

rush vi to dash forward. * n a headlong advance; hurry; a reed; an unedited film print.

rusk n a light hard cake or biscuit.

rust n the red oxide formed on iron exposed to moisture; a parasite fungus.* vi to contract rust; to degenerate in idleness.

rustic adj rural; homely; not polished.

rusticate vi to dwell in the country. * vt to banish from a university for a time.

rustle vi, vt to make a sound as of rubbing of dry leaves. * n the crinkling sound of blown leaves.

rusty adj covered with rust; impaired by inaction.

rut n the track of a wheel; a groove; routine.

ruthless adj cruel; pitiless.

rye n a cereal plant and its seed; a whiskey made from rye.

S

Sabbath n a day of rest and worship, observed on a Saturday by Jews, Sunday by Christians and Friday by Muslims.

sabbatical n a year's leave from a teaching post, often paid, for research or travel.

sabotage n a deliberate damage of machinery, or disruption of public services, by enemy agents, disgruntled employees, etc, to prevent their effective operation. *vt to practise sabotage on; to spoil, disrupt.

saccharin n a non-fattening substitute for sugar.

sachet n a small bag for perfume, etc.

sack n a bag made of coarse cloth used as a container; pillage of a town. * vt to pillage; to dismiss.

sacrament n a solemn religious ordinance; a sacred symbol or pledge.

sacred adj set apart for a holy purpose; consecrated; religious.

sacrifice n something given up in the interests of another; loss; the thing offered up. * vt to give up.

sacrum n the bone at base of vertebral column.

sad adj sorrowful; gloomy.

sadden vt to make sad. * vi to become sad.

saddle n a seat for a rider on a horse or bicycle. * vt to put a saddle on.

sadism n sexual pleasure obtained by inflicting cruelty on another; extreme cruelty.

safari n a journey or hunting expedition, esp in Africa.

safe adj secure; free from danger; trustworthy. * n a strong box for securing valuables; a burglar-proof chamber; a cupboard.

safeguard n a defence; protection. * vt to guard.

safety n freedom from danger, hurt, or loss.

safety belt n a belt worn by a person working at great height to prevent falling; a seatbelt.

safety valve n a valve that opens when the pressure of steam in a boiler becomes too great.

sag vi (pt **sagged**) to sink in the middle; to droop.

sagacity n shrewdness; high intelligence.

sage adj wise; grave. * n a wise man; an aromatic plant.

Sagittarius n the archer, a sign of the zodiac.

sail n a canvas spread to catch the wind; a voyage in a sailing vessel. * vi, vt to move by means of sails; to glide; to navigate.

sailor n a seaman; a mariner.

saint n one eminent for piety.

sake n behalf; purpose; benefit; interest.

salad n raw herbs, such as lettuce, cress, etc, with a dressing.

salary n a fixed, regular payment for work.

sale n act of selling; the exchange of goods or services for money; the market or opportunity of selling; an auction; the disposal of goods at reduced prices.

salesman n one employed to sell goods.

salience n projection; protrusion.

salient adj springing; projecting; conspicuous.

saline adj consisting of salt; salt.

saliva n the fluid secreted by glands of mouth that aids digestion.

sallow adj having a sickly, yellowish colour. * n a kind of willow.

sally n a sudden attack or outburst; a lively remark, a quip.

salon n a reception room; a gallery.

saloon n a spacious apartment; main cabin of a steamer.

salsa n (the music for) a type of Puerto Rican dance; a spicy tomato sauce.

salt n a substance for seasoning and preserving food; a compound produced by the combination of a base with an acid; savour; an old sailor. * vt to sprinkle with salt.

saltire n a cross (X) dividing heraldic shield into four parts.

salubrious adj health-giving; wholesome.

salutary adj beneficial, wholesome.

salutation n a greeting; a salute.

salute vt to greet; to welcome; to greet with a bow; kiss, etc. * vi to make a salute.

salvable adj that may be saved.

salvage n the saving of a ship or its cargo at sea; the saving of property from fire; payment for such service.

salvation n redemption of man from sin.

salve n a healing ointment; remedy. * vt to apply salve to.

salver n a small tray.

salvo n a salute of guns; a sudden burst.

same adj identical; exactly similar; unchanged; uniform; monotonous.

sample n a specimen; a small part representative of the whole.

sanatorium n an establishment for the treatment of convalescents or the chronically ill.

sanctification n a purifying from sin; consecration.

sanctified adj made holy; consecrated.

sanctify vt to make holy.

sanctimonious adj making a show of sanctity; hypocritical.

sanction n permission; authority; a penalty by which a law is enforced. * vt to ratify; to authorize.

sanctity n saintliness; holiness.

sanctuary n a sacred place; part of a church where the altar is placed; a sure refuge.

sanctum n a sacred place; a private room.

sand n fine particles of stone; pl tracts of sand on the seashore, etc.

sandal n a shoe consisting of a sole strapped to the foot.

sandpaper n paper coated with sand for smoothing and polishing.

sandstone n a stone composed of compressed sand.

sandwich n slices of bread, with meat or savoury between. * vt to fit between two other pieces.

sane adj sound in mind; sensible.

sanguine *adj* full of blood; cheerful; hopeful.

sanitary *adj* healthful; hygienic.

sanitation *n* measures for securing good health in a community; hygiene; drainage and disposal of sewage.

sanity *n* soundness of mind.

Sanskrit *n, adj* the ancient language of Hindus.

sap *vt, vi* to undermine. * *n* a trench; vital juice of plants.

sapient *adj* wise; sage; discerning.

sapling *n* a young tree.

sapphire *n* a precious stone of a rich blue colour.

sarcasm *n* a bitter cutting jest; gibe.

sarcastic *adj* biting; taunting; satirical.

sarcophagus *n* (*pl* **sarcophagi**) a coffin of stone.

sardonic *adj* bitter; mocking; grimly jocular.

sartorial *adj* pertaining to a tailor.

sash *n* a long band or scarf worn for ornament; a window frame.

Satan *n* the devil; the adversary of God.

satchel *n* a little bag for carrying books, papers, etc.

sate *vt* to satisfy the appetite of; to glut.

satellite *n* a small planet revolving round a larger; a man-made object orbiting the earth to gather scientific information, etc.

satiate *vt* to satisfy fully; to surfeit. * *adj* glutted.

satin *n* a glossy close-woven silk cloth.

satire *n* a composition in prose or verse, ridiculing or censuring manners and customs of the time.

satirize *vt* to ridicule; to hold up to scorn.

satisfaction *n* pleasure; contentment; atonement; payment.

satisfactory *adj* adequate; up to expectation.

satisfy *vt, vi* to gratify fully; to convince.

saturate *vt* to soak thoroughly.

saturation *n* state of being soaked or filled with another substance to utmost limit.

Saturday *n* the seventh day of the week.

Saturn *n* a planet.

sauce *n* a liquid relish or seasoning for food.

saucepan *n* a deep cooking pan with a handle and a lid.

saucer *n* a curved plate in which cup is set.

saucy *adj* pert; impudent; rude.

saunter *vi* to stroll about idly. * *n* a stroll.

sausage *n* minced seasoned meat, esp pork, packed into animal gut or other casing.

savage *adj* wild; barbarous; brutal. * *n* a barbarian.

savagery *n* cruelty; barbarity.

save *vt* to preserve; to protect; to rescue; to spare. * *vi* to be economical. * *prep* except.

saving *adj* thrifty; preserving; excepting. * *n* what is saved. * *prep* excepting.

saviour *n* a preserver; rescuer; (*with cap*) Jesus Christ).

savory n a Mediterranean aromatic herb used for flavouring.

savour n taste; flavour; a distinctive quality. * vi to have a particular taste.

savoury adj tasty; palatable; spicy not sweet.

saw n a cutting instrument with toothed edge; a maxim * vt, vi (pp **sawn**) to cut with a saw.

sawdust n small fragments of wood produced in sawing.

sawmill n a mill for sawing timber.

say vt, vi (pt, pp **said**) to utter in words; to speak; to declare; to relate.

saying n a proverb; maxim.

scab n crust formed over a sore on healing; itch; mange.

scabbard n the sheath of a sword.

scabies n contagious itching skin disease.

scaffolding n a framework to aid in building houses, etc.

scald vt to burn with hot liquid. * n a burn from hot liquid or steam; scurf.

scale n a thin flake on skin of animals; instrument for weighing; series of steps; gradation; a measure; rank; series of musical notes. * vt to weigh; to strip of scales; to climb. * vi to peel.

scallop n an edible shellfish; a curving or indentation on edge. * vt to indent or curve edges.

scalp n the skin and hair of top of head. * vt to cut off scalp.

scalpel n a short, thin, very sharp knife.

scamp n a knave; rogue.

scamper vi to scurry. * n a hurried run.

scan vt to look through quickly; to examine with a radiological device; to mark the rhythm of verse.

scandal n a disgraceful event or action; a feeling of moral outrage; shame.

scandalous adj shameful; disgraceful.

scant adj limited; meagre. * vt to stint; to grudge. * adv scarcely.

scapegoat n one who bears the blame of others.

scapula n the shoulder blade.

scar n the mark of a wound; a blemish; a cliff; a steep bare bank. * vt to form a scar; to wound.

scarab n Egyptian beetle; a gem cut in the form of a beetle.

scarce adj rare; deficient; hard to find.

scarcity n dearth; deficiency.

scare vt to terrify; to scare. * n a causeless alarm; panic.

scarecrow n anything set up to scare away birds.

scarf n a broad band or sash for neck wear; a joint in timber.

scarify vt to make small incision in the skin; to shock; to criticize savagely.

scarlet n, adj a bright red colour.

scarp n a precipitous slope.

scathing adj severe; bitterly critical; withering.

scatter vt to disperse; to throw loosely about, to occur at random. * vi to straggle apart.

scatterbrain n a giddy, thoughtless person.

scenario n an outline of events, real or imagined; the plot or script of a film etc.

scene n a stage; a distinct part of a play; a painted device on the stage; place of action; a view; display of emotion.

scenery n the painted scenes and hangings of the stage; landscape; view.

scenic adj relating to natural scenery.

scent n an odour left by an animal, by which it can be tracked; a perfume; sense of smell. * vt to discern by smell.

sceptic n a doubter; disbeliever.

sceptical adj doubting; doubting truth of revelation.

scepticism n doubt; incredulity.

sceptre n the rod borne by a ruler as a symbol of power.

schedule n a timetable; a list or inventory. *vt to plan.

scheme n a plan of proceedings; a system; a project. * vt, vi to plan; project; plot.

schism n a separation; a disruption.

scholar n a school pupil; a learned person.

scholarship n learning; an annual grant to a student, usu won by competitive examination.

school n a place of instruction; a body of pupils; disciples; sect or body; a shoal (of fishes). * vt to instruct; to train.

schooner n a vessel with two masts.

sciatica n neuralgia of the sciatic nerve.

science n knowledge; knowledge reduced to a system; study of natural laws and principles; trained skill.

scientific adj skilled in science.

scientist n a specialist in a branch of science.

scimitar n a short curved sword.

scintillate vi to sparkle; to twinkle.

scion n a cutting; a young shoot; a descendant.

scissors npl a cutting instrument of two blades, whose edges slide past each other.

sclerosis n a hardening of tissue.

scoff n an expression of scorn; a gibe. * vi to jeer; to mock. * vt to mock at.

scold vi, vt to rebuke angrily; to find fault with harshly; to tell off.

scoop n a short-handled shovel for grain, etc; a coal scuttle; a hollowing out spoon or gouge for cheese, etc. * vt to hollow out.

scooter n a child's two-wheeled vehicle with a footboard and steering handle; a motor scooter.

scope n an aim or end; range; opportunity.

scorch vt, vi to singe; parch; shrivel; to drive at reckless speed.

score n a notch; a line; a furrow; an account or reckoning; runs, points, etc, made in games; twenty; reason; copy of concerted musical piece. * vt to mark; record; register.

scorn n extreme contempt. * vt to disdain; to deride. * vi to feel or show scorn.

scornful adj disdainful; mocking; contemptuous.

scotch vt to stamp out.

scoundrel n a rogue, rascal.

scour vt, vi to clean by rubbing; to purge violently; to pass swiftly over.

scourge n a lash; a whip; a grievous affliction; a plague. * vt to lash; to afflict sorely.

scout n an exploring or reconnoitring messenger; a person employed to find new talent. * vi to act as scout.

scowl vi to frown in anger. * n a sullen frowning look.

scraggy adj lean and bony; gaunt.

scramble vi to clamber on all fours; to push rudely; to break and stir eggs; to make unintelligible in transit. * n a pushing and struggling for something.

scrambling adj irregular; straggling.

scrap n a small piece; a fragment; a cut-out picture.

scrape vt, vi to rub with something hard; to grate; to erase; to gather money laboriously; to make a grating noise. * n a rasping sound; serious trouble.

scratch vt, vi to tear or mark with something sharp; to tear with nails; to erase or cancel * n a slight mark or wound; starting line; competitor without start. * adj haphazard.

scrawl vt, vi to scribble. * n slovenly writing.

scream vi to shriek. * n a shrill cry.

screen n a shield from draughts, heat, etc; a sieve; a partition in a church; a sheet on which pictures are projected; an electronic display. * vt to shelter; to conceal; to sift.

scree npl debris of rocks; shingle.

screw n a cylinder with a spiral ridge; a screw propeller; a twist or turn. * vt to fasten by a screw; to twist; to oppress.

screwdriver n an instrument for turning screw nails.

screw nail n a nail grooved like a screw.

scribble vt, vi to write carelessly. * n a scrawl.

scribe n a writer; copyist.

scrimp vt to make too small or short. * adj scanty.

script n handwriting; type imitating handwriting; the text of a play or a film.

scripture n any sacred writing.

scroll n a roll of paper; a first draft; a spiral design.

scrotum n the bag that contains the testicles.

scrounge vt, vi to seek or obtain (something) for nothing.

scrub vt to rub hard; to make clean or bright. * n a stunted tree or bush; a mean person.

scrubby adj stunted; niggardly.

scruple n (usu pl) a moral principle or belief causing one to doubt or hesitate about a course of action. *vt, vi to hesitate owing to scruples.

scrupulous adj conscientious; exact.

scrutinize vt, vi to examine closely; to investigate.

scrutiny n close search; careful investigation.

scuffle n a confused struggle. * vi to strive confusedly at close quarters.

scull n a short oar, used in pairs. * vt to propel by sculls.

scullery *n* a back kitchen where dishes, etc, are washed.

sculptor *n* an artist in stone, wood, clay, etc.

sculpture *n* the art of carving wood or stone into images; an image in stone, etc.

scum *n* impurities that rise to the surface of liquids; refuse; despicable people.

scupper *n* hole to carry off water from a ship's deck. * *vt* to sink deliberately.

scurrilous *adj* foul-mouthed; abusive.

scurry *vt* to hurry. * *n* hurry; haste.

scurvily *adv* basely; shabbily.

scurvy *n* a disease caused by an insufficiency of vitamin C. * *adj* vile; mean.

scuttle *n* a pail for coals; a hatchway; a short run; a quick race. * *vt* to sink by making holes in (a ship). * *vi* to scurry.

scythe *n* an implement for cutting grass, etc.

sea *n* an expanse of salt water; ocean or part of it; a vast quantity; a great wave.

seagoing *adj* applied to vessels going to foreign ports.

seal *n* a stamp or die with a motto or device; wax with stamp impression; guarantee; carnivorous marine animal. * *vt* to set a seal to; to confirm; to close.

sea level *n* the level of the sea's surface.

seam *n* the joining line of edges of cloth; a vein of metal; a scar.

seamy *adj* sordid; disagreeable; shabby.

séance *n* to try to communicate with the dead; a meeting of spiritualists.

seaport *n* a town on the sea or estuary accessible to ocean-going ships.

sear *vt* to brand; to burn; to deaden.

search *vt* to look or rummage for; to explore, examine. * *n* quest; pursuit; inquiry.

searching *adj* penetrating; severe; testing.

seashore *n* land beside the sea or between high and low water marks.; the beach.

seasick *adj* affected with sickness by the rolling of a ship.

seaside *n* the seashore.

season *n* a division of the year; a suitable time; time of greatest activity. * *vt* to accustom; to acclimatize; to flavour.

seasonable *adj* opportune; timely.

seasonal *adj* of or relating to a season.

seasoning *n* salt, spices, etc, used to enhance the flavour of food.

seat *n* that on which one sits; a chair, stool, etc; place of sitting; a right to sit; residence; station; manner of sitting. * *vt* to place on a seat; to settle.

seatbelt *n* an anchored strap worn in a car or aeroplane to secure a person to a seat.

seaward *adj, adv* toward the sea.

seaweed *n* a mass of plants growing in or under water; a sea plant, esp a marine alga.

sebaceous *adj* containing fatty matter.

secede *vi* to withdraw from fellow-ship.

secession *n* disruption; withdrawal from membership.

secluded *adj* retired; remote; private.

seclusion *n* solitude; privacy.

second *adj* next after the first; inferior; other. * *n* one who comes next after first; one who supports another; to place in temporary service elsewhere; a 60th part of a minute. * *vt* to support.

secondary *adj* subordinate; not elementary; inferior.

secrecy *n* concealment; seclusion; habit of keeping secrets.

secret *adj* not made public; concealed from others; hidden; private; remote. * *n* something hidden; a mystery; a hidden cause.

secretariat *n* an administrative office or staff, as in a government.

secretary *n* a person employed to deal with correspondence, filing, answering telephone calls etc; head of a state department; executive officer of company.

secrete *vt* to hide; to produce and release (a substance) out of blood or sap.

secretion *n* act or process of secreting; matter secreted, as bile, etc.

secretive *adj* given to secrecy; reticent.

sect *n* a body of persons united in doctrine; a denomination.

sectarian *adj* pertaining to a sect; bigoted. * *n* member of a sect.

section *n* a cutting; part cut off; subdivision of chapter, etc; slice; distinct part; the plane figure formed when solid is cut through.

sectional *adj* made up of sections; partial.

sector *n* part of circle between two radii; a mathematical instrument.

secular *adj* worldly; temporal; not sacred.

secularize *vt* to free from religious influence; to hand over church property to state.

secure *adj* free from care or danger; safe; confident. * *vt* to make safe; to seize and confine; to guarantee; to fasten.

security *n* safety; confidence; protection; a guarantee; a surety; *pl* bonds, stocks, etc.

sedate *adj* staid; sober; calm; composed.

sedately *adv* calmly; tranquilly.

sedative *adj* soothing. * *n* a soothing drug.

sedentary *adj* inactive; requiring much sitting.

sediment *n* that which settles to the bottom of liquids; matter deposited by water or wind.

sedition *n* action or speech against law and order.

seditious *adj* inciting to rebellion; inflammatory.

seduce *vt* to lead astray; to corrupt.

seduction *n* allurement; temptation; attraction.

seductive *adj* enticing; alluring.

sedulous *adj* assiduous; diligent.

see¹ *vb* (*pt* saw, *pp* seen) *vt* to perceive by the eye; to notice; to understand; to ascertain; to consult.

* *vi* to have the power of sight; to make inquiry; to consider; to reflect; to understand. * *interj* look!

see² *n* diocese or sphere of a bishop.

seed *n* the small hard part of a plant from which a new plant grows; the source of anything; sperm; descendant. * *vt, vi* to sow; to produce seed.

seedling *n* a plant that is reared from a seed.

seedy *adj* abounding with seeds; shabby; out of sorts.

seeing *n* vision, sight. * *adj* having sight; observant. * *conj* in view of the fact that; since.

seek *vt, vi* (*pt, pp* **sought**) to search for; to ask for; to resort to.

seem *vi* to appear; to look as if; to pretend.

seemingly *adv* apparently.

seemly *adj* becoming; decent.

seer *n* a prophet.

seesaw *n* a swinging movement up and down; a children's game on balanced plank; vacillation.

seethe *vi* to be very angry outwardly.

segment *n* a section; part of circle cut off by straight line; a portion.

segregate *vt* to set apart or separate from others; to isolate.

seismic *adj* pertaining to earthquakes.

seismology *n* the science of earthquakes.

seize *vt, vi* to lay hold of forcibly; to apprehend; to attack, as fear, illness, etc.

seizure *n* act of seizing; a sudden attack of illness.

seldom *adv* rarely; not often.

select *vt* to choose; to pick out. * *adj* chosen.

selection *n* process of choosing; things chosen.

self *n* (*pl* **selves**) one's individual person or interest. * *adj or pron* same; uniform.

self-conscious *adj* thinking about one's self overmuch; shy.

self-defence *n* the act of defending oneself.

self-denial *n* the forbearing to gratify one's desires; unselfishness.

self-esteem *n* high opinion of one's self; vanity.

self-evident *adj* obvious; needing no proof.

self-important *adj* pompous.

self-imposed *adj* voluntarily undertaken.

selfish *adj* absorbed in one's self; not generous.

self-respect *n* proper pride.

self-righteous *adj* stressing one's own goodness; pharisaical.

self-seeking *adj* selfish.

self-sufficient *adj* needing no help.

sell *vb* (*pt, pp* **sold**) *vt* to give for a price; to betray. * *vi* to practise selling; to be sold.

semaphore *n* a system of visual signalling using the operators arms, flags etc.

semblance *n* similarity; appearance.

semibreve *n* a musical note = 2 minims.

semicircle *n* a half circle.

semicolon *n* the point (;) marking a longer pause than a comma.

seminal *adj* pertaining to seed; germinal.

seminar *n* a group of students engaged in research or study under supervision; any group meeting to pool and discuss ideas.

seminary *n* a school, academy, or college.

semiquaver *n* half a quaver in music.

semolina *n* granular flour.

senate *n* a legislative or deliberative council; governing body in some universities.

senator *n* a member of a senate.

send *vt* (*pt, pp* **sent**) to cause to go or be carried; to transmit; to dispatch.

senile *adj* aged; doting; tottering.

senility *n* a state of being mentally weakened by old age.

senior *adj* older; higher in rank or standing. * *n* one older in age or office.

seniority *n* priority in rank or office.

sensation *n* perception through the senses; feeling; a thrill.

sensational *adj* causing an excited feeling; emotional.

sense *n* one of the five senses, sight, hearing, taste, smell, touch; understanding; good judgment; discernment; meaning.

senseless *adj* stupid; foolish; meaningless; purposeless.

sensibility *n* acuteness of perception; delicacy of feeling.

sensible *adj* having good sense; judicious; reasonable; appreciable.

sensitive *adj* susceptible to impressions; easily affected; touchy; tender.

sensitize *vt* to make (paper) susceptible to rays of light.

sensory *adj* relating to the senses; conveying sensation.

sensual *adj* bodily, relating to the senses rather than the mind; arousing sexual desire.

sensuous *adj* giving pleasure to the body or the mind through the senses.

sentence *n* opinion; judgment of a court; a number of words conveying a complete thought. * *vt* to pass sentence upon; to condemn.

sententious *adj* abounding in maxims; terse; judicial.

sentient *adj* making use of the senses.

sentiment *n* tenderness of feeling; thought prompted by emotion; a toast.

sentimental *adj* apt to be swayed by feelings; romantic.

sentinel *n* a guard; sentry.

sentry *n* a soldier on guard to give warning of danger.

separable *adj* that may be separated; capable of separation.

separate *vt* to put or set apart; to sever; to divide apart. * *vi* to go apart. * *adj* detached; distinct.

separation *n* the act of separating or the state of being separate; a formal arrangement of husband and wife to live apart.

separatist *n* one who advocates separation; a seceder.

sepia *n* a brown pigment.

September *n* the ninth month of the year.

septenary adj consisting of or proceeding by sevens; lasting seven years.

septennial adj occurring every, or lasting, seven years.

septic adj promoting or causing putrefaction.

septicaemia n blood poisoning.

septuagenarian n a person seventy years of age.

septum n (pl **septa**) a membrane separating organs or cavities.

sepulchral adj having to do with a grave; (voice) deep and gloomy.

sepulchre n a tomb; a burial vault.

sequel n that which follows; a consequence; issue.

sequence n a coming after; succession; series.

sequential adj arranged or following in a sequence.

sequester vt to set apart; to withdraw; to seize goods till debt is paid; to confiscate.

sequestrate vt to seize and dispose of goods for benefit of creditors.

sequestration n confiscation of debtor's goods in interest of creditors.

serenade n music played at night under a person's window, esp by a lover. * vt, vi to perform a serenade.

serene adj clear; bright; calm; unruffled.

serenity n calmness; peace; equanimity.

sergeant n a noncommissioned officer above corporal in the army etc; a police officer.

serial adj appearing periodically. * n a story issued in parts.

series n a succession of things; sequence.

serious adj grave; earnest; attended with danger; important; critical.

sermon n a religious discourse; an admonition.

serpentine adj spiral; winding; crafty. * n a mineral.

serrated adj notched; toothed.

serum n the watery part of bodily fluid, esp liquid that separates out from the blood when it coagulates; such fluid taken from the blood of an animal immune to a disease, used as an antitoxin.

servant n a domestic; an attendant.

serve vt to work for and meet the needs of; to minister to; to deliver or execute; to supply with (food). * vi to be a servant; to suit.

service n work of a servant; employment; kindness; official duties; public worship; liturgy; table dishes; (pl) the army, navy, etc.

serviceable adj useful; beneficial.

serviette n a table napkin.

servile adj slavish; fawning; subservient.

servility n meanness of spirit; excessive deference.

servitude n slavery; bondage.

sessile adj without a stalk; growing direct from stem.

session n the meeting of a court; a series of such meetings; a period of study; a university year.

set vb (pres p **setting**, pt, pp **set**) vt to place in position; to fix; to appoint; to regulate or adjust; to fit to music; to adorn; to spread (sails). * vi to sink below horizon; to solidify; to tend; to point out game; to apply one's self. * n direction; tendency; attitude; bent; collection of things used together; a group of games; persons associated.

settee n a short sofa.

setting n descent below horizon; hardening of plaster; the mounting of a gem; fitting to music; a background scene; environment.

settle vt, vi to fix permanently; to quiet; to decide; to pay; to agree; to subside; to become calm; to clarify; to take up residence.

settled adj established; steadfast.

settlement n an arrangement; a newly established colony; subsidence (of buildings).

settler n a colonist.

seven adj one more than six.

sevenfold adj seven times.

seventeenth adj, n the ordinal of seventeen.

seventh adj the ordinal of seven.

seventieth adj, n the ordinal of seventy.

seventy adj, n seven times ten.

sever vt to separate; to divide into parts; to break off.

several adj separate; more than two but not very many.

severally adv separately.

severance n separation.

severe adj serious; grave; harsh; searching; austere.

severity n harshness; cruel treatment; intensity.

sew vt, vi (pp **sewn**) to make by needle and thread.

sewage n waste matter carried off by sewers.

sewer n a subterranean drain to carry off water, filth, etc.

sewerage n the system of sewers; sewage.

sex n the characteristics that distinguish male and female organisms on the basis of their reproductive function.

sexagenarian n a person sixty years of age.

sexism n discrimination on the basis of sex.

sextant n an instrument for measuring angles and altitudes.

sextuple adj sixfold.

sexual adj pertaining to sex.

sexual intercourse n the act of copulation.

sexuality n state of being sexual.

shabbily adv in a shabby manner; with shabby clothes; meanly.

shabby adj threadbare; mean; stingy.

shackle n a fetter; a manacle. * vt to fetter; hamper.

shade n interception of light; obscurity; darkness; a shady place; a screen; dimness; gradation of light; a ghost.

shading n light and shade in a picture.

shadow adj a figure projected by interception of light; shade; an inseparable companion; a spirit. * vt to shade; to cloud; to follow closely.

shadowy adj faint; dim; unsubstantial.

shady adj abounding in shade; (inf) of doubtful character.

shaft n the handle of a tool, etc; the body of a column; pole of carriage; a critical remark or attack; well-like entrance to mine.

shaggy adj long and unkempt; rough; untidy.

shake vb (pt **shook**, pp **shaken**) vt to move quickly to and fro; to agitate. * vi to tremble. * n a tremor; shock; a trill.

shaky adj unsteady; feeble.

shale n a clay rock with a slaty structure.

shall vb aux (pt **should**) in first person it is a future tense; in the second and third it implies authority.

shallow adj not deep; superficial; simple. * n a shoal.

sham n a pretence; a fraud. * adj false. * vt, vi to feign; pretend.

shambles npl a place of great disorder.

shambling adj walking with awkward, unsteady gait.

shame n a painful emotion excited by guilt, disgrace, etc * vt to make ashamed; to disgrace.

shameful adj disgraceful; infamous.

shameless adj immodest; impudent.

shampoo n a liquid cleansing agent for washing the hair. *vt to wash the hair with shampoo.

shandy n beer diluted with a nonalcoholic drink (as lemonade).

shank n the leg; the shinbone; the stem or shaft of tool, anchor, etc.

shanty n a hut or mean dwelling; sailors' song.

shape vt to form; to mould. * vi to suit. * n form or figure; make; a model.

shapely adj well-proportioned.

shard n a fragment of pottery.

share n a part, lot or portion; ploughshare; one of equal parts of company's capital. * vt, vi to divide; to apportion among others; to have part.

shareholder n an owner of shares in company.

shark n a voracious sea fish; a swindler.

sharp adj having a cutting edge or point; keen; shrewd; piercing; biting; barely honest. * n a note raised a semitone.

sharpen vt to make sharp; to whet.

sharpshooter n an expert shot; a sniper.

shatter vt, vi to break in pieces; to smash.

shave vt (pp **shaved** or **shaven**) to cut hair close with razor; to pare; to miss narrowly; to graze; to fleece. * n a cutting off of the beard; a narrow escape.

shaving n a thin slice pared off.

shawl n a loose covering for the shoulders.

she pron the female person or thing named before or in question. * n a female person or animal.

sheaf n (pl **sheaves**) a bundle of stalks of wheat, etc; a collection of papers tied in a bundle.

shear vt, vi (pp **sheared** or **shorn**) to clip or eat through; to remove (a sheep's fleece) by clipping; to break off.

shears npl large kind of scissors.

sheath n a close-fitting cover, esp for a blade; a condom; a straight dress.

sheathe vt to put into a sheath; to protect by a casing.

shed vt, vi (pt, pp **shed**) to cast off; to diffuse; to let fall in drops; to spill. * n a watershed; a hut; a roofed shelter.

sheen n brightness; gloss.

sheer adj mere; downright, utter; extremely steep, precipitous; delicately fine. * vi to swerve; to shy.

sheet n a broad, thin piece of anything; broad expanse; bed linen; a single piece of paper; a newspaper.

shelf n (pl **shelves**) a horizontal board fixed in position to support books, etc; a ledge.

shell n hard outer crust or case; an explosive projectile. * vt to strip of shell; to fire shells.

shellfish n an aquatic animal with a shell covering.

shelter n a protection; asylum; refuge. * vt to protect. * vi to take shelter.

shelve vt to place on a shelf; to defer consideration. * vi to slope.

shelving n shelves collectively.

shepherd n a person who looks after sheep.

sheriff n a chief law officer or judge of a county.

sherry n a fortified wine of southern Spain.

shield n a protective covering or guard; a piece of armour carried for defence on the left arm. * vt to protect; to screen.

shift vi to change; to move; to contrive; to manage. * n a change; expedient; a dodge; relay time.

shiftless adj improvident; useless; without resource.

shifty adj unreliable; changeable; tricky.

shillyshally vi to wobble; to vacillate.

shimmer vi to glisten softly. * n a flicker.

shin n the front of the lower leg.

shine vi (pt, pp **shone**) to emit light; to beam; to be bright, lively or conspicuous.

shingle n thin wood used in roofing; loose gravel. *vt to roof with shingles.

shingles n a viral disease marked by a painful rash of red spots.

shining adj bright; illustrious.

shinty n a form of hockey.

ship n a large seagoing vessel; *vt, vi to put or take on board; to transport for service in a ship; to fix in place.

shipmate n a fellow sailor.

shipment n a consignment; goods shipped.

shipper n one who exports or imports goods by sea.

shipping n ships in general; the business of transporting goods.

shipshape adj in seaman-like fashion; trim.

shipwreck n the wreck of a ship; the loss of a vessel at sea.

shipyard n a shipbuilding establishment.

shirk vt, vi to try to evade a duty.

shirt n a sleeved garment of cotton etc for the upper body.

shiver vt to shatter. * vi to tremble, as from cold; to shudder. * n a splinter; shaking fit.

shoal *n* a large number of fish swimming together.

shock *n* a violent collision; a sudden emotional disturbance; the effect of an electrical charge on the body. * *vt* to horrify; to disgust.

shocking *adj* dreadful; offensive.

shoddy *adj* made of cheap material; trashy.

shoe *n* outer covering for foot; metal plate on hoof of horse; a drag for a wheel.

shoehorn *n* a curved piece of horn (or metal) to aid in putting on shoe.

shoot *vb* (*pt*, *pp* **shot**) *vt* to discharge with force; to hit or kill with missile; to propel quickly.* *vi* to dart along; to sprout. * *n* a young branch or bud; a chute.

shooting *n* killing game; land rented to shoot over.

shop *n* a place where goods are sold by retail; a workshop. * *vi* to visit shops.

shore *n* land along edge of sea; coast; a prop. * *vt* to prop up.

short *adj* not long or tall; scanty; concise; curt; brittle. *npl* short trousers. * in short, briefly.

shortage *n* a deficit.

shortcoming *n* a defect.

shorten *vt* to make short; to reduce amount.

shorthand *n* abbreviated writing.

short-sighted *n* unable to see far; lacking foresight.

shortwave *n* a radio wave sixty metres or less in length.

shot *n* act of shooting; a projectile; a bullet; range or reach; a marksman.

shoulder *n* the joint connecting an arm, foreleg or wing to a body; a projection. * *vt* to jostle; to put on the shoulders.

shout *vi* to utter a loud cry. * *n* a loud cry.

shove *vt, vi* to push forward; to jostle. *n* a push.

shovel *n* a spade with a slightly curved blade. * *vt* (*pt* **shovelled**) to move or lift with a shovel.

show *vb* (*pp* **shown** or **showed**) *vt* to display to view; to let be seen; to prove. * *vi* to appear. * *n* display; pageant; pretence; a theatrical performance.

shower *n* a brief fall of rain, etc; a copious supply. * *vt, vi* to rain; to pour down; to bestow liberally.

showroom *n* a room in which goods are exhibited.

showy *adj* bright and attractive but not necessarily good.

shrapnel *n* an artillery shell filled with small pieces of metal that scatter on impact.

shred *vt* to tear into small pieces. * *n* a fragment or scrap.

shrew *n* a scold; a kind of mouse.

shrewd *adj* astute; clever.

shrewish *adj* given to scolding.

shriek *vi* to scream * *n* a shrill cry.

shrill *adj* piercing in sound; strident.

shrine *n* a hallowed place; an altar; a tomb.

shrink *vi* (*pt* **shrank**, *pp* **shrunk**) to contract; to shrivel; to flinch.

shrive *vt* to confess and absolve.

shrivel *vi, vt* (*pt* **shrivelled**) to shrink into wrinkles; to wither up.

shroud n a burial cloth; anything that covers or conceals.

shrub n a bush with separate stems from same root.

shrubbery n a plantation of shrubs.

shrug vt, vi to raise one's shoulders in surprise, doubt, indifference, etc.

shudder vi to tremble with fear; to quake. * n a tremor.

shuffle vt to shove one way and the other; to confuse; to mix cards. * vi to quibble; to drag one's feet. *n an evasion; a shuffling gait or step.

shuffling adj moving with irregular gait; evasive.

shun vt to avoid; to refrain from.

shunt vi, vt in railways, to switch from one track to another.

shut vt, vi (pt, pp shut) to close or stop up; to bar.

shutter n a movable screen for a window.

shuttle n a boat-shaped contrivance for shooting cross threads in loom; an aircraft, spacecraft, etc, making back-and-forth trips over a given route.

shuttlecock n a cork stuck with feathers, used in badminton.

shy adj timid; retiring; very self-conscious; coy. * vi, vt to start aside, as horse; to throw. * n a throw.

shyness n reserve; coyness.

sibilant adj hissing. * n a letter uttered with a hissing as s and z.

sic adv as written (used in text to indicate that an error or doubtful usage is reproduced from the original.

sick adj ill; disgusted; unhealthy; vomiting.

sicken vt to make sick; to disgust. * vi to become sick.

sickening adj disgusting.

sickle n a reaping hook.

sickness n disease; ill-health.

side n the broad or long surface of a body; edge, border; slope (of hill); bias (of ball). * vi to support, espouse (a cause). * adj oblique.

sideboard n a piece of furniture used to hold dining utensils, etc.

sidelong adv indirect. * adj oblique.

sidetrack vt to prevent action by diversionary tactics; to shunt aside.

sideways adv toward one side; on one side.

siding n a short line of rails for shunting purposes.

siege n the surrounding of a fortified place to cut off supplies and compel its surrender; the act of besieging; a continued attempt to gain something.

sienna n a reddish-brown pigment.

siesta n a midday nap.

sieve n a utensil with holes for straining; a person who cannot keep secrets. * vt to sift.

sift vt to separate coarser parts from finer with a sieve.

sifter n a sieve.

sigh vi to draw a deep and audible breath, as in grief, weariness or relief. * n a long and deep breath.

sight n act or power of seeing; view; visibility; estimation; a show. * vt to see.

sightless adj blind.

sightseeing n the visiting of interesting places.

sign n a mark, token, stamp, or symbol; an emblem; indication; gesture. * vt, vi to affix a signature; to make a sign.

signal n a sign to give information, orders, etc, at a distance. * adj notable. * vt, vi (pt **signalled**) to convey by signs.

signally adv remarkably; notably.

signatory n a party to the signing of a treaty or other agreement.

signature n one's name written by oneself; a printed sheet when folded before being used.

signboard n a board marked with a person's name or business.

significant adj weighty; important; highly expressive; momentous.

signify vt to make known; to mean; to imply.

silence n quiet; secrecy; stillness; absence of sound. * vt to still; to cause to be quiet.

silent adj mute; taciturn; making no noise.

silhouette n a shadow outline of a shape against light. * vt to show up in outline; to depict in silhouette.

silica n a hard mineral, a compound of oxygen and silicon, found in quartz and flint.

silicon n a nonmetallic element whose oxide is silica.

silk n the fine thread produced by silkworm; cloth made of silk.

silky adj like silk; smooth and glossy.

sill n the timber or stone at foot of window.

silly adj foolish; unwise; frivolous; being stunned or dazed.

silo n a pit or tower for storage (fodder).

silt n sediment from moving water.

silver n a ductile, malleable, precious metal of a white colour used in jewellery, cutlery, etc. * vt, vi to coat with silver.

silvering n coating with silver or quicksilver.

silversmith n a worker or dealer in silver.

silver-tongued adj persuasive; musical.

similar adj like; resembling.

similarity n likeness; resemblance.

simile n a figure of speech containing a comparison.

similitude n likeness; resemblance.

simmer vi to boil gently.

simper vi to smile in a silly manner. * n an affected smile.

simple adj not complex; single; artless; plain; silly; easy to understand or solve.

simplicity n sincerity; artlessness; innocence; folly.

simplify vt to make simple.

simulate vt to pretend to have or feel; to feign.

simulation n reproducing specific conditions or conduct.

simultaneous adj taking place at the same time.

sin n a transgression of the divine law; iniquity; a wicked act; an offence. * vi to do wrong.

since adv from that time; ago. * prep after. * conj because that.

sincere adj genuine, real, not pretended; honest; straightforward.

sincerity *n* honesty of mind; freedom from pretence.

sinecure *n* a paid office with few, if any, duties.

sinew *n* the fibrous cord which joins muscle to bone.

sinful *adj* wicked; erring.

sing *vi, vt* (*pt* **sang**, *pp* **sung**) to utter melodious sounds; to celebrate in song.

singe *vt* to burn surface. * *n* a slight burn.

single *adj* being one or a unit; individual; unmarried; sincere. * *vt* to select individually (with **out**).

singly *adv* one by one; sincerely.

singular *adj* denoting only one person or thing; remarkable; quaint; rare. * *n* singular number.

singularly *adv* peculiarly; remarkably.

sinister *adj* left; evil; malevolent; ominous.

sink *vb* (*pt* **sank**, *pp* **sunk**) *vi* to fall below surface (water); to subside; to fall in value, strength, etc. * *vt* to immerse; to dig (shaft); to degrade. * *n* a drain or receptacle to carry off dirty water.

sinking *adj* depressing, as in feeling.

sinner *n* a transgressor; offender; a person who sins.

sinuate *vt* to wind. * *adj* winding.

sinuosity *n* a wavy line; a bend.

sinuous *adj* winding; curved; tortuous.

sinus *n* an air cavity in the skull that opens in the nasal cavities.

sip *vt* to drink in small quantities. * *n* a drop; a taste.

siphon *n* a bent tube for drawing off liquids.

sir *n* a word of respect used to men; a title.

siren *n* a device producing a loud wailing sound as a warning signal; a sea nymph who lured sailors to destruction; an alluring, dangerous woman.

sirloin *n* the upper part of loin of beef.

sirocco *n* a hot wind blowing over southern Europe from the south.

sister *n* a female born of the same parents; a member of an order of nuns.

sister-in-law *n* a husband or wife's sister.

sit *vt, vi* (*pres p* **sitting**, *pt, pp* **sat**) to rest oneself on the buttocks, as on a chair, to perch (birds); to incubate; to have a seat (in Parliament); to suit; to take an examination.

site *n* situation; a building plot; the scene of something.

sitter *n* one who sits for his portrait.

sitting *n* a session, as of a court.

situated *adj* placed; located; provided with money etc.

situation *n* position; station; post.

six *adj, n* one more than five.

sixfold *adj, adv* six times.

sixteen *adj, n* six and ten.

sixteenth *adj* ordinal of sixteen.

sixth *adj* ordinal of six.

sixtieth *adj, n* ordinal of sixty.

sixty *adj, n* six times ten.

size *n* magnitude; the dimensions or proportions of something; a thin pasty glue used by painters to glaze paper, etc. * vt to arrange according to size; to cover with size.

skate n a steel bar fastened to boot for moving on ice; a coarse flat fish. * vt to go on skates.

skateboard n a short, oblong board with two wheels at each end for standing on and riding.

skein n a small hank of thread.

skeleton n the bony framework of an animal; outline.

sketch n an outline; a first rough draught quickly made. * vt to draw; to outline.

skewer n a pin for fastening meat.

ski n (pl **skis**) a long narrow runner of wood, metal or plastic that is fastened to a boot to enable movement across snow. * vi to travel on skis.

skid vt, vi to slide without rotating; to slip sideways as cycle, aeroplane, etc. * n a drag to reduce speed.

skiff n a small light boat.

skilful adj skilled; dexterous; adroit.

skill n ability; expertness; aptitude; proficiency.

skim vt to remove the scum from the surface of; to glance over (book). * vi to glide along (water).

skin n the natural outer coating of animals; a hide; rind. * vt to strip the skin from; flay.

skin-deep adj superficial.

skinflint n a mean person.

skinny adj very thin.

skip vb (pt **skipped**) vi to leap; to bound; to spring. * vt to omit. * n a light leap; a skipper; the captain of a curling or bowling team.

skipper n the captain of a ship.

skirmish n a minor fight in a war. * vi to fight when reconnoitring.

skirt n lower part of a coat; woman's garment that hangs from the waist; border. * vt, vi to border; to pass along edge.

skit n a short humorous sketch.

skittish adj excitable; frisky; fickle.

skulk vi to lurk; to keep out of sight; to shirk duty.

skull n the bony case that contains the brain, the cranium.

sky n the vault of heaven.

skylight n a window in a roof.

skyward adj, adv towards the sky.

slab n a flat piece of stone, wood, etc. * adj thick and slimy.

slack adj loose; easy-going; not busy; relaxed. * n the loose part of a rope, etc. * vt, vi to idle, be less active; to slacken.

slacken vi to become slack; * vt to relax; to reduce; to loosen.

slag n fused dross of metal, clinkers.

slake vt to quench; to mix (lime) with water.

slam vt, vi (pt **slammed**) to shut with a bang. * n a bang; the winning of 12 or 13 tricks at bridge.

slander n a false and injurious report. * vt to vilify; to defame.

slang n, adj expressions in common use but not approved as good English; jargon.

slant adj sloping. * vt, vi to slope; to incline; to tell in such a way as to have a bias.* n a slope.

slap n a blow with the open hand. * vt (pt **slapped**) to strike with the open hand.

slapdash *adv* carelessly; at random.

slash *vt, vi* to strike at wildly with knife, sword, etc; to slit, as a sleeve. * *n* a long cut; slit.

slate *n* rock which splits into thin layers; a thin roofing slab; a writing plate. * *vt* to cover with slates; to criticize harshly.

slater *n* one who slates buildings.

slating *n* the roof or roofing; harsh criticism.

slaty *adj* of or like slate.

slaughter *n* a slaying; carnage; massacre. * *vt* to slay; to kill for market.

slave *n* a person without freedom or personal rights.

slaver *n* saliva dripping from mouth. * *vt, vi* to let saliva drip; to fawn upon.

slavery *n* bondage; drudgery.

slavish *adj* servile; oppressively laborious.

slay *vt* (*pt* **slew**, *pp* **slain**) to kill by violence; to murder.

sledgehammer *n* a large, heavy hammer for two hands.

sledge *n* a vehicle on runners used over snow; a sleigh.

sleek *adj* smooth and glossy; plausible.

sleep *vi, vt* (*pt, pp* **slept**) to rest with mind and body inactive; to slumber; to lie dormant. * *n* slumber; repose; death.

sleeper *n* one who sleeps; a beam for support joists, floors, rails, etc; a sleeping car (railway).

sleepy *adj* drowsy; sluggish; not alert.

sleet *n* hail or snow mingled with rain.

sleeve *n* part of a garment enclosing arm.

sleight *n* manual dexterity; **sleight of hand** jugglery.

slender *adj* thin; slim; scanty.

slice *vt* to cut into thin pieces; a stroke that makes the ball curl to the right (golf). * *n* a thin broad piece cut off.

slide *vi, vt* (*pt, pp* **slid**) to slip or glide over surface, as ice. * *n* a slope or track for sliding on.

slight *adj* small; trifling; frail. * *n* intentional disregard. * *vt* to treat as of no account.

slim *adj* slight; slender; cunning.

slime *n* a half-liquid sticky substance; mucus.

sling *vt* (*pt, pp* **slung**) to hurl; to suspend; to place in a sling. * *n* a contrivance for hurling stones; a hanging bandage for injured limb.

slink *vt* (*pt, pp* **slunk**) to steal away.

slip *vi* to move smoothly along; to glide; to miss one's foothold; to let go (anchor); to err; to escape (memory). * *n* act of slipping; omission; error; leash; narrow strip (paper, etc); incline on which ships are built.

slipper *n* a light soft shoe for household wear.

slippery *adj* causing to slip; unreliable.

slipshod *adj* down at heels; slovenly.

slit *vi* (*pt, pp* **slit**) to cut lengthwise. * *n* a long cut or opening.

sliver *n* a splinter.

slobber *vi, vt* to drool; to run at the mouth.

slogan n a catchy phrase used in advertising or as a motto by a political party etc.

sloop n a sailing vessel with one mast.

slop vt to spill. * n unappetising; semi-liquid food; spilled water; poor liquor; (pl) dirty or waste water.

slope n a slant.* vt, vi to incline.

sloppy adj careless; untidy; slovenly.

slot n a long narrow opening; a slit. *vt to fit into a slot.

sloth n indolence; laziness; a slow-moving mammal.

slouch n to sit or move in a drooping or ungainly manner * vi, vt to move with drooping gait.

slouching adj awkward; crouching.

slough n cast skin of snake. * vi, vt to cast or come off (skin).

slovenly adj untidy; dirty; careless.

slow adj not rapid; tardy; dull; stupid.

sludge n mire; soft mud; sediment.

sluggish adj lazy; slothful; slow.

sluice n a gate for regulating flow of water in canal, etc. * vt, vi to scour with water.

slum n an overcrowded area.

slumber vi to sleep; to doze. * n a light sleep.

slump n sudden fall in value or slacking in demand. * vt to lump together; to fall heavily (shares).

slur vt to pronounce or speak indistinctly; to run together (words). * n a stain, stigma.

slush n ·sludge or soft mud; half-melted snow.

slut n a slovenly or immoral woman; a slattern.

sly adj cunning; crafty; wily.

smack vi to make a sharp noise with lips; to taste. * vt to slap. * n a loud kiss; a slap; a taste; a fishing vessel.

small adj little; petty; short; narrow-minded; mean.

small arms npl rifles, pistols, etc, as distinguished from artillery.

smallpox n a contagious disease, now rare, marked by pustules on skin.

small talk n light, social talk.

smart n a quick, keen pain. * adj keen; clever; quick; brisk; witty; spruce. * vi to feel a sharp pain.

smarten vt to make smart.

smash vt to dash or go to pieces. * n a crash; ruin; failure.

smattering n a superficial knowledge.

smear vt to daub with anything greasy.

smell vt, vi (pt, pp **smelt** or **smelled**) to perceive by the nose; to give out an odour. * n sense of smell; scent; odour.

smelt vt to melt, as ore. * n a small fish allied to salmon.

smile vi to show joy by the features of the face. * n a look of pleasure.

smirk vi to smile affectedly. * n an inane smile; simper.

smite vt, vi (pt **smote**, pp **smitten**) to strike; to slay; to afflict.

smock n a chemise; a smock frock.

smocking n a fancy stitch in sewing.

smoke n sooty vapour from burning substance; vapour; act of smoking (pipe, etc). * vi, vt to emit smoke; to use tobacco; to fumigate.

smoking n the use of tobacco. * adj emitting smoke.

smoky adj giving out smoke; filled with smoke.

smooth adj even on the surface; glossy; pleasant. * vt to make smooth; to level.

smother n to cover over quickly * vt, vi to stifle; to suffocate.

smoulder vi to burn and smoke without flame.

smudge vt to stain with dirt. * n a stain; a smear.

smug n complacent; self-satisfied.

smuggle vt to import or export secretly without paying duty.

smuggling n the importing or exporting goods without paying duty.

smut n a spot or stain; a flake of soot; obscene language.

smutty adj soiled with smut; obscene.

snack n a light meal between regular meals.

snag n a short projecting stump; a knot; a stumbling block.

snake n a limbless, scaly reptile with a long tapering body, often with salivary glands modified to produce venom.

snap vt, vi to bite or seize suddenly; to break with a sharp sound. * n a sudden bite; spring catch; sharp noise.

snapshot n a hasty shot at a moving animal; an instantaneous photograph.

snare n a running noose for catching animals; a pitfall; a trap. * vt to catch in snare; to trap.

snarl vi to growl with bared teeth, as an angry dog; to speak rudely; to become entangled. * n a growl.

snarling adj snappish; peevish.

snatch vt to seize abruptly or without permission. * vi to grasp (at). * n a sudden seizing; a small portion.

sneak vi, vt to go slyly; to steal off; to behave meanly. * n a telltale; a mean wretch.

sneer vi to show contempt by a look; to jeer. * n a scoff; a jeer.

sneeze vi to emit air violently and audibly through nose.

snick vt to cut; to clip; to snip.

sniff vi to smell; to inhale through the nose audibly.

snigger vi to giggle; to laugh in sly fashion. * n a partly suppressed laugh.

snip vt to cut off at a stroke. * n a single cut; small piece; a certainty.

snipe vt to lie in wait and pick off enemy by rifle fire.

snippet n a small part cut off; pl odds and ends.

snivelling adj whining; tearful.

snob n a person who wishes to be associated with those of a higher social status, whilst acting condescendingly to those whom he or she regards as inferior.

snooze n a short sleep. * vi to take a short nap.

snore vi to breathe noisily in sleep; noisy breathing in sleep.

snorkel n a breathing tube extending above the water, used in swimming just below the surface. * vi (pt **snorkelled**) to swim using a snorkel.

snort vi to eject air violently through nose, as horses. * n an explosive breath sound.

snout n an animal's nose or muzzle.

snow n vapour frozen in the air and falling in flakes.

snowball n a ball of snow pressed together for throwing.

snowboard n a board shaped like a large ski which a person can stand on to slide across snow.

snowdrift n a bank of drifted snow.

snowdrop n an early spring flower.

snowplough n an implement for clearing snow from roads.

snub vt (pt **snubbed**) to humiliate with words or a look; to slight. * n a check; rebuke.

snuff vt, vi to sniff; to smell; to take snuff; to crop or trim (wick). * n charred part of wick; powdered tobacco.

snuffle vi to speak through the nose. * n a nasal twang; cant; pl cold in the head.

snug adj neat; trim; cosy.

snuggle vi to lie close for warmth; to nestle.

so adv in this or that manner; to that degree; thus; very. * conj provided that; therefore.

soak vt, vi to become saturated; to wet thoroughly.

soap n a compound of fat with an alkali, used in washing; (inf) a soap opera. * vt to rub with soap.

soap opera n (inf) a daytime radio or television serial melodrama

soar vi to fly upwards; to tower.

sob vi to weep convulsively. * n a short choking sigh.

sober adj temperate; not drunk; staid; grave; thoughtful.

sobriety n temperance; saneness; gravity.

sobriquet n a nickname.

soccer n a football game played on a field by two teams of 11 players with a round inflated ball.

sociable adj fond of companions; social.

social adj living or organized in a community, not solitary; genial; affable.

socialism n a theory of social organization aiming at cooperative action and the nationalization of capital and land.

socialist n one who advocates socialism.

social security n financial assistance for the unemployed, disabled, etc, to alleviate economic distress.

society n the social relationship between human beings or animals organized collectively.

sociologist n one versed in social science.

sociology n the science of the history, nature, etc, of human society; social science.

sock n a short stocking covering the foot and lower leg.

socket n a cavity into which anything is fitted.

sod n small square piece of turf.

soda n the alkali, carbonate of sodium.

sodden adj saturated; soaked and soft.

sofa n a couch with cushioned seat, back, and arms.

soft adj yielding easily to pressure;

delicate; smooth; not harsh; quiet.

soften vt, vi to make or become soft; to tone down; to melt; to relent.

softly adv gently; tenderly.

soil vt, vi to make dirty; to tarnish. * n dirt; top layer of earth; mould; country.

sojourn vi to reside for a time. * n a temporary stay.

solace vt to cheer or console. * n consolation; comfort.

solar adj pertaining to or proceeding from sun; sunny.

solder vt to unite metals by a metal alloy. *n an alloy capable when fused of cementing metals together.

soldier n a person in military service.

sole n the under side of the foot; the bottom of a shoe; a flatfish. * vt to furnish with a sole. * adj single; only; alone.

solecism n a grammatical error; a breach of rules of syntax.

solely adv singly; alone; only.

solemn adj grave; formal; impressive; awe inspiring.

solemnity n gravity; a solemn ceremony.

solicit vt, vi to ask earnestly; to invite.

solicitation n supplication; entreaty.

solicitor n a lawyer.

solicitous adj anxious; very concerned.

solid adj resisting pressure; not liquid or gaseous; not hollow; compact; firm; strongly constructed. * n a compact body.

solidarity n unity of interest and action.

solidity n density; firmness.

soliloquy n the act of talking to oneself.

solitaire n a gem in a single setting; a stud; a game for one player.

solitary adj being alone; lonely; not frequented. * n a recluse.

solitude n loneliness; a lonely place.

solo n a tune or air for a single performer. * vi to perform by oneself.

soloist n a solo singer or performer.

solstice n the time when the sun is farthest north or south of equator, 21st June and 21st Dec. respectively.

solubility n quality of being soluble.

soluble adj capable of being dissolved in a fluid; capable of solution, as a problem.

solution n the dissolving of a solid in a liquid; explanation; result.

solve vt to explain; to make clear; to unravel.

solvency n ability to pay debts.

solvent adj having the power of dissolving; able to pay all debts. * n a fluid that dissolves another substance.

sombre adj dark; gloomy; dismal.

some adj an indefinite number; considerable; more or less. * pron an indefinite part, quantity, or number; certain individuals.

somebody n some person; a person of importance.

somehow adv one way or another.

somersault n a leap in which the heels turn over the head.

something n a thing unspecified; part or portion. * adv to some degree.

sometime adv once; by and by. * adj former.

sometimes adv now and then; at times.

somewhat n more or less. * adv in some degree.

somewhere adv in some place.

somnambulism n the act of walking in sleep.

somnolence n sleepiness.

somnolent adj sleepy; drowsy.

son n a male child or descendant.

song n that which is sung; vocal music; a lyric; the call of certain birds.

sonic adj of, producing or involving sound waves.

son-in-law n a daughter's husband.

sonnet n a poem of fourteen pentameter lines with varying rhymes.

sonorous adj resonant; deep-toned.

soon adv in a short time; quickly; readily.

soot n a black substance formed from burning matter.

sooth adj true. * n truth; reality.

soothe vt to calm; to comfort; to relieve pain.

soothsayer n one who foretells the future.

sop n something dipped in broth or liquid food; bribe given to pacify.

sophism n false reasoning but with appearance of truth.

soporific adj causing sleep. * n a drug that induces sleep.

soprano n the highest female voice; a singer with such a voice.

sorcerer n a wizard; a person who uses magic powers.

sorceress n a female sorcerer.

sorcery n magic; enchantment; witchcraft.

sordid adj mean; vile; base; squalid.

sore adj painful; tender. * n an ulcer, wound, etc.

sorely adv seriously; grievously.

sorrow n grief; distress of mind; sadness; regret. * vi to grieve.

sorrowful adj full of sorrow.

sorry adj feeling sorrow or pity; grieved; wretched.

sort n nature or character; kind; species; a set. * vt to arrange in order; to sort.

soufflé n a light dish of baked egg whites.

soul n the spiritual element in man; conscience; essence; a person.

sound adj whole; firm; healthy; orthodox; just. * n a narrow channel of water; a strait; that which is heard; noise. * vt, vi to measure the depth of; to examine medically; to try to discover the opinion, etc, of; to make a noise; to probe; to pronounce; to be spread or published.

sounding adj resounding. * n the ascertaining depth of water.

soundings npl the depths of water in rivers, harbours, etc.

soundtrack n the sound accompanying a film; the area on cinema film that carries the sound recording.

soup n a kind of broth.

sour adj acid to the taste; tart; peevish; distasteful or unpleasant. * vt to make sour; to embitter.

source n that from which anything rises; the fountainhead; origin.

souse vt to pickle; to immerse.

south n one of four compass points; position of sun at noon. * adj being in or toward the south.

southeast n the point midway between south and east. * adj pertaining to or from the southeast.

southerly adj lying toward the south; coming from the south.

southern adj belonging to the south; southerly.

southward adv, adj toward the south.

southwest n the point midway between south and west. * adj pertaining to or from the southwest.

souvenir n a keepsake; a memento.

sovereign adj supreme in power; chief * n a monarch; a ruler.

sovereignty n supreme power; dominion.

sow¹ vt, vi vb (pp **sown** or **sowed**) to scatter seed over; to spread abroad.

sow² n an adult female pig.

spa n a resort for medicinal water.

space n the limitless three-dimensional expanse within which all objects exist; outer space; a specific area; an interval; empty area; room; an unoccupied area or seat. *vt to arrange at intervals.

spacious adj roomy; capacious.

spade n an instrument for digging; one of the suits of cards.

span n reach or space from thumb to extended little finger; nine inches; short space of time; spread of arch. * vt to extend across; to measure with the fingers extended.

spank vt to slap with the flat of the hand, esp on the buttocks.

spanner n a tool with a hole or jaws to grip and turn nuts or bolts.

spar n a long piece of timber; a pole; a crystalline mineral; boxing match. * vi to box; to bandy words.

spare adj scanty; thin; held in reserve. * vt, vi to use frugally; to dispense with; to be saving; to forbear; to have mercy on.

sparing adj frugal; economical.

spark n a particle of burning matter; a flash of light from an electrical discharge. * vi to emit fiery particles.

sparkle n a little spark; lustre. * vi to emit sparks; to glitter.

sparkling adj glittering; lively.

sparse adj thinly scattered; scanty.

spartan adj rigorously severe.

spasm n a violent contraction of muscles; a convulsive fit.

spasmodic adj intermittently.

spastic n a person who suffers from cerebral palsy. *adj affected by muscle spasm.

spate n a sudden heavy flood; a large amount.

spatial adj pertaining to space.

spatter vt to scatter a liquid on; to sprinkle.

spatula n a broad thin blade, used in spreading plasters, paints, etc.

spawn n the eggs or ova of fish, etc. * vt, vi to deposit spawn.

speak vi, vt vb (pt **spoke**, pp **spoken**) to utter words; to talk; to deliver a speech; to pronounce.

speaker n one who speaks; the presiding official in a legislative assembly.

spear n a long, pointed weapon; a

lance. * vt to pierce with a spear.

special adj particular; distinctive; uncommon.

specialist n one who concentrates on a particular subject; an expert.

speciality n special characteristic; something made or sold exclusively by certain traders; a special pursuit; a special product.

specialize vt, vi to apply one's self to a particular subject.

species n sing, pl a kind, sort, or variety; a class of plants or animals; subdivision of a genus.

specific adj pertaining to a species; definite; precise. * n a remedy for a special disease; a sure remedy.

specifically adv definitely; precisely.

specification n a requirement; detailed statement of particulars for carrying out contracts, etc.

specify vt to make specific; to state in detail.

specimen n a sample; a part to typify the whole.

specious adj superficially correct; plausible.

speck n a small spot; a flaw; a particle.

speckled adj spotted.

spectacle n a show; an exhibition; a pageant; pl glasses to assist vision.

spectacular adj impressive; astounding.

spectator n an onlooker.

spectral adj shadowy; ghostly.

spectre n an apparition; a ghost.

spectroscope n the instrument employed in decomposition of rays of light.

spectrum n (pl **spectra**) the coloured bands produced by passing light through a prism.

speculate vi to theorize; to conjecture; to gamble in stocks, land, etc.

speculation n act of speculating; theory; hazardous financial transactions.

speculative adj risky; contemplative.

speculator n one who takes undue risks in business.

speech n the faculty of speaking; language; talk; a formal discourse; oration.

speechless adj silent; unable to speak.

speed n success; velocity; haste. * vi (pt, pp **sped**) to make haste; to prosper; to fare. * vt (pt, pp **speeded**) to drive (a vehicle) at an illegally high speed.

speedometer n indicator for showing speed of motors, cycles, etc.

spell n a charm; fascination; a period of · work. * vt (pt, pp **spelt** or **spelled**) to give in correct order the letters of words.

spend vt, vi (pt, pp **spent**) to pay out, as money; to squander; to pass, as time; to exhaust of force.

spendthrift n, adj a prodigal; wasteful.

spent adj wearied; exhausted.

sperm n semen; the male reproductive cell.

spew vt, vi to vomit; to flow or gush forth.

sphere n an orb; a ball; a sun, star, or planet; extent of motion, action, etc.

spheric, spherical *adj* globular.

spheroid *n* a body like a sphere, as earth, orange, etc.

sphincter *n* a ring-like muscle closing an opening an orifice.

sphinx *n* a fabled monster, half human, half lion.

spicate *adj* spiked; pointed.

spice *n* an aromatic seasoning for food; relish; flavour. * *vt* to flavour; to season.

spicy *adj* pungent; piquant; racy.

spider *n* a small wingless creature (arachnid) with eight legs, and abdominal spinnerets for spinning silk threads to make webs.

spike *n* a piece of pointed iron; an ear of corn, etc. * *vt* to fasten with spikes; to transfix; to plug a hole (cannon).

spill *vt, vi* (*pt, pp* **spilt** *or* **spilled**) to let run out or overflow; to shed. * *n* a piece of wood or twisted paper for lighting candle, etc; a fall.

spin *vt, vi* (*pres p* **spinning**, *pt* **span**, *pp* **spun**) to draw out and twist into threads; to protract; to whirl; to rotate swiftly. * *n* a rapid run.

spinach *n* a plant with large green edible leaves

spinal *adj* pertaining to the spine.

spinal cord *n* the cord of nerves enclosed by the spinal column.

spindle *n* a tapering rod on which thread is wound; an axis; a yarn measure; a slender stalk.

spine *n* a prickle; a pointed spike in animals; the backbone.

spinnaker *n* a triangular sail used in running before wind.

spinster *n* an unmarried woman.

spiral *adj* winding like thread of screw. * *n* a helix or coil.

spirally *adv* in spiral fashion.

spire *n* a cone-like structure; a steeple.

spirit *n* the breath of life; the soul; a spectre; vivacity; courage; mood; essence; a volatile liquid; *pl* alcoholic liquor.

spirited *adj* lively; animated.

spiritless *adj* dejected; depressed.

spirit level *n* an instrument for testing when a thing is horizontal.

spiritual *adj* not material; mental; holy; divine.

spiritualism *n* the doctrine that soul, spirit, is only reality; belief that communication can be obtained with the dead.

spiritualist *n* one who believes in spiritualism.

spirituality *n* quality of being spiritual; spiritual nature.

spit *vt, vi* (*pres p* **spitting**, *pt, pp* **spat**) to eject from the mouth, as saliva.

spit *n* a prong on which meat is roasted; low land running into the sea. * *vt* (*pt* **spitted**) to put on a spit; to pierce.

spite *n* ill-will; rancour; malice.

spiteful *adj* malignant; malicious.

spittle *n* saliva.

spittoon *n* a vessel to receive discharges of spittle.

splash *vt, vi* to bespatter with liquid matter. * *n* water or mud thrown on anything; noise of heavy body striking water; a spot of mud.

splay *vt* to slope or form with an angle. * *adj* turned outward, as a person's feet.

spleen *n* a large lymphatic organ in the upper left part of the abdomen which modifies the blood structure; spitefulness; ill humour.

splendid *adj* brilliant; showy; famous.

splendour *n* brilliancy; magnificence; grandeur.

splenetic *adj* morose; sullen; spiteful.

splice *vt* to unite, by interweaving, as ropes, or overlapping, as timber. * *n* union by interweaving or joining.

splint *n* a rigid structure to keep a broken limb in position.

splinter *n* a piece of wood split off * *vt* to split into small pieces.

split *vt, vi vb* (*pt, pp* **split**) to cleave; to rend; to burst; to separate. * *n* a rent; fissure; breach. * *adj* divided; rent.

splutter *n* a confused noise; a stir. * *vi* to speak incoherently; to spit when speaking.

spoil *n* pillage; booty; plunder. * *vb* (*pt, pp* **spoilt** *or* **spoiled**) *vt* to plunder; to impair; to over indulge a child. * *vi* to grow useless; to decay.

spoke *n* one of bars or rays of a wheel; rung (of ladder). * *vi pt* of speak.

spoken *adj* oral; speaking (as in fairspoken).

spokesman *n* one who speaks on behalf of others.

sponge *n* a plant-like marine animal with an internal skeleton of elastic interlacing horny fibres; a piece of natural or man-made sponge for washing or cleaning. * *vt* to wipe with a sponge. * *vi* (*inf*) to scrounge.

sponger *n* one who lives on others; a parasite.

sponsor *n* a person or organization that pays the expenses connected with an artistic production or sports event in return for advertising; in US, a business firm, etc that pays for a radio or TV programme advertising its product. * *vt* to act as sponsor for.

spontaneity *n* voluntary action; readiness.

spontaneous *adj* arising naturally; instinctive.

spook *n* a ghost; an apparition. * *vt* to frighten.

spool *n* a reel, esp to wind thread or yarn on.

spoon *n* a domestic utensil used in feeding or cooking.

spoor *n* the track or trail of an animal.

sporadic *adj* scattered; occurring here and there.

spore *n* the reproductive body of a flowerless plant.

sport *n* a game; good humoured joking; out-of-door recreation; jest. * *vt, vi* to play; to trifle; to wear publicly.

sporting *adj* indulging in sport; belonging to sport.

spot *n* a speck, a blemish; a flaw; a locality. * *vt* to stain; to note.

spotless *adj* blameless; stainless.

spouse 329 **square**

spouse *n* a husband or wife.

spout *n* a nozzle; projecting mouth of a vessel; a waterspout. * *vt, vi* to gush forth; to mouth one's words.

sprain *vt* to twist or tear, as muscles or ligaments of a joint. * *n* a violent strain of a joint.

sprawl *vi* to spread the limbs untidily.

spray *n* a twig; collection of small branches; windblown water. * *vt* to sprinkle with a fluid.

spread *vt, vi vb* (*pt, pp* **spread**) to stretch or expand; to distribute; to apply a coating; to emit; to diffuse. * *n* extent; a meal or banquet.

spree *n* a merry frolic; a carousal.

sprig *n* a small shoot or spray; a twig with leaves on it.

sprightly *adj* lively; gay.

spring *vb* (*pt* **sprang**, *pp* **sprung**) *vi* to leap; to start up; to dart; to warp. * *vt* to cease to operate suddenly; to start or rouse. * *n* a leap; resilience; elastic spiral; an issue of water; source of supply; season of the year.

springboard *n* an flexible board used in vaulting, etc.

spring-clean *vi* to clean (a house, etc) thoroughly.

sprinkle *vt, vi* to scatter in small drops.

sprint *n* a short foot race; a spurt. * *vi* to go at top speed.

sprit *n* a small spar to extend and raise sail.

sprite *n* a spirit; a goblin; a dainty person.

sprout *vi* to bud; to push out new shoots. * *n* a shoot of a plant; *pl* Brussels sprouts.

spruce *adj* neat; trim. * *n* a pine tree yielding valuable timber.

spry *adj* nimble; active; lively.

spume *n* froth; foam; surf. * *vi* to froth.

spur *n* a goad or rowel worn on horsemen's heels; a stimulus; an incentive; an outgrowth; a ridge running off from a main range. * *vt* to prick with a spur; to incite.

spurious *adj* counterfeit; false.

spurn *vt* to drive away, as with the foot; to reject or treat with disdain.

spurred *adj* wearing spurs.

spurt *vt, vi* to spirt; to exert one's whole strength (in a race). * *n* a gush of liquid; a special effort.

sputter *vi* to emit saliva in speaking; to speak hastily and indistinctly.

sputum *n* spittle.

spy *vt* to gain sight of; to explore. * *vi* to pry. * *n* a secret agent; an informer.

squabble *vi* to wrangle; to quarrel noisily. * *n* a scuffle; a brawl.

squad *n* a small group of soldiers.

squadron *n* a unit of cavalry or of a fleet.

squalid *adj* sordid; wretched; dirty.

squall *vi* to scream loudly. * *n* a loud scream; a violent gust of wind.

squalor *n* wretchedness; foulness.

squander *vt* to spend lavishly; to waste.

square *adj* having four equal sides and four right angles; forming a right angle; just; honest. * *n* a parallelogram having four equal sides and right angles; an area with houses in form of square; an instrument for drawing right angles; product of a number multiplied by itself * vt, vi to make square; to adjust; to settle (accounts); to suit.

squash vt to crush; to beat into pulp.

squat vi to crouch down on the heels; to crouch; to settle on land without authority.

squatter n one who settles on land or property without a title.

squawk vi to cry with a harsh voice; as of a bird.

squeak vi to utter a high pitched sound. * n a high pitched sound.

squeal vi to cry with a sharp, shrill voice. * n a shrill, sharp cry.

squeamish adj easily made sick or feeling sick; easily shocked or upset.

squeeze vt to subject to pressure; to hug. * vi to press; to crowd. * n pressure; an embrace.

squint adj looking obliquely. * n a oblique look. * vi to half close or cross the eyes.

squire n an attendant on a knight; a country gentleman. * vt to escort.

squirm vi to wriggle; to writhe.

squirrel n a rodent with a long bushy tail.

squirt vt to throw out in jets. * vi to spirt. * n a syringe; a jet.

stab vt, vi to pierce with a pointed weapon; to pain suddenly and sharply. * n a thrust with dagger, etc; a secret injury.

stability n steadiness; firmness.

stable adj firm; steadfast. * n a build-

ing for horses, etc * vt to put or keep in a stable.

stabling n accommodation for horses.

staccato adj in music, a sign for separate emphasis on each note.

stack n a large, regularly built pile of hay, records, papers, etc; a chimney head; a tall chimney. * vt to pile together.

stadium n an arena.

staff n (pl **staves, staffs**) a stick or rod; a prop or support; a baton; the five parallel lines on which musical notes are written; the officers assisting generals, etc; in any body of assistants, e.g. in schools.

stag n a full grown male deer.

stage n a raised platform, esp for actors; a theatre; a halting place; distance between two halting places; field of action; degree of progress. * vt to put on the stage.

stagger vi, vt to reel; to totter; to amaze. * n a lurch; an involuntary swaying of body.

staging n scaffolding.

stagnant adj not flowing; motionless; with a foul smell; sluggish.

stagnate vi to cease to flow; to become foul.

stagnation n state of being motionless; sluggishness.

staid adj sober; grave; sedate.

stain vt to discolour; to soil; to disgrace; to dye. * n a discoloration; disgrace.

stainless adj untarnished; pure.

stair n a series of connected steps.

staircase n a flight of stairs with bannisters.

stake n a sharpened piece of wood; a post; that which is pledged or wagered; (*preceded by* **at**) hazard. * vt to mark with stakes; to pledge; to wager.

stalactite n a mass of calcareous matter hanging from roof of cave.

stalagmite n a spike-like calcareous mass rising from floor of cave.

stale adj not fresh; musty; trite. * vt to make stale.

stalemate n a draw in chess through one player not being able to make any move except one that puts his king in check; a deadlock.

stalk n the stem of a plant; a strut. * vi, vt to walk in stately fashion; to follow game warily; to follow a person obsessively.

stalker n one who stalks deer or a person.

stall n a compartment in a stable; a bench or shed where goods are exposed for sale; a seat near the orchestra in a theatre; a seat in the chancel or choir of a church. *vt, vi to play for time; to postpone.

stallion n a male horse for breeding purposes.

stalwart adj stout-hearted; tall and strong.

stamen n the organ of flower that produces pollen.

stamina n staying power; strength.

stammer vi, vt to stutter; to halt in speech. * n a stutter.

stamp vt, vi to strike by thrusting foot a down; to impress; to imprint; to affix a postage stamp to; to coin. * n an instrument for crushing or making impressions; the mark imprinted; a postage stamp; character; sort.

stampede n· a sudden panicky rush (esp of cattle). * vi, vt to make or cause a sudden rush.

stance n posture; the attitude taken in a particular situation.

stanchion n a supporting prop or post.

stand vi, vt vb (pt, pp **stood**) to be erect; to stop; to endure; to be on end; to become a candidate; not to fail; to pay for. * n a halt; a station; a small table; a booth for exhibiting; a tiered platform for spectators.

standard n a flag; an ensign; a rule or measure; a test; a grade; an upright.

stand-in n a substitute.

standing adj upright; erect; permanent; stagnant. * n rank; position.

standpoint n point of view; opinion.

stanza n a verse or connected number of lines of poetry.

staple n a principle commodity of trade or industry of a region, etc; a main constituent; a U-shaped thin piece of wire for fastening. *vt to fasten with a staple.

star n a celestial body other than the sun or moon; a figure with radiating points; a badge of honour; an asterisk (*); an outstanding artiste. * vt to adorn with stars. * vi to shine as a star; to be pre-eminent.

starboard n, adj the right-hand side of a ship.

starch n a vegetable substance, employed for stiffening linen, etc.

starchy *adj* stiffened with starch; precise; formal.

stare *vi* to look fixedly. * *vt* to affect or abash by staring. * *n* a fixed look.

stargazer *n* an astronomer; an astrologer.

stark *adj* bare; plain; blunt. * *adv* wholly.

starless *adj* having no stars visible.

starlight *n* the light from the stars.

starry *adj* abounding with stars; like stars.

start *vi, vt* to spring up; to set out; to begin; to wince; to startle. * *n* a sudden movement; a jump; a handicap; outset.

starter *n* a device for starting motor engine; one who gives signal for setting off; the first course in a meal.

startle *vi* to move suddenly. * *vt* to frighten.

startling *adj* surprising; alarming.

starvation *n* state of being starved.

starve *vi* to suffer or die through lack of food. *vt* deprive (a person) of food; to deprive (of) anything necessary.

state *n* condition; situation; rank; pomp; a nation; civil power. * *adj* national; public. * *vt* to narrate.

statecraft *n* skill in managing affairs of state.

stated *adj* fixed; regular.

stately *adj* imposing; dignified; lofty.

statement *n* something stated; narrative.

statesman *n* a well-known and experienced politician.

static *adj* fixed; stationary; at rest. * *n* electrical interference causing noise on radio or television.

station *n* position; situation; rank; class; a stopping place for trains etc. * *vt* to assign a position to.

stationary *adj* fixed; not moving.

stationery *n* writing materials, esp paper.

statistic *n* a fact expressed in numbers.

statistician *n* one versed in statistics.

statue *n* an image of a human figure or animal moulded in marble, bronze, etc.

statuesque *n* statue-like.

statuette *n* a small statue.

stature *n* height; tallness.

status *n* social position; rank; state of affairs.

statute *n* a law enacted by parliament.

statutory *n* enacted by statute.

staunch *adj* loyal, dependable. * *vt* to stop from running (as blood).

stave *n* a pole; one of segments in side of cask; a stanza; in music, the staff. * *vb* (*pt, pp* **stove** *or* **staved**) *vt* to make a hole in. * *vi* to stave off, to put off; to delay.

stay *vt* to prop; to stop; to delay; * *vt* to remain; to reside. * *n* sojourn; stop; obstacle; a prop; support; in place.

steadfast *adj* firm; constant; resolute.

steady *adj* firm; constant; regular. * *vt* to make or keep firm.

steak *n* a slice of beef or fish for grilling or frying.

steal vt, vi (pt **stole**, pp **stolen**) to gain secretly; to take from someone dishonestly.

stealth n a manner of moving quietly and secretly.

steam n the vapour of boiling water; energy. * vt, vi to emit steam; to expose to steam.

steamy adj damp; misty; full of condensation.

steel n iron hardened by addition of carbon; a knife sharpener; sternness. * adj made of steel; hard. * vt to harden; to temper.

steep adj sloping greatly; precipitous. * n a cliff. * vt to soak.

steepen vi to become steep.

steeple n a spire; a pointed tower, usu of a church.

steeplechase n a race over obstacles, esp cross-country.

steer vt, vi to direct and govern, as a ship; to guide. * n a young ox, a bullock.

stellar adj pertaining to stars, starry.

stem n the stalk of a tree, shrub, etc; stock of a family; the prow of a vessel. * vt (pt **stemmed**) to dam up; to check.

stench n a foul smell.

stencil n a thin plate with a pattern cut through it, used for marking surface beneath. * vt to paint by means of a stencil.

stenographer n one who is skilled at writing in shorthand.

stentorian adj loud-voiced.

step vi to walk. * vt to measure by steps; to fix a mast. * n a pace; a grade; a degree; a rise; footprint;

rung of ladder. * prefix related by remarriage of a spouse or partner.

stepladder n a portable self-supporting ladder.

stepping stone n a stone to raise the feet above a stream or mud; a means of advancement.

stereo n a hi-fi or record player with two loudspeakers; stereophonic sound. * adj stereophonic.

stereophonic adj (of a sound reproduction system) using two separate channels for recording and transmission to create a spatial effect.

stereotype n a fixed general image of a person or thing shared by many people.

sterile adj barren; unfruitful; free from bacteria.

sterility n barrenness; unfruitfulness; freedom from bacteria.

sterilize vt to make sterile; to rid of bacteria by boiling, etc.

sterling adj genuine; pure; denoting standard British money.

stern adj austere; harsh. * n the hind part of a ship.

sternum n the breastbone.

stertorous adj marked by laboured and noisy breathing.

stethoscope n an instrument for sounding the chest, lungs, etc.

stevedore n one who loads or unloads vessels.

stew vt to boil slowly in a closed vessel. * vi to be cooked slowly. * n meat stewed; state of anxiety.

steward m, **stewardess** f n one who manages affairs for another; one who helps to manage a public function; an attendant on ship or aeroplane passengers.

stick vt, vi (pt, pp **stuck**) to pierce or stab; to fasten; to fix; to adhere. * n a rod or wand; a staff.

stickler n a person who is scrupulous or obstinate about something.

sticky adj adhesive; gluey.

stiff adj rigid; formal in manner; stubborn; difficult; not flexible or supple.

stiffening n substance used to make anything stiff.

stifle vt, vi to suffocate; to suppress; to smother.

stigma n (pl **stigmas** or **stigmata**) a mark or brand; a mark of infamy; top of pistil of a flower.

stigmatize vt to hold up to reproach.

stiletto n a small dagger; a pointed instrument for making eyelet holes; a shoe with a long pointed heel.

still adj at rest; calm; silent; not carbonated. * vt to make still; to appease or allay. * adv to this time; yet * n a distilling apparatus.

stillborn adj dead at birth.

still life n a painting of inanimate objects such as fruits, flowers, etc; objects without life.

stilt n either of a pair of poles, with a rest for the foot on which one can walk.

stilted adj pompous; unnaturally formal.

stimulant adj energizing. * n a drug that increases energy for a time; an intoxicant.

stimulate vt to rouse up; to incite; to spur on.

stimulating adj rousing; invigorating.

stimulus n (pl **stimuli**) an incentive to action; a spur; a response in a living organism.

sting vt (pt, pp **stung**) to pierce, as wasps; to prick, as a nettle. * n a sharp-pointed defensive organ of certain animals; secreting poison (plants); any acute mental or physical pain.

stinging adj sharp; keen; painful.

stingy adj very mean; scanty.

stink vi (pt **stank**, pp **stunk**) to emit a strong offensive smell. * n a foul smell.

stint vt to restrict. * vi to cease. * n limit; restriction.

stipend n yearly allowance; salary.

stipple vt to engrave by means of dots.

stipulate vi to specify as terms of an agreement.

stipulation n a condition; item in a contract.

stir vt to set in motion; to agitate; to rouse. * vi to be in motion; to be up and doing. * n bustle; noise.

stirring adj rousing; exciting.

stirrup n a foot support in riding.

stitch n a sharp pain; movement of a needle in sewing. * vt, vi to join by stitches.

stoat n a kind of weasel, valuable for its fur.

stock adj a post; stem of a tree; wooden piece of a rifle; lineage; capital; shares in state funds; goods in hand; cattle; a thick gravy for soups; a garden plant; (pl) an old instrument of torture for offenders; shares; frame on which a ship is built. * *adj* standing; permanent.

stockade *n* an area fenced round for protection; an enclosure.

stockbroker *n* one who deals in stocks and shares.

stockbroking *n* the business of a stockbroker.

stockholder *n* an owner of shares.

stocking *n* a close-fitting covering for foot and leg.

stock market, stock exchange *n* place where shares are bought and sold.

stockpile *n* a reserve supply of essentials.

stocktaking *n* a periodical valuation of goods in a shop, etc.

stodgy *adj* damp; heavy; indigestible.

stoic *n* one indifferent to pleasure or pain; one imperturbable and serene whatever fortune brings.

stoicism *n* impassiveness; serenity of spirit.

stoke *vt* to stir and keep supplied with fuel, as a fire.

stole *n* a vestment worn round neck and with hanging ends.

stolid *adj* dull; unresponsive.

stomach *n* the principal organ of digestion; appetite.

stone *n* a hard mass of earthy or mineral matter; a pebble; a concretion in the kidneys or bladder; the nut of a fruit; a measure of 14 pounds/6.35 kilograms. * *vt* to pelt with stones; to free from stones.

stony *adj* abounding in or like stone; hard; frigid; unfeeling.

stool *n* a portable seat, without a back, for one person; matter evacuated from the bowels.

stoop *vi* to bend forward and downward; to yield; to condescend. * *n* a downward bend of body; a veranda; a flagon.

stop *vt, vi* to halt; to hinder or check; to suspend; to close up; to stay; * *n* pause; punctuation mark; device for regulating musical sounds.

stopcock *n* a tap to regulate flow of water, gas, etc.

stopgap *n* a temporary expedient.

stoppage *n* a halt.

stopper *n* that which closes a small vent or hole.

stopwatch *n* a watch that can be started and stopped instantaneously.

storage *n* act of storing; charge for storing goods; the storage of goods in a computer memory.

store *n* a large quantity for supply; a warehouse; abundance. * *vt* to amass; to hoard up.

storeroom *n* a room for reception of stores.

storey *n* a floor of a building, also story.

stork *n* a large heron-like bird.

storm *n* a heavy fall of rain, snow etc with strong winds; tempest; a tumult. * *vt, vi* to assail; to take by assault; to rage.

stormy *adj* tempestuous; violent.

story *n* a narrative; a tale; a fiction; a falsehood.

stout *adj* bold; valiant; corpulent. * *n* a dark-brown malt liquor.

stove *n* an apparatus for warming a room, cooking, etc.

stow *vt* to store; to pack closely.

stowaway *n* one who hides himself on a ship to avoid paying the fare.

straddle *vt* to have one leg or support on either side of something.

straggle *vi* to stray; to be scattered.

straggler *n* one who wanders from main body; a laggard.

straight *adj* continuing in one direction, not curved or bent; not crooked; upright.

straighten *vt* to make straight.

straightforward *adj* honest; open.

strain *vt, vi* to stretch tightly; to exert to the utmost; to sprain; to filter. * *n* violent effort; tenor; theme; a poem; tune; race.

strained *adj* overstretched; forced or unnatural.

strainer *n* a filter or sieve.

strait *adj* confined; narrow; strict. * *n* a narrow passage of water; distress (often *pl*).

straiten *vt* to make narrow; to embarrass; to distress.

straitjacket *n* a strong garment used to bind the arms of violent people to their bodies.

strait-laced *adj* puritanical; strict in morals.

strand *n* the shore, beach; a single piece of thread or wire twisted to make a rope, etc. * *vt, vi* to drive or be driven ashore; to leave helpless without transport or money.

strange *adj* foreign; wonderful; odd.

stranger *n* a foreigner; an alien; a visitor.

strangle *vt* to choke; to throttle.

strangulate *vt* to strangle; to stop circulation by pressure.

strangulation *n* compression of the windpipe; constriction.

strap *n* a narrow band of leather, metal, etc; a razor strop. * *vt* to fasten with a strap.

strapping *adj* tall and well made.

stratagem *n* a device or plan to deceive an enemy; a ruse.

strategic, strategical *adj* pertaining to strategy.

strategy *n* the planning and conduct of war; a political, economic, or business policy.

stratification *n* arrangement in layers.

stratify *vt* to form or deposit in strata.

stratum *n* (*pl* **strata**) a layer of rock, earth, etc.

stratus *n* a low horizontal layer of clouds.

straw *n* the stalk of threshed grain, pulse, etc.

stray *vi* to wander; to err. * *adj* strayed; straggling.

streak *n* a long mark of contrasting colour; a stripe. * *vt* to mark with streaks.

stream *n* a small river or brook; a current. * *vi, vt* to move in a stream; issue forth.

streamer *n* a banner; a long decorative ribbon.

streamline *vt* to shape (a car, boat, etc) in a way that lessens resistance through air or water; to make more efficient; to simplify.

street *n* a road in a town, village or city lined with trees.

strength *n* force or energy; power; numbers of an army, fleet, etc. * On the strength of, in reliance upon.

strenuous *adj* earnest; energetic; vigorous.

stress *vt* to emphasize. * *n* pressure; mental or physical tension; emphasis.

stretch *vt, vi* to draw out tight; to extend; to strain; to exaggerate. * *n* strain; scope; expanse.

stretcher *n* a portable frame for carrying sick or wounded.

strew *vt vb* (*pp* **strewed** *or* **strewn**) to spread by scattering; to scatter loosely.

stricken *adj* suffering from an illness; afflicted, as by something painful.

strickle *n* a hone; a grindstone.

strict *adj* rigid in enforcing rules; exact; severe.

stricture *n* an unnatural contraction of throat, intestines, etc; censure.

stride *vi* (*pt* **strode**, *pp* **stridden**) to walk with long steps. * *n* a long step.

strident *adj* harsh; grating.

strife *n* conflict; discord; quarrel.

strike *vb* (*pt, pp* **struck**) *vi* to hit with force; to sound (clock); to cease work to enforce a demand for better conditions. * *vt* to smite; to mint; to come sharply against; to lower (flag); to take down (tent). * *n* a cessation of work; a military attack.

striking *adj* surprising; impressive.

string *n* a slender cord; twine; a se-ries; cord or wire of musical instrument. * *vt* (*pt, pp* **strung**) to thread on a string.

stringency *n* severity; pressure.

stringent *adj* strict; severe; binding.

strip *vt* to lay bare; to skin. * *vi* to undress. * *n* a long narrow piece.

stripe *n* a streak; a band; a lash; a weal.

stripper *n* a striptease artist; a device or solvent that removes paint.

striptease *n* an erotic show in which a person removes his or her clothes slowly and seductively to music.

strive *vi vb* (*pt* **strove**, *pp* **striven**) to endeavour; to struggle; to vie.

stroke *n* a blow; calamity; attack; striking of a clock; touch; a line; a gentle rub; the sweep of an oar; the aft-most rower who sets time to others. * *vt* to rub gently with hand.

stroll *vi* to ramble; to saunter. * *n* a short leisurely walk.

strong *adj* powerful; robust; firm; forcible; ardent.

stronghold *n* a fort; a keep; a centre of strength or support.

strongroom *n* a room where valuables are kept.

strop *n* a strip of leather for sharpening razors, etc.

structural *adj* pertaining to structure.

structure *n* a building of any kind; manner of building; make; form; organization.

struggle *vi* to strive; to contend. * *n* a violent effort; contest; strife.

strum *vi, vt* (*pt* **strummed**) to play noisily on a stringed instrument.

strut *vi* (*pt* **strutted**) to walk with affected dignity. * *n* a pompous gait; a support for a rafter or framework.

strychnine *n* a highly poisonous alkaloid.

stubble *n* the stumps of cornstalks left after reaping.

stubborn *adj* obstinate; wilful; mulish; dogged.

stucco *n* a fine plaster; work made of stucco.

stuck-up *adj* giving one's self airs; proud; pompous.

stud *n* a post; a nail with a large head; an ornamental button; a set of breeding horses.

student *n* a scholar; one given to study.

studied *adj* deliberate; well-considered.

studio *n* the workplace of a painter or sculptor; a building or room where motion pictures are made or TV and radio programmes are recorded.

studious *adj* given to study; earnest.

study *n* application to learning; subject studied; room set apart for study; thought, reflection. * *vt, vi* to apply mind to; to investigate; to reflect on.

stuff *n* material; textile fabrics; trash. * *vt, vi* to pack; to cram.

stuffing *n* padding; seasoning packed into meat, fowls, etc, in cooking.

stuffy *adj* close; stifling; poorly ventilated.

stultify *vi, vt* to make ineffectual or foolish.

stumble *vi* to trip; to err; to light on by chance. * *n* a stagger; trip.

stump *n* part of felled tree left standing; part of limb left after amputation; a wicket (cricket). * *vt* to lop; to dismiss batsman off his ground; to pay (up).

stun *vt* to make senseless; to stupefy; to amaze.

stunning *adj* strikingly attractive.

stunt *vt* to dwarf * *n* a check in growth; a showy `turn; a feat of strength or skill.

stunted *adj* dwarfed.

stupefaction *n* insensibility; amazement.

stupefy *vt* to astound; to dull the senses.

stupendous *adj* immense; awe-inspiring.

stupid *adj* foolish; dull-witted.

stupidity *n* dullness of mind; folly.

stupor *n* torpor; insensibility.

sturdy *adj* stout; strong; hardy.

stutter *vi* to stammer. * *n* a stammer.

sty[1] *n* a pen for swine; a foul place.

sty[2], **stye** *n* a small swelling on the edge of the eyelid.

style *n* manner of doing anything; title; fashion. * *vt* to designate; to term.

stylish *adj* fashionable.

stylist *n* a master of style.

stylus *n* the component in a record player that contacts with the groove of a record and transmits sound to the amplifier.

suave *adj* gracious in manner; pleasant.

sub *n* (*inf*) short for submarine, substitute, subscription, subeditor, etc.

sub- *prefix* under, below; subordinate, next in rank to.

subconscious adj happening without one's awareness. *n the part of the mind that is active without one's conscious awareness.

subcutaneous adj immediately below the skin.

subdivide vt to divide into smaller parts.

subdue vt to overcome; to overpower; to tone down.

subeditor n an under or assistant editor.

subject adj ruled by another; liable. * n one who owes allegiance to a ruler or government; theme; topic; the nominative of a verb. * vt to subdue; to expose.

subjection n authority; control.

subjective adj relating to the conscious subject, opposed to objective.

subjugate vt to subdue; to conquer.

subjunctive adj, n (of) the mood of a verb that expresses condition, hypothesis, doubt.

sublet vt (pres pto let to another person what oneself holds as tenant.

sublime adj awe-inspiring; noble; majestic. * The sublime, the awe-inspiring in the works of nature or of art, as opposed to the beautiful.

subliminal adj under the threshold of consciousness; subconscious.

sublimity n loftiness of style or feeling; grandeur.

submarine adj being under surface of the sea. * n a submersible boat.

submerge vt, vi to put under water; to sink.

submersed adj being or growing under water.

submersible adj capable of being submerged and propelled under water. * n a submarine.

submission n surrender; obedience; resignation.

submissive adj humble, compliant.

submit vt, vi to yield or surrender; to refer to another's judgment; to suffer without complaint.

subordinate adj secondary; lower in rank. * n one who ranks below another. * vt to place in a lower rank.

subordination n inferiority of rank; subjection.

subpoena n a summons to give evidence in law court. * vt to serve with a subpoena.

subscribe vt to pay to receive regular copies (of a magazine, etc); to donate money (to a charity, etc); to support or agree with (an opinion, etc).

subscriber n one who subscribes; a contributor.

subscript adj written below.

subscription n sum subscribed to receive copies (of a magazine) or to be a member of a club.

subsection n a division of a section.

subsequent adj following; next.

subservience n servility; obsequiousness.

subservient adj serving to further some end; helpful; servile; inferior.

subside vi to sink or fall to the bottom; to abate; to settle.

subsidence n a sinking down of land or sea; a landslip.

subsidiarity n the devolution of power to the lowest effective level.

subsidiary *adj* minor; subordinate; supplementary.

subsidize *vt* to assist with money; to purchase help by a subsidy.

subsidy *n* government financial aid to assist an enterprise.

subsist *vi* to have existence; to live.

subsistence *n* existence; livelihood.

subsoil *n* the stratum of earth just below surface.

substance *n* that of which a thing consists; material; a body; essence.

substantial *adj* of considerable value or style; real; solid; strong.

substantiate *vt* to give proof for; to verify.

substantive *adj* expressing existence; real. * *n* a noun.

substitute *vt* to put in the place of another; to exchange. * *n* a deputy.

substructure *n* a foundation; basis.

subterfuge *n* an artifice; evasion.

subterranean *adj* underground.

subtitle *n* an explanatory, usu secondary, title of a book; a printed translation superimposed on a foreign language film.

subtle *adj* thin; acute; sly; artful.

subtlety *n* nicety of distinction.

subtract *vt* to take from; to deduct.

subtraction *n* the taking of a number from a greater.

suburb *n* an outlying residential part of a city.

suburban *adj* situated in the suburbs.

subvention *n* a government grant; a subsidy.

subversion *n* the act of undermining the authority of a government or institution.

subversive *adj* destructive.

subvert *vt* to ruin utterly; to overturn.

subway *n* an underground passage.

succeed *vt* to follow in order; to come after. * *vi* to ensue; to become heir; to accomplish what is attempted.

success *n* favourable result; good fortune.

successful *adj* prosperous; fortunate.

succession *n* a following in order; lineage.

successive *adj* coming in succession; consecutive.

successor *n* one who succeeds or follows another.

succinct *adj* brief; concise.

succour *vt* to help when in difficulty; to aid. * *n* aid; help.

succulent *adj* full of sap; juicy.

succumb *vi* to yield; to submit.

such *adj* of like kind or degree; similar.

suck *vt, vi* to draw (liquid etc) into the mouth.

sucker *n* a person who is easily taken in or deceived.

suckle *vt* to nurse at the breast.

suckling *n* an unweaned child or animal.

suction *n* act of sucking; the sucking up of a fluid by exhaustion of air.

sucrose *n* sugar.

sudden *adj* happening without warning; abrupt.

sue *vt* to bring a legal action against.

suet *n* white, solid fat in animal tissue, used in cooking.

suffer *vt* to endure; to permit. * *vi* to undergo pain.

sufferance n endurance of pain; passive consent.

suffering n the bearing of pain; distress.

suffice vi to be sufficient. * vt to satisfy.

sufficiency n an ample supply; competence.

sufficient adj adequate; enough.

suffix n a letter or syllable affixed to the end of a word.

suffocate vt, vi to stifle; to choke; to be stifled.

suffrage n a vote; right of voting; the franchise.

suffuse vt to spread over or fill, as with colour or light.

sugar n a sweet granular substance manufactured from sugar cane, maple, beet, etc. * vt to sweeten.

sugary adj sweet; flattering.

suggest vt to hint; to propose; to intimate.

suggestion n a hint; a tentative proposal.

suggestive adj hinting at; stimulating; prompting thought; rather indecent.

suicidal adj fatal; self-destructive.

suicide n self-murder or self-murderer.

suit n a petition; a courtship; an action at law; a set of matching garments. * vt, vi to adapt; to fit; to satisfy.

suitable adj fitting; appropriate; becoming.

suite n a retinue; a set, as of rooms.

suitor n a wooer.

sulk vi to be sullen or pettish.

sulky adj sullen; morose.

sullen adj ill-natured; morose; sour; dismal.

sully vt, vi to soil; to tarnish.

sulphur n brimstone; a yellow nonmetallic element.

sulphurous adj impregnated with sulphur; like sulphur.

sultry adj very hot; oppressive.

sum n the whole; aggregate; essence; substance; a quantity of money; an arithmetical problem. * vt to add up; to review main facts.

summarize vt to set forth the main facts; to make an abstract or outline.

summary adj concise; brief; dispensing with formalities. * n an abridged account; an abstract.

summation n addition; aggregate.

summer n the warmest season of year; between spring and autumn.

summit n the top; highest point.

summon vt to call by authority; to cite to appear in court.

summons n a notice to appear, esp in court; an earnest call.

sumptuous adj very costly; magnificent.

sun n the star around which the earth and other planets revolve that gives light and heat to the solar system; the sunshine. * vt to expose oneself to the sun's rays.

sunbeam n a ray of the sun.

sunburn vt inflammation of the skin from exposure to the sun.

Sunday n the day after Saturday; the Christian day of worship; the Christian Sabbath.

sunder vt to part; to separate.

sundial n an instrument to show time by a shadow cast by sun.

sundry adj miscellaneous; various.

sunglasses npl tinted glasses to protect the eyes from sunlight.

sunlit adj lit by the sun.

sunny adj like the sun; bright or cheerful.

sunrise n first appearance of the sun in the morning.

sunset n descent of sun below the horizon.

sunshine n the light of the sun; warmth; brightness.

sunstroke n an acute illness caused by overexposure to the sun's rays.

sup vt to sip; to imbibe. * vi to take supper. * n a sip; a small mouthful.

super adj (inf) fantastic; excellent. * n (inf) a superintendent, as in the police.

superannuation n regular contributions from employee's wages towards a pension scheme.

superb adj magnificent; grand; of the highest quality.

supercilious adj haughty; scornful.

superficial adj being on the surface; shallow.

superfluous adj needless; redundant.

superhuman adj more than human.

superimpose vt to lay upon something else.

superintend vt to supervise; to direct; to manage.

superintendent n one who manages or supervises; a rank of police officer.

superior adj higher; better; preferable. * n one higher in rank; head of monastery, convent.

superiority n pre-eminence.

superlative adj highest in degree; supreme. * n the highest degree of adjectives or adverbs.

supermarket n a large, self-service shop selling food and household goods.

supernatural adj that which cannot be explained by nature.

superpower n a nation with great economic and military strength.

superscribe vt to write upon or over.

supersede vt to set aside; displace; supplant.

supersensitive adj oversensitive.

supersonic adj faster than the speed of sound.

superstition n credulity in regard to the supernatural; a belief without reason.

superstitious adj credulous.

superstructure n anything resting on a foundation; a building.

supervise vt to oversee and direct; to superintend.

supervision n oversight.

supine adj lying on the back; indolent.

supper n the evening meal.

supplant vt to supersede; to oust, esp by craft.

supple adj pliant; flexible.

supplement n an addition; appendix. * vt to make additions to.

supplicant adj suppliant. * n one who begs earnestly for some favour.

supplication n earnest prayer; entreaty.

supply vt to furnish; to satisfy. * n

store; *pl* stores; money provided for government expenses; a substitute.

support *vt* to uphold; to prop; to maintain; to endure; to back up. * *n* a prop; aid; maintenance.

supporter *n* a defender; adherent; prop.

suppose *vt* to assume; to imagine; to imply; to expect.

supposition *n* assumption; surmise.

suppress *vt* to put down; to quell; to conceal; to crush.

suppression *n* concealment; stoppage.

suppressive *adj* tending to suppress.

suppurate *vi* to form or discharge pus.

suppuration *n* a gathering of pus.

supremacy *n* supreme authority.

supreme *adj* highest in authority; sovereign; paramount.

surcharge *vt* to overload; to charge an additional sum. * *n* an excessive load; an additional tax or charge.

sure *adj* certain; positive; unfailing; stable.

surety *n* security against loss, etc; guarantee; bail.

surf *n* the swell of sea breaking on shore.

surface *n* the outside part of anything; external appearance.

surfeit *n* an excess of food or drink; satiety. * *vt, vi* to feed to excess.

surge *n* the swelling of a wave; a billow. * *vi* to swell; to heave.

surgeon *n* a person skilled in surgery.

surgery *n* the operative branch of medical practice; a doctor's consulting room.

surgical *adj* pertaining to surgery.

surly *adj* morose; churlish.

surmise *n* a supposition; conjecture. * *vt* to guess; to suspect.

surmount *vt* to rise above; to overcome.

surname *n* the family name of an individual.

surpass *vt* to go beyond; to excel.

surplus *n* an excess beyond what is required; balance.

surprise *n* act of taking unawares; astonishment. * *vt* to take unawares; to startle; to astonish.

surprising *adj* amazing; remarkable.

surrender *vt* to deliver up; to resign; to cede. * *n* a yielding or giving up. * *vt* to yield.

surreptitious *adj* done by stealth; underhand.

surrogate *n* a person or thing substituting for another, esp bearing a child.

surround *vt* to encompass. * *n* a border around the edge of something.

surrounding *n* an environment (generally in *pl*).

surveillance *n* a keeping watch over; oversight.

survey *vt* to oversee; to inspect; to measure and value as land, etc. * *n* a general view; examination; plan.

surveying *n* the art or practice of measuring land.

surveyor *n* a measurer; an inspector.

survival *n* a living or continuing longer; a relic or custom of the past.

survive *vt* to outlive; to outlast; to endure.

susceptible *adj* easily affected; sensitive.

suspect vt to mistrust; to conjecture. * n a suspected person.

suspend vt to hang; to postpone; to discontinue; to debar temporarily from a privilege etc.

suspender n a supporting strap or brace.

suspense n uncertainty; anxiety.

suspension n abeyance; temporary cessation of office; postponement; (*chem*) a dispersion of fine particles in a liquid.

suspension bridge n a bridge suspended by cables anchored to towers at either end.

suspensory adj giving support.

suspicion n act of suspecting; mistrust; a belief held or formed without sure proof; a trace.

suspicious adj mistrustful; doubtful.

sustain vt to hold up or support; to maintain; to endure.

sustenance n nourishment.

suture n a seam; the line of junction of bones of skull; the stitching of a wound.

swab n a wad of absorbent material, usu cotton, used to clean wounds, take specimens, etc; a mop. * vt to clean with a swab.

swaddle vt to swathe; to bind tight with clothes.

swagger vt to strut; to bluster. * n swinging gait.

swallow vt to receive through the gullet into the stomach; to engulf; to accept without question. * n the act of swallowing; a migratory bird.

swamp n a bog; a fen. * vt to overwhelm; to capsize, as a boat.

swap vt (*pt* **swapped**) to barter; to exchange.

swarm n a multitude, esp of insects. * vi to throng together; to leave hive in a body; to climb a tree, etc.

swarthy adj tawny; dark-complexioned.

swashbuckler n an adventurous person.

swath n a line of mown grass or grain; sweep of a scythe.

swathe vt to wrap around, as with a bandage.

sway vi to move backwards and forwards; to vacillate in judgment or opinion * n influence; control.

swear vi, vt (*pt* **swore**, *pp* **sworn**) to make a solemn declaration; to curse; to use obscene language.

sweat n perspiration; labour. * vi, vt to emit moisture through pores.

sweater n a knitted pullover.

sweaty adj moist with sweat.

sweep vb (*pt, pp* **swept**) vt to remove (rubbish, dirt) with a brush; to carry along. * vi to pass with swiftness or pomp; to move with a long reach. * n reach; range; rapid survey; one who sweeps chimneys.

sweeping adj comprehensive.

sweepstake n a gamble in which the stakes go to drawers of winning horses etc.

sweet adj agreeable to the taste; having the taste of honey or sugar; fragrant; melodious; kind; gentle. * n a dessert; pl confectionery.

sweetheart n a lover.

swell vb (*pp* **swelled** or **swollen**) vi to grow larger; to heave; to bulge out.

* *vt* to expand. * *n* gradual increase; a rise of ground; the movement of the sea.

swelling *n* an inflammation.

swelter *vi* to suffer from heat; to perspire.

swerve *vi* to turn aside; to alter course suddenly.

swift *adj* speedy; fleet; prompt. * *n* a species of swallow.

swig *n* a long drink, esp from a bottle.

swill *vi* to drink greedily; to rinse with a large amount of water.* *n* a liquid refuse fed to pigs.

swim *vb* (*pres p* **swimming**, *pt* **swam**, *pp* **swum**) *vi* to float; to move through water; to be dizzy. * *vt* to pass by swimming. * *n* act of swimming.

swimmingly *adv* smoothly; with great success.

swindle *vt* to cheat. * *n* a gross fraud.

swindler *n* a cheat.

swine *n sing, pl* a pig; *pl* pigs collectively.

swing *vb* (*pt, pp* **swung**) *vi* to move to and fro; to turn round at anchor; to change opinion or preference. * *vt* to achieve; to bring about. * *n* sweep of a body; rhythm; apparatus for swinging on; free course; a form of jazz music.

swipe *vt, vi* to strike with sweeping blow. * *n* a sweeping blow.

swirl *vi* to turn with a whirling motion.

swish *vt* to move with a soft, whistling sound.* *n* swishing sound.

switch *n* a sudden change; a swap; a device for changing the course of an electric current. * *vt* to change.

swivel *n* a coupling that permits parts to rotate. * *vt* (*pt* **swivelled**) to turn as if on a pivot.

swoon *vi* to faint.

swoop *vi* to dart upon prey from a height. * *n* the pounce or dart as of a hawk.

sword *n* a weapon with a long blade and a handle at one end.

sworn *adj* bound by oath.

sycophant *n* a person who flatters to win favour.

syllable *n* a sound or combination of sounds uttered with one effort.

syllabus *n* an outline or summary, esp of a course of study.

sylph *n* a slender, graceful female.

sylviculture *n* forestry.

symbol *n* a sign; an emblem; a type; a figure.

symbolism *n* the lavish use of symbolic language.

symbolize *vt* to represent by a symbol; to typify.

symmetry *n* the corresponding arrangement of one part to another in size, shape and position.

sympathetic *adj* compassionate; showing sympathy.

sympathy *n* fellow feeling; compassion.

symphony *n* unison of sound; an orchestral piece of music.

symposium *n* (*pl* **symposia**) a discussion on a subject by experts.

symptom *n* a bodily sensation indicative of a particular disease; an indication.

symptomatic *adj* indicative; relating to symptoms.

synagogue *n* a place where Jews assemble for worship and religious study.

synchronize *vi, vt* to agree or make to agree in time.

synchronous *adj* happening at the same time; simultaneous.

syncopate *vt* to contract words by omission of middle letters; in music, to pass from one bar to another by a slur.

syncopation *n* word shortening; interruption of musical rhythm.

syndicate *n* a company formed for a special purpose.

synonym *n* a word having same meaning as another.

synonymous *adj* of similar meaning; interchangeable.

synopsis *n* a summary.

syntax *n* correct arrangement of words in sentences.

synthesis *n* the combining of parts to make a whole; the production of a compound by a chemical reaction.

synthetic *adj* artificially produced.

syringe *n* a hollow tube with a plunger and a sharp needle at either end by which liquids are injected or withdrawn, esp in medicine. * *vt* to inject or cleanse with a syringe.

syrup *n* a thick sweet substance made by boiling sugar with water; the concentrated juice of a fruit or plant.

system *n* a method of working or organizing by following a set of rules; the body as a functional unity; a plan; method.

T

tab *n* a small flap; a tag.

table *n* an article of furniture with a flat surface set on legs; fare; persons round a table; a list or index. * *vt* to lay on a table; to put forward, submit; to postpone.

tableau *n* (*pl* **tableaux**) a picture; a striking group or dramatic scene.

table d'hôte *n* dinner served in a hotel or restaurant at a fixed price.

tableland *n* a plateau.

tablet *n* a set of ivory or paper slips for memoranda; a slab bearing an inscription; a small cake, as of soap etc.

tabloid *n* a small format newspaper.

taboo *n* a ban or prohibition. * *vt* to forbid approach to or use of.

tabular *adj* in form of a table; flat.

tacit *adj* implied, but not expressed; silent.

taciturn *adj* of few words; silent.

tack *n* a small nail; a stitch; course of a ship as regards the wind. * *vt* to fasten by tacks; to attach slightly. * *vi* to change course of a ship to catch the wind.

tackle *n* gear or apparatus; pulleys, ropes, rigging. * *vt* to grapple with; to seize.

tact *n* fineness of touch; judgment; taste; adroitness.

tactical *adj* pertaining to tactics.

tactics *n* stratagem; ploy; the science or art of military manoeuvring.

tactile *adj* having the sense of touch.

tactless *adj* lacking tact.

taffeta *n* a silk fabric.

tag *n* a metallic point to end of a lace; an appendage; a catchword.

tail *n* appendage to hinder part of animal's body; hinder part; reverse of a coin.

tailor *n* a maker of clothes, esp for men.

taint *vt* to defile; to infect. * *vi* to be infected. * *n* infection; a stain.

take *vt, vi* (*pt* **took**, *pp* **taken**) to receive or accept; to capture; to understand; to employ; to be infected; to bear; to conduct.

taking *adj* alluring; attracting.

talc *n* a smooth mineral used in ceramics and talcum powder.

talent *n* any innate or special aptitude.

talisman *n* a charm; a mascot.

talk *vi* to utter words; to converse. * *vt* to discuss. * *n* familiar conversation; rumour; discussion.

talkative *adj* garrulous; fond of talking.

tall *adj* high in stature; lofty.

talon *n* the claw of a bird of prey.

tambourine *n* a percussion instrument.

tame *adj* domesticated; spiritless; insipid. * *vt* to make tame; to subdue.

tamper *vi* to meddle or interfere; to use bribery.

tampon *n* a plug of absorbent material inserted in the vagina during menstruation.

tan *vt* (*pt* **tanned**) to convert into leather, as skins; to make sunburnt. * *n* bark used for tanning.

tandem *adv* one behind another. * *n* a pair of horses yoked single file; a bicycle with riders single file.

tang *n* a taste; characteristic flavour; part of tool which fits into handle.

tangent *n* a straight line touching a circle but not cutting it.

tangible *adj* perceptible to touch; real; actual.

tangle *vt* to interweave; to involve. * *n* a knot; a muddle; complication.

tango *n* a Latin American ballroom dance.

tank *n* a large cistern; a reservoir; a covered armoured car with caterpillar wheels and containing men and weaponry.

tankard *n* a large drinking vessel with a lid.

tannery *n* a place for tanning leather.

tanning *n* process of converting hides into leather.

tantalize *vt* to torment by raising false hopes.

tantamount *adj* equal; equivalent.

tantrum *n* a fit of bad temper.

tap *n* pipe for drawing off liquor; a spigot; a stopper or plug; a touch. * *vt, vi* to broach; to strike lightly.

tape *n* a narrow band of linen; magnetic tape, as in an audio cassette or videotape.

taper *n* a long wick coated with wax. * *adj* narrowing to a point. * *vt* to narrow to a point.

tapestry *n* rich woven hangings of wool and silk, with pictorial representations.

tapeworm *n* a long tape-like worm found sometimes in intestines.

taproot *n* main root of a plant.

tar *n* a thick, dark, viscous substance obtained from pine, coal, etc; a sailor. * *vt* to smear with tar.

tarantella *n* a lively Italian dance.

tardily *adv* slowly.

tardy *adj* slow; late; backward.

target *n* a circular shield; a shooting mark or butt.

tariff *n* a schedule of dutiable goods; a scale of charges.

tarnish *vt, vi* to sully; to dim.

tarpaulin *n* canvas covered with tar.

tarry *vi* to stay; to delay. * *vt* to wait for.

tart *adj* sharp to the taste; acid; snappish. * *n* a small fruit pie.

tartan *n* a woollen chequered cloth of many colours.

task *n* a piece of work imposed by another; lesson to be learned; toil. * *vt* to burden.

tassel *n* a small ornament with hanging threads.

taste *vt, vi* to perceive flavour of by tongue or palate; to partake slightly of; to experience; to have a flavour. * *n* flavour; trial; sample; discernment; good style.

tasteful *adj* showing good taste.

tasteless *adj* stale; void of taste.

tasty *adj* savoury; palatable.

tatter *n* a loose hanging rag.

tattle *vi* to talk idly; to gossip. * *n* idle talk.

tattoo *n* military call to quarters; military exhibition. * *vt* to prick ink into skin.

taunt *vt* to reproach; to upbraid. * *n* a bitter reproach.

Taurus *n* the Bull, one of the twelve signs of the zodiac.

taut *adj* tight; stretched.

tautology *n* repetition of the same meaning in different words.

tavern *n* an inn.

tawdry *adj* showy but inelegant.

tawny *adj* tan-coloured; yellowish-brown.

tax *n* a charge made by government on income, etc; a burdensome duty. * *vt* to place tax on; to accuse.

taxation *n* act of levying taxes; the aggregate of taxes.

taxidermy *n* the art of stuffing animals.

tea *n* dried leaves of an Eastern shrub; beverage made from them.

teach *vt, vi vb* (*pt, pp* **taught**) to instruct; to inform; to give instruction.

teacher *n* one who teaches; a schoolmaster.

teaching *n* act or business of instructing.

teak *n* an Indian tree producing hard durable timber.

team *n* a brood; a litter; two or more draught animals harnessed together; a side in a game, match, etc.

tear¹ *n* a drop of water appearing in, or falling from, the eye.

tear² *vt, vi* (*pt* **tore**, *pp* **torn**) to pull in pieces; to wound; to pull with violence. * *n* a rent.

tease vt to pull apart fibres of; to torment.

teat n the nipple.

technical adj pertaining to arts, crafts, or sciences.

technicality n something peculiar to a special art, craft, etc.

technique n manner of artistic execution; manipulative skill.

technology n the science of the industrial arts.

techy, tetchy adj peevish; fretful.

tedious adj tiresome; fatiguing.

tedium n irksomeness.

tee n the target in quoits, curling, etc; the starting place for each hole in golf.

teem vi to pour (with rain); to be prolific.

teeming adj fruitful; prolific.

teens npl the years of one's age having ending teen.

teeth npl of tooth.

teethe vi to cut one's first teeth.

teetotal adj totally abstaining from intoxicants.

telegram n a telegraphic message.

telegraph n a deivce for sending messages to a distance, esp by electricity and with or without wires. * vt to send a telegraph.

telepathy n the transference of thought from mind to mind without aid of senses.

telephone n an instrument transmitting sound to a distance by electricity. * vt to transmit by telephone.

telescope n an optical instrument for viewing distant objects.

television n the transmission of visual images and sound via electrical and sound waves; a television receiving set; television broadcasting.

tell vt, vi vb (pt, pp **told**) to number; to relate; to explain; to report; to inform; to bid.

teller n a bank clerk in charge of cash; one appointed to count votes.

telling adj very effective.

telltale adj revealing; informative. * n a blabber; a betrayer of secrets.

temerity n contempt of danger; rashness.

temper vt to mix in due proportion; to moderate; to harden. * n due mixture; disposition of mind; passion; mood; quality.

temperament n disposition; nature.

temperance n moderation, esp in regard to alcoholic drink.

temperate adj moderate; calm.

temperature n degree of heat or cold.

tempered adj disposed; hardened, as steel.

tempest n a violent storm.

tempestuous adj very stormy; violent.

temple n a place of worship; a church; the side of the head above either cheekbone.

tempo n musical time.

temporal adj pertaining to time; secular; worldly; civil, secular.

temporarily adv for a time only; provisionally.

temporary adj lasting but for a time; provisional.

temporize vi to hedge; to wait and see; to trim.

tempt *vt* to entice; to put to test; to allure into evil.

temptation *n* enticement to evil.

tempting *adj* attractive; alluring.

ten *adj, n* the number next after nine; the symbol for this (10).

tenable *adj* able to be held; defensible; sound.

tenacious *adj* holding fast; unyielding; tough; stubborn.

tenacity *n* doggedness; toughness.

tenancy *n* the holding of land, etc, as a tenant.

tenant *n* an occupier who pays rent.

tend *vi* to incline; trend; aim * *vt* to attend; guard; to look after.

tendency *n* inclination; bias; proneness.

tender *n* a small vessel carrying stores, etc, to larger one; the part of a locomotive carrying fuel and water; an offer; an estimate. * *vt* to offer or present; to send in an estimate. * *adj* fragile; delicate; sensitive; compassionate; weak.

tendon *n* a sinew; fibrous band joining muscles to bones.

tendril *n* a slender, twining shoot by which some plants cling or climb.

tenebrous *adj* dark; gloomy.

tenement *n* block of buildings divided into separate houses.

tenet *n* a doctrine, opinion, or dogma.

tenfold *adj* ten times more.

tennis *n* a game with balls and rackets.

tenon *n* the end of piece of wood shaped to fit into mortise or hole in another piece.

tenor *n* a prevailing course; purport; drift; higher of two kinds of men's voices; one with tenor voice.

tense *n* verbal inflection to express time. * *adj* stretched tight; strained.

tensile *adj* of or relating to tension; stretchable.

tension *n* act of stretching; tightness; strain; anxiety.

tensor *n* a muscle that extends or tightens a part.

tent *n* a portable shelter of canvas.

tentacle *n* a threadlike organ of various animals, serving as a limb or feeler.

tentative *adj* experimental.

tenterhook *n* one of hooks on cloth-stretching frame. *(with on) in a state of anxiety or suspense.

tenth *adj* ordinal number of ten.

tenuity *n* thinness; rarity.

tenuous *adj* thin; slender.

tenure *n* a holding or conditions of holding land, office etc.

tepid *adj* lukewarm.

tercentenary *adj* comprising three hundred years. * *n* the three-hundredth anniversary.

term *n* a limit; boundary; period of session, etc; rent day; a word; *pl* conditions. * *vt* to name; to call.

terminable *adj* capable of being ended or bounded.

terminal *adj* pertaining to the end. * *n* an extremity; the clamping screw at each end of a voltaic battery; a computer keyboard and monitor.

terminate *vt, vi* to bound; to limit; to end.

terminology *n* the terms special to a science, art, etc.

terminus *n* (*pl* **termini**) a boundary; a limit; end of a transport line.

terrace *n* a raised level bank of earth; a row of houses.

terracotta *n* a reddish-brown pottery or its colour.

terrestrial *adj* pertaining to the earth; worldly.

terrible *adj* awful; terrifying.

terrific *adj* terrifying; dreadful.

terrify *vt* to scare; to frighten.

territory *n* a large tract of land; a region.

terror *n* extreme fear; dread.

terrorism *n* the use of violence to intimidate.

terrorize *vt* to intimidate by means of terror.

terse *adj* concise; pointed.

tertiary *adj* third; applied to a geological formation.

tessellated *adj* resembling mosaic.

test *n* a putting to the proof; examination; trial. * *vt* to try.

testament *n* in law, a person's will; (*with cap*) one of two divisions of the Bible.

testamentary *adj* bequeathed by will.

testator (*f* **testatrix**) *n* one who leaves a will at death.

testicle *n* either of the two male reproductive glands that produce semen.

testify *vi, vt* to bear witness; to affirm on oath.

testimonial *n* a recommendation of one's character or abilities.

testimony *n* evidence; declaration.

testy *adj* fretful; peevish.

tête-à-tête *adv* face to face. * *n* a private talk.

tether *n* a rope confining animal within certain limits. * *vt* to confine with a tether.

tetragon *n* a plane figure having four angles.

tetrahedron *n* a solid body having four equal triangles as its faces.

text *n* a main part of a printed work; a topic; a textbook.

textbook *n* a standard book of instruction; a manual.

textile *adj* woven. * *n* a fabric made by weaving.

texture *n* the grain or feel of a thing.

thallus *n* a plant showing little difference between leaf, stem, and root.

than *conj* introduces second member of comparison.

thank *n* almost always in *pl* expression of gratitude. * *vt* to give thanks to.

thanksgiving *n* act of giving thanks, esp to God.

that *adj, demons pron* (*pl* **those**) pointing out a person or thing at a distance; the farther of two. * *rel pron sing, pl* equivalent to who or which. * *conj* introducing noun clause; in order that.

thatch *n* straw used as cover for roofs or stacks. * *vt* to put thatch on.

thaw *vi, vt* to melt, as ice or snow; to become genial. * *n* the melting of ice or snow.

the *def art* denoting particular person or thing.

theatre *n* a playhouse; an operating room; sphere of action.

theatrical *adj* artificial; showy; pompous.

theft *n* act of stealing.

their *poss adj, pron* belonging to them * **theirs** possessive case of they, used without noun.

theism *n* belief in gods.

them *per pron* the objective case of **they**.

theme *n* a subject or topic.

themselves *per pron pl* of himself, herself, etc.

then *adv* at that time. * *conj* from that place or time; therefore.

thenceforth *adv* from that time.

thenceforward *adv* from that time onward.

theocracy *n* direct government by God; a state so governed.

theologian *n* a person well versed in theology.

theology *n* the study of religious doctrine and divine things.

theorem *n* a proposition capable of being proved.

theoretical *adj* not practical; hypothetical.

theorize *vi* to conjecture; to speculate.

theory *n* speculation; hypothesis to explain something.

therapeutic *adj* pertaining to the healing art; curative.

there *adv* in or at that place.

thereafter *adv* after that; accordingly.

thereby *adv* by that means.

therefore *adv, conj* for that or this reason; consequently.

thereupon *adv* upon that or this; immediately.

therewith *adv* with that or this.

thermal *adj* pertaining to heat; warm; hot.

thermodynamics *n* the science of heat as a force.

thermometer *n* an instrument for measuring degree of temperature.

thermos *n* a vacuum flask used to keep liquids warm.

thermostat *n* an appliance for regulating steam pressure and temperature.

thesaurus *n* a reference book of synonyms and antonyms.

these *pronominal adj pl* of **this**.

thesis *n* (*pl* **theses**) a subject for discussion; a theme; an essay.

thespian *adj* relating to dramatic acting.

they *per pron pl* the plural of he, she or it.

thick *adj* dense; close; foggy; crowded; dull.

thicket *n* a copse; a tangle of shrubs.

thickset *adj* thickly planted; stumpy.

thief *n* (*pl* **thieves**) a person who steals.

thieve *vi, vt* to steal.

thigh *n* the leg above the knee.

thimble *n* a metal cover for finger in sewing.

thin *adj* not thick; sparse; slim; lean; poor. * *vt, vi* to make or become thin.

thing *n* an inanimate object; any separate entity; *pl* clothes; baggage, etc.

think *vi, vt* (*pt, pp* **thought**) to have

the mind working; to reflect; to judge; to believe.

third *adj* ordinal of three.

thirst *n* the desire or distress occasioned by want of water; eager desire after anything. * *vi* to feel thirst; to desire vehemently.

thirteen *adj, n* ten and three.

thirty *adj, n* thrice ten.

this *adj, pron* (*pl* **these**) that which is near or present.

thong *n* a strap of hide or leather.

thorax *n* the human chest.

thorn *n* a prickly tree or shrub.

thorough *adj* complete; entire.

thoroughbred *adj* of pure stock.

thoroughfare *n* a public or open road.

thoroughgoing *adj* downright; extreme.

those *adj, pron pl* of that.

though *conj* notwithstanding.

thought *n* the power of thinking; opinion; judgment; care.

thousand *adj, n* ten hundred.

thrash, thresh *vt* to beat out grain from husk; to flog.

thread *n* a fine cord; any fine filament; spiral part of a screw; general purpose. * *vt* to pass thread through; to make one's way through.

threadbare *adj* worn out; trite.

threat *n* declaration of intention to punish or hurt.

threaten *vt* to use threats towards.

threatening *adj* impending; menacing.

three *adj, n* the number next after two; the symbol for this (3).

threescore *adj* three times a score; sixty.

thresh *vt* to beat out grain from husks.

threshold *n* a door sill; entrance.

thrice *adv* three times.

thrift *n* frugality; a plant.

thriftless *adj* wasteful.

thrifty *adj* frugal; saving.

thrill *vt, vi* to send a quiver through. * *n* a quiver; a tingling feeling.

thrilling *adj* exciting.

thrive *vi* to prosper; to flourish.

throat *n* the opening downward at back of mouth.

throb *vi* to beat, as the heart; to palpitate.

throe *n* extreme pain; agony.

throne *n* a royal seat.

throng *n* a crowd. * *vi, vt* to crowd together.

throttle *n* the windpipe; the gullet; engine's steam or petrol regulator.

through *prep* from end to end of; by means of * *adj, adv* from end to end.

throughout *prep* quite through. * *adv* in every part.

throw *vt, vi* (*pt* **threw**, *pp* **thrown**) to fling or cast; to propel; to twist or wind; to utter. * *n* a cast at dice, etc; a venture.

thrum *n* coarse yarn. * *vt, vi* to drum; to strum.

thrush *n* a singing bird; an oral fungal infection.

thrust *vt, vi vb* (*pt, pp* **thrust**) to push with force; to shove; to stab; to intrude. * *n* a violent push; a stab.

thumb *n* the first short thick finger of

the human hand. * vt to soil with marks of the thumb or fingers.

thump n a dull, heavy blow. * vt, vi to strike with something heavy.

thunder n the sound which follows lightning; any loud noise. * vi to make a loud noise.

thunderbolt n a shaft of lightning.

thunderclap n a peal of thunder.

thundering adj resounding.

thunderstruck adj amazed.

Thursday n the fifth day of the week.

thus adv in this manner.

thwart adj transverse. * vt to cross; to frustrate. * n rowers' seat athwart boat.

thyme n a small aromatic herb or shrub.

tiara n a diadem for head.

tibia n the shin bone.

tick n the beat of watch or clock; a tapping; a dot. * n insect. * vt, vi to mark with a dot; to sound, as watch.

ticket n a label; a piece of cardboard giving right of entry, travel, etc.

tickle vi, vt to touch lightly in certain places and cause involuntary laughter; to please; to puzzle.

ticklish adj difficult; critical.

tidal adj pertaining to tides.

tide n time; season; the ebb and flow of sea.

tidings npl news; information.

tidy adj clean and orderly; neat; trim * vt to make tidy.

tie vt to fasten; to constrain; * n a fastening; a necktie; bond; an equality in numbers.

tier n a row; a rank.

tiff n a slight quarrel.

tiffany n a gauze or very thin silk.

tight adj compact; well-knit; fitting close or too close; scarce, as money; tipsy.

tights npl a one-piece garment covering the legs and lower body.

tile n a slab of baked clay for roofing, flooring, etc; a drain pipe. * vt to cover with tiles.

till n a money drawer in shop counter. * prep until. * vt to cultivate; to plough and prepare for seed.

tiller n the handle of a rudder.

tilt vi to joust; to lean or slope. * n a slant; a joust; an awning for cart or boat.

timber n wood for building purposes.

timbre n characteristic quality of musical note.

time n the measure of duration; a point of duration; occasion; season; epoch; present life; rhythm * vt to regulate or measure.

timely adj opportune. * adv early.

timeous adj timely.

timetable n a table of school hours and classes; a schedule.

timid adj fearful; shy.

timorous adj full of fear.

tin n a malleable white metal.

tincture n a tinge, tint, or shade; flavour; extract or solution of drug in alcohol. * vt to tinge.

tinder n an inflammable substance used for kindling fire from a spark.

tine n a prong; tooth of harrow, etc.

tinge vt to tint; to imbue. * n a tint; a slight colour.

tingle vi to feel a thrilling sensation.

tinker n a mender of kettles, etc. * vt, vi to mend; to patch up.

tinkle vi to make small, sharp sounds; to clink. * n a sharp, ringing sound.

tinplate n thin sheet iron coated with tin.

tinsel n glittering thread or foil; something gaudy but of little value; mere glitter.

tint n a tinge; hue. * vt to tinge.

tintinnabulation n a jingling, as of bells.

tiny adj very small; puny.

tip n a small end or point; a tap; a gratuity; a dump; a hint. * vt to cant, as a cart; to put tip on; to give gratuity to.

tipple vi, vt to drink strong liquors frequently; to imbibe often.

tipsy adj mildly intoxicated.

tiptoe vi to walk very quietly.

tiptop adj excellent; first-rate.

tirade n a violent speech, denunciation.

tire n band or hoop of iron or rubber round wheels; headdress. * vt to fatigue; to weary; to attire.

tiresome adj wearisome; tedious.

tissue n delicate fabric; thin paper sheet; substance (muscle, fat, etc) composing parts of animals and plants; a fabrication.

titanic adj huge; gigantic.

titbit n a tasty morsel.

titillation n a pleasant feeling, a teasing, esp sexual.

title n an inscription; heading; name; appellation of dignity; a right.

titled adj having a title.

title deed n the legal document proving right to property.

title page n the page of book containing its name, author, etc.

titter vi to giggle. * n a half-suppressed laugh.

titular adj nominal.

to prep denoting motion towards.

toadstool n a mushroom-like fungus.

toady n a base sycophant; a sponger. * vt to fawn upon.

toast vt to dry and brown before the fire; to drink health of * n toasted bread; person or sentiment whose health is drunk.

tobacco n a narcotic plant whose leaves when dried are used for smoking or snuff.

toboggan n a snow sledge.

toddle vi to walk with uncertain steps, as a child.

toddy n a mixture of spirit, hot water, and sugar.

toe n one of the five extremities of the foot.

toffee n a sweetmeat made of butter and sugar.

toga n a loose robe.

together adv in company.

toil vi to labour; to drudge. * n hard work; a snare.

toilet n the lavatory; the act of washing and dressing oneself.

toilsome adj laborious.

token n a mark; symbol; keepsake.

tolerable adj passable; middling.

tolerance n forbearance.

tolerant adj indulgent; broad-minded.

tolerate vt to allow or permit; to put up with.

toll n a tax charged for use of road, bridge, etc; sound of a bell. * vi to ring bell slowly.

tomb n a grave; burial vault.

tombstone n a stone erected over a grave.

tome n a volume; a large book.

tomfoolery n nonsense; silly acts.

tomorrow n the day after the present.

tone n sound or character of sound; timbre; temper; colour scheme. * vt, vi to tone down, to soften.

tongs npl an appliance for lifting coal, sugar, etc.

tongue n the organ of speech and taste; speech; language; clapper of bell.

tonic adj strengthening; bracing. * n a bracing medicine; keynote.

tonight n the present night.

tonnage n weight of ship's freight; duty on ships.

tonne n a metric ton, 1,000 kilograms.

tonsil n one of glands on each side of throat.

tonsillitis n inflammation of tonsils.

too adv over; as well; also.

tool n an instrument to work with.

tooling n skilled work with a tool.

tooth n (pl **teeth**) one of the bony projections from gums used for chewing.

toothache n a pain in teeth.

toothed adj jagged; indented.

top n the highest part; summit; toy for spinning. * vi, vt to excel; to be at top.

top-heavy adj overweighted above and apt to fall over.

topic n a theme or text.

topical adj local; full of allusions.

topography n scientific description of a district; local geography.

topple vi to fall over; overbalance.

torch n a light to be carried in the hand.

toreador n a Spanish bullfighter.

torment n torture; anguish. * vt to torture; to tease.

tornado n (pl **tornadoes**) a hurricane.

torpedo n (pl **torpedoes**) a kind of electric eel; a self-propelled explosive submarine projectile.

torpid adj numb; inactive.

torpor n apathy; numbness.

torrent n a rushing stream.

torrid adj parched; violently hot.

torsion n act of twisting; amount or force of twist.

torso n a headless, limbless trunk, esp of statue.

tort n wrong; injury.

tortilla n a round thin maize pancake usually eaten hot with a topping or filling.

tortuous adj crooked; winding.

torture n extreme pain; agony. * vt to rack; to harass.

toss vt, vi to throw upward; to jerk, as head; to roll about. * n a throw; a fall.

tot n anything small; a sum in addition. * vt to add.

total adj, n whole; complete.

totem n a tribal emblem.

totter vi to stagger; to reel.

touch vt, vi to come in contact with; to handle lightly; to reach; to move feelings of * n contact; feeling; skill in some art.

touching adj affecting. * prep concerning.

touchstone n a stone for testing purity of gold and silver; a test or criterion.

touchy adj irritable; sensitive.

tough adj flexible; tenacious; stubborn.

tour n a long trip, esp for pleasure. * vt to make a tour.

tourist n one who makes a tour.

tournament n a contest in which individuals or sides are pitted against one another.

tourniquet n an appliance for stopping flow from cut artery.

tousle vt to ruffle; to disarrange.

tout vi to seek for custom openly; to canvas obtrusively. * n a shameless canvasser.

tow vt to haul by a rope. * n haulage; fibres of flax or hemp.

toward, towards prep in the direction of * adv at hand.

towel n a cloth for drying.

tower n a lofty narrow building; a fortress. * vi to soar.

towering adj lofty; violent.

town n an urban centre, smaller than a city and larger than a village.

toxic adj poisonous.

toxin n a poisonous substance.

toy n a plaything; a trifle. * vi to dally; to trifle.

trace n a mark left by anything; footstep; track; one of straps by which a carriage is drawn. * vt to track out; to copy by marking over.

trachea n the windpipe.

track n a footprint; rut made by wheel; beaten path; course. * vt to trace; to follow step by step.

trackless adj pathless; untrodden.

tract n wide region; a short treatise.

tractable adj docile; manageable.

traction n act of drawing, esp vehicles.

trade n employment; commerce; traffic. * vi, vt to buy and sell.

trademark n a distinctive mark put by manufacturer on his goods.

trades union n a union of workers in a trade to protect their interests.

tradition n knowledge handed down orally; a custom.

traduce vt to slander; defame.

traffic n trade; commerce; intercourse; conveyance of passengers or goods on railways, roads, etc. * vi to trade.

tragedy n an elevated drama with fatal ending; any dreadful event.

tragic, tragical adj fatal; disastrous.

trail n a track or scent. * vt to drag along the ground; to hang downwards.

trailer n a climbing plant; a vehicle towed by another.

train vt to draw along; to drill; to exercise; to teach; to take aim * n something drawn along; a series of railway carriages coupled with engine; trailing part of skirt; a retinue; process.

training n exercise; education; practice.

trait n a distinguishing feature.

traitor n one guilty of treason.

trajectory n the path of a moving body, as bullet, comet, etc.

tram n a tramway line; a tramcar.

trammel n a net for birds or fishes; a

shackle; a handicap; a hindrance. * *vt* (*pt* **tramelled**) to impede.

tramp *vt*, *vi* to tread under foot; travel on foot. * *n* a journey on foot; a vagrant.

trample *vt* to tread on heavily; to ride roughshod over.

trance *n* a state of insensibility; a swoon.

tranquil *adj* calm; serene.

transact *vt*, *vi* to carry through.

transaction *n* management; performance; *pl* report of proceedings of societies.

transcend *vt* to rise above; to surpass.

transcendent *adj* of surpassing merit; pre-eminent; supernatural.

transcribe *vt* to write out fully from notes or a tape recording.

transcript *n* a written copy.

transcription *n* act of transcribing; a copy.

transfer *vt* to convey from one place or person to another. * *n* conveyance of titles, etc, from one to another; a design that can be printed off on another surface.

transfigure *vt* to change in form or shape.

transfix *vt* to piece through.

transform *vt* to change the form of; to convert.

transformation *n* a complete change of appearance or nature.

transfuse *vt* to transfer, as blood, from one person to another.

transgress *vt* to break or violate. * *vi* to do wrong.

transgression *n* fault; offence.

transient *adj* passing quickly; fleeting.

transit *n* a passing across; passage of planet across sun's disc or of star across meridian of a place; conveyance.

transition *n* passage from one place or state to another.

transitive *adj* in grammar, said of action passing from subject to object.

transitory *adj* fleeting.

translate *vt* to remove from one place to another; to render into another language.

translation *n* removal; a turning into another language; a version.

translucent *adj* semi-transparent.

translucid *adj* translucent.

transmissible *adj* able to be passed through or along.

transmission *n* a passing through; act of sending.

transmit *vt* to convey or effect conveyance of news, light, etc; to hand down.

transmogrify *vt* to transform; to change.

transmute *vt* to change from one form into another.

transom *n* a strengthening cross beam over door or window.

transparency *n* clearness; obviousness; picture visible only when light passes through.

transparent *adj* clear; not opaque; frank.

transpiration *n* emission of vapour or moisture through pores.

transpire *vt* to emit through pores of skin. * *vt* to exhale; to become known.

transplant vt to remove and plant in another place.

transport vt to carry from one place to another; to banish; to enrapture. * n conveyance for goods; a ship for carrying troops, etc; rapture.

transpose vt to change the order of things.

transposition n change in order of words for effect.

transubstantiate vt to change to an-other-substance.

transude vi to pass through pores.

transversal adj lying across. * n line cutting other straight lines.

transverse adj lying across; cross-wise.

trap n a contrivance for catching ani-mals; an ambush; a contrivance in drains to prevent foul air rising; a light uncovered vehicle; an igneous rock. * vt, vi to snare; to take una-wares; to set trap for.

trap door n a door in a floor or ceil-ing or roof.

trapeze n a swing for gymnastic ex-ercises.

trapezium n (pl **trapezia**) a plane four-sided figure of which two sides are parallel.

trappings npl finery; adornment, esp for horses.

trash n rubbish; refuse.

travail vi to labour; to toil. * n toil and pain; childbirth.

travel n journey to a distant country. * vi to journey.

traverse adj transverse. * n a cross-piece; denial of a plea in lawsuit; barrier across a trench. * vt to cross; to journey through; to deny. * adv athwart; crosswise.

travesty n a wilful misrepresenta-tion.

trawl vi to fish by trailing a net. * n a large net for deep-sea fishing.

trawler n a fishing vessel with a trawl net.

tray n a broad, flat, rimmed utensil for carrying dishes, etc.

treacherous adj faithless; deceitful.

treachery n betrayal of trust; per-fidy; treason.

treacle n the syrup obtained in the re-fining of sugar.

tread vb (pt **trod**, pp **trodden**) vi to step or walk. * vt to trample; dance. * n step; the part of a shoe, tyre, etc that touches the ground.

treason n treachery; disloyalty to king or country.

treasonable adj involving treason.

treasure n great wealth; something greatly valued. * vt to prize highly.

treasurer n one who has the charge of funds.

treasury n place where public money is stored; government department that controls finance.

treat vt, vi to handle; to act towards; to discourse on. * n an entertain-ment; a rare pleasure.

treatise n an essay; pamphlet.

treatment n mode of dealing with.

treaty n an agreement between na-tions.

treble adj threefold. * n highest part in music; soprano.

tree n a woody plant with trunk and branches.

trefoil n a three-leaved plant, as clover; a sculptured tracery like clover.

trek vi to migrate by wagon.

trellis n a latticework structure.

tremble vi to shake; to quiver.

tremendous adj terrible; huge.

tremor n an involuntary trembling; a shivering.

tremulous adj trembling; quavering.

trench vt, vi to dig a ditch in; to turn over and mix, as soil. * n a long narrow cutting; a deep ditch with a rampart.

trenchant adj cutting; severe.

trend vi to incline towards. * n direction; tendency.

trepidation n consternation; fear.

trespass vi to intrude on another's land; to transgress; to sin. * n a sin; offence; intrusion on another's property.

tress n a lock of hair.

trestle n a frame for supporting things.

trial n a putting to the test; ordeal; attempt; hardship.

triangle n a figure having three sides and three angles.

triangular adj having form of triangle.

tribe n a division of a people; family; race.

tribulation n deep affliction; suffering.

tribunal n a court of justice.

tributary adj paying tribute; subordinate. * n a stream flowing into another.

tribute n merited praise.

trice n an instant.

trick n an artifice; fraud; a knack; a habit; a prank. * vt to deceive; to cheat.

trickery n cheating; fraud.

trickle vi to fall in drops.

trickster n a knave; cheat.

tricycle n three-wheeled cycle.

trident n three-pronged sceptre.

tried adj approved; reliable.

triennial adj happening every three years.

trifle n thing of little value; a confection or pudding. * vt, vi to toy; to idle.

trifling adj trivial; frivolous.

trigger n the catch by which a gun is fired.

trigonometry n the science dealing with measurement of triangles and ratios of their angles.

trilateral adj three-sided.

trill n a tremor of voice in singing. * vt to warble.

trilogy n a series of three connected dramas, poems, etc.

trim vt to put in order; to prune; to adjust (cargo). * adj spruce; neat. * n readiness; good condition.

trimming n an embellishment, esp of garment; pl accessories; parings.

trinity n a union of three in one.

trinket n a trifling ornament.

trio n a set of three; composition for three performers.

trip vi to step lightly; to skip; to stumble. * vt to cause to stumble. * n a stumble; an excursion or jaunt.

tripartite adj divided into three; made between three parties.

tripe n stomach of sheep, cow, etc, prepared as food.

triple adj threefold; treble.

triplet n three of a kind; pl three children at one birth.

triplicate adj threefold.

tripod n a three-legged stand.

tripper n a day excursionist.

trisect vt to cut into three equal parts.

trisyllable n a word consisting of three syllables.

trite adj commonplace; well-worn.

triumph n a rejoicing for victory; a great victory. * vi to gain a victory; to exult.

triumphal adj pertaining to a triumph.

triumphant adj victorious; exultant.

triumvirate n a coalition of three men in office.

trivet n a tripod for kettle, etc.

trivial adj common; trifling.

trod, trodden pt and pp of tread.

troglodyte n a cave dweller.

troll vt, vi to sing in chorus or succession; to fish by trailing bait. * n a part song; a fishing reel; a dwarfish elf.

trolley, trolly n a small truck.

trollop n a slattern.

trombone n a deep-toned wind instrument.

troop n a collection of people or animals; a cavalry company; pl soldiers in general. * vi to gather in large numbers.

trooper n a cavalryman; a mounted policeman.

troopship n a ship used for transport of military forces.

trophy n a token or memorial of victory.

tropic n one of the two parallel lines of latitude on either side of the equator; (pl) the regions lying between these lines.

tropical adj excessively hot; relating to the tropics.

trot vi (pt **trotted**) to run with small steps. * n a medium pace.

troth n truth; faith.

trouble vt to disturb; to distress. * n distress; affliction.

troublesome adj annoying; tiresome.

trough n a long shallow drinking vessel; a hollow.

trounce vt to beat severely.

troupe n a company of performers.

trousers npl a garment for men, covering legs.

trousseau n a bride's outfit.

trowel n a hand tool for spreading mortar, etc.

truant n one who stays from school without leave. * vi to play truant.

truce n a temporary stoppage of fighting; armistice.

truck n a heavy motor vehicle for transporting goods. *vt to convey by truck. * vi to drive a truck.

truculence n ferocity.

truculent adj aggressive; overbearing.

trudge vi to walk, esp with heavy steps.

true adj conformable to fact; genuine; loyal; honest; exact.

truffle n an edible fungus growing underground.

truism n a self-evident truth.

truly adv really; according to truth.

trump n a winning card; one of the favoured suit for time being; a real good fellow. * vt to take with a trump card; to concoct (with up).

trumpet n a metal wind instrument. * vt to proclaim; to sound.

truncate vt to cut off; to lop.

truncated adj cut short.

truncheon n a short staff; a baton of authority.

trundle vi to roll or bowl. * n a little wheel.

trunk n the stem of a tree; body of an animal; chest for containing clothes, etc; proboscis of an elephant, etc.

trunk line n main line of railway, telephone, etc.

truss n a bundle, as of hay; a bandage; crossbeams to support roof * vt to tie up (fowl) for cooking; to strengthen; to bind firmly.

trust n reliance; confidence; hope; credit; a business combine; money or property entrusted to individuals (trustees) for use in specified ways. * vt, vi to rely upon; to credit; to entrust.

trustee n one appointed to hold property for benefit of others.

trustworthy adj faithful; honest.

trusty adj reliable; staunch.

truth n conformity to fact or reality; integrity; constancy; reality.

try vt to test; to afflict; to examine judicially; to attempt.

trying adj severe; searching.

tryst n an appointment to meet; a rendezvous.

tub n an open wooden vessel; a small bath.

tube n a pipe; a hollow cylinder.

tuber n an underground fleshy stem or root.

tuberculosis n a disease marked by presence of tubercles in tissues; consumption.

tubing n material for tubes series of tubes.

tubular adj like a tube; consisting of tubes.

tuck vt to gather in a fold. * n fold in garment; roll of drum; eatables.

Tuesday n the second work day of the week.

tuft n a cluster; clump.

tug vt, vi to pull with effort. * n a strong pull; steam towing vessel.

tuition n instruction; business of teaching.

tulle n a thin silk fabric.

tumble vi to roll about; to fall. * vt to overturn. * n a fall.

tumbler n an acrobat; a drinking glass.

tumid adj swollen; bombastic.

tumour n an abnormal growth of tissue in any part of the body.

tumult n uproar; riot.

tumultuous adj turbulent; disorderly.

tundra n flat, treeless arctic plain.

tune n a short air or melody; harmony; correct intonation; frame of mind; mood. * vt to put into tune; to adapt.

tunic n a loose garment sometimes worn by both sexes; a military jacket; a covering membrane.

tuning fork n a two-pronged fork which when struck gives a standard musical note.

tunnel n an arched underground passage, esp on railways.

turban n a headdress.

turbid adj muddy; dense.

turbine n a horizontal water wheel; a rotary motor driven by steam, water, etc.

turbulence n disorder; tumult.

turbulent adj disorderly; riotous.

tureen n a large deep dish for soup.

turf n the grassy layer on the surface of the ground; a sod. **the turf** the business of horse racing.

turgid adj swelling; bombastic.

turmeric n an Asian plant whose root is used as a dye, a drug and a flavouring.

turmoil n uproar; disorder.

turn vt to cause to move round; to shape by a lathe; to alter course; to reverse; to change. * vi to revolve; to bend or curve; to become sour. * n a revolution; a bend; a short walk; purpose; a short spell.

turncoat n one who deserts his or her party or principles.

turning n a turn; a bend; the art of shaping articles on a lathe.

turnstile n a revolving barrier that serves as an entrance gate.

turpentine n a resin obtained from certain trees; oil distilled from this.

turpitude n baseness; depravity.

turquoise n a greenish blue precious stone.

turret n a little tower forming part of a building; a rotating iron tower to protect guns and gunners on a warship.

tusk n a long pointed tooth projecting from the mouth as in an elephant or boar.

tussle n a struggle; a scuffle.

tussock n a clump of grass.

tutelage n guardianship; guidance by a tutor.

tutelar adj protecting.

tutor n a private teacher.

twaddle vi to prate; to chatter. * n silly talk.

twang vi to pluck a taut string or wire. * n sound of a taut string plucked.

tweak vt to pinch; twist.

tweed n a twilled woollen fabric.

tweezers npl small pincers to pluck out hairs, etc.

twelfth adj the ordinal of twelve.

twelve adj, n ten and two.

twentieth adj the ordinal of twenty.

twenty adj, n twice ten.

twice adv two times.

twiddle vt, vi to twirl idly.

twig n a small shoot or branch.

twilight n the faint light after sunset and before dawn.

twill n a textile fabric with parallel ribs.

twin n one of two born at a birth. * adj double.

twine n strong thread or cord. * vt, vi to twist; to coil.

twinge n a sudden darting pain.

twinkle vi to sparkle; to blink. * n a sparkle.

twirl vt, vi to turn round rapidly; to rotate. *.n a curl; a flourish.

twist n something twined, as a thread; roll of tobacco; a wrench; a turn. * vt, vi to twine; to writhe; to pervert.

twitch vt to pluck; to jerk. * n a quick pull; a muscular jerk.

two adj, n the number next above one; the symbol for this (2, II, ii).

two-faced adj deceitful; hypocritical.

tymbal n a kettledrum.

tympanum n (pl **tympana**) the drum of the ear.

type n a distinguishing mark; emblem; model; letter used in printing; such letters collectively.

typewriter n a machine for producing printed letters by inked type.

typhoid n enteric fever; a low fever with acute intestinal pain.

typhoon n a violent hurricane.

typhus n a dangerous fever.

typical adj characteristic; symbolic.

typify vt to represent; exemplify.

typography n the art of printing.

tyrannical adj despotic; overbearing.

tyrannize vi to act the tyrant; to oppress.

tyranny n oppressive government; despotism.

tyrant n a despot; an oppressor.

tyre n a protective ring, usu rubber round the rim of a wheel.

tyro n a novice, a beginner.

U

ubiquitous adj existing everywhere; omnipresent.

udder n the milk gland of cows, sheep, etc.

ugly adj unattractive; unsightly; repulsive; ill-tempered.

ulcer n a festering sore.

ulceration n an ulcerous condition.

ulster n a long loose overcoat.

ulterior adj not evident; on further side; (motives) hidden .

ultimate adj utmost; final.

ultimatum n a last or final offer.

ultra prefix, adj beyond; extreme.

ultramarine n a vivid blue pigment.

ululate vi to howl, as with pain.

umbilical adj pertaining to the navel.

umbra n the dark central part of a shadow.

umbrage n resentment; offence.

umbrella n a folding frame with handle and covering, etc, as protection from rain; general protection.

umpire n a judge or referee. * vt, vi to enforce rules in sport; to arbitrate.

un- prefix that negates or reverses the original meaning, as untrue, not true. The sense of these 'u' words is in most cases self-evident, and only those in common use are given below, together with a fairly complete list of those whose meaning is less obvious.

unable *adj* not able; unequal to some task.

unacceptable *adj* unwelcome.

unaccountable *adj* inexplicable, puzzling; not responsible.

unaccustomed *adj* unusual.

unacknowledged *adj* ignored.

unacquainted *adj* not familiar with.

unadorned *adj* plain; simple.

unaffected *adj* simple; sincere; unmoved.

unaided *adj* without aid.

unalterable *adj* unchangeable.

unanimity *n* complete agreement (the 'un' here stands for *unus*, 'one').

unanimous *adj* being of one mind.

unanswerable *adj* conclusive.

unappreciated *adj* not duly prized.

unapproachable *adj* inaccessible.

unarmed *adj* defenceless.

unassailable *adj* impregnable.

unassuming *adj* modest.

unattended *adj* solitary; alone.

unattractive *adj* uninteresting.

unauthorized *adj* unwarranted.

unavailing *adj* of no avail.

unavoidable *adj* bound to happen, inevitable; necessary, compulsory.

unaware *adj, adv* unconscious; ignorant.

unawares *adv* unexpectedly.

unbearable *adj* intolerable.

unbecoming *adj* unseemly.

unbend *vi* to make straight.

unbiased *adj* impartial; just.

unbounded *adj* boundless, vast.

unbridled *adj* unrestrained.

unburden *vt* to rid of a load or burden.

uncanny *adj* weird; mysterious.

unceasing *adj* continual.

uncertain *adj* doubtful; variable.

unchallenged *adj* unopposed.

unchanging *adj* constant; immutable.

uncharitable *adj* harsh; ungenerous.

uncivil *adj* rude; discourteous.

uncivilized *adj* barbarous.

uncle *n* the brother of one's father or mother.

unclean *adj* dirty; impure.

uncomfortable *adj* ill at ease.

uncommunicative *adj* reserved; taciturn.

uncompromising *adj* unyielding.

unconditional *adj* unqualified.

unconnected *adj* separate; rambling.

unconscionable *adj* inordinate.

unconscious *adj* insensible; unaware.

unconstitutional *adj* not according to the principles of the constitution.

uncontrollable *adj* headstrong.

unconventional *adj* free and easy.

unconverted *adj* unchanged.

uncouple *vt* to set loose, as dogs on leash.

uncouth *adj* odd in appearance.

uncover *vt* to divest of a cover.

unctuous *adj* oily; greasy.

uncultivated *adj* not tilled; boorish.

undaunted *adj* intrepid; fearless.

undecided *adj* wavering; irresolute.

undemonstrative *adj* reserved; placid.

undeniable *adj* indisputable; true.

under *prep* below; beneath; subject to; inferior. * *adv* in a lower condition or degree. * *adj* lower; subordinate.

underclothes *npl* clothes worn under others or next the skin.

undercurrent *n* a current below another.

undergo *vt* to bear; to suffer.

undergraduate *n* a student who has not taken his or her degree.

undergrowth *n* shrubs, plants, etc, growing among trees.

underhand *adj* sly; dishonest.

underline *vt* to mark with a line underneath for emphasis.

undermine *vt* to sap; to injure by underhand means.

underrate *vt* to undervalue.

undersized *adj* dwarfish; small.

understand *vt, vi* to comprehend.

understanding *n* comprehension; discernment; knowledge; agreement.

understudy *n* one who gets up a theatrical part to be ready as substitute.

undertake *vt, vi* to take in hand.

undertaker *n* one who manages funerals.

undertaking *n* a task; project; promise.

undertone *n* an undercurrent of feeling.

undertow *n* the backward suction of a wave breaking on shore; undercurrent.

underwear *n* underclothes.

underworld *n* the world of criminals.

underwrite *vt* to sign one's name as answerable for a certain amount of insurance.

undisguised *adj* open; candid.

undisturbed *adj* calm; tranquil.

undo *vt* to reverse what has been done.

undoing *n* reversal; ruin.

undoubted *adj* certain; unquestionable.

undress *vt vi* to take off one's clothes.

undue *adj* unnecessary; excessive.

undulation *n* a waving motion; a gentle slope; vibratory motion.

undulatory *adj* wavelike.

unearned *adj* unmerited; (income) not earned by labour or skill.

unearth *vt* to discover; to reveal.

unearthly *adj* weird; ghostly.

uneasy *adj* restless; awkward; anxious.

unendurable *adj* intolerable.

unequable *adj* changeful; fitful.

unequal *adj* ill-matched.

unequivocal *adj* undoubted; clear.

uneven *adj* unequal; rough; odd.

unexceptionable *adj* irreproachable.

unexpected *adj* not looked for; sudden.

unexplored *adj* unvisited.

unfading *adj* always fresh.

unfailing *adj* sure.

unfair *adj* unjust; biassed.

unfaithful *adj* disloyal; false.

unfamiliar *adj* strange; unaccustomed.

unfasten *vt* to loose; to undo.

unfavourable *adj* adverse.

unfeeling *adj* devoid of feeling; harsh.

unfit *adj* unsuitable; incompetent.

unflinching *adj* resolute; firm.

unfold *vt, vi* to open the folds of; to display.

unforeseen *adj* unexpected; sudden.

unforgiving *adj* relentless; implacable.

unfortunate *adj* unlucky; unhappy.

unfounded *adj* false; groundless.

unfrequented *adj* rarely visited; solitary.

unfurl *vt* to spread out (flag, etc).

unfurnished *adj* without furniture.

ungainly *adj* clumsy; awkward.

ungenerous *adj* stingy; mean.

ungovernable *adj* headstrong; unruly.

ungraceful *adj* inelegant.

ungrammatical *adj* not according to grammar.

ungrateful *adj* not thankful; irksome.

ungrudging *adj* generous; hearty.

unguent *n* an ointment.

unhappily *adv* unfortunately.

unhappy *adj* miserable; sad; unlucky.

unhealthy *adj* sickly; unwholesome.

unheeded *adj* ignored; disregarded.

unheeding *adj* careless.

unhesitating *adj* instant; prompt.

unhinge *vt* to loosen; to derange.

unholy *adj* profane; wicked.

uniform *adj* regular; unvarying. * *n* regulation dress of certain persons.

uniformity *n* sameness; agreement; conformity to one type.

unify *vt* to form into one.

unimpaired *adj* uninjured.

unimpeachable *adj* irreproachable.

uninhabited *adj* deserted; desolate.

unintelligent *adj* dull; stupid.

unintelligible *adj* incapable of being understood; meaningless.

unintentional *adj* accidental.

uninteresting *adj* tedious; wearisome.

uninterrupted *adj* continuous; unbroken.

uninviting *adj* unattractive.

union *n* concord; a league; a trade union.

unionist *n* a trade unionist.

unique *adj* being the only one of its kind.

unison *n* harmony; concord.

unit *n* a single thing or person; an individual; a standard quantity.

unite *vt, vi* to combine; to connect.

unity *n* harmony; oneness; the number 1.

universal *adj* all-embracing, total.

universe *n* the whole creation; the world.

university *n* educational institution for higher learning and research.

unjust *adj* unfair; bad; biassed.

unkempt *adj* uncombed; rough.

unknowingly *adv* unwittingly.

unlace *vt* to unfasten.

unlawful *adj* illegal.

unless *conj* if it be not that.

unlicensed *adj* without legal permission.

unlike *adj* different; dissimilar.

unlimited *adj* unbounded; limitless.

unlooked-for *adj* unexpected.

unlucky *adj* unfortunate; ill-fated.

unman *vt* to weaken the courage of; to make effeminate.

unmanageable *adj* beyond control.

unmannerly *adj* rude; ill-bred.

unmask *vt* to strip off mask; to expose.

unmeasured *adj* excessive; boundless.

unmerciful *adj* ruthless; cruel.

unmerited *adj* undeserved.

unmitigated *adj* unqualified; absolute.

unnatural *adj* inhuman; affected.

unnavigable *adj* incapable of being navigated.

unnerve *vt* to unman; to deprive of power.

unobtrusive *adj* retiring; modest.

unoccupied *adj* empty; at leisure.

unopposed *adj* meeting with no opposition.

unorthodox *adj* unconventional.

unpack *vt* to empty a pack, trunk, etc.

unpalatable *adj* unpleasant to taste.

unparalleled *adj* unequalled; matchless.

unpardonable *adj* inexcusable.

unpleasant *adj* disagreeable.

unpractised *adj* raw; unskilful.

unprecedented *adj* unparalleled.

unpretentious *adj* modest.

unprincipled *adj* immoral; wicked.

unproductive *adj* barren.

unprofessional *adj* contrary to professional etiquette.

unprofitable *adj* fruitless; futile.

unqualified *adj* untrained; incompetent.

unquestionable *adj* indisputable.

unravel *vt* to disentangle; to solve.

unreadable *adj* illegible.

unreal *adj* sham; visionary.

unreasonable *adj* immoderate; absurd.

unrecorded *adj* not placed on record.

unrelenting *adj* hard; pitiless.

unreliable *adj* untrustworthy.

unremitting *adj* ceaseless; constant.

unrequited *adj* unrewarded.

unreserved *adj* frank; full; open.

unrest *n* disquiet; uneasiness.

unrestrained *adj* unbridled; loose.

unripe *adj* immature.

unrivalled *adj* peerless.

unroll *vt, vi* to unfold; to display.

unruffled *adj* calm; composed.

unruly *adj* disorderly.

unsatisfactory *adj* not up to expectation.

unsavoury *adj* insipid; not pleasing.

unscathed *adj* uninjured.

unscrupulous *adj* unprincipled.

unseemly *adj* unbecoming, improper.

unsentimental *adj* matter-of-fact.

unserviceable *adj* useless.

unsettle *vt* to upset; to derange.

unshapely *adj* ill-formed.

unsightly *adj* ugly; repulsive.

unsociable *adj* reserved; solitary.

unsolicited *adj* not sought.

unsophisticated *adj* natural; artless.

unsound *adj* diseased; faulty.

unspeakable *adj* unutterable.

unstable *adj* unsteady; fickle.

unsteady *adj* changeable; unsafe.

unstinted *adj* lavish; generous.

unsubstantial *adj* visionary; flimsy.

unsuitable *adj* unfit; unbecoming.

unsullied *adj* pure; stainless.

unsung *adj* not celebrated in song or poetry.

unsurpassed *adj* not excelled.

unsuspecting *adj* free from suspicion.

unswerving *adj* steadfast; straight.

untenable *adj* not fit to be occupied.

unthinkable adj inconceivable.

unthinking adj careless; heedless.

untidy adj slovenly; careless.

untie vt to loosen; to undo.

until prep, conj up to the time that; till.

untimely adj ill-timed; unseasonable.

untiring adj unwearied.

unto prep to.

untold adj countless; vast; unrecorded.

untouched adj unscathed; unmoved.

untoward adj unseemly; unfavourable.

untried adj not attempted; inexperienced.

untroubled adj calm; unruffled.

untrue adj incorrect; faithless.

untrustworthy adj unreliable; false.

unusual adj rare; peculiar.

unutterable adj unspeakable.

unvarnished adj plain; unadorned.

unvarying adj uniform.

unveil vt to uncover; to disclose to view.

unwarrantable adj unjustifiable; illegal.

unwavering adj steady; staunch.

unwearied adj tireless; incessant.

unwieldy n huge; cumbersome.

unwilling adj reluctant; loath.

unwind vt to wind off.

unwitting adj ignorant; unaware.

unworthy adj base; worthless.

unwritten adj understood though not expressed; traditional.

unyielding adj stubborn; unbending.

up adv aloft; in or to a higher position; upright; out of bed. * prep from below to a higher point.

upbraid vt to reproach; to taunt.

upbringing n training; breeding.

upheaval n great social or political changes.

uphold vt to support; to sustain.

upholster vt to furnish (chairs, sofas, etc) with springs, stuffing, etc.

upkeep n maintenance.

upon prep up and on; on.

upper adj higher in place or rank.

uppish adj snobbish.

upright adj erect; trustworthy.

uproar n a great tumult.

uproarious adj noisy; boisterous.

uproot vt to tear up by roots.

upset vt (pt, pp upset) to overturn; to discompose. * n act of upsetting. * adj fixed.

upshot n final issue; end.

upstairs adj, adv in or towards upper story of building; house, etc.

upstart n one who has suddenly risen in position; an arrogant person.

urban adj belonging to a city.

urbane adj sophisticated; polite.

urchin n a small mischievous boy.

urge vt to press to do something.

urgent adj pressing; imperative.

urine n fluid excreted from kidneys and bladder.

urn n a kind of vase.

us pron the objective case of we.

usage n treatment; customary practice.

use n employment practice; need. * vt to put to use; to avail one's self of; to employ.

user n one who uses.

useful adj helpful; serviceable.

usher n a doorkeeper; an assistant.

usual *adj* customary; common.

usurer *n* one who takes exorbitant interest.

usurp *vt* to seize and hold without right.

usury *n* extortionate interest for loan.

utensil *n* a kitchen implement.

uterus *n* the female organ in which offspring are developed until birth, the womb.

utility *n* usefulness; profit.

utilize *vt* make use of.

utmost *adj* the highest degree.

utopia *n* an ideal state or government.

utopian *adj* ideally perfect; visionary.

utter *adj* complete; total. * *vt* to speak; pronounce; spread abroad.

uvula *n* small fleshy body hanging from back palate.

V

vacancy *n* empty space; an unfilled post.

vacant *adj* empty; unfilled; silly.

vacate *vt* to quit possession of.

vacation *n* holiday time.

vaccinate *vt* to inoculate against disease.

vaccine *n* a preparation for inoculation.

vacillate *vi* to waver; to be undecided.

vacuous *adj* empty; void; vacant.

vacuum *n* a space void of air; empty space; a vacuum cleaner.

vagabond *adj* roaming; idling. * *n* a tramp.

vagina *n* in female mammals and humans, the canal connecting the uterus and the external sex organs.

vagrant *adj* wandering. * *n* a tramp.

vague *adj* indefinite; hazy.

vain *adj* empty; fruitless; conceited. * In vain, to no purpose.

vale *n* a valley.

valedictory *n* farewell.

valentine *n* a love gift or missive sent on St Valentine's day (14 February).

valet *n* a manservant.

valiant *adj* brave; heroic.

valid *adj* well grounded; sound.

validate *vt* to corroborate; to legalize.

validity *n* justness; soundness.

valise *n* a small suitcase.

valley *n* low ground between hills.

valour *n* bravery; courage.

valuable *adj* of great worth. * *npl* precious belongings.

valuator *n* an appraiser or valuer.

value *n* worth; importance; price. * *vt* to estimate; to prize; to appraise.

valve *n* a lid or flap for an opening, giving passage in one direction only.

vampire *n* a fabled blood-sucking creature; a person who preys on others; a bat.

van *n* a covered motor vehicle.

vandal *n* a barbarian; a person who wilfully damages property.

vane *n* a weathercock; the blade of a windmill, etc.

vanguard *n* front part of an army; the leading position of any movement.

vanilla *n* a flavouring prepared from tropical orchid.

vanish *vi* to disappear; to pass away.

vanity *n* idle show; craving for praise; emptiness; conceit.

vanquish *vt* to conquer; overcome.

vapid *adj* spiritless; flat; dull.

vaporize *vt* to convert or pass off into vapour.

vapour *n* a gas or fume given off by a body when sufficiently heated.

variable *adj* fickle; changeable.

variance *n* dispute; quarrel.

variant *n* an alternative form.

variation *n* change; alteration.

varicose *adj* (*veins*) enlarged.

varied *adj* diverse; various.

variegated *adj* diversified in colour.

variety *n* diversity; change in assortment; a species.

various *adj* different; several.

varnish *n* a resinous solution used to give gloss to wood, paper, etc; a gloss; a sham.

vary *vt, vi* to change; to alter; to differ; to disagree.

vascular *adj* pertaining to vessels, ducts, etc, of organic bodies.

vase *n* a jar-shaped vessel for ornament or use.

vast *adj* of great extent; immense.

vat *n* a huge tub or tank for holding liquors.

vaudeville *n* a light comedy with dances and songs.

vault *n* an arched roof; cellar; a leap. * *vi* to leap.

vaunt *vi, vt* to brag; to exult. * *n* a boast.

veal *n* the flesh of a calf.

veer *vi* to change direction.

vegetable *adj, n* (of) a plant grown for food.

vegetarian *n* a person who consumes a diet that excludes meat and fish.

vegetate *vi* to live a plant's life; to lead an aimless life.

vegetation *n* plants in general.

vehement *adj* ardent; forcible.

vehicle *n* a conveyance such as a car, bus or truck for carrying people; a medium.

veil *n* a screen; a face shade; a disguise. * *vt* to conceal.

vein *n* a blood vessel that returns blood to heart; sap tube or rib in leaves; a seam of ore; disposition; mood; streak.

velocity *n* rate of motion; speed.

velvet *n* a rich soft fabric.

venal *adj* base; corrupt.

vend *vt* to sell.

vendetta *n* a feud.

vendor *n* one who sells.

veneer *n* a thin facing of fine wood glued on a less valuable sort; a gloss. * *vt* to overlay with a veneer; to gloss.

venerable *adj* worthy of respect and admiration.

venerate *vt* to revere; honour.

vengeance *n* punishment in return for an injury.

venial *adj* pardonable; slight.

venison *n* the flesh of deer.

venom *n* poison; spite; malice.

venomous *adj* poisonous; spiteful.

venous *adj* pertaining to a vein.

vent *n* an outlet; a flue; expression. * *vt* to emit; utter.

ventilate *vt* to give air to; to discuss freely.

ventilator n an appliance for ventilating a room; a device for enable a patient to breathe normally.

ventral adj abdominal.

ventricle n a small cavity in body, esp one of those in heart or brain.

ventriloquist n one able to disguise his voice so that it seems to come from another speaker.

venture n a risky undertaking. * vi to dare. * vt to risk.

venturesome adj bold; hazardous.

venue n the appointed place of trial (law); meeting place.

veracious adj truthful; accurate.

veracity n truthfulness.

veranda, verandah n a portico or balcony along front of house.

verb n the predicative word in a sentence.

verbal adj spoken; oral.

verbally adv by word of mouth.

verbatim adv word for word.

verbiage n the use of too many words.

verbosity n superabundance of words; wordiness.

verdant adj green; simple; gullible.

verdict n the finding of a jury; considered opinion.

verdigris n the green rust of copper.

verdure n green vegetation.

verge n border; margin; brink. * vi to incline; to border.

verification n a proving true.

verify vt to prove to be true; to confirm.

verisimilitude n the appearance of truth; probability.

veritable adj true; real; actual.

verity n truth.

vermicular adj wormlike.

vermilion n a beautiful red colour.

vermin n noxious animals or insects as rats, lice, etc.

verminous adj infested by vermin.

vernacular adj native. * n mother tongue.

vernal adj pertaining to the spring.

versatile adj readily turning; variable; many-sided.

verse n a line of poetry; metre; poetry; a stanza; a short section of any composition.

versed adj having knowledge, skilled.

version n a translation; rendering.

versus prep against.

vertebra n (pl **vertebrae**) one of the bones of the spine; pl the spine.

vertebrate adj having a backbone.

vertex n (pl **vertexes, vertices**) the highest point; apex; zenith.

vertical adj upright; plumb.

vertigo n giddiness.

verve n spirit; energy.

very adj true; real. * adv truly.

vesicle n a small bladder or blister.

vessel n a hollow utensil for holding things; a ship.

vest n a waistcoat; an undergarment. * vi to furnish with (power, property, etc). * vt to invest.

vestal adj sacred to the goddess Vesta; vowed to chastity; pure. * n a virgin who served in the temple of Vesta in ancient Rome.

vested adj robed; established.

vestibule n lobby or hall of house.

vestige n footprint; mark or trace.

vestment n a garment, esp priestly garment.

vestry n room where clerical vestments are kept.

vesture n dress; clothing.

veteran adj long experienced, esp in war.

veterinary adj pertaining to diseases of domestic animals.

veto n the right to reject or forbid. * vt to refuse assent to.

vexatious adj annoying; troublesome.

vexed adj annoyed; much disputed.

via prep by way of.

viaduct n an arched bridge over a valley.

vial n a small glass bottle.

vibrant adj vibrating; tremulous.

vibrate vt, vi to wave to and fro; to swing; to quiver.

vibratory adj causing to vibrate.

vicarious adj acting for, or on behalf of, another.

vice n a blemish; moral failing; profligacy; an instrument for gripping things firmly.

vice- prefix denoting a depute or one who acts in the place of another, e.g. vice-president.

vicinity n neighbourhood.

vicious adj malicious; bad-tempered.

vicissitude n one of ups and downs of life.

victim n a person who has suffered injury; a dupe.

victimize vt to make a victim of.

victor n conqueror; winner.

victory n defeat of enemy or rival; triumph.

victual n food provided; provisions (usu in pl). * vt to supply with food or stores.

vide (Latin) see; refer to.

video n the transmission or recording of television programmes or films using a television set and a video recorder and videotape. * vt to record on videotape.

videotape n magnetic tape on which images and sounds can be recorded for reproduction on television.

vie vi to contend; to compete.

view n a look; inspection; survey; range of vision; scene; intention. * vt, vi to see; to survey; to consider.

vigil n a watching, esp devotional.

vigilance n watchfulness.

vigilant adj watchful.

vignette n an engraving on a title page, etc, without a definite border; a picture without definite edges.

vigorous adj full of vigour.

vigour n energy; force; strength.

vile adj base; depraved.

vilify vt to slander.

villa n a country or suburban house.

village n a collection of houses smaller than a town.

villain n a criminal; a scoundrel.

villainous adj base; vile; wicked.

vim n vigour; energy.

vinaigrette n a salad dressing of oil, vinegar and seasoning.

vindicate vt to justify; uphold.

vindictive adj revengeful.

vine n a plant that bears grapes.

vinegar n a liquid containing acetic acid, used as a condiment and preserve.

vineyard n a plantation of vines.

vintage n the yearly produce of vine; wine of particular year.

vintner *n* a wine seller.

viola *n* a large violin; genus of plants including violet, pansy, etc.

violate *vt* to injure; to outrage.

violation *n* infringement.

violence *n* great force; injury.

violent *adj* vehement; furious.

violin *n* a four-stringed musical instrument.

virago *n* a bad tempered woman.

virescent *adj* slightly green.

virgin *n* a person who has never had sexual intercourse. * *adj* untouched; pure.

virginal *adj* of or pertaining to a virgin. * *n* a kind of spinet.

virile *adj* sexually potent; strong.

virtual *adj* in effect, but not in name.

virtue *n* moral goodness; admirable quality.

virtuoso *n* a person highly skilled, esp in playing a musical instrument.

virtuous *adj* moral; upright.

virulent *adj* poisonous; malignant.

virus *n* a microorganism capable of causing ill-health; illness caused by virus; (computing) an unauthorized computer program which inserts itself into computer systems and causes disruption to existing software.

visa *n* an endorsement on a passport allowing the holder to travel in the country of the government issuing it.

visage *n* the face or countenance.

vis-à-vis *adv* face to face.

viscera *npl* the entrails.

viscid *adj* sticky or adhesive.

viscous *adj* glutinous; viscid.

visible *adj* perceivable by the eye.

vision *n* sight; object of sight; a dream.

visionary *adj* imaginary; fanciful. * *n* an impractical person.

visit *vt* to call upon; to afflict. * *vi* to make calls. * *n* a call.

visor, vizor *n* the movable face-guard of a helmet.

vista *n* an extended view.

vital *adj* mortal; essential.

vitality *n* vital force; energy.

vitals *npl* parts essential to life.

vitamin *n* an essential element in the diet.

vitiate *vt* to make faulty; to impair.

vitreous *adj* glassy.

vitrify *vt* to convert into glass.

vitriol *n* sulphuric acid.

vituperate *vt* to abuse; to revile.

vivacious *adj* lively; sprightly.

vivid *adj* bright; striking.

vivify *vt* to animate.

viviparous *adj* giving birth to live young.

vivisection *n* act of experimenting on a living animal.

vixen *n* a female fox; a shrew.

vocabulary *n* a list of words with definitions; an individual's command or use of words.

vocal *adj* pertaining to the voice.

vocalist *n* a singer.

vocation *n* a calling; occupation.

vociferous *adj* clamorous; noisy.

vogue *n* temporary fashion.

voice *n* the sound uttered by the mouth; utterance; speech; sound emitted; vote; a form of verb inflection. * *vt* to utter or express.

void *adj* empty; null. * *n* an empty space. * *vt* to make vacant; to nullify.

volatile *adj* readily passing off in vapour; flighty.

volcano *n* a mountain formed by ejections of lava, ashes, etc, through an opening in the earth's crust.

volition *n* will; power of choice.

volley *n* a simultaneous discharge of missiles.

volleyball *n* a team game played by hitting an inflated ball over a net with the hands; the ball used.

volt *n* unit of electromotive force.

volubility *n* fluency of speech.

voluble *adj* over fluent; glib.

volume *n* an amount of space; mass or bulk; a book.

volumetric *adj* pertaining to measurement by volume.

voluminous *adj* bulky; copious.

voluntary *adj* acting of one's own free will; without remuneration.

volunteer *n* a person who undertakes military or other service of his or her own free will. * *vi* to offer one's services.

voluptuous *adj* fond of bodily pleasures; physically attractive through shapeliness or fullness of the body.

vomit *vi*, *vt* (*pt* **vomited**) to throw up from stomach; to eject; matter ejected from stomach.

voracious *adj* greedy; ravenous.

vortex *n* (*pl* **vortices** *or* **vortexes**) a whirling motion as in whirlpool, whirlwind.

vote *n* the recording of opinion for or against proposal; suffrage. * *vi*, *vt* to give a vote; to grant by vote.

votive *adj* promised by vow.

vouch *vt* to attest; to guarantee.

voucher *n* a written record of a transaction; a token that can be exchanged for something else.

vouchsafe *vt* to condescend to grant.

vow *n* a solemn promise; an oath. * *vt* to promise solemnly.

vowel *n* a simple vocal sound; letter denoting it.

voyage *n* a journey, esp by ship.

vulcanite *n* a rubber hardened by treating with sulphur.

vulgar *adj* coarse in manners.

vulgarity *n* rudeness of manners.

vulnerable *adj* liable to injury.

vulpine *adj* crafty; foxy.

vulture *n* a large bird of prey; a rapacious person.

vulva *n* the external genitals of human females.

W

wad *n* a fibrous mass; a bundle of paper money.

wadding *n* any soft material for use in packing, padding, etc.

waddle *vi* to walk with a rolling gait.

wade *vi* to walk through water; to walk with difficulty.

wafer *n* a thin crisp cracker or biscuit.

waft *vt* to sail or bear along gently.

wag vt, vi (pt **wagged**) to shake up and down or to and fro. * n a wit; joker.

wage vt to stake; to carry on, esp war; * n salary; hire; usu. in pl

wager n a bet; subject of bet. * vt to stake.

wagon, waggon n a four-wheeled cart; a truck.

waif n a homeless, neglected child.

wail vi to lament; to cry aloud. * n a moaning cry.

waist n part of body from ribs to hips.

waistcoat n a sleeveless undercoat; a vest.

wait vi to stay in expectation; to attend; to serve at table. * n period of waiting.

waiter n a servant in attendance at table.

waive vt to forgo; give up.

wake vb (pt **woke**, pp **woken**) vi to be awake. * vt to arouse. * n a vigil over the dead; track left by a ship.

waken vt, vi to arouse; wake.

walk vi to advance step by step. * n a ramble; a road, path; sphere of life.

wall n a rigid vertical structure for enclosing, dividing or protecting.

wallet n a flat pocketbook for paper money, cards, etc.

wallow vi to roll in mud, to indulge oneself in emotion.

waltz n a whirling dance or its music. * to dance a waltz.

wand n a magician's rod.

wander vi to ramble; to roam; to err.

wane vt to grow less; to decline.

want n need; longing; dearth; poverty. * vt, vi to lack; need.

wanton adj frisky; lustful. * n a lewd person.

war n a fight between nations; enmity; a contest.

warble vt, vi to sing like a bird; to trill.

ward vt to guard; to fend off * n guard; custody; one under a guardian; a division of a town or country; apartment of an hospital.

warden n a guardian; head of college or hostel.

warder n a guard; a keeper.

wardrobe n a cabinet or closet for keeping clothes; one's stock of clothes.

ware n merchandise; goods (usu in pl). * adj wary.

warehouse n a building for storing wares, goods.

warfare n military service; war.

warm adj moderately hot; zealous; excited; lively. * vt, vi to make or become warm or animated.

warmth n gentle heat; cordiality.

warn vt to caution; to advise.

warning n caution; previous notice.

warp vt, vi to twist; to pervert. * n lengthwise threads in loom; a twist.

warped adj twisted by shrinking; perverted.

warrant vt to guarantee; to authorize; to justify. * n a guarantee; writ or summons; voucher.

warranty n warrant; guarantee.

warrior n a gallant soldier.

wart n a hard dry growth on skin.

wary adj cautious; prudent.

was pt of to be.

wash vt, vi to cleanse with water; to

colour lightly. * *n* flow or dash of
water; a lotion; thin coat of colour.

washer *n* a ring of metal, rubber, etc,
for tightening nut on screw.

washing *n* clothes washed; a cleansing.

wasp *n* a stinging winged insect.

waspish *adj* like a wasp; venomous;
irritable; snappish.

wastage *n* lost by use or waste.

waste *vt, vi* to ravage; to damage; to
squander; to grow less. * *adj* unused; devastated. * *n* a wilderness;
useless spending; decrease; refuse.

waste pipe *n* a pipe to carry off waste
water.

watch *n* a guard; vigilance; sentry; a
timepiece. * *vt, vi* to guard; to observe carefully; to await.

watchful *adj* vigilant; cautious.

watchmaker *n* one who makes or repairs watches.

watchword *n* a password; a slogan; a
motto.

water *n* the commonest of liquids,
clear and transparent when pure.
* *vt, vi* to supply with water; to irrigate; to dilute; to take in water.

watercolour *n* a pigment ground up
with water and gum instead of oil; a
picture painted with watercolours.

watercourse *n* a channel for water.

waterfall *n* a stream falling over
rocks; a cascade.

waterlogged *adj* soaked or filled
with water.

waterproof *adj* impervious to water.
* *n* cloth so made.

watershed *n* dividing ridge between
river systems.

waterspout *n* a column of water
sucked up by whirlwind.

watery *adj* like water; tasteless.

wave *vi, vt* to move up and down, or
to and fro; to brandish; to beckon.
* *n* a rising motion on surface of
water, etc; a waving of hand as signal.

waved *adj* undulating.

waver *vi* to move to and fro; falter;
flicker.

wax *n* secretion by bees; anything
like wax. * *vt* to rub with wax; to
grow larger.

waxwork *n* modelling in wax; *pl* figures in wax.

way *n* a track, path, or road; distance
traversed; direction; condition;
method; course.

wayfarer *n* a traveller.

waylay *vt* to lie in wait for; to accost.

wayside *n* the side of a road.

wayward *adj* wilful; perverse.

we *pron* plural of I.

weak *adj* feeble; frail; foolish; vacillating.

weaken *vt, vi* to make or become
weak.

weakling *n* a weak creature.

weal *n* a raised mark on skin.

wealth *n* riches; abundance.

wean *vt* to break off from any habit;
to discontinue giving mother's
milk.

weapon *n* any instrument of offence
or defence.

wear *vb* (*pt* **wore**, *pp* **worn**) *vt* to
have on, as clothes; to waste by rub-
bing; to exhibit. * *vi* to last; to exhaust.

wearisome *adj* tiresome; tiring.

weary *adj* tired; jaded. * *vt* to wear out strength or patience; to become weary.

weather *n* the general atmospheric conditions at any particular time. * *vt* to affect by weather, as rocks; to bear up against (storms, etc).

weathercock *n* a vane turning with wind.

weatherglass *n* a barometer.

weave *vt vb* (*pt, pp* **wove** *or* **weaved**) to form by interlacing threads; to compose or fabricate.

web *n* woven cloth; tissue or texture; film; membrane between toes of waterfowl.

webbed *adj* having the toes united by a membrane.

webbing *n* a strong narrow band used for girths, etc.

wed *vt, vi vb* (*pt, pp* **wedded** *or* **wed**) to marry; to unite together.

wedding *n* marriage; nuptials.

wedge *n* a block sloping to thin edge at one end. * *vt* to cleave, fix, or fasten with wedge.

wedlock *n* marriage.

Wednesday *n* fourth day of week.

weed *n* a useless plant; tobacco; * *vt* to remove weeds.

week *n* seven consecutive days.

weep *vi, vt* (*pt, pp* **wept**) to shed tears; to mourn.

weft *n* cross-threads of web.

weigh *vt* to find heaviness of; to reflect on; to raise anchor. * *vi* to have weight; to bear heavily.

weight *n* heaviness; gravity; heavy mass; pressure.

weir *n* a dam across a stream.

weird *n* fate. * *adj* unearthly; queer.

welcome *adj* pleasing. * *n* a kind reception.

weld *vt* to fuse together, esp metal; to unite.

welfare *n* health; state provision of financial aid to the unemployed, sick, etc.

well *n* a spring; a pit sunk for water; staircase or lift space. * *vi* to bubble up; to issue forth.

well *adv* rightly; smartly. * *adj* hale; hearty.

wellington *n* a high waterproof boot.

welter *vi* to wallow; to roll. * *n* a confused mass.

went *pt* of go.

west *n* one of the four compass points; the sun's setting place.

western *adj* in or from west.

wet *adj* covered with water; moist; rainy. * *n* water; rain. * *vt* to make wet.

whale *n* largest of sea animals.

whaler *n* a ship employed in whale fishery.

wharf *n* (*pl* **wharfs, wharves**) a loading place for ships, a quay.

wheat *n* a cereal from which flour is obtained.

wheaten *adj* made from wheat.

wheel *n* a round spoked frame turning on an axis; anything like a wheel. * *vt, vi* to revolve or cause to revolve.

wheelbarrow *n* a hand carriage with one wheel.

wheelwright *n* a maker of wheels and carts.

wheeze vi to breathe hard and audibly.

welk n a shellfish; a periwinkle.

when adv, conj at what or which time; while; whereas.

whence adv, conj from what place.

where adv, conj at or in what place.

whereas conj that being so.

whereby adv, conj by which or what.

wherefore adv, conj for which reason; why.

whereon adv, conj on which or on what.

whereupon adv upon which.

wherever adv at whatever place.

whet vt to sharpen; to edge; to stimulate.

whether pron which of two. * conj, adv which of two or more.

whetstone n a sharpening stone.

which pron an interrogative pronoun; a relative pronoun, the neuter of who.

whiff n a puff of air, smoke, smell.

while n a short space of time. * conj during that time that. * vt to pass (time) pleasantly.

whilst adv while.

whim n a sudden fancy.

whimper vi to whine. * n a pathetic cry.

whimsical adj fantastic; odd.

whine vi utter plaintive cry. * n a wail.

whip vt to lash; to flog; to beat into froth. * n a piece of leather attached to a handle used to punish people or drive on animals; an officer in parliament who maintains party discipline.

whippersnapper n a forward but insignificant person.

whir vi to fly with buzzing sound.

whirl vt, vi to revolve rapidly.

whirlpool n a whirling eddy of water.

whirlwind n a whirling eddy of air.

whisk vt to stir or move rapidly. * n a jerking motion; small brush; an egg-beater.

whisker n hair on cheeks.

whisky, whiskey n spirit distilled from barley, etc.

whisper vt, vi to speak very softly. * n a low voice.

whist interj hush! * n a game of cards.

whistle vi to make a shrill sound with lips or instrument. * n a shrill sound; a small wind instrument.

white adj snow-coloured; pure.

whitewash n lime and water for whitening walls, etc; to conceal the truth.

whither adv to what or which place.

whittle vt to pare down.

who pron what or which person; that.

whole adj hale and sound. * n the total; all.

wholesale n sale of goods in large quantities. * adj extensive.

wholesome adj healthy; salutary.

wholly adv entirely.

whoop n a loud shout.

whooping cough n an infectious disease, esp of children, causing coughing spasms.

whose pron the possessive case of who or which.

why adv, conj for what reason.

wick n the thread of a lamp or candle.

wicked adj bad; sinful; roguish.

wicket n a small gate; the three upright stumps in cricket.

wide *adj* broad; extensive.

widen *vt*, *vi* to make or grow wide.

widow *n* a woman whose husband is deceased.

widower *n* a man whose wife is deceased.

width *n* breadth.

wield *vt* to handle; to exercise.

wife *n* (*pl* **wives**) a married woman.

wig *n* an artificial head of hair.

wigwam *n* a North American Indian domed shelter.

wild *adj* in a state of nature; untamed; stormy.

wilderness *n* a desert; waste.

wildfire *n* sheet lightning.

wile *n* fraud; trick. * *vt* to entice.

wilful *adj* stubborn; headstrong.

will *v aux* expressing futurity or resolve. * *vt*, *vi* to determine by choice; to wish; to bequeath. * *n* wish; choice; determination; purpose; last testament; feeling.

willing *adj* ready; instant; ungrudging.

willow *n* a tree or shrub, valuable for basket-making, etc; a cricket bat.

wily *adj* cunning; sly.

win *vb* (*pt*, *pp* **won**) *vt* to gain; to allure. * *vi* to gain victory.

wince *vi* to shrink, as from pain.

winch *n* crank of wheel or axle; a windlass.

wind[1] *n* a current of air; breath; flatulence. * *vi* to blow, as a horn. * *vt* to put out of breath; to rest.

wind[2] *vb* (*pt*, *pp* **wound**) *vt* to twist; to coil. * *vi* to twine; to meander.

windfall *n* fruit blown down; an unexpected financial gain.

winding *adj* bending; twisting. * *n* a turn; a bend.

windlass *n* a kind of hoisting machine; a winch.

windmill *n* a mill driven by wind.

window *n* a glazed opening in wall for light.

windpipe *n* the air passage to lungs; trachea.

windward *n* the point from which the wind blows.

wine *n* the fermented juice of grapes.

winepress *n* an apparatus for pressing juice from grapes.

wing *n* organ of flight; side extension of building, army, etc; side. * *vt* to fly; to wound.

wink *vi* to shut and open eyelids; to give hint by eyelids; to connive. * *n* a winking or hint given by it.

winning *adj* attractive; charming.

winnow *vt* to fan chaff from grain; to sift.

winsome *adj* attractive; winning.

winter *n* the cold season of year. * *vi* to pass the winter.

wipe *vt* to clean by gentle rubbing; to efface.

wire *n* a thread of metal; a telegram * *vt* to bind with wire. * *vi* to telegraph.

wiry *adj* wire-like; sinewy.

wisdom *n* sound judgment and knowledge; prudence.

wise *adj* learned; judging rightly.

wish *vi* to have a desire; to long. * *vt* to express desire. * *n* a desire.

wisp *n* a small bundle of straw, etc; anything slender.

wistful *adj* pensive; yearning.

wit *vt, vi* to know; to be aware; **to wit** namely; that is to say. * *n* understanding; humour; a humorist.

witch *n* a woman who practises magic and is considered to have dealings with the devil.

witchcraft *n* the practice of magic.

with *prep* expressing nearness or connection; among; possessing.

withdraw *vt* to draw back; to retract. * *vi* to retire.

wither *vi* to fade or shrivel.

withers *npl* ridge between shoulder bones of horse.

withhold *vt* to hold back; not to grant.

within *prep* inside. * *adv* inwardly.

without *prep, adv* outside.

withstand *vt, vi* to oppose; to resist.

witness *n* testimony; evidence; one who gives sworn evidence. * *vt, vi* to see; to attest; to sign as witness.

witticism *n* a witty remark.

witty *adj* humorous; smart and droll.

wizard *n* a magician; conjuror.

wizen, wizened *adj* shrivelled.

wobble *vi* to sway from side to side.

woe *n* grief; misery.

woebegone *adj* grief-stricken.

wolf *n* (*pl* **wolves**) a wild animal of the dog family.

woman *n* (*pl* **women**) an adult female; the female sex.

womanhood *n* the state or qualities of a woman.

won *pt, pp* of **win**.

wonder *n* something very strange; a marvel; feeling excited by something strange. * *vi* to be struck with wonder; to marvel.

woo *vt* to court with a view to marriage.

wood *n* a collection of growing trees; timber.

wooden *adj* made of wood; stiff.

woodwork *n* carpentry.

wool *n* the fleece of sheep, goats, etc.

woolgathering *n* idle dreaming.

woollen *adj* made of wool. * *n* cloth made of wool.

word *n* an articulate sound expressing an idea; information; a saying; motto; promise; *pl* a quarrel; *pl* lyrics. * *vt* to put into words; to flatter.

wording *n* the mode of expressing in words.

wordy *adj* using many words; verbose.

work *n* effort; employment; a task; achievement; a book or other composition; a factory. * *vi* to labour, toil; to be employed; to ferment. * *vt* to bring about; to influence; to fashion.

working class *n* people who work for wages, esp manual workers.

workman *n* an artisan; a skilled worker.

workmanship *n* skill of a worker or quality of his work.

workshop *n* a place where some craft is carried on.

world *n* the whole creation; the earth; mankind; the public.

worldly *adj* relating to this world or this life; experienced.

worm *n* a small creeping animal; thread of screw; spiral pipe in a condenser. * *vi* to work slowly and secretly. * *vt* to undermine; to extract.

worn *pp* of **wear**.

worry *vt* to harass; to fret. * *n* anxiety.

worse *adj* bad or ill in greater degree; inferior.

worship *n* religious service; adoration; reverence; title of honour. * *vt* to adore; to perform religious service.

worshipful *adj* honourable.

worst *adj* bad or evil in highest degree. * *vt* to defeat.

worsted *n* woollen yarn used in knitting.

worth *adj* equal in value to; deserving of * *n* value; price.

worthy *adj* deserving; befitting. * *n* a notable person.

would-be *adj* wishing to be; pretended.

wound *n* a cut or stab, etc; injury. * *vt, vi* to inflict a wound; to pain.

wove *pt* of **weave**.

wrack *n* seaweed generally; wreck; a thin flying cloud.

wrangle *vi* to dispute angrily. * *n* a dispute.

wrap *vt* to fold or roll; to envelop. * *n* a shawl or rug.

wrapper *n* a loose morning gown; cover for postal packets, as books, etc.

wrath *n* violent anger; rage.

wreak *vt* to inflict, execute (vengeance etc).

wreath *n* a twisted rin of leaves, flowers, etc; something like this in shape.

wreathe *vt* to entwine; to encircle.

wreck *n* ruin; destruction of ship at sea. * *vt* to ruin; destroy.

wreckage *n* remains of wrecked ship.

wrench *n* a violent twist; tool for screwing nuts, etc. * *vt* to pull with a twist.

wrest *vt* to twist; to distort.

wrestle *vi* to contend by grappling and trying to throw down.

wretch *n* a miserable person; base creature.

wretched *adj* unhappy; worthless.

wriggle *vi, vt* to twist about.

wright *n* an artisan; a carpenter.

wring *vt(pt, pp* **wrung**) to twist and squeeze; to extort.

wrinkle *n* a crease in skin; furrow; hint. * *vt, vi* to crease.

wrist *n* the joint uniting hand to arm.

writ *n* a written court order.

write *vt, vi* (*pt* **wrote**, *pp* **written**) to form by a pen, etc; to set down in words; to communicate by letter; to compose.

writer *n* an author; a clerk; a law agent.

writer's cramp *n* spasms in the fingers from excessive writing.

writhe *vt, vi* to turn and twist, as in pain.

wrong *adj* not right; false. * *n* an injury. * *vt* to treat unjustly.

wrongful *adj* injurious; unjust.

wrought *adj* beaten or rolled into shape.

wry *adj* contorted; twisted; ironic.

WWW *abbr* World Wide Web.

wynd *n* a narrow alley; a lane.

X

xanthic *adj* yellowish; of or relating to xanthine.

xanthine *n* a compound related in structure to uric acid, found in urine, blood and some tissues.

xenophobia *n* fear or dislike of foreigners or strangers.

xerography *n* photocopying by using light to form an electrostatic image.

X-ray, x-ray *n* a radiation of very short wavelengths, capable of penetrating solid bodies. * *vt* to photograph by X-rays.

xylophone *n* a musical instrument of wooden bars freely suspended and vibrating when struck.

Y

yacht *n* a light sailing vessel for pleasure or racing.

yahoo *n* a rude or brutish person.

yak *n* a Tibetan ox.

yam *n* a tropical plant and its edible root.

yap *vi* to talk constantly.

yard *n* a standard measure of 3 feet; an enclosure; a spar hung across a mast to support a sail.

yardarm *n* either end of a ship's yard.

yarn *n* any spun thread; a spun-out story.

yaw *vi* to swerve suddenly in sailing.

yawl *n* a ship's small boat; a small yacht.

yawn *vi* to open the jaws involuntarily, as from drowsiness. * *n* act of yawning.

year *n* the period of earth's complete revolution round sun; 12 months; 365 or 366 days.

yearling *n* a one-year-old animal.

yearn *vi* to be filled with longing, love, or pity for.

yeast *n* a fermenting substance for raising bread.

yell *vi* to scream * *n* a shrill cry.

yellow *adj, n* a bright golden colour.

yelp *vi* to utter a sharp bark.

yen *n* the monetary unit of Japan; (*inf*) a yearning, an ambition.

yes *adv* a word of affirmation or consent.

yesterday *n* the day before the present.

yet *adv* in addition; still. * *conj* nevertheless.

yew *n* a large evergreen tree.

yield *vt* to produce in return for labour, etc; to afford; to give up. * *vi* to submit. * *n* product; crop.

yodel *vt, vi* (*pt* **yodelled**) to sing with changes from the natural to falsetto voice.

yoga *n* a system of exercises for attaining bodily and spiritual control .

yoke n a neckpiece of wood binding oxen together in drawing; a pair of draught oxen; a bond or link; part of a garment that is fitted below the neck. * vt to couple.

yokel n an unsophisticated country person.

yolk n the yellow part of an egg.

yonder adv over there.

you pron 2nd person sing and pl the person or persons spoken to.

young adj not old; youthful. * n offspring; young persons.

youngster n a boy; young person.

youth n period from childhood to manhood; a young man; young people.

Yule n Christmas.

Z

zany adj comical; eccentric.

zeal n eagerness; ardour; fanaticism.

zealot n an extreme partisan; a fanatic.

zebra n a striped wild animal related to the horse.

zenith n the point of heavens right overhead; highest point.

zephyr n the west wind; any soft breeze.

zeppelin n a rigid, cigar-shaped airship.

zero n a cipher; nothing; the point from which marking of a scale begins.

zest n relish; keen enjoyment.

zigzag adj, n a line with short sharp turns. * vi (pt **zigzagged**) to turn sharply this way and that.

zinc n a soft bluish white metal.

zip vb (pt **zipped**) vi (inf) to move at high speed, to dart. * vt to fasten with a zipper. * n a zipper.

zipper, zip-fastener n a slide fastening device on clothing, etc, with interlocking teeth.

zither n a flat, stringed musical instrument.

zodiac n the tract in the heavens within which the apparent path of sun, moon, and planets is confined, and containing the twelve constellations, or signs of zodiác.

zone n a girdle or belt; one of the five great belts of the earth; any well-defined tract.

zoolite n a fossil animal.

zoology n the science of animal life.

zoom vi to climb rapidly and sharply; to increase rapidly; to move very quickly.

zoophyte n a plant-like animal, as sponge, coral.

Zoroastrian n a believer in the religion of Zoroaster, founder of Parseeism, or fire worship.

zymotic adj caused by or relating to an infection or an infectious disease; producing fermentation.

zymurgy n the chemistry of fermentation in brewing etc.